C000227995

Claire

with my best wishes

Richard

Mrs. D

The Life of Anne Damer (1748-1828)

Mrs. D

The Life of Anne Damer (1748-1828)

RICHARD WEBB

BREWIN BOOKS

First published by
Brewin Books Ltd, 56 Alcester Road,
Studley, Warwickshire B80 7LG in 2013
www.brewinbooks.com

© Richard Webb 2013.

All rights reserved.

ISBN: 978-1-85858-500-0

The moral right of the author has been asserted.

A Cataloguing in Publication Record
for this title is available from the British Library.

Typeset in Minion Pro
Printed in Great Britain by
Berforts Information Press Ltd.

CONTENTS

Foreword — vii

1. Setting the Scene — 1
2. Childhood and Adolescence — 11
3. Launched into Society — 30
4. Three Weddings and a Funeral — 36
5. Going Solo: Stringency and Statuary — 54
6. Antiques and Animals — 72
7. Abused — 79
8. The 1784 Election — 86
9. Sculpture and the Theatre — 92
10. My Straw Berrys — 111
11. Travels on the Continent — 118
12. Letters to and from Italy and Life in England — 134
13. Proposals — 151
14. A Difficult Choice — 169
15. Two Deaths and a Removal — 184
16. Nelson and Napoleon — 196
17. Belmour — 220
18. Sculpture from Life — 226
19. The March of Time — 238
20. Princess Caroline and a Dash to Paris — 251
21. The Final Curtain — 267

Envoi — 273
Personae Dramatis — 274
Main Sources used — 292
Family Trees — 294
List of Anne Damer's Sculptures — 296
Index — 299

FOREWORD

My attention was first drawn to Anne Damer by my late mother-in-law, Diana Neave, later Baroness Airey of Abingdon. Diana had inherited some early works of Anne Damer from her mother, a direct descendant of Louisa Johnston, to whom Anne left her estate. She was fascinated by Anne Damer's friendships, especially those with Horace Walpole and Mary Berry. Sadly she never found time to write her own biography of Anne.

She encouraged her goddaughter, Dorothy Abel-Smith, to research Anne's life, drawing Dorothy's attention to "what I found to be the remarkable relationship between ASD and Horace Walpole, that they shared a great affection for Mary Berry … and that this triangle constituted a fascinating FRIENDSHIP". In setting out her own plan for a biography, Diana continued: "I seek really to make Friendship, whether between men and/or women, my theme, as it seems to me that few people today have time for Friendship, so obsessed are they by sex." In 1999 Dorothy produced a synopsis of Anne's life and work in memory of, and as a tribute to Diana and her late husband Airey Neave. I would like to thank Dorothy for making her research available to me.

I would also like to acknowledge other help that I have received in writing this book. I am afraid that lack of space precludes my mentioning everyone who has assisted me, and my apologies to the many helpers not mentioned by name. I hasten to say that your advice was in all cases much appreciated. In particular I would like to thank those that have helped me in my chase to find and understand Anne Damer's sculptures, including the Campbell-Johnston family, James Peill, Curator at Goodwood House, Stephen Lloyd, curator at Knowsley, Giovanna Giusti for making me welcome at the Uffizi gallery, Florence, and to Alain Pougetout, curator at Malmaison.

I must thank Anna Chalcraft who introduced me to the Friends of Strawberry Hill, through whom I met Maggie Powell, Sue Walker and the staff of the Lewis Walpole Library. Access to the treasure trove of 18th century history contained at Farmington was made even more rewarding by the warmth of their welcome.

Other notable biographical assistance was received from Desmond Hillary Archivist at Combe Bank School, from Edward Clive at Christies, who led me to Christies sale of John Damer's household contents, and from Dr Jonathan Gross who discussed and sent me a copy of his edition of Anne Damer's novel *Belmour*.

Library and museum staff at the British Library Rare Manuscripts Reading Room, the British Museum, Victoria and Albert Museum, National Portrait Galleries of

England and Scotland, the Rangers House Greenwich, Edinburgh Register House and National Gallery of Scotland have all encouraged and helped me. Thanks are due too to County Archives staff in Dorset, Hull, West Sussex and Warwickshire.

I must thank and congratulate Jane Manley who edited my spelling, grammar, punctuation and much more, with her customary skill and tact. It has been a pleasure to work with Alan and Alistair Brewin, publishers of this book. Their enterprise may be small in size, but it is huge in enthusiasm and enterprise. The chief and last accolade must go to my wife Marigold who has flown, driven and walked with me, to innumerable Damer destinations, and photographed and noted their contents. At times I have been accused of having been married to Mrs Damer, (not historically auspicious for me), and for any inattention to more pressing matters, I apologise.

Chapter 1

SETTING THE SCENE

Anne Seymour Conway was born on 8th November 1748, at Combe Bank, a substantial country house in the village of Sundridge, near Sevenoaks, in Kent. The property belonged to her maternal grandfather, Colonel John Campbell. 18th century prints of Combe Bank depict a symmetrical house with turrets at all four corners. An elegant landscape of trees and lawns, flanked by paths and ornamental urns, leads to twin summerhouses looking out on to parkland where sheep and cattle graze and shepherd and milkmaid go about their business. The Palladian house had been designed by the architect Roger Morris, on Colonel Campbell's instructions, and was built in the 1720s. On the ground floor, the high-ceilinged rooms with fine plasterwork were ideally proportioned. However, almost all visitors found it extremely cold. Today the house, much enlarged in the early 20th century, is a private girls' school. Nowadays an hour's drive from the centre of London, it was then a day's journey.

The England into which Anne was born was very different from that of today. There were far fewer people. The total population of the country was some 7 million, as compared with 61 million today. London then had around 800,000 inhabitants; today 8 million. Even so, population increase was still a concern; by the time that Anne had reached the age of 50, Malthus had published his essay, *The Principles of Population*. In the first national census in 1801 England's total population numbered around 8 million, coincidentally the same number as present day London.

Travel and communication were much slower than today. The journey from London to Paris could take four to five days: crossing the Channel required favourable wind and weather, and shipwrecks were frequent. Until a semaphore system was invented in France in the 1790s, there was no signalling system more advanced than lighting beacons, and the quickest way to deliver a message was by a mounted horseman. There was little urgency for diplomacy, when the snows of Russia delayed messages by months. Wars could only be waged during the summer months, as it was impossible to move armies and their baggage trains in winter.

The political system was also markedly different. Parliament included members from England, Scotland and Wales, but not from Ireland, although that land was part of the United Kingdom. Suffrage was restricted largely to male householders, although in some Rotten boroughs other more ancient methods of selection were preferred. In the late 18th century out of 405 elected members of parliament, 293 were chosen by fewer than 500 voters. Almost all of the 293 were controlled by the landed aristocracy, which divided broadly between Whigs, the "anti-Court" party, who believed that the power of the crown should be diminished, and Tories, the "Court party", who were broadly satisfied with the status quo. The Whigs were controlled by a small number of often closely-related families, headed by dukes, marquesses and earls. They were geographically strong in the Home Counties and in the Presbyterian areas of south Scotland. The Tories were traditionally the party of the landed gentry, including a share of the aristocracy, with particular strengths geographically in former Jacobite areas in the western and northern fringes of England. From the accession of George I in 1714 to the death of George II in 1760, the Whigs virtually monopolised government. By this time the traditional terms "Whig" and "Tory" meant little in terms of political expression, though some families and some areas of the country were still traditionally aligned. A Tory could certainly be distinguished by a lack of ambition for government, a Whig by desire for office.

The government of the day also controlled appointments to profitable office. The profits were made not so much from the small salaries paid by the Crown, as from the income involved in the job itself. A tax collector who held on to the money he collected before remitting it to the Treasury could happily use the funds as a banker. A network of sinecures and placements existed to bind both MPs in Parliament and local officials in the provinces to one of the governing family factions, Rockinghams, Grenvilles, or Bedfords. To the student of 21st-century politics, the system may seem undemocratic, venal, and corrupt, but for its protagonists it worked. They believed firmly that an enlightened oligarchy was good for the nation, for its people, and for themselves. It was the political system that would take England through the American War of Independence, the French Revolution, and the Napoleonic Wars. Essentially it was not changed radically until the great Reform Bill of 1832.

If the political structure was static at the accession of George III, society seemed equally so. In the words of a verse of the 19th-century hymn, now missing from modern hymn books: "The rich man in his castle, the poor man at his gate, God made them high or lowly, and ordered their estate". In a country which was predominantly made up of small towns and villages, the landed classes, both aristocracy and gentry, ruled the roost. There was virtually no interference by central government in local affairs. Executive power lay with the justices of the peace who all came from the established landed interest. The squire would be on easy terms with those whom he met on a daily basis, from his solicitor in the town, his priest in the parish church, or the steward who looked after his land. It was a local partnership facilitated by the existence of unquestioned social distinctions.

It was difficult, but certainly not impossible, to break into this closed society, though it might take three generations to do so. Wealth was certainly a help, and a returning nabob from the East India Company like Clive or Warren Hastings, or a wealthy brewer like Samuel Whitbread would aspire to join the Establishment. Foreigners, especially those with a trained eye, often see more clearly than the locals, and the observant Swiss miniaturist painter Jean Rouquet wrote that "the Englishman always has in his hands an accurate pair of scales in which he scrupulously weighs up the birth, the rank, and above all the wealth of the people he meets, in order to adjust his behaviour towards them accordingly". But the transition still took time. William Pitt, later Lord Chatham, was the grandson of "Diamond" Pitt, the former Governor of Madras, whose wealth was largely funded by the sale of an enormous diamond to the Duke of Orleans for £135,000, and whose powerbase was built by the purchase, with the proceeds, of the voting rights in the pocket borough of Old Sarum. Pitt was sent to school at Eton and University at Trinity College Oxford, thus providing him with a suitable upbringing for a future statesman.

A classical education was also a prerequisite for those in the circles of power. Schooling in early 18th century England depended, as today, on where you lived, and your ability to fund the cost. Elementary education was available in some villages but not in others. These schools would be run on a charitable basis, buildings and teaching staff funded by the local squire and parson, and subject to the rules of the Church of England's Society for the promotion of Christian knowledge. In the towns, schools might alternatively be run by a Methodist committee. However, many children received no formal education at all. At secondary level, the grammar schools offered a mind-improving grounding in Latin and Greek, at the same time providing literacy skills in English, and from the better grammar schools, the opportunity to proceed to University and a career in the law, education or the church.

Those members of the landowning, professional, and merchant trading families who could afford to pay, commenced their children's education at home with a tutor or governess, and then sent the boys on to Eton, Harrow, Winchester or Westminster. Thence they would proceed to the universities of Oxford or Cambridge, to study classics, philosophy, natural sciences, literature and history. Undergraduates did not have to cope with the pressures of modern university life; at Oxford there were no exams, and many used that time to acquire more worldly tastes and a liking for brandy. Yet at the same time there was among the more intelligent of the ruling landowning establishment, a general wish, perhaps as never before in England, to be a master of the classics, to be a cultivated gentleman, guided by Reason, a worthy member of the Age of Enlightenment. An essential part of a gentleman's education, was the Grand Tour; today it would be called a Gap Year. This took the form of a journey around Europe, from the salons of Paris to the classical antiquities of Florence, Naples, and Rome. There were no cameras to record events, and so the fashionable visitor, whilst in Italy, would have commissioned Pompeo Battoni to paint his portrait against a background of antiquity. For the young man who wanted education, and who could afford it, the opportunity had never been so good.

For girls generally the chances were less favourable. The grammar schools, public schools and universities were a male preserve. Small private seminaries were available at local level for the female children of the gentry. Here among the better academies a girl might expect to learn the rudiments of the classics, and rather more essential skills such as conversation, playing a musical instrument, dancing, sewing, needlework, and other attributes necessary to run a future household. However for a girl who wished and was in a position to join "*le ton*", something more would be required. *Le ton* (pronounced 'tone') was the term used to describe the select and narrow group that made up high society, and from which the aspiring leaders of the nation would select their brides. The ideal wife would be expected to be impeccably bred, to be an heiress, to be beautiful, to be a little educated in the classics, to be a sparkling conversationalist, and a competent dancer. She would have grown up learning the unwritten rules of fashionable behaviour from her immediate family circle; she would have had a teacher, probably a governess, who would teach her Latin and French, English and French literature, appreciation of painting and music, and competence in the latter.

The girl who had all the ideal attributes could expect to make a good marriage. If she expected to find an ideal and faithful husband, she would very probably be disappointed. The essential role of a wife was to produce a male heir, and to be the organiser and hostess of a grand household. The pleasurable mission of her husband, when freed from the responsibilities of power, was to find a mistress. In general terms the higher a person's social ranking, the more unfaithful he could be without fear of disapproval by *le ton*. As soon as one bed was vacated, the ensuing empty space could be quickly filled, and in the top strata of Society wives frequently found lovers while their husbands dallied elsewhere. Such *amours* were the talk both of *le ton* and the town. The more important the lovers, the greater the publicity, the innuendo and the fabrication, produced and preserved for posterity both in the letters and diaries of Society gossip, and in the anonymous scribbling of political pamphlets and news sheets. Of course there were many couples who led blameless lives untouched by scandal, but as is the way of the world, these secured little public mention.

For those girls born to *le ton*, and its endless round of masquerades, theatres and balls, it could be difficult to escape its clutches. But it was not impossible. Earlier in the 1730s Lady Margaret Harley, only child of the second Earl of Oxford and granddaughter of Robert Harley, the great Tory Prime Minister, had befriended Elizabeth Robinson, who had been educated by her grandfather, Doctor Middleton, a celebrated Cambridge don. Margaret who had grown up amongst connoisseurs, collectors, and writers at Wimpole Hall was a great heiress in her own right and after marriage made her the Duchess of Portland she made her home at Welbeck Abbey a centre not only for collecting but also for the arts in general. Elizabeth Robinson married Edward Montagu, who had family mining interests in Northumberland, and as Elizabeth Montagu set up a salon in Hill Street London where tea and intellectual discussions took the place of cards and wine. At her meetings, ladies with an intellectual bent, who became known as the Blue Stockingers, mingled with some of the leading male celebrities of the day. Doctor Johnson, David Garrick the actor, and Sir Joshua Reynolds were all attendees. The name Blue Stocking may have arisen from the fact that blue stockings were worn as informal day dress, whilst black was reserved for formal and evening meetings. An eccentric and male invitee, Dr Stillingfleet, is said to have remarked that he had no black formal wear, and had been told to come in "your blue". The Blue Stockingers was very much an informal gathering, whose members were of differing backgrounds. Elizabeth Vesey was a daughter of the Bishop of Ossory, Elizabeth Carter's father was a clergyman, Hannah More's was a schoolteacher, and Anna Barbauld's combined the role of Head Master of a Dissenting Academy with that of a minister of the Presbyterian Church. For the majority of these women, their parents' roles in church and school were invaluable in providing them with an education which would otherwise have been impossible. However they were still very much a minority in society; only Lady Margaret Harley came from the great landowning aristocracy, and her family were not Whigs.

This was the England into which Anne Seymour Conway was born and would grow up. On the surface it appeared a stable society; any undercurrents which might be stirring, were not yet apparent. For members of the leading Whig aristocracy, life was very pleasant, and Anne's family very much fitted into this category. Her father, Henry Seymour Conway, was the younger son of Francis Lord Conway of Ragley, whose wife Charlotte was the sister of Catherine, wife of the great British Prime Minister Sir Robert Walpole. The Seymours were direct descendants of the Dukes of Somerset. Henry's elder brother, Francis, was to become the first Marquis of Hertford, and to marry a daughter of the Duke of Grafton.

Anne's mother, born Miss Caroline Campbell, had been married at the age of 18 to Charles Bruce, Earl of Ailesbury, then aged 57. They had one daughter, Mary, born in 1741. In 1746 the Earl of Ailesbury died, and in 1747 Lady Ailesbury married Henry Seymour Conway. As was the custom in those days, although her husband was a commoner, she retained her former married title as Caroline Lady Ailesbury; this could have been the cue for the poet Shenstone to describe her, following a visit to his landscape garden at the Leasowes, as "Peerless Ailesbury". It could, of course, also have been that he did think her beyond compare; for she, as her mother before her, was a very special woman. The clan Campbell, of which Caroline was a member, was the powerbase of the Scottish Whigs. They were Southern Highlanders and they were

Presbyterians and the sworn enemies of the Catholic Jacobite Highlanders. Their clan chieftain was the third Duke of Argyll, based in his fortress at Inveraray Castle. That Duke was to die without a male heir in 1761, when the title and headship of the clan passed to Caroline's father, Colonel Campbell, as fourth Duke of Argyll. The infant Anne Seymour Conway was therefore a fusion of the two greatest Whig families in England and Scotland. Her breeding could not be faulted.

What sort of characters were her parents? Her father, Henry Seymour Conway, or Harry, as he was generally known within his family, was born in 1719. His mother, Charlotte, was the granddaughter of Sir John Shorter, a former Lord Mayor of London, and sister of Catherine, wife of Sir Robert Walpole. He was educated at Eton, where he had arrived in 1732 and where one of his contemporaries was his cousin Horace Walpole, younger son of Sir Robert. Following school, he entered the army in 1737 as a lieutenant in Molesworth's Regiment of Dragoons. It should be noted that for the wealthy and well-connected, soldiering was a part-time occupation, as the campaigning season was restricted to the good-weather months and closed down during the winter. This, for instance, allowed Harry to join his cousin Horace Walpole, and his friend the poet Thomas Gray, for three months in Rheims during the winter of 1739-40, where they jointly studied the French language. During the War of the Austrian succession he served in the First Foot Guards at the battle of Fontenoy, where he distinguished himself as one of only 24 in his company to survive. In 1746 he took part in the Battle of Culloden, which brought the 1745 Jacobite rising to an end. He then returned to the continent in April 1747, and fought at the battle of Lauffeldt on 2nd July 1747, where he had a narrow escape. Horace Walpole, in a letter, tells that his cousin "was overpowered and flung down when one French hussar held him by the hair, while another was going to stab him: at that instant an English sergeant with a soldier came up, and killed the latter; but was instantly killed himself; the soldier attacked the other, and Mister Conway escaped; but he was afterwards taken prisoner; is since released on parole, and may come home to console his fair widow." He was in fact released three days after capture, thus enabling him to return within one week to England.

At the same time as being a soldier on active service, Harry was also beginning a political career. In 1741 he was returned unopposed as an Irish MP for Antrim County, and as an English MP for Higham Ferrers, both on the recommendation of Sir Robert Walpole. It paid to have a relation as Prime Minister. During this period he would spend the summer, which was the open season for military activity, with the army, and the winter, when weather conditions brought fighting and manoeuvring to a standstill, in politics. In 1747 he was elected MP for Penryn, a Cornish borough in the pocket of the Boscawen family. It was thus both as an MP and as an officer that in 1747 he wed Caroline Countess of Ailesbury.

As a man, Harry was a curious mixture of soldier and man of action, and of poet and dilettante. After Eton he received a course of instruction in mathematics and fortification, and then went straight into the army. He elected not to attend university. He was a do-er before a thinker. However he was still very much a man of the 18th century Enlightenment. He accompanied his cousin Horace Walpole to Italy on the Grand Tour, he wrote verse, and cultivated and distilled lavender on a commercial scale at his home at Park Place. He also invented an industrial process for distillation. He was tall and good-looking, a good and brave soldier, although it was later said of him that "he was a better general than a politician, and a better soldier than a general". He seemed to have been universally liked, and a model husband, in an era when many were not.

As a politician he had entered Parliament in 1741, the same year as his cousin Horace. Here he was to show himself a competent speaker, "the beauty of his person and the harmony of his voice" marking him out for attention. The philosopher David Hume, his secretary from 1766 to 1768, described him as "the most reasonable, equal tempered, and gentlemanlike man imaginable". However he was not an original thinker. He often relied on the advice of his cousin Horace Walpole to form his political opinions; indeed in their early days in parliament their respective talents worked to each other's advantage. Horace was the brains working amongst the varying Whig factions, offering ideas, propounding policies, finding the *modus vivendi*. Harry was the polished orator, the man who could be trusted, the speaker who could clearly express what Horace and he had agreed.

We have to speculate as to what sort of father he might have been to Anne; she was an only child and it may well be that he had wished she had been a son. As a small child she was often dispatched to stay with her uncle and godfather Horace Walpole (hereinafter also referred to as HW) while her father was away soldiering, or on other activities. Little if any correspondence exists between father and daughter, and Anne's mentions of her father are admiring and respectful as to his abilities, but silent on his personality. It is unfortunate that she directed that following her death all her letters should be destroyed and that her executor carried out her instructions. It would have been enlightening to have been able to find some correspondence between them. In the event her father married her off immediately after she had been presented at Court, to the first wealthy young man who proposed to her, and whose suitability was summed up as having an income of £20,000 per annum. Harry may well have been an ideal husband but he was not necessarily the fondest of fathers.

Harry fell in love with Caroline Ailesbury while stationed with the army in Stirling following the battle of Culloden. HW's delicate antennae had heard something by 24th October 1746, when he wrote to Conway as follows: "Harry, Scotland is the last place on earth I should have thought of for turning anybody poet: but I begin to forgive it half its treasons in favour of your verses, for I suppose you don't think I am the dupe of the Highland story that you tell me: the only use I shall make of it is to commend the lines to you, as if they really were a Scotsman's. There is a melancholy harmony in them that is charming and a delicacy in the thoughts that no Scotch man is capable of, though a Scotch woman might inspire it. I beg … that you would continue your *de tristibus* till I have an opportunity of seeing your Muse … *Reprends ta musette, berger amoreux!*"

Caroline Campbell was the only daughter of Colonel "Handsome Jack" Campbell and his wife Mary Bellenden. The latter had been a Lady of the Bedchamber to the Princess of Wales in the reign of George I. She was a noted beauty, to whom the Prince of Wales was much attracted. It was not mutual. In 1720 she quietly married Colonel Campbell, a fellow courtier, and one of the Grooms of the Bedchamber to the Prince. The marriage was for love and not for money. The bridegroom was one of thirteen children of an impoverished younger son. Although he was ultimately to become fourth Duke of Argyll, there seemed no prospect of this at the time of marriage. The couple had four sons and one daughter. John the eldest was to become fifth Duke of Argyll and to marry Elizabeth, Duchess of Hamilton, one of the celebrated and beautiful Gunning sisters. The second brother, Harry, was ADC to Sir John Ligonier, and died at the battle of Lauffeldt. The third son, William, became a sailor and married Sarah Izard, of Charleston, California, of which state he was to become the last governor. A fourth brother, Frederick, married Mary, widow of Earl Ferrers.

The one daughter was Caroline, born in 1721 and named after her godmother, Caroline Princess of Wales. When her mother died she was only 15 years old; her father was continually abroad on active military service and believed that an early marriage would provide Caroline with a home and security. Lord Bruce, the suitor who appeared three years later, was a widower and, aged 57, older than her own father. Any reservations which Caroline may have had counted for little, and her friends, led by Lady Suffolk, advised her to accept his proposal. Mrs Delaney's sister wrote that "Miss Campbell is to be married to my Lord Bruce, her father can give her no fortune, she is very pretty, well-behaved, and just eighteen, has £2000 a year jointure, and £400 pin money. They say he is cross, covetous, and threescore years, and this unsuitable marriage is the admiration of the old and the envy of the young."

They were wed in 1739, and shortly afterwards Mrs Delaney remarked on Lady Bruce's dress "in lemon colour, richly embroidered with silver and colour", at a party given by Frederick Prince of Wales. In 1741 Lord Bruce's father died, and he succeeded as third Earl of Ailesbury. Their daughter, Lady Mary Bruce, was born that year. By the time of Lord Ailesbury's death six years later, on 10th February 1747, Caroline's affections had obviously transferred to Harry, as one week later Lord Pulteney wrote to Charles Hotham: "Colonel Conway is to be married to Lady Ailesbury immediately, notwithstanding my Lord is not yet buried; the only reason I can give for her violent hurry is that Mr Conway is to go to Flanders in a little while, and she has a mind to make sure of him whilst she can."

Caroline had been left a wealthy widow. She received a jointure of £3000 a year and half the Ailesbury jewels, the other half and £30,000 going to her daughter Mary. In addition Caroline was left their London home, Savile House, Leicester Square, afterwards occupied by Frederick Prince of Wales. She was not only beautiful and accomplished, but also very well endowed.

The wedding was delayed, possibly out of respect to the late Earl of Ailesbury, or perhaps indeed by Harry's absence in the army. Flanders did call, and with it the battle of Lauffeldt where, whilst Harry Conway was captured and put on parole, Caroline's brother, Harry Campbell, was killed. Harry Conway, writing to HW after the battle, refers to him as "Poor Harry Campbell, we have had no account of his being killed but knowing his excessive forwardness in exposing himself and having not been able to hear a word of him since the action, I am afraid we have too little room to doubt of it." Following the battle, Harry had to kick his heels while on parole.

The word 'parole' stems from mediaeval French and essentially means to give one's word of honour. The parole system has disappeared from modern warfare. Essentially prisoners of war would be released to rejoin their friends and family on condition that they were paroled to take no further part in warfare usually with a time limitation. If both sides had taken prisoners it was possible to arrange for an exchange to take place, on completion of which all parties would be released from their parole.

On this occasion an agreement was signed at Liège on 31st August 1747, requiring that Frenchmen who were prisoners of war, including those captured in the Mediterranean area, were sent back to France within six weeks. If this did not happen, Englishmen currently on parole would be required to return to France. In the event, the Frenchmen were not returned within the stipulated time because, according to Lord Chesterfield, despite every arrangement having been made for their delivery, the French had not sent "the necessary remittances of money for their officers, demanded long ago". Marshal Saxe, the French commander, immediately demanded the return of the English officers, headed by General Ligonier. Harry reported that the English commanding officer, the Duke of Cumberland, was angry with the French for insisting on keeping to exact dates, but that he thought that our people were more to blame "for neglecting or wilfully breaking that promise". In the event the onset of winter brought both the outstanding paroles and the campaigning season to an end.

Harry's mind was still very much on his Scottish widow. He reported that the Duke of Cumberland "jokes with me sometimes about a certain affair; perhaps you will do so too, for many of my friends do, but if I had a mind I could stop your mouth by telling you I grow very serious about it, and it's worth my while I am sure, for you're a formidable enemy on those occasions; indeed, Horry, I do, I grow wondrous serious;

perhaps you'll be surprised, for you think me without resolution, but if another person can be as serious as myself, we shall actually commit the most serious folly in the world." In the event the marriage actually took place on 19th December 1747.

In spring 1748 the campaigning season was due to start again. Harry and Caroline left London about 20th March. On 7th April they were in Rotterdam, where Harry was forced to leave Caroline and her friend Lady Ancram "at a villainous inn". He joined the Duke of Cumberland's headquarters as the Duke passed through Rotterdam *en route* to Breda. At the end of April, Harry wrote to HW to give his view of the state of the campaign. This unfortunately was not favourable; the French army was double in numbers to that of Cumberland, the Allied army was divided, half observing the siege of Maastricht and the other half, under the Stadtholder, assembled at Breda; reinforcements of 30,000 Russian troops were somewhere in western Poland. "In short, heaven preserve us, I think we are in a woeful scrape and shall be much obliged to those, be they militant or civil, who will get us out of it. … Lady Ailesbury stays at Rotterdam, I mean hitherto." Luckily affairs were overtaken by events and following the surrender of Maastricht the preliminaries of the Peace of Aix La Chapelle were signed on 30th April.

In June the married couple spent a fortnight together in Holland where he saw "some fine Dutch paintings, a great deal of fine china and the Stadt House at Amsterdam which besides the queerness of the country and the absurdity of the people is, I think, all there is worthy of remark." This was not quite true as he could not resist telling HW: "I must tell you how they lie and then I'll have done actually … the Prince and Princess in a great bed of state, the room well lighted up, curtains all open, and nothing but a single sheet of fine Holland over their persons, and with this all the nurses and children, four or five of them at least, in the room. This is really propagating in state and I suppose the Stadtholder's children must be got as well as born in public." Horace replied that he was delighted with the description of the bedchamber of the house of Orange: "the sight itself must have been very odious, as the hero and heroine are so extremely ugly." He enquired whether Lady Ailesbury was not tired by now of her travels, hinting that his new house at Strawberry Hill had plenty of room to hold a married pair.

In September Harry wrote from Eindhoven expressing dislike at the sameness and dullness of life, despite having Caroline with him, especially because of "the condition she is in, you may guess what that is, and at this distance from home, I rarely can't be a moment satisfied; especially as there is and has been lately a good deal of sickness in the army. I have asked the Duke's leave for us both to go through Flanders, so that I think to see her safe landed at Dover and then return; she does not care to go to the last moment that is proper." HW was meanwhile writing a book the dedication of which shall be "addressed to your son that is coming". That son was in fact a daughter, Anne Seymour Conway.

Chapter 2

CHILDHOOD AND ADOLESCENCE

It is reasonable to suppose that the infant Anne's first Christmas was spent at Combe Bank, and that Harry also stayed there with wife, daughter and father-in-law. It was apparently not a comfortable abode. Mary Berry, when visiting it some years later, thought that it united every possible discomfort, and the newly married couple did not linger long there. The Seymour Conways' London address was Conway House, Warwick Street, Soho. From there Harry went about his Parliamentary business, and Caroline took up with gusto her new role as a leading society hostess. At the same time they were searching for a country house, and in 1749 they rented Latimer's, near Chesham in Buckinghamshire, the property of Mrs Cavendish, for three years.

Harry wrote to HW on 14th September, saying that before they left London at the end of the summer season, Horace had promised to visit and that they had been looking forward to it ever since. He teases Horace knowing that "such a farmer and such a country gentleman as you, I mean so busy a one, such a builder and such a gardener must be greatly taken up and that your hours are very sacred; however, when your affairs permit and a few days may be stolen from your occupations, know that there is to be entered upon immediately, if you please, a great old house, lying and being in the County of Bucks and parish of Chesham, about 12 miles from Uxbridge, which will give you a very great welcome, is in a healthful airy situation and shall be insured to stand during your term though contemporary with Queen Elisabeth's grandfather, is neither haunted with ghosts, rats, nor country neighbours, and if its cold will have good fires before Michaelmas." Later in September, Horace arrived; he did not seem impressed. "This house which they have hired is large and bad and old but of a bad age finely situated on a hill in a beech wood with a river at the bottom, and a range of hills and woods on the opposite side belonging to the Duke of Bedford. They are fond of it, but the view is melancholy."

For the longer term Harry determined that he should buy his own country seat, and not rent somebody else's. In July 1750 he wrote to HW: "I am much obliged to you for the care you promise to take for us about an house, which we both long for most impatiently, and really I think not with an unreasonable patience neither, as the sooner we get it the longer we shall enjoy it: more time to plant and improve, and age steals on with a silent foot, you know, and upon none so fast as your planters, who as their trees grow upwards, never think how they are hastening downwards themselves, of which tendency in myself my grey hairs admonish me daily."

He told Horace in October 1750 that he had looked at several places: Eversley and Holt Forest in Hampshire, and somewhere else in the neighbourhood of Strawberry Hill, which they thought too near to London. "I should indeed upon the strength of what you say, as you seem to imagine it would do for us, have concluded you'll have heard some particulars of the beauties of the place, as wood, water, hill and vale, the concave and convex of Mr Kent etc, and something of this kind I should be obliged to you if you would ask him for us, if you see him and have not; and what sort of country, whether wet or dry, this being the sort of examination we make of every place that comes before us; for as our intention is to buy, which is wedding a place for life, you'll own too much caution can't be used."

In January 1751 Harry voted with Pitt against the government's proposal to reduce the number of seamen in the Navy. This may have counted against him in his wish to command a regiment of home-based dragoons. By summer 1751 the Conways still had not found a house suitable for their requirements when Harry was ordered to proceed to Minorca to join his new regiment, the 34th Foot, to which he had been transferred as Colonel. Caroline and Anne were left at home at Latimer's. Harry wrote to HW from Paris, *en route*, and in September from Minorca, which he intensely disliked. "'Tis such a complication of ugliness, dullness and *ennui*; rocks, sands, mountains, bareness, brownness, barrenness, no mirth, no joy, no society, much ignorance, much poverty and superstition! 'Tis a horrid little spot indeed, an abominable one beyond all other abominations." He did not stay there long. HW had already warned Horace Mann in July to expect Harry in Florence: "I need not recommend him to you; but you will see something very different from the staring boys that come in flocks to you new, once a year, like woodcocks. Mister Conway is deservedly reckoned one of the first and most rising young men in England. He has distinguished himself in the greatest style both in the army and in Parliament. This is for you: for the Florentine ladies, there is still the finest person and the handsomest face I ever saw – no, I cannot say that all this will be quite for them; he will not think any of them so handsome as my Lady Ailesbury."

At the beginning of November Caroline wrote to HW hoping to join her husband in Florence. Her visit never took place, but Harry arrived in Florence in early December, having missed an earlier boat from Minorca to Leghorn (the modern Livorno). By January 1752 he was in Rome awaiting news of a new military posting, whilst taking time to view the celebrated antiquities. He wrote regularly to Caroline bemoaning the fact that he had still heard nothing. In mid-February Caroline told Horace Walpole "I am afraid you will think I plagued you to death about my husband but I must tell you that I have just received another letter from him of February 6th in which he complains of not having had any letter from England in near a fortnight, and concludes I am either sick or dead, but as he has some hopes in the midst of all his fears, he is come to a resolution of waiting only one week longer at Rome, and then setting out for Paris to know his fate. I desire to know your thoughts upon the subject, and that you will condole with me a little upon this occasion." In the event Harry returned home in March 1752.

They were not to remain long in England. On 1st May Harry and Caroline left for Ireland where Harry was to join his regiment. On this occasion, and probably the first of several times, the infant Anne, now aged three, was left in the care of her cousin Horace Walpole at Strawberry Hill. A letter dated 15th May from HW to Horace Mann informs him that "Mr Conway and Lady Ailesbury are gone to his regiment in Ireland for four months, which is a little rigorous, not only after an exile in Minorca, but more especially unpleasant now, as they have just bought one of the most charming houses in England, Park Place, which belonged to Lady Archibald Hamilton and then to the Prince. You have seen enough of Mr Conway to judge how patiently he submits to his duty. Their little girl is left with me."

On 2nd May Harry wrote to Horace: "Dear Horry, You'll be surprised perhaps at my hurry in troubling you with this; but not so much at Lady Ailesbury's having something to say about Miss; I say Lady Ailesbury though we are both Parties in the affair, which is that having agreed the country air is proper for her after the smallpox we shall beg the favour if it is equally convenient that you'll send for Missy to Strawberry instead of keeping her in town; but if it is not entirely so to desire you'll be so good as to let her go with Mathews, our servant, who will still be in town to Park Place till the time you go to Strawberry when upon your summons, she shall be immediately conveyed to you; where I don't doubt she will be as happy and as much obliged to you for your goodness as we are for that you have already showed in desiring to be troubled with brats before your time."

The remark "after the smallpox" is interesting. This disease was the scourge of the 18th century world. George Washington and Abraham Lincoln caught it and recovered; Louis XV died of it. It affected about 10% of the European population, and of those, around 15% died. The virus *variola* came in two forms, major and minor; the latter was less severe, and rarely caused death. In England there was a major epidemic from 1751-53, starting in London in December 1751. During 1752, in London alone, 3500 died from the disease.

Earlier in the 18th century, Lady Mary Wortley Montagu, wife of the British ambassador to the Ottoman Empire, noticed that the Turks inoculated against the disease with success. They placed a small pustule or scab, taken from a sufferer of the less severe form, into a scratch between an infant's finger and thumb; the virus would enter the body in a weakened form, the body would build its own anti viral protection, and provide lifelong protection from all forms of smallpox. Any pustules on young soft skin soon disappeared without trace. Despite the remonstrations of the embassy chaplain, who claimed that it was not a Christian operation, and therefore would not succeed with Christian babies, she had her own infant successfully inoculated.

On her return to England she reported on the Turkish practice to the Princess of Wales, who arranged that six felons, three male and three female, convicted to be hanged, would be inoculated by the eminent doctor Charles Maitland. If they did not catch the smallpox, they would be pardoned. The experiment went ahead, the felons remained healthy and were freed with a lifelong protection against smallpox. As Voltaire remarked, they had escaped death twice. This experiment was followed by a similar test on five orphan children, with equally successful results. The Princess's own children were subsequently successfully inoculated, or variolated, as it was described, and the process was taken up by those members of society who could afford it. It was this "variolation" which the infant Anne had experienced.

Horace replied to Harry's letter on a lighter note, on 5th May. He alludes to Lady Mary Coke, a Campbell cousin of Caroline's, who had separated from her husband, the heir to the Earl of Leicester, as soon as she was able, following their marriage in 1747. He had locked her into their home at Holkham Hall in Norfolk; she had refused him his conjugal rights. It had taken until 1750 to agree terms of separation, and the marriage was only terminated by the husband's death in 1753.

"I now entirely credit all that my Lord Leicester and his family have said against Lady Mary Coke and her family, and am convinced that it is impossible to marry anything of the blood of Campbell without having all her relations in arms to procure a separation immediately! Pray, what have I done? Have I come home drunk to my wife within these first four days? Or, have I sat up gaming all night and not come home at all to her, after her Lady Mother had been persuaded that I was the soberest young nobleman in England, and had the greatest aversion to play? Have I kept my bride awake all night with railing at her father, when all the world had allowed him to be one of the bravest officers in Europe – in short, I have a mind to take counsel, even of the wisest lawyer now living in matrimonial cases, my Lord Coke … my wife shall neither run to Italy after lovers and books, nor keep a dormitory in her dressing room at Whitehall for Westminster schoolboys, your Frederick Campbells and such like, nor yet shall she reside at her mother's house; but shall absolutely set out for Strawberry Hill in two or three days, as soon as her room can be well-aired, for to give her her due, I don't think her to blame, but flatter myself that she is quite contented with the easy foot we live upon; separate beds, dining in her dressing room when she is out of humour, and a little toad-eater that I had got for her, and whose pockets and bosom I have never examined to see if she brought any *billets-doux* from Tommy Lyttelton, or any of her fellows. I shall follow her myself in less than a fortnight, and if her family don't give me any more trouble – why, who knows, but at your return you may find your daughter with qualms and in a sack? If you should happen to want to know any more particulars, she is quite well, has walked in the park every morning, or has the chariot as she chooses, and in short, one would think that I or she were much older than we really are, for I grow excessively fond of her…"

Harry was quite satisfied by this reply, and wrote from his regiment in Belturbet, County Cavan: "I should have thanked you before for your ready compliance with our parental injunctions but was in such a continual hurry during the few days I stayed in Dublin I had not a moment to command; and now that you have complied and as I have great ambition to see my daughter in a sack and to become a grandfather, I think I may promise you shall have no farther trouble from her parents, for to do you and her justice she has yet made no complaint at all … I now see you settled at Strawberry, you and her and the boy in all sorts of matrimonial comfort and harmony of which I desire you'll wish her joy in my name. I am not vain enough to send you congratulations, though I rarely flatter myself sometimes she makes a tolerable wife; a little capricious I doubt and subject to humour now and then, but agreeable enough in her gayer hours, and even engaging when she pleases. However if you don't like her upon trial (what few parents would), on our return we'll take her off your hands again towards the month of August or so…"

While her parents enjoyed the brief pleasures and vicissitudes of Ireland, Anne stayed happily with HW at Strawberry Hill. And what a man and what a place with whom and in which be left! Born in 1717, two years before his cousin Harry Seymour Conway, Horace Walpole was the youngest son of Sir Robert Walpole, England's first Prime Minister. He was 11 years younger than his five siblings and Sir Robert and his wife Catherine were leading separate lives at the date of his birth. Sir Robert certainly accepted him as his son, but whilst the Walpoles generally exuded good health and the roast beef colouring which the French expect of the English, Horace was slim, pale and unsubstantial. It was believed that Catherine had been having an affair with Carr Lord Hervey; Horace's physical characteristics were more akin to that family.

He was educated at Eton, leaving in 1735 for a rather intermittent university career at King's College Cambridge. Here he remained until he came of age, by which time, thanks to his father's generosity, he was already financially independent. Sir Robert Walpole had secured for him the lifetime position of Usher of the Exchequer, worth about £900 a year, and two other offices as Clerk of the Escheats and Controller of the Pipe, producing another £300 a year jointly. The duties of these roles were immaterial, as he employed somebody else to carry them out, pocketing any profits arising from them and paying the employees out of the proceeds. In the 21st century this arrangement might exercise the minds of scrutineers of Parliamentary privileges and expenses, but in 1741 it was the accepted norm.

Financially independent, Horace had set off on the Grand Tour, taking with him his Eton contemporary, Thomas Gray the poet. They started in France and from Paris went to Rheims for three months to learn French. There they were joined by Harry Seymour Conway. And it was probably here that cousinly acquaintance was transformed into a lifetime friendship. From France Horace went on to spend 12 months in Florence with the British Envoy, Horace Mann. He had returned in September 1741 to take his seat as Member of Parliament for Callington in Cornwall, a pocket Borough for which he had been elected in his absence.

When Anne was born in 1748, Horace was well into his wonderful letters to a number of different recipients. The first of these had been penned in 1735, and for more than 60 years they would describe current political and social affairs, and paint pen portraits of the leading personalities of the era. They are written with wit, spirit, and perspicacity. Intended both for his contemporaries and for posterity, Horace's letters have proved fascinating to both. Contemporary writers appreciated them; Sir Walter Scott called them the best in our language; Byron said that they were incomparable. They have stood the test of time and are as enjoyable and relevant today as they were 250 years ago.

Horace was a bachelor born and bred. Sexually he would appear to have been pretty inactive; he showed no real appetite for either sex. If he had a penchant at all it was for dowagers. Seemingly weak, his constitution was in fact pretty strong; he walked in all weathers without a hat, and would regularly sit through the small hours of the night writing his letters. From middle age he was frequently and very painfully afflicted with gout; though this was probably one name to cover several afflictions. Nevertheless he was to live to be eighty, a very good age at that time. Though occasionally peevish, he was essentially a kindly man. He had a brilliant mind and carefully developed tastes. He delighted in contrary views, of which his Gothick Castle at Strawberry Hill is the best known instance.

Strawberry Hill overlooked the River Thames at Twickenham. The river, which was often easier to traverse than the roads, provided both a thoroughfare and a viewpoint. It was in an especially sought-after area, easy to reach from London, but at the same time in the country. Twickenham was but a small village. He purchased the house from Mrs Chevenix, a toy-shop owner from Charing Cross. Describing the property, Horace wrote to Harry Conway on 8th June 1747, some 18 months before Anne's birth: "You perceive by my date that I am got into a new camp, and have left my tub at Windsor. It is a little plaything house that I got out of Mrs Chevenix's shop, and it is the prettiest bauble you ever saw. It is set in enamelled meadows, with filigree hedges:

A small Euphrates through the piece is roll'd,
And little finches wave their wings in gold.

Two delightful roads, you would call dusty, supply me continually with coaches and chaises: barges as solemn as barons of the Exchequer move under my window; Richmond Hill and Ham Walks bound my prospect; but, thank God! the Thames is between me and the Duchess of Queensberry. Dowagers as plentiful as flounders inhabit all around, and Pope's ghost is just now skimming under my window by a most poetical moonlight. I have about land enough to keep such a farm as Noah's, when he set up in the Ark with a pair of each kind; but my cottage is rather cleaner than I believe his was after they had been cooped up together forty days."

This little cottage was to be transformed over the next few years, coinciding with Anne's childhood and adolescence, into the Gothick castle of Strawberry Hill. While his more conventional contemporaries were still designing and building concentric Palladian country houses of exact geometrical proportions, HW was designing his Gothick Castle to be as asymmetrical as possible. Where his peers chose Bath or Portland stone, Horace constructed in wood and papier-mâché. Where they looked for their buildings to last for ever, Horace was doubtful whether his creation would survive his lifetime. In the event, today Strawberry Hill is restored to its former glory, whilst many of its contemporary buildings have disappeared.

It was here, too, that in 1757 he established his own printing house, the Strawberry Hill Press, run by Thomas Kirgate, where many of his first editions were printed, as well as works by other authors, such as his friend, Thomas Gray.

Indeed life must have been entertaining for the little girl. Horace writing to George Montagu says: "we lead quite a rural life, have had a sheep shearing, a haymaking, a syllabub under the cow, and a fishing … of three goldfish out of Poyang [the Chinese name given by Horace to his gold fish pond] for a present to Madam Clive … Mr Bentley is with me, finishing the drawings for Gray's Odes; there are some Mandarin-cats fishing for goldfish, which will delight you." Madam Clive was the celebrated comedy actress, Kitty Clive, who lived at the end of the garden at Little Strawberry Hill; Mr Bentley was Richard Bentley, son of the Master of Trinity, a founding member of HW's Committee of Taste and an expert draughtsman. Thomas Gray, the poet had been a friend of HW at Eton, and had accompanied him on the Grand Tour. His celebrated *Ode on the Death of a Favourite Cat Drowned in a Tub of Goldfishes* was written at Strawberry Hill in 1748.

There is little recorded mention of Anne's formal education during childhood and adolescence. At various times she is recorded as having a nurse or nanny, who accompanied her wherever she went. Her extensive knowledge, wit, and conversation came very much from being part of the learned literary and artistic society in which she was to grow up. In addition she would have had the advantage of being able to use at will the extensive libraries both at Park Place and at Strawberry Hill. She might well have had access to a game housed at Strawberry Hill called "The Impenetrable Secret". This was a combination firstly of a conjuring trick: "Take a card, and don't show me which – memorise one particular proverb, witticism or adage, listed upon the card", followed by: "And this was the saying which you chose", selected from another pack of cards. Secondly, it was an educational process, providing a wealth of source material for future conversation: "Good nature is a great misfortune when it is not managed with prudence", or "The greatest of prodigals is he who bestows benefits on the undeserving", or "Wedding a woman for her beauty is like eating a bird for its singing". The game provided one hundred of these witty or improving answers, to be memorised informally. Visions of the *enfant terrible*, little Miss Know All, spring to mind, but Miss Elizabeth Jones, the nursemaid in the nursery wing was probably up for it.

Anne's first stay at Strawberry Hill came to an end in June 1752, to the chagrin of HW who wrote to Harry regretting that "I shall certainly see you with less pleasure than ever as our meeting is to be attended with a resignation of my little charge. She is vastly well, and I think you will find her grown fat. I am husband enough to mind her beauty no longer, and perhaps you will say husband enough too, in pretending that my love is converted into friendship; but I shall tell you some stories of her understanding that will please you, I trust, as much as they have done me."

The move from Strawberry Hill to Park Place exchanged two sources of delight, the first marvellously quirky, the second conventionally outstanding. Park Place, in the parish of Remenham, just to the north of Henley-on-Thames, was a large rectangular country house, handsomely placed on a hill overlooking the River Thames running below. It had been built in 1719 by Lord Archibald Hamilton and was subsequently a country residence of Frederick Prince of Wales, father of George III. Harry was delighted with this purchase and was to spend his whole life enjoying and improving it.

Here Anne was to find a new companion, brought by her father from Minorca. This was described by HW as "originally from Africa, a 'Jeriboo', to be sure you know what that is, if you don't, I will tell you, and then I believe you will scarce know any better. It is the composition of a squirrel, a hare, a rat, and a monkey, which altogether looks very like a bird in that it is about the size of the first, with much such a head, except that the top of the nose seems shaved off, and the remains are like a human hair-lip; the ears and its timidity are like a hare. It has two short little feet before like a rat, but which it never uses for walking, I believe, never but to hold its food, the tail is naked like a monkey's, with a tuft of hair at the end; striped black and white in rings. The two hindlegs are as long as Granville's with feet more like a bird than any other animal, and upon these it hops so at a distance you might take it for a large thrush. It lies in cotton and is brisk at night, eats wheat and never drinks; it would, but drinking is fatal to them. Such is a 'Jeriboo'." Was it what we know as a gerbil?

Horace was also helping to increase the livestock population at Park Place. Towards the end of August Harry wrote to him thanking him for an offer of pigs, cows and bantams. The cows would be Alderneys, a much sought after breed from the Channel Islands, rich red in colour, and suppliers of extremely creamy milk. Harry was delighted to receive all of these, providing that the Alderneys were free of cattle distemper, a disease endemic at the time, but of which Berkshire was then free. The bantams were to come in a basket on the London stage coach. The pigs took longer to arrive; they were a very special Chinese pair, boar and sow, brindled in colour, and very stout. They were due to make the trip from Strawberry Hill to Park Place by water, in a barge on the River Thames. However at the first attempt, the men in charge of herding them to the barge were drunk, and accused the porcine pair of being wild and unruly. The next boarding party was more successful, and on 16th November Harry wrote to HW: "I do thank you, my dear Horry, very heartily for your charming brindled couple; I waited to do it till I saw 'em safe arrived which did not happen till this morning; they have been eight days on their voyage and the poor Lady Ticchi-Micchi no doubt horribly seasick; notwithstanding which they are come in all the glory of their fat with their bellies sweeping the ground ... Ticchi-Micchi himself is of a wildness and Majesty not to be described; his high bristles on his neck and his low belly forming a most complete line of beauty; in short, they are all perfection and we all thanks." He went on to invite Horace to stay and join them with Sir George and Lady Lyttelton and their son Tommy.

In the spring of 1753 Harry rejoined his Regiment in County Sligo, returning to Park Place in late June. Caroline and Anne remained in England. The summer and autumn were spent planting and improving the grounds at Park Place. Horace visited them at least twice and the parents visited Stowe and Hagley. In March 1754 Horace told George Montagu that he had gone with Lady Ailesbury and Mr Conway and Miss Anne to hear the rehearsal of Mrs Clive's new farce which was very droll with very pretty music. In May Harry was back with his regiment in Athlone, returning to Park Place in time to arrange to receive goldfish from Horace in July.

Towards the end of July Harry received a new command as the Colonel of the 4th Horse (later to become the 7th Dragoon Guards). In September Horace again looked forward to a further visit to Park Place, and to teasing Harry, who had narrowly escaped royal displeasure when his horse kicked the Duke of Cumberland on the leg whilst on parade. *The Daily Advertiser* reported the incident and was relieved that his Highness, "having on a strong boot, received little injury." In an October letter to Horace, in which he expressed hopes for a future appointment as Groom of the Bedchamber to the King, Harry sent "the compliments of Lady Ailesbury and your little wife's love, which is more."

In April 1755, Harry received an unexpected but not unwelcome promotion, though not in the military field. The Marquess of Hartington had been appointed Lord-

Lieutenant of Ireland and had accepted the position on condition that Harry, who was an acquaintance, but not a close friend, should accompany him as secretary and Minister. This was an important posting, as it entailed executive control of the administration under the Lord-Lieutenant. Harry was already a member of the Irish parliament, and his previous experience with his regiment in Ireland would have made him a very suitable choice for the position.

The political situation in Ireland was messy. Calls for Irish independence from a Patriot faction, and a possible French invasion, gave cause for concern and Hartington reported to Newcastle after a few days that "I own I shall not flatter myself that things will go quietly, until I have some further proofs of their good intentions." It is not surprising that in the circumstances Caroline and Anne were left in London. Caroline reported that she had just been to the Tower of London to inspect the menagerie there. This would have been a forerunner of London Zoo, and possibly it had been a treat for Anne.

During June, the Lord-Lieutenant and his Minister went on Progress through the province of Munster to inspect fortifications and review the troops. Colonel Conway was presented with the freedom of the cities of Dublin and Cork, and of Kinsale. With each freedom came a silver presentation box. By now Harry had decided that Ireland was sufficiently safe to accommodate Caroline and Anne. He sailed from Dublin on 9th July to report to the Prime Minister, Newcastle, on the current political situation and also to collect his wife and daughter. He returned to Dublin on 16th September. The voyage was not a happy one; it took 40 hours from Holyhead. Caroline was very sick and Anne a little. Both recovered speedily. Horace professed mock worry lest Anne should come to harm, "as my Lady is a little coquette herself, and loves crowds and admiration and a court life, it will be very difficult for her to keep a strict eye upon Missy. The Irish are very forward and bold…. I say no more; but it would hurt you both extremely to have her marry herself idly; and I think my lord chancellor has not extended his matrimonial foresight to Ireland. However, I have much confidence in Miss Elizabeth Jones: I am sure when they were here, she would never let Missy whisper with a boy that was old enough to speak." It would seem that Anne and her nurse had been staying again with Horace a little earlier.

Harry seemed confident that Anne would hold her own. "Missy has many followers and pretenders as you may imagine; but as she does not know the merit of broad shoulders and strong legs, and is more taken with the charms of conversation, and is not quite reconciled to a story told with a brogue, I hope she may be tolerably safe for this session, especially as I think they seldom begin to ravish 'em under nine years old." In December the Duke of Devonshire died, and the Marquess of Hartington, Harry's boss, succeeded him. In January Harry reported that Missy was being strongly solicited by a sturdy little fellow who kissed and played with her from morning to night and swore that he would marry her. Horace replied fearing that he must resign his claim: "I never was very proper to contest with an Hibernian hero."

In the meantime Irish elections were taking place, political machination continued unabated, and Lisbon suffered a disastrous earthquake. The New Year in 1756 saw Caroline writing to Horace stating that "Missy is sitting by me, throwing all the ink and sand about, and tormenting me to death to read fairy tales to her." At the same time she told Horace that she hoped that in six weeks they would be home. She was to be disappointed. Harry, who had been appointed a major-general in January, wrote to Horace dreading a prolongation of the session of the Irish parliament. He looked forward to "his plough and his cabbages more than can be expressed", complaining that in Ireland he was indeed no major-general but a mere secretary. Horace in reply lamented that Harry never told him of any of Missy's *bon mots*. "I hope she has not resided in Ireland till they are degenerated into bulls!" It was the end of April before Harry was able to write with the news that they were shortly to come home and in the event he reached London on 17th May 1756.

Back at Park Place in June, Caroline wrote to HW saying that she was in need of a sideboard table, about 6 feet long, for Park Place, and since Horace might be going to an auction of Mr Pestre's furniture, she would be obliged if he would bid for her if he saw anything suitable. She was also in need of chair frames which would be good enough to hold her needlework. She was acknowledged by her contemporaries as being outstanding in the art and skill of embroidery, and she gave Horace two of her firescreens for Strawberry Hill. The Conways visited Horace at Strawberry Hill for two days in June, and he returned to them at Park Place in July. Anne would have had plenty of time and opportunity to catch up with her godfather.

While the domestic scene may have seemed peaceful, in Europe and beyond the Seven Years War was brewing. This was to be the first global conflict in history. The ancient enemies France and Austria combined to take on Frederick the Great's Prussia, backed by Hanoverian George II's England. England's interests were primarily overseas and directed towards advancing her colonial empire in India and the New World at the expense of France, and latterly Spain. The war lasted from 1756 to 1763 terminating in the Treaty of Paris. Overseas the British were successful in Canada and America and in India. On the continent the fortunes of war swayed to and fro. At one time Prussia was facing the combined might of France, Austria and Russia, and when, following the death of George II in England, the new monarch decided to withdraw subsidies to Prussia, things looked bleak for Frederick the Great. However another timely death saw Peter III succeed the Empress Elizabeth in Russia. Peter was a staunch admirer of Frederick the Great and directed a reversal of Russia's policy to support Prussia. In 1762 the battles of Burkersdorf and Reichenbach saw Frederick gaining decisive victories over the Austrians, reclaiming all the lands lost hitherto.

In England, the political scene was controlled until 1760 by a partnership between William Pitt in the House of Commons and the Duke of Newcastle in the Lords. Pitt provided the drive to the war effort; Newcastle kept the coalition together by careful manipulation of the varying Whig factions and interests, and managed the increasing war debt. Whilst in Ireland, Harry had been kept informed of political events by HW; back in England he took a keen interest in matters both political and military, sometimes attending Parliament, more often military camps across the country. However he still found time for visits to view the houses and grounds of his colleagues, and to entertain them at Park Place. Caroline often accompanied him on his travels, and acted as hostess on home ground, where she would undoubtedly have been ably supported by Missy Anne.

In July 1757 Harry was summoned once more to military action. As second-in-command to Sir John Mordaunt, he was to embark with troops to an unknown destination, which he believed might be to relieve the Duke of Cumberland on the mainland. A few days later the mission was revealed as a projected secret expedition to Rochefort, the well fortified French naval base, not far from La Rochelle, and facing the Atlantic seaboard. It was an expedition dreamed up by William Pitt and the Cabinet Council. At first both naval and military commanders had declared the expedition impracticable; however later advice from a French pilot caused them to change their minds and to support the venture. A large fleet assembled, lying off Newport in the Isle of Wight, which caused consternation along the French Channel coast. The destination remained secret. Eventually the men of war and troopships assembled off Cowes, the winds were declared propitious, and on 7th September 1757 the expedition set sail

On 23rd September the fleet arrived off Rochefort, and captured a small island and fort commanding the river Charente and the approach to Rochefort. This was achieved by Captain Howe in command of the *Magnamine*, who approached the island under French fire and when his ship was within a ships-length of the fortress wall, commenced a cannonade which in thirty-five minutes flattened the French defences. Harry had been standing by with three battalions to occupy the island, but in the event was not required to do so.

A week later, Harry wrote to HW stating that he would be surprised to hear that they were already on their way back to England. The expedition had not been a success. The naval and military commanders had not agreed matters between themselves, and the military commanders, having agreed that a direct attack on Rochefort was not possible, had then disagreed on alternative targets. Major-General Conway had been in favour of attacking the smaller position of Fouras, or the Ile d'Oléron, but Mordaunt, his commanding officer, and the other senior officers had disagreed. Harry eventually acquiesced to their opinion, and the expedition therefore returned having achieved nothing.

The writer has navigated the river Charente as far as Rochefort. The port was designed and fortified by Vauban, Louis XIV's great military architect. It was well protected, and at least 3 miles upriver. It is extremely difficult to see how it could have been attacked and taken from the seaward side. The moral must be "never trust a French pilot".

Harry was chary of the reaction back home to the expedition's failure. "I gave my opinion against an undertaking I thought impracticable, as then proposed. I have ever since been labouring to prevent the disgrace of coming away so poorly as I think we shall." On 2nd October Caroline wrote to HW from Park Place, worried that she had heard nothing. On 7th October he let her know that the expedition had docked at Portsmouth the previous day. Harry had asked Horace to keep a weather eye open as to reactions to the expedition in London while he was busy disembarking the troops. On 14th October Caroline joined him at Portsmouth, and on the 16th, he arrived in London after a short stop at Park Place.

Both the King and William Pitt, the Prime Minister, were furious at the failure of the expedition, and wished to have all the military leaders court-martialled, a threat of which Harry had been apprehensive. In the event only Mordaunt was court-martialled, and subsequently acquitted unanimously. However the Rochefort expedition had done no good to Harry's reputation as a general. The following year, 1758, he was bypassed for inclusion in another expedition, almost equally unsuccessful, to Brittany to attack St Malo. General Ligonier told Harry that the King had made all the appointments and that for the present he was required in England to help defend the country.

Staying in England led to a round of accompanying Caroline on visits to friends and relations in the great country houses, and entertaining them at Park Place in return. In July they went on what they described as "the Northern circuit" including the Straffords at Wentworth Castle and the Devonshires at Chatsworth. Caroline went to take the waters at Harrogate and in an interesting snippet of correspondence, Lady Caroline Fox described to her sister Lady Kildare a letter written by Caroline to her daughter Mary, by now Duchess of Richmond. The letter in question was "the only one she has received from her in six weeks. It's a pretty letter, with an account of Harrogate, which is a strange place, but not the least like the letter of a mother to a daughter, a coldness and form in it that astonishes me. Dear siss, how could you ever take to anybody that has such a cold, reserved disposition … Such a want of frankness and openness … I can't conceive how Conway and she ever could produce a child with such icy dispositions, but to speak seriously, I do think there is in mother and daughter as much insensibility and want of that sort of cordial unreserved affection in their natures which I can't describe … than ever I saw in any people." The child referred to was Anne, who was accompanying her parents on their journey; she was then aged 9½, and seemed already to display a lack of warmth or *simpatia*.

Harry was much impressed by Wentworth: "no other place was ever in greater beauty; how much that is improved by the good and agreeable company of the owners you can tell. We are at present confined to our *parti carré*, Missy goes for nothing, and clever as this is you can't imagine how much we agree in wishing for you to spoil it," presumably by taking her off their hands again. They continued to Chatsworth, taking in Worksop, seat of the Duke of Norfolk, *en route*. By September they were back at Park Place, and Harry, resigned to not having been asked to join a further military expedition to the West Indies, used his vigour and skills in the alternative role of farmer. "I neither read Aristotle nor Plato…. but I read Tull upon husbandry, and grow a prodigious farmer. I visit my farm almost every day. I have seen my hops picked and dried and bagged; I have visited my barns and my fields. The only fault is I don't grow rich; on that head I really am ashamed of myself. I talked of buying estates, building roads, etc, and find I have no money." Towards the end of 1758 Henry did at last get a military assignment, but possibly a more pedestrian one than he had hoped for. He was asked to go and arrange terms with the French for an exchange of prisoners, and this was achieved in February 1759.

During 1757 Mary Bruce was married to Charles, third Duke of Richmond, before she had reached her 17th birthday. Horace recorded that "the Duke of Richmond has made two balls for his approaching wedding with Lady Mary Bruce. It is the prettiest match in the world: youth, beauty, riches, alliances and all the blood of all the Kings from Robert Bruce to Charles II. They are the prettiest couple in England, excepting the father-in-law and mother." During the following year the Duke of Richmond, aged 23, commanded the 72nd Regiment and accompanied the Duke of Marlborough's expedition to the coast of France. While he was away, the Duchess of Richmond stayed with her mother and half-sister, mostly at Park Place. They also paid constant visits to Strawberry Hill.

Also in 1758 Horace stayed for another week at Park Place, "where one of the bravest men in the world who is not permitted to contribute to our conquests, was indulged in being the happiest by being with one of the most deserving women, for Campbell goodness no more wears out than Campbell beauty. All their good qualities are huckaback." Huckaback is described in Johnson's dictionary as "a kind of linen with raised figures". Its significance was that it was the most hard-wearing and long-lasting of materials. Elsewhere Horace describes Caroline and her cousin, Lady Strafford, as "huckaback beauties that never wear out." It may have been during this visit that Horace noticed Anne modelling characters from Edmund Spenser's *Faerie Queene* with a wax candle and silk, feathers and tinsel picked out from the silk. She had produced a miniature knight and his squire, smaller than a fingers length, in costumes as described by Spencer.

On 2nd February 1759, while Harry was negotiating prisoners on the continent, another family wedding took place and Caroline gained a notable sister-in-law. On this occasion the bridegroom was Caroline's brother, Colonel John Campbell, who was to become Marquess of Lorne, the courtesy title of the eldest son of the Duke of Argyll, when her father, "Handsome Jack" Campbell, succeeded as fourth Duke of Argyll in April 1761. His bride was the noted beauty Elizabeth Duchess of Hamilton, one of the Gunning sisters, whose previous husband had married her on St. Valentine's Day 1752, the day of their first meeting, with a wedding ring plucked from a bedroom curtain. He had died in January 1758 at the age of 33, as a result of cold caught out hunting. As was the fashion of the day, she retained her former title as Duchess of Hamilton until her husband succeeded as fifth Duke of Argyll in 1770.

Thus Horace was able to write on 2nd June 1759: "Strawberry Hill is grown a perfect Paphos, it is the land of beauties. On Wednesday Lady Ailesbury and the Duchesses of Hamilton and Richmond dined there, the two latter stayed all night. There never was so pretty sight as to see them all three sitting in the shell. A thousand years hence, when I begin to grow old, if that can ever be, I shall talk of this event, and tell young people how much handsomer the women of my time were than they will be then. I shall say women alter now. I remember Lady Ailesbury looking handsomer than her daughter, the pretty Duchess of Richmond, as they were sitting in the shell on my terrace with the Duchess of Hamilton, one of the famous Gunnings." The Shell was a magnificent wooden garden seat, carved to resemble an enormous scallop shell, rising with a curved fan shaped back.

By this time the war in Europe was getting dangerously close to home. The county militias were raised and armed. The unmilitary Horace described their appearance: "the regimentals, too, are very becoming, scarlet faced with black, buff waistcoats, and buttons. How knights of shires, who have never shot anything but woodcocks, like this warfare, I don't know; but the towns through which they pass adore them: everywhere they are treated and regaled." Anne must have seen the Oxfordshire militia parading through Henley. By late summer Harry was employed in the task of licking this amateur army into shape, an uncongenial posting for a regular officer. This time he was at Chatham camp. On 1st August he told the Duke of Devonshire that the Surrey Yeomanry were expected shortly, and in October he wrote to Horace telling him that he had reviewed the Regiment, and that Horace would be able to read in the patriotic press how excellently the troops had performed. His real feelings as to their competence he kept to himself.

Harry was still without military command on active service. In August he and Caroline visited Ragley, where a major session of the card game Loo was in progress. HW excused himself from the party as he was suffering for the first time from an extremely painful attack of gout. In September Harry was back on duty inspecting the militia in Kent and Essex. In spring 1761 he was at last asked to join the Army as second-in-command to Lord Granby in Germany. On this occasion he was accompanied both by Caroline and Anne, and Caroline's Campbell cousin, Lady Mary Coke. While Harry went campaigning, Caroline remained in The Hague whence she sent gifts of snuff and bonbons to Horace. In July she sent a further gift of Dutch china, and Horace, writing to thank and talk about the coming wedding and coronation of George III, mentioned that "if Miss Conway has a mind to be in fashion at her return she must take some David or other to teach her the new twing twang, twing twing tang of the guitar." On 27th September Horace wrote again to Caroline including his regards to Miss Conway.

Six months later in March 1762 Horace complained of a bad cold but believed that with the assistance of James's powder for four nights, he would recover, and "if Miss Conway does not come back with *soixante et douze quartiers* and the hauteur of a landgravine, I think I shall still be able to run down the precipices at Park Place with her .... this is to be understood, supposing that we have any summer." In a postscript to this letter, Horace thanked Caroline for sending Anne's drawings, which were of a Dutch officer, an English officer in his morning dress, a German officer, a French officer and an English alehouse man, plus a sketch of Madame Paganzikar of Osnabrück. He ended: "My compliments to Miss Conway's drawing." This is the first instance recorded of Anne's artistic talents, and interestingly the daughter of a soldier had been encouraged to draw soldiers.

By July 1762 Caroline and Anne had obviously returned home, as Horace wrote inviting them to visit him at Strawberry Hill. On 26th September 1762 Horace in return visited Park Place where, writing to Harry, still in Germany, he had found "Your Countess is handsomer than fame and your daughter improving every day and your plantations more thriving than the poor woods about Marburg and Cassel. Chinese pheasants swarm there." In the event, Harry remained on the continent with the army until the spring of 1763 when, following the Peace of Paris, he was put in charge of bringing the British troops back to England.

On 1st May 1763 HW wrote to Harry, primarily about John Wilkes, who had been committed to the Tower of London on a warrant for treason contained in his publication *The North Briton*. He went on to talk about designs for a cottage or greenhouse at Park Place, and mentions the Infanta (Anne) "whose progress in waxen statuary I hope advances so fast, that by next winter she may rival Rackstrow's old man." Anne, by now aged 15, had modelled a bas-relief shock dog in wax, along with oval wax profiles in the manner of Isaac Gosset. Working with wax was considered a fit occupation and a desirable skill for a lady. "Rackstrow's old man" is Horace at his hyperbolic best. There was no way in which Anne could have rivalled the old man produced in plaster of Paris, life-size and coloured like a model from Madame Tussaud's. It had been exhibited in the 1763 exhibition of the Free Society, and had had to be withdrawn from view "on having frightened an apothecary".

By summer 1763 Harry was back at Park Place, supervising the building of a Gothick cottage, to be followed by a bridge taking the Henley to Wargrave road over the valley that flowed down from the house to the Thames. In the autumn he moved to London and an active role in the House of Commons, where for a few months his cousin HW was also an active attendee. In the opening debate on Thursday 17th November 1763 both cousins voted against the government in a division concerning the rights and privileges of members of parliament. They went on to oppose the government again in defending Parliamentary privilege in the case of John Wilkes and *The North Briton*, and in doing so incurred the instant displeasure of His Majesty, and an implied threat to relieve Harry of his dual positions as Colonel of his Regiment and Gentleman of the Bedchamber. The Parliamentary session finished in December with riots in London, protesting against the unpopularity of the Court party, and Wilkes arrested and back in the Tower of London.

Parliament reassembled in January, and on Friday, 3rd February Harry made a dramatic and telling attack on the government. On February 14th and 17th he again voted with the opposition against the legality of general warrants. Two months later, a day after parliament had been prorogued, he received his reward for integrity from the government. On 20th April *St James's Chronicle*, the government record, reported "His Majesty has been pleased to appoint the Right Hon. The Earl of Pembroke to the Regiment late General Conway's, who has resigned." Conway himself did not hear of his dismissal until 22nd April. At the same time he was also dismissed from his position as Groom of the Bedchamber. He bore this loss, which severely dented his annual income, with dignity. Horace offered to pay him £6000 as a gesture of support, and he received further offers of financial support from the Duke of Devonshire, Lord Strafford, and his brother-in-law, the Earl of Hertford. He refused all offers of help and retired back to his family, to Park Place, and to measures of economy.

In July Horace records sending gifts of a small bull for Lady Ailesbury, and seven bantams for the Infanta (Anne). In August he visited Park Place where his fellow guests were Lord and Lady William Campbell. Lord William was Caroline's brother, a naval captain, who had married Sarah Izard, an American from South Carolina, the previous year.

During this visit Lady Ailesbury, Anne, and Lord and Lady William Campbell, were fishing in a boat on the River Thames, close to Henley, when they heard a man calling out "Boat! Boat!", several of which passed not far off without taking any notice. Eventually a man appeared at the point of a nearby island, shouting that there was a man drowning. Lord William and the ladies immediately set off, and rowed to the place, where they were shown something lying on the river bed. "His lordship stirred it with the pole of his boat, which was 20 feet long; but as the pole had no hook to it, and his Lordship finding it was losing too much time, he instantly pulled off his coat (his Lady and sisters being in the boat) and jumped into the water, which was 16 feet deep; and although the man was under the trunk of an old tree, he brought him up and swam to shore with him. His Lordship then ordered him to be blooded, and by his great care of him, he soon began to draw breath, and being carried home was perfectly recovered." This incident left a deep impression on Anne. Her uncle William became something of a cult hero to her. The gallant naval captain, who was later to become governor of South Carolina, and to serve together with the young Nelson under Admiral Parker, was to surface again years later as an ideal of gallantry in her novel *Belmour*.

In October Harry received an unexpected windfall, being left a legacy of £5000 by the Duke of Devonshire, described in the following terms: "I give to General Conway £5000, as a testimony of my friendship for him; and of my sense of his honourable conduct, and friendship for me." The Duke and the Cavendish interest had been firm supporters with Harry of the Opposition. In November HW, who was planning a visit to Paris where his cousin and Harry's brother, Lord Hertford, was ambassador, again visited Park Place, where he was able to report that the bridge was now completed.

In January 1765 parliament met again, and on the opening day Harry spoke forcefully concerning the iniquity of dismissing military officers for civil reasons. It was a remarkably good speech and together with an even stronger performance on 23rd January, did much to confirm his skills as an orator and put down a marker for high office in the event of a change of government. This was to be another six months in arrival. The alliance between Grenville and Bedford staggered on until June, arguing between themselves, the opposition, and the King.

Eventually George III could tolerate them no longer, and in June a new administration was formed with Rockingham as First Lord of the Treasury and Harry Conway as Secretary of State for the North. HW was extremely upset not be offered a post in the new administration, even though he would certainly have refused to take it. Other relations had fared better: Harry's brother Lord Hertford became Lord-Lieutenant of Ireland, and his place as ambassador to France was taken by the Duke of Richmond, Harry's stepson-in-law.

HW decided to take up the invitation of Lord Hertford, the shortly-to-be-departing ambassador to France, to visit him in Paris. Harry, who had depended on Horace's advice in political matters, was furious to see him absent himself for a matter of months. Although by October a friendly correspondence had been resumed, Horace's resentment at being passed over lingered on, and the cousins' previous close relationship was never quite the same.

One important change resulting from a shift around in offices was that the philosopher David Hume, who had been secretary to Hertford in Paris and had carried on as *chargé d'affaires* until the Duke of Richmond arrived to take over, now returned to London, and early in 1767 became secretary to Harry.

The new Secretary of State found his workload hard. By the end of November he suggested to HW that they took a trip to Naples together and said that he was missing the pleasures of Park Place. In January 1766 Hertford wrote to Horace that "my brother writes me word that he is overloaded with business before that of Parliament is added to it". Indeed it would have been hard work. Rockingham and the majority of office-holders were members of the House of Lords, whilst in the Commons where, as today, the main action occurred, Harry's only ministerial support was from Chancellor of the Exchequer Dowdeswell, the MP for Tewkesbury, and Charles Townsend, who, although brilliant on occasions, was inconstant in his loyalty. By March 1766 Harry became ill from overwork, though he had recovered by April. Politics were not his only worry; his daughter Anne's education was complete and she was launched on London society.

Anne herself has been mentioned only in passing during this chapter. But in studying the activities and movements of her parents it is possible to get a pretty good idea of her upbringing. We have no record of any formal education, but we know that she spoke excellent French. She may have visited France during the years from 1763-67 when both her uncle and half brother-in-law were successively ambassadors to France, though there is no record of this. She was conversant with Latin and had a smattering of Greek. She was extremely well-read, and able to comment intelligently on the theatre. She must have picked up these attributes from listening to and talking with the highly educated members of her parents' circle. In addition both she and her half-sister would have had formal training from governesses. She had begun modelling in wax and shown herself skilful in this art. In short she was educationally fully-rounded, and a credit to her parents. Outwardly she was pretty and attractive, and her conversation accomplished. However her personality lacked warmth and spontaneity, and she did not make friends easily. She was an only child and she was a daughter. In all probability Harry the soldier would have preferred a son to carry on the Conway name. In an era when large families were the norm, and especially so in the Campbell clan, her only sibling was her half-sister Mary, six years her senior. Like many children who grow up in an adult world without the constant companionship of others of a similar age, she could be unbending and cold to her contemporaries. She was fond of her parents, and by 18th century Whig standards they were very good to their daughter. However they did not spend too many hours with her. Harry, firstly as soldier and latterly as politician, had his hands fully occupied; while Caroline's never-ending round of visits and calls, dinners and suppers and nightly sessions of Loo, left little time available for bringing up children. This was still a time when children should be seen but not heard, and, at that, only seen on selected occasions. Anne was a child of her Age, fair but frigid, accomplished but awkward.

Chapter 3

LAUNCHED INTO SOCIETY

In June 1766 Lady Sarah Lennox wrote to Lady Susan O'Brien that "Miss Conway is come about, she is grown very pretty and agreeable". A little later, at the end of August 1766, Lady Mary Coke recorded that Lady Ailesbury and General Conway had taken her to see a portrait of Anne which was being completed by Angelica Kauffman, a newly arrived painter from Italy. The picture was described by Lady Mary as being a good likeness and well done, but as being too large, "you would take it for a very big Woman". It is in fact a charming picture showing Anne as the goddess Ceres, seated facing to the left in a classical landscape of mountains and trees. In her left hand she holds a bunch of olive twigs and pink roses. She has long dark brown hair plaited and curled around her head, surrounded by a leafy garland. Intelligent blue eyes, long straight nose and a quizzical smile help complete a pretty picture of a young lady.

The portrait, painted to be exhibited before being hung in the family home, pronounced to Society that Miss Conway had been launched into their midst. The transition from schoolgirl to eligible bride was a sudden one, and from Anne's parents point of view it required an equally rapid solution. "Marry your daughter betimes for fear she should marry herself" is a timeless proverb. In the eyes of 18th century parents the purpose of a daughter was to make herself as attractive as possible, so that they, the parents, might find a suitable and willing husband for her. Caroline Ailesbury had been no exception, married at 18 to an earl aged 57; and in her view what was good enough for the mother would be fine for the daughter. The most visible marketplace for young brides was Almacks Assembly Rooms in King Street, St James's. Opened in February 1765, this fashionable institution offered for a subscription of 10 guineas a weekly Wednesday ball. Anyone wishing to attend these balls, must first have passed the scrutiny of a selection panel, "the committee" of senior leading lady members of "*le ton*".

Lady Mary Coke was appointed as sponsor and chaperone. A Campbell cousin of Caroline Ailesbury, she had also been the victim of an arranged and desperately unhappy marriage to Lord Coke, from which she had only been rescued by her husband's premature death. She recorded in her diary on 16th January 1767: "At a little after nine, I was ingaged to call on Miss Conway & Lady Charlotte Ponsonby to go with them to Almacks. The Princess Amelia just went in before us: The ball did not begin till near ten o'clock. I was glad that the two young ladies that were with me got partners: one danced with the Duke of Buccleuch & the other with Mr Howard. But I observed that the Duke danced his last dance with Lady Bell Stanhope & led her down to supper." On this occasion Lady Mary had certainly succeeded in her task, as both young men mentioned were among the most eligible bachelors of the day, Mr Howard being heir to the Duke of Norfolk, and the Duke of Buccleuch, to the Duke of Queensberry. Chaperones could carry out the introductions; after that it was up to the girls themselves to make their mark. Lady Mary's rather unkind postscript is in character, but probably to the point.

The following day Lady Mary visited Lady Dalkeith, mother of the Duke of Buccleuch. She told her how, on the previous evening at Almacks, she had noted her son dancing with Lady Bell Stanhope and taking her down to supper. She went on to say that she had nothing against the lady in question, but that the young man would do better to cast his eye over all the young ladies that might be "proper for him to marry". Lady Dalkeith had agreed and said that at the forthcoming Queen's birthday ball, she would ensure that he danced with Lady Betty Montagu.

A few days later, Lady Mary received a visit from Caroline Ailesbury. She complained that the Duke of Buccleuch had previously been very friendly towards Anne, but that over the last four or five days, he had refused to speak to her. Furthermore Lady Dalkeith had never asked Anne to visit her house or taken the least notice of her. Their behaviour had made Caroline suspect that someone else was being lined up for the Duke. Caroline had continued, somewhat unconvincingly, that although the Conways would be extremely happy if the Duke liked Anne, they were in no hurry to marry her off. She explained that her daughter would have a very considerable fortune, and was a good catch for anybody. Indeed, she exclaimed, Lady Berkeley had thought Anne extremely suitable for her son, Lord Berkeley, but she had thought Anne could do better. Lady Mary replied that Lady Dalkeith had frequently said that provided that her son chose a well educated girl from a good family, she would leave the decision to him. Lady Mary had gone on to say that there must have been some mistake with regard to the lack of invitation, and that she would try to rectify the omission.

Sadly matters did not improve. On 17th February Caroline Ailesbury, who shared a box at the Opera with Lady Mary, sent a note to her saying that she was unable to go that evening. Lady Mary therefore invited Anne Conway to join her in her mother's place. The Duke of Buccleuch was at the Opera and pointedly failed to greet them, or to assist in finding their servants when leaving. Lady Mary was unable to account for his behaviour but went home "not having been much pleased or amused".

On 24th February Lady Mary recorded excitedly that she had been told by the Duke of Buccleuch's sister, Lady Frances Scott, that he had asked her to find out from their mother whether Lady Betty Montagu would be acceptable to her as a daughter-in-law. She had not as yet had the opportunity to speak to her mother but she had no doubt that she would be delighted. Later in the day Lady Dalkeith had visited Lady Mary to say "that was the Choice in the World she wished him to make", and that she was going home to write her son a letter to let him know how happy he had made her. Two days later Lady Mary received a note from Lady Dalkeith saying that her son had had supper with her on the previous evening, asking her to go and see Lady Betty's mother, the Duchess of Montagu, to seek her approval for him to propose to her daughter. The following day Lady Mary reported that the Duchess of Montagu had received the proposal, and replied that, though nothing would give her husband and herself more pleasure, they had agreed that Lady Betty make her own choice of husband, and she could say no more until the latter had been consulted. The following day brought news that Lady Betty had consented.

The rigid protocol for arranging this marriage was customary. On this occasion it was left to the bride to make her choice, and Lady Betty revealed a little later that she had already turned down three or four previous suitors. However, Lady Dalkeith's earlier remark that she would insist that her son danced with Lady Betty Montagu at the Queen's birthday ball might imply that mother and daughter-in-law-to-be were hunting together. At 23 she was three years older than her prospective husband, and must have been on the marriage market for all of those three years. She was also five years more mature than Anne, who was effectively straight out of school.

On 1st March, almost immediately after the prospective marriage had been announced, Lady Mary dined with Harry and Caroline. "I fear'd the Duke's marriage would be a disappointment at that House, as I fancy they wish'd him for Miss Conway, tho' rather from the Amiableness of his disposition than any consideration for his great Fortune. Had that been his Choice there cou'd have been no objection since her birth was equal to anybody's and She herself extremely well behaved." The dinner party considered whether the bride-to-be was possessed of a great fortune, and came to no conclusion, going on to discuss politics, where the Administration, for which Harry was responsible in the Commons, had been defeated over the Land Tax. It would seem probable that his mind was on other matters than the marriage prospects of his daughter.

On 5th March Lady Mary recorded in her diary that she had forgotten an invitation from Caroline to go and see Miss Conway dance. Nine days later, on 14th March, she noted that Mr Damer had called on Anne in the box at the Opera which she shared with Caroline, and that she expected an engagement might be in the offing. "Before the Opera was over I was persuaded my conjectures were well grounded." The next day was Sunday, and Lady Mary went to church where "Miss Conway's marriage to Mr Damer was own'd; everybody wished General Conway joy".

On 19th March HW wrote to Sir Horace Mann: "Mr Conway is in great felicity, going to marry his only daughter to Lord Milton's eldest son, Mr Damer. The estate in Lord Milton's possession is already three and twenty thousand pounds a year. Seven more are just coming from the author of this wealth, an old uncle in Ireland of ninety-three [John Damer of Shronehill, Tipperary, d.1768]. Lord Milton gives up five thousand a year in present, and settles the rest; for his two other boys are amply provided for. Miss Conway is to have a jointure of two thousand five hundred, and five hundred pin-money. Her fortune, which is ten thousand, goes in jewels, equipage, and furniture. Her person is remarkably genteel and pleasing, her face very sensible and agreeable, and wanting nothing but more colour … It is the more creditable as Lord Milton sought the match. Mr Conway gives up all the money he has in the world, and has no East India bonds."

The pre-nuptial arrangements for this match seemed eminently satisfactory. Lord Milton had provided his son with an income of £5000 a year, and provided for the future by settling an expectancy of a further £25,000 a year. From this the bride was guaranteed a jointure of £2500; this was an annual payment to be made following the death of a husband, which in days of high mortality was a very necessary insurance provision. In addition he would provide her with £500 a year "pin money" to spend on personal requirements. To put matters in perspective, £5000 a year in 1767 is the equivalent of around £500,000 a year in 2012 using the equivalent of the retail price index.

Who was this wealthy young man who had proposed and been accepted with such alacrity? John Damer was aged 23, five years older than Anne. He was the eldest son of Lord Milton. His mother had been Lady Caroline Sackville, daughter of the first Duke of Dorset. He had been educated at Eton, to which he had given a leaving portrait of himself by Sir Joshua Reynolds. In this he is depicted handsomely-clad in a dark green gown overlaid with heavy gold embroidery, a fine lace cravat around his neck, and the finest lace around his cuffs. Dark-haired and brown-eyed, he appears handsome enough, but his eyes look not at the artist, but to his right, at something unseen, and there is a hint of petulance in the mouth. The picture is dated May 1762, and describes him as 'John Damer of Trinity College, Cambridge' born in 1744, and at Eton from 1755-60. He had appeared in Anne's life like a bolt from the blue, and with precious little form to assess his character and suitability. However he, and his brothers had already been picked up by HW's antennae. In February 1765, writing to Sir Horace Mann in Florence, he thanked him on behalf of Lord and Lady Milton for "your civilities to Mr Damer". Mann had replied on 23rd March asking Horace to pay his respects to Lord and Lady Milton for their appreciation in his attempt "to be civil to their sons". He regretted that in due course, the parents were likely to hear that there had been a drunken riot in Rome when George Damer, John's younger brother, and his friend, Sir Thomas Gascoigne, had wounded four men, one of them mortally. Fortunately for Damer and Gascoigne, the Governor of Rome, Signor Piccolomini, had hushed the affair up, and promised "an act of oblivion" in return for compensation to those wounded, and a pension to the widow of the deceased. Mann continued that the Damer brothers had left for Venice. He advised

Horace not say anything of the affair to Lord Milton, but let the brothers explain it themselves. He had been forced to make a report to Lord Halifax but had restricted himself to saying that the insolence of the coachmen had caused the row, and that the young men had only been defending themselves. Gascoigne had claimed that it was all George Damer's fault, and that he himself had been absent, having gone home for his pistols, when the fatal blow was struck.

Later in May 1765 Horace acknowledged Mann's letter: "I have been so cautious as not to mention a single word of the affair of the young Damers, and am glad I was so prudent, for I have not heard it from a soul; and I should have been very sorry the family should have thought it came from you. The eldest, at least, is returned for I saw him t'other day. The whole to be sure will come out by degrees from the English abroad. I did not even make your compliments to my Lord and Lady, lest they should suspect you will have told me. I suppose it is to conceal it, that they appear unconcerned."

There is also mention of a Mr Damer, very likely to be John, as he was about in London, meeting with the eminent author and financial guru, Adam Smith, author of *The Wealth of Nations*, in February 1767. They were having breakfast together, and Smith, who was notably absent-minded, took a piece of bread and butter, rolled it around, popped it into a teapot, and then poured water over it. A few minutes later he complained that it was the worst tea he had ever drunk. The young man replied that this was not surprising, as he had rolled up his bread and butter and put it in the pot. This story at least illustrates that John Damer had sufficient clout to be able to breakfast with the great man. It might call in to question his common sense in bandying the story about, but that would have been a temptation very hard to resist.

Otherwise there is a complete silence at the time of his engagement as to his character, appearance, and general disposition. Both HW and Lady Mary Coke remark on him as an escort to Anne, but neither mentions him for good or ill; possibly they knew little more about him.

The family wealth came from John's great-uncle, who had made a large fortune as a moneylender in Dublin. A trusted former cavalry commander of Oliver Cromwell's Ironsides, he had settled in Ireland where he lived to a great age. John's father, Joseph, was a wealthy and ambitious man, anxious to be accepted into the highest ranks of society. In 1752 he had purchased the Milton Abbey estate in Dorset. The original Abbey had been founded c.933 AD, with a large endowment of land by King Athelstan of Wessex, to commemorate the death at sea of his brother Edwin. In 1309 the abbey was burnt to the ground and its replacement, built in stone, thrived as a Benedictine institution. At the time of the Dissolution of the Monasteries it was sold for £1000 to Sir John Tregonwell, a solicitor employed by Henry VIII in his divorce proceedings against Catherine of Aragon. The Tregonwell family and their descendants had continued as owners until the estate was bought by Joseph Damer.

After purchasing the estate, Damer had wasted little time in altering it on a grand scale. In the fashion of the time, he planned to remove the town of Middleton, south of the Abbey, and to replace it with the new model village of Milton Abbas, half-a-mile to the south east. Change is always unpopular; the townspeople of Middleton proved reluctant to give up their homes, even for an idyllic thatched cottage village. It took 25 years and a flood before the transition was completed. The new house, on the site of the decaying buildings adjacent to the Abbey, took less long. Damer employed John Vardy, the architect of The Horse Guards in London, who worked both on Milton Abbey and on a town house in Park Lane. This was later to become Dorchester House, and the site of the present Dorchester Hotel. He also set about establishing his lineage, claiming descent from the ancient Irish barons, the Damoreys. In 1764 Damer was created Baron Milton. Duly ennobled, he enlisted the great landscaper Lancelot 'Capability' Brown to design the grounds at Milton. In 1765 Vardy died and was succeeded as architect by Sir William Chambers. The latter was instructed to complete the house in the Gothick style, but after several quarrels between architect and client, the architect resigned, leaving the completion of the interior to James Wyatt, who also 'restored' the Abbey Church. The final result was the impressive mansion in its valley setting, now a public school.

While the great house and its surrounding landscape were being constructed, Damer had ensured that his wealth was being used to consolidate his position in society. In 1741, at the age of 21, he had been elected to support the Whig party as one of 4 MPs for the rotten Borough of Weymouth. In 1742 he married Lady Caroline Sackville, daughter of the first Duke of Dorset. He continued as an MP, representing Bramber in Sussex in 1747, and returning to Dorset in 1754 as MP for the county town of Dorchester. In 1753 he was given an Irish peerage as Lord Milton of Shrone Hill, Co Tipperary, and in 1762 he became Lord Milton of Milton Abbey.

By 1766, it was time for his eldest son John, who had just reached his majority, to emulate his father and marry a suitable wife. She should come from blue-blooded and Whig stock, and be attractive and capable. Anne Seymour Conway was descended on one side from Lord Protector Somerset and Sir Robert Walpole, and on the other from the Dukes of Argyll, heads of the clan Campbell. Her father was Secretary of State, and her mother was anxious to marry her off. Lord Milton lost no time in offering a family alliance, which was accepted with alacrity. The prospective bride and groom had played little part in the negotiation.

Their engagement lasted from March until their marriage in June. By aristocratic 18th century standards, this was a long time. Indeed, on 7th June Mme du Deffand had written to HW, saying she had imagined that the wedding had been cancelled. If there were any premarital rifts, history does not relate them.

Chapter 4

THREE WEDDINGS AND A FUNERAL

John and Anne were married on Sunday 14th June 1767, at Park Place. The announcement in the *London Evening Post* for Saturday 13th June to Tuesday 16th June 1767 read as follows: "Sunday, was married at Park Place, the Hon. Mr Damer, eldest son of Lord Milton, to Miss Conway, daughter of the right Hon. Henry Seymour Conway, Esq; who, together with his Lady, the Countess of Ailesbury, and several persons of distinction, set out that morning to be present at the marriage ceremony."

An extract from the marriage register in Remenham parish church reads as follows: "The Honble. John Damer, Bachelor, eldest son of the Right Honourable Joseph, Lord Milton, and the Honourable Anne Seymour Conway, Spinster, Daughter of the Right Honble. Henry Seymour Conway, one of His Majesty's Principal Secretarys of State, and with his consent, were Married in this Parish by Special License at his Seat at Park Place, this fourteenth day of June, in the Year 1767, by me, William Stockwood, Rector of Henley on Thames."

This Marriage was   John Damer
solemnised between Us   A.S.Conway
In the presence of   Milton
                                 H.S.Conway

Their nuptials were evidently only attended by a few hand-picked close relations, as was usual at the time. There is no other record of the event. Later that week the newly-married couple came up to London, accompanied by the bride's mother. The latter confided to Lady Mary Coke that Mrs Damer's ear-rings had cost £4000. She much regretted that the Court was in mourning, as it prevented her daughter's finery from being seen.

Anne was aged eighteen, launched into Society only a few months previously, married, and mistress of a substantial household in a new house at the top of Tilney Street, overlooking Hyde Park. Friends of her own age were few, since as a single child she had lived life to date mainly with her parents' generation. She had to learn both how to run her household and how to make new friends of her own age. For a teenager, with newly acquired wealth and husband, the path of pleasure lay open. She set out to explore it.

What was the world of *le ton* like in 1767? In addition to being a marketplace for young brides, the Season also provided entertainment for all ages. The beautifully-bred were interspersed with politicians, raconteurs, wits and blackguards. Every night there would be an event, a ball in one of the great houses, by invitation only, or an evening playing cards, either in a private house or, for the men, in the new clubs at Almack's (shortly to become Brooks's) or White's. There were theatres or the Opera, or a masquerade in fancy dress. In addition, there were the Assembly Rooms at Almack's, scene of Anne's first foray into Society, or the Gardens at Ranelagh or Vauxhall. The balls may have been exclusive, but in the masquerades and Gardens, high society mixed with charlatans and cardsharpers. There was certainly no shortage of pleasures. In the words of Dr Johnson. "When a man is tired of London, he is tired of life."

The London Season started with the recall of Parliament in January and continued until July, with a minor season from the end of September to the end of October. Should there be any requirement for a change, there were ample attractions elsewhere. In England, the spa town of Bath had active rivals at Tunbridge Wells or Cheltenham. Further afield, the delights of Paris, subject to the country not being at war with France, competed with fine Italian weather and antique remains, and more restorative waters at Spa in Belgium. Out of the Season, the great aristocratic families retreated to their country estates, with house parties, playing cards and amateur theatricals in the evening, hunting or shooting, dependent on the time of year, or enjoyment of the landscape during daylight hours.

In the world of *le ton*, marriage was not necessarily an institution for the faithful. Following the lead of the Royal Family, it was almost obligatory for a great aristocrat to have a mistress, in addition to a wife. Fidelity was the exception rather than the rule. Caroline and Harry were noted, almost by exception, for their exemplary behaviour and devotion to each other; it was an example that the next generation seemed reluctant to follow. It was not unusual for a nobleman to have a mistress both before and after marriage; the husbands of two of Anne's greatest friends, the future Lady Melbourne and the future Duchess of Devonshire, brought mistresses with them when they married. Peniston Lamb was enamoured of the singer Harriot Powell, whilst the Duke of Devonshire's current belle, Charlotte Spencer, was caring for their baby daughter at the time of his wedding. As a generalisation, the more exalted the ranking in the peerage, the more libertine the behaviour.

Girls were expected to remain virgins until they were married. There was an unwritten law that wives should remain faithful to their husbands until such time as they had produced a male heir. After that, provided that discretion was observed, they could be freed to take one or more lovers. Of Elizabeth Melbourne's six children, only one, her eldest son Peniston, was definitely fathered by her husband. Once Georgiana

Devonshire had produced her son and heir, Hart, she too was free to find solace with Lord Grey, and to have a daughter, Eliza, by him. Her mistake was to flaunt her lover openly, and not to use the required discretion.

How did Anne Damer figure in this raffish society? She seems to have taken time to become accustomed to a new world, gradually making friends and entering into its spirit and activities. At first, whilst finding her feet, Anne seems to have depended much on the company of her family and premarital acquaintances. Lady Mary Coke recorded two visits to the opera with Anne in March 1768. At one of these Anne had recounted a robbery at her father's house. A surveyor, recommended by the Duke of Richmond, a previous employer, had been employed by Harry, and worked at his London residence Conway House. This man was married to Anne's maid and was friendly with her father's servants. On a recent evening, he had spent the evening with them until 10 o'clock at night, when he left, ostensibly to go home. In fact, he remained in the house locking himself into an unused garret. At 2 am when he thought the house asleep, he went downstairs and lit a candle from the ashes in the hall grate. He went to a drawer in the table in which Harry kept his money, in the forms of bills drawable on the bank. He removed the bills amounting to £900, put the candle on top of the table and paper on top of the candle, which quickly caught fire. He speedily removed himself from the house, climbed a tree next to the garden boundary wall, and dropped down on the other side, then waited until he saw smoke indicating that the house was on fire. The next morning he turned up at the house for work, surprised to find the library burned, and many books and pictures damaged or destroyed. He was even more surprised to find that the drawers which had contained the money had not burned. He quickly realised that Harry would now know that the bills had been stolen and would swiftly inform the bank. He needed to get there first. He immediately set out to the bank and changed the bills for cash, signing his name by the pseudonym Thomas Williams. Harry was too late at the bank, but immediately recognised "Williams's" signature as being in the surveyor's handwriting.

Harry and the Duke of Richmond hatched a plan to catch the thief. Richmond sent for him to look over some plans, with Harry in attendance. While he was examining them, two men were admitted to the room on business with the Duke. One of the men handed the Duke a paper, and Harry immediately took hold of the surveyor, saying "You are the man who robbed me and set my house on fire". The two men were the bank clerks who had recognised the surveyor as "Thomas Williams". At first the surveyor denied the charge but after a few moments he confessed, and was subsequently committed to prison. Here he also confessed to stealing 20 guineas from the King's Messenger in Paris whilst employed by Richmond, at that time ambassador to France. He was subsequently hanged, despite Harry's pleas for clemency. History does not relate the reactions of Anne, or of her widowed maid.

Meanwhile, there were other changes in family circumstances. When Parliament rose on 1st July 1767, Harry, wishing the government to take a more moderate line in respect of both the American colonists and the East India Company, threatened to resign as Secretary of State. HW told Sir Horace Mann at the end of October 1767 that Harry had waived his salary of £5000 a year as Secretary of State, "contenting himself with the profits of Lieutenant-General of the Ordnance, which do not exceed eleven hundred, and awaiting for a Regiment." In January 1768, the Bedford faction came to power and Harry was able to resign as Secretary of State. He continued as Lieutenant-General of the Ordnance, and in February 1768 was named as Colonel of the Fourth Dragoons. HW, too, decided to step down from membership of Parliament before the election of 1768.

Whilst the old Whig guard bowed out, there was no shortage of new blood to take their place. Elections to Parliament took place that spring, and on 12th April 1768 the *London Gazette* recorded that John Damer had been returned as member for Gatton, one of the most rotten of the rotten boroughs, returning two members with an electorate of fewer than ten voters. The two seats were in the gift of two persons. In 1768 one of these was John Tattersall, who sold it to John Damer; the other was in the gift of Sir George Colebrooke, banker and MP for Arundel, who placed another banker, Joseph Martin, in his slot. This deal marked Colebrooke out as more than a passing acquaintance of John Damer. Some years later, HW was to describe John Damer as "grave, cool, reasonable, and reserved." He was not at first sight a man who would wish to join the nightlife of the swinging 1760s.

On 9th May 1768, the newly-married couple were together to give Lady Mary a lift home after dinner with the Spanish ambassador, whilst she left her coach for Caroline who was to leave later. Both would have had to run the gauntlet of the London mob, which was out in force that night in support of the jailed John Wilkes. On this occasion, Anne and John had been together as a couple; at other times, they went their separate ways. This was not a problem for either. It was not unusual for a wife not to be accompanied by her husband in the evenings. During the Season, gentlemen were generally only available for social activities on Wednesday and Saturday evenings while Parliament was sitting. The lure of the gaming tables, or the convivial conversation of friends and drinking companions in London gentlemen's clubs such as Brooks's or White's, followed by a visit to one's mistress were popular alternatives. Wives were free to join with other ladies for the theatre or Opera, or for a card game, or simply to wait at home for the return of their husbands. Anne preferred the former, and especially the theatre. Her mother shared a box with Lady Mary Coke, and she made good use of this whenever the opportunity arose. At this stage of her life, she was entirely untouched by rumour or scandal. No son and heir appeared, but there was plenty of time. Anne's immediate female Campbell relations were not prolific breeders; in an age of large but not long-lived families, Caroline had only one child by each husband, Anne's half-sister Mary was barren, as was Lady Mary Coke. Anne's upbringing as a daughter of a faithful mother, with her Presbyterian Campbell origins, may have made Anne, at this stage of a marriage, more straitlaced than some of her contemporaries. She may also have lacked some of their feminine warmth, though perfectly able to converse and correspond at length with members of the opposite sex.

If John Damer found Anne frigid, and not much fun to come home to, there was always the temptation to gamble. In July 1769 HW noted the gambling in East India stock, in which "fortunes were made and lost every day. Panchaud, a banker from Paris, broke yesterday for seventy thousand pounds by buying and selling stock; and Sir Laurence Dundas paid in an hundred and forty thousand pounds for what he had bought." Nor was speculation in East India stock the end of the affair. In January 1770 Horace told Sir Horace Mann that the gambling at Almack's now surpassed that at White's. Young men were losing five, ten, fifteen thousand pounds in the evening there. Lord Stavordale, who had not yet reached the age of 21, had lost £11,000 in one night, and then recovered it in one hand at hazard. His only comment was "now, if I had been playing deep, I might have won millions." A little later in the year Horace again complained to Horace Mann about the profligacy of young men of fashion: "I know a younger brother who literally gives a flower woman half a guinea every morning for a bunch of roses for the nosegay in his buttonhole."

It was the time of the *macaroni* and the masquerade. The former was the name given to a society of more or less fashionable young fops, younger members of Brooks's who spent their money on outrageous and expensive clothing. Travel on the continent was a prerequisite of inclusion in their society. The latter was the masked fancy dress entertainment which gave patrons of both sexes the opportunity to be seen flaunting their newly-purchased costumes among their peers; or clad in dominos, hooded cloaks with eye slits, they could remain *incognito* to the world, and free for whatever clandestine engagement the night might provide.

Percy Noble, a previous biographer of Anne, states that at first the newly-married couple were much in love, that they visited Park Place during the summer months, and also paid several visits to Lord and Lady Milton at Milton Abbey. A contrary contemporary view was given by that most observant of commentators, Mme du Deffand. Writing from Paris to HW, only two weeks after the wedding, she noted that "people say that your little cousin does not care for her husband, and doesn't mind; I pity her, for it is sad to live with someone you find stupid or silly". The reality was that husband and wife had little in common. The history of their marriage was to be one of gradual estrangement. There would be no children to give a shared love and interest. Anne would grow to like life in the fast lane, John to detest it. Reference to Anne, other than in passing, totally disappears from HW's correspondence from shortly after her marriage until 1773. If they did write to each other, and Anne later destroyed the letters, there is no mention of her in letters to other of his correspondents. She also, over time, appeared less regularly in Lady Mary Coke's diary. Both were members of the Campbell family clan in London, and continued to see each other, especially on family occasions, but mentions of Anne gradually became more disparaging as she mixed with a younger generation.

In August 1768 HW wrote to Harry saying that he intended to join him at Park Place for a couple of days *en route* to Ragley. He noted "the treasures that are pouring in upon your daughter by the old Damer's death". Old John Damer, aged 95, had died at Shronehill in Ireland. The *Lloyds Evening Post* reported that "this gentleman having a great estate in Limerick left by his uncle Joseph Damer (who also died at above 90 years of age) has made it his constant residence for above 70 years doing infinite good by his exemplary piety and unconfined charities. Dying without issue, he is succeeded by his nephew Lord Milton." The Damer referred to was an older John, great-uncle of Anne's husband, who had been a moneylender in Ireland. In fact Anne was to see no benefit from his estate, which went to Lord Milton, young John's father.

It is possible that Horace in writing disapprovingly to his correspondents about the gambling and profligacy of the young, fully realised that the Damers were very much a part of them, but, fiercely proud of his family's good reputation, he made no mention of their involvement. Besides he had his old age well planned, and it did not really include the younger generation. "My plan is to pass away calmly; cheerfully if I can, sometimes to amuse myself with the rising generation, but to take care not to fatigue them, nor weary them with old stories, which will not interest them, as their adventures do not interest me. Age would indulge prejudices if it did not sometimes polish itself against younger acquaintance; but it must be the work of folly if one hopes to contract friendships with them, or desires it, or thinks one can become the same follies, or expects that they should do more than bear one for one's good humour. In short, they are a pleasant medicine, that one should take care not to grow fond of."

The year 1769 saw Anne's time divided between family, mainly of the older generation, and newly-acquired friends of her own age. On 3rd February 1769 Anne was at a card party of her mother's; the game was Loo. Other guests included Lady Mary Coke and Lady Lyttelton, the second of whom was, like Anne, a great francophile, and admirer of the French Ambassadress. They had insisted that she was well-bred, though Lady Mary had remarked acidly that "few people are of that opinion". A few days later on 9th February Lady Mary was again at Caroline's, and recorded that among fellow guests were Anne, Lord Strafford, and the Dowager Lady Waldegrave. Lady Mary recorded it as an unhappy occasion, made worse by the fact that Anne and Maria Waldegrave whispered and giggled with each other. Maria who was Anne's cousin and had previously been Miss Walpole, had been widowed when

Lord Waldegrave died in 1763. She was 12 years older than Anne, and nine years younger than Lady Mary.

One particular new friend appeared in London. On 13th April 1769 Elizabeth Milbanke had wed Peniston Lamb, a marriage which was to have a great effect on Anne's life. Elizabeth was aged 17 at the time of her marriage, some three years younger than Anne. Her father was a North Yorkshire baronet. Her husband, the son of a very wealthy lawyer, Sir Matthew Lamb, was a member of Parliament, entering the Commons, like John Damer, in 1768, though to remain there much longer. She was ambitious, beautiful, lively and intelligent; he was silent, acquiescent and rather dull. However he was extremely rich, thanks to his inheritance of a fortune created by his grandfather and increased by his father, who had also married an heiress. Marriage brought Elizabeth from the North Yorkshire moors to fashionable London, starting in her husband's bachelor quarters in Sackville Street. They were not to remain there long; Elizabeth's driving ambition and determination to be a leading Whig hostess required a substantial residence in which to entertain. Melbourne House in Piccadilly, renamed after Peniston Lamb had been made Lord Melbourne in the Irish peerage, was purchased from Lord Holland in April 1770 for £16,500. A month later Elizabeth gave birth to a son, also named Peniston Lamb, and presented her husband with an heir to his title and estates. Work on the new house began in 1771 and finished in 1774 at a cost of £40,000. Now better known as Albany, it stands next to the Royal Academy, facing Fortnum & Mason. Elizabeth lost no time in befriending Anne Damer, three years her senior. She was a near neighbour, had an impeccable Whig background, and was also newly-married. Anne was to help in the decoration both of Melbourne House and of the Melbourne's country estate at Brocket Park in Hertfordshire.

On 9th June 1769, back with the family, Anne was the only younger guest at a family dinner party given by HW at Strawberry Hill; the others present were Harry and Caroline, Lord and Lady Frederick Campbell, Caroline's brother and sister-in-law, Lady Lyttelton and Lady Mary Coke. The latter wrote in her diary that Anne was clad in an English-style dress but had her hair dressed in the style of her French friends. Whether these were French friends in England, or new friends made in unrecorded visits to France is unclear. The Duke of Richmond, a previous ambassador to France, was also Duc d'Aubigny in France, and had many French friends who came to England. One in particular, Madame de Cambis, was to become his mistress. Her family circle centred around a raffish literary circle headed by her uncle and aunt Le Chevalier and Madame de Boufflers. Lady Mary recorded another disagreeable evening, during which she lost 13 guineas at Loo.

Gradually Anne mastered her role as a hostess, extended her circle of friends, and appeared regularly at Court. A newspaper report dated 21st January 1771 stated that "The Court was extremely brilliant last Friday …. the most distinguished for dress beauty and elegance were the Duchesses of Ancaster, Northumberland, and Richmond, the Hon. Mrs Damer, Lady Holdernesse, Lady Paget, Lady Craven, Lady Jersey…"

Others of her new close friends were Lady Harrington's daughters, Isabella, who had become Lady Molyneux, and Harriot Stanhope. Their mother, a daughter of the Duke of Grafton, had been ardently admired by Harry before her marriage. He had been dissuaded from marrying her himself by Horace Walpole, who told him that he could not afford her. In June 1771 Lady Harrington, Harriot and Anne went riding, stopping at Notting Hill to call, without warning, on Lady Mary Coke at 2.30pm. This was again unpopular with Lady Mary, who wished to be ready to dine at her usual hour of 3pm, and was only half dressed. The visitors did not stay long; they went over the house, out into the garden, picked some roses and then departed. By this time Anne was very much out of favour with Lady Mary. (A repeat visit was to take place three years later on 1st July 1774. Anne, again in company with Lady Harrington and Harriot, visited Lady Mary, recently returned from France. Once more the visit was unpopular; this time Lady Mary was interrupted in the process of paying her bills.)

Later in June 1771 the family were together again for a long weekend at Park Place. Lady Mary arrived in the early Saturday afternoon, to be joined by HW in the evening. Sunday was passed pleasantly enough, despite cloud and a cold wind which continued on Monday, when Horace departed for Strawberry Hill. That evening they were joined by the politicians Lord Lyttelton and Lord Camden, and the actor David Garrick and his wife. Lord Camden departed that evening but the others stayed on. By Wednesday the weather had improved, the house party played bowls and went for walks. Cards were banned during the period that these more important guests were being entertained. Lady Mary departed on Thursday, noting in her diary that Caroline was determined to take Anne and John to Scotland with her, to see and meet the Campbell relations. Harry would be unable to accompany them, as he had to remain behind in charge of work on the fortifications at Portsmouth.

The family journey to Scotland was scheduled to take six weeks, starting out in August, and included a stay at Wentworth Castle, the seat of Lord Strafford, *en route*. Lady Strafford was Lady Mary Coke's sister and Caroline's cousin, and had married William Wentworth, second Earl of Strafford, creator of an inspirational landscape at Wentworth Castle, near Barnsley in South Yorkshire. Before they departed, Lady Harrington gave a ball, at which she had encouraged Lord Villiers to propose to her daughter, Harriot. On 6th August 1771, just after the Scottish expedition was due to set out, Lady Mary recorded in her diary that she had been visited by Lord Villiers, together with Lord Petersham, Lord Harrington's son and heir. She had been unable to ask Villiers, in Harriot's brother's presence, how the romance was progressing. She noted that society gossip suggested that Harriot would no longer speak to Villiers, as a result of being advised by Anne Damer to look elsewhere. Lady Mary suggested to her sister that Anne might explain further, "as I imagine she is now with you". In the event, Villiers married someone else that year, and Harriot had to wait until 1776 to marry Lord Foley. Again there is the inference that Anne was *persona non grata* with Lady Mary.

Outside the family circle, Anne was branching out with Elizabeth Melbourne. On 30th April 1772 they attended a masquerade at the Pantheon. Sir Joshua Reynolds was there in a domino, and noted Oliver Goldsmith and his friend Mr Cradock, in old English dresses. The fourteen rooms blazed with light and decorations. The suppers and wine were in keeping with the rank of the best part of the company. Many of the ladies were in male dominoes "and appeared as masculine as many of the delicate *macaroni* things we see everywhere, the 'Billy Whiffles' of the present age." These ladies included the Duchess of Ancaster, Lady Melbourne and Mrs Damer.

A few weeks later, Anne was at the masquerade at Mrs Cornelys's in Soho Square. Numbers attending were said to be not very numerous, but to include the most distinguished company since the King of Denmark's Ball. "The characters were not only various and elegant but were supported with a greater deal of vivacity than usual in this country. There were so many of the first nobility (chiefly in dominoes), that it would be tedious and altogether unnecessary to enumerate them. Lady Harrington and family (Lady Sefton excepted) with the Hon. and amiable Mrs Damer, formed a most beautiful assemblage of Arcadians…" Another group, (Mr Andrews, Captain Jones, Mr Crawford and Mr Villeneuve) appeared as a Dancing Bear with attendants, "*à la mode de Maccaroni's*". The bear rather resembled a clumsy ape; it was led by a sailor accompanied by a blind fiddler. The sailor distributed printed handbills, "which contain so fine a piece of satire on the *macaronis*, that if it does not laugh them out of countenance, we must pronounce them absolutely incorrigible." The bill announced: "Just arrived, the noted She Bear brought from Terra Incognita on board the Discovery with Captain Exotic, who has spent twenty-five years of his life in search of wild beasts and cockle shells. This surprising animal from her long and intimate commerce with the human species, has adopted their manners. She is as tame as a lamb, and harmless as a *macaroni*. She teaches grown gentlemen to dance minuets, *allemandes* and *cotillons*."

Others noted attending the party included among the cross-dressers the elegant Mrs Garnier in a man's domino, and Mr B…. as a French *fille de joie*. Also present were Mr Abell Drugger, a quack doctor, a Highlander, a Queen of Cards, several milkmaids, a mendicant friar, two harlequins, and a Pantaloon. A Mr Damer was noted in the Carlisle party, which included Lady Carlisle, Lady Betty Hamilton, and Lady Juliana Howard. However, there was no indication as to which of the Mr Damers it might have been. On 30th May 1772 the *Morning Chronicle* reported another masquerade with a large turnout of leading members of society, which included Charles James Fox and Anne.

In the following year, in March 1773, HW noted a more formal location and occasion, the French ambassador's Ball. Here Anne was performing in one of the set pieces: "The quadrilles were very pretty: Mrs Damer, Lady Sefton, Lady Melbourne, and the Princess Czartoriski in blue satin, with blond and *collets montés à la reine Elizabeth*; Lord Robert Spencer, Mr Fitzpatrick, Lord Carlisle, and I forget whom, in like dresses with red sashes, *de rouge*, black hats with diamond loops and a few feathers, began."

At another private party at Epsom in 1774, a *fête champêtre* given by Lord Stanley, shortly to succeed his father as the 12th Lord Derby, most of the guests were "dressed with much propriety". However, some had come in fancy dress, including the Duke and Duchess of Grafton, Lady Betty Hamilton (shortly to marry Lord Stanley), Mrs Fitzroy and Mrs Damer. The classical pastoral simplicity of the ladies' dresses ensured that "the most delightful picture … ever painted in the Fields of Sicily, was by no means to be compared with the real festivity at the Oaks on Thursday evening." The Oaks was Lord Derby's house and gave its name to the Classic race for three-year-old fillies, whilst Lord Derby himself is commemorated by the Classic counterpart for colts, both of which take place annually in June on the Downs above his house. There is no indication that Anne took any interest in the Sport of Kings.

Anne also relished the pleasures of life abroad, whilst John Damer preferred to remain in England. She spoke fluent French and adequate Italian and German. She had accompanied her parents abroad in her teens, and acquired a taste for travel. Her health, and especially her chest, gave her cause for concern, and doctors would generally prescribe a curative rest overseas. In late summer 1772 she left England for France, and seems to have taken John Damer with her, anyway for part of the trip. Madame du Deffand, writing to HW in July, reported that Anne had been a great success, pleasing everybody and especially Madame de Mirepoix. In September Mme du Deffand wrote to Horace that she hoped she would have the good fortune to please Mrs Damer, but didn't dare to flatter herself too much on that score. Anne had apparently departed a month before to travel in the country; and before she had left the capital she had developed "*une grande passion*" for Mme de Cambis. In general she had been pleasing and likeable. John Damer had appeared to Mme du Deffand to be a very good and honest man. Anne returned to England in October, when she was presented at Court. In a disparaging tone, by now to be expected, Lady Mary remarked that she was said to be very well dressed *à la mode de Paris*, but regretted that she had increased the amount of "ruge" in her make up; she had already worn too much before she departed for France. In December HW confided to Caroline that he found Anne to be better, though he would not be satisfied until her night sweats had gone. He remarked that she was very good, and came to see him often, despite the fact that "I preach to her". Preaching was presumably an avuncular recommendation to mend her ways. Horace noted that she was about to leave London to stay with her half-sister at Goodwood, which though a cold house, was dry and wholesome with good air.

In July 1773 Mme du Deffand remarked that John Damer was in Paris by himself, and that Anne had sent her six beautiful pineapples. In the same letter she noted with approval the Vicomtesse du Barry, who resembled Louis XV's mistress, Mme de Châteauroux.

A further trip abroad was planned in October 1774, not entirely for health reasons, as HW had written to Harry in September that "I never saw Mrs D better in her life, nor look so well. You may trust me, who am so apt to be frightened about her". It was an occasion for a family party. Caroline, Anne, and Harriot Stanhope set out first. For Caroline it was a first-time visit, looked forward to with much excitement. They were joined on the 5th November by Harry, who had been on a mission to Prussia to meet up with Frederick the Great and discuss military matters. Harriot's father, Lord Harrington, also joined the Paris trip, according to Horace "packing up his decrepit bones". Horace himself refused the invitation to increase the family party, citing as excuses his fear of a return of the gout, a distrust of French doctors, and misgivings about French cleanliness. He also advised caution, and to have a very strong lock for your *portefeuille*. He warned that in the hotels the staff had double keys to every lock, that they went through and examined your papers, and pilfered every bit of clothing that took their fancy. He also asked Harry to make the acquaintance of Mme du Deffand, his wonderful elderly correspondent, to whom he had written requesting her to give Harry his letters to her so that he might have them for safekeeping.

Originally the stay was intended to last until early December, but the visitors enjoyed themselves so much that they did not return home until 21st February 1775. On her return, Anne officially parted from her husband. HW complained that Anne said nothing to him, but that he was in favour of her intention (presumably to part from John), and believed her silence to him was on her mother's advice.

Back in England Anne was to make a new friend. On 7th June 1774 Lady Georgiana Spencer had married the fifth Duke of Devonshire. Summer and autumn had been spent at Chatsworth, by the end of which time the new Duchess had become painfully aware that hers too was a loveless marriage. In January 1775 the Devonshires returned to London, to a new role for Georgiana as the fresh leader of *le ton*. She caused an immediate sensation and very soon became close friends both with Elizabeth Melbourne and Anne Damer. All three had husbands who were unsatisfactory, unfaithful, or inattentive. Anne was nine years older than Georgiana, who was six years younger than Elizabeth Melbourne. The young Duchess depended for advice on her elder colleagues. Elizabeth, ever the opportunist, sought to use the

Devonshires' superior social standing to her own advantage, and took her existing friend, Anne Damer, with her.

In 1775, while the American War of Independence got under way and John Damer got into debt, Anne, now separated from her husband, embarked on a life of pleasure. The next 18 months were to be a wild succession of balls, masquerades, amateur theatricals, and visits to the Opera and the theatre. Typical would have been the masquerade at the Opera House described in the *Middlesex Journal* for 25th April 1775. This was an Italian masked country fair; the theatre was set out with a number of shops with several pretty shopkeepers dealing in millinery, perfumes, trinkets, toys, gloves, ribbons, and feathers. Cox's Good-Future Lottery-Office had a fine piece of machinery to attract customers, whilst other retailers included Thomas Hall, the exhibitor of stuffed birds. Mr Breslaw practised feats of dexterity, though the reader is left to guess the context, whilst one of his performers played the fiddle, and the Sieur Gaetana imitated bird calls. The company was not overcrowded but everyone had made a great effort to come elegantly dressed. There was "uncommonly good and comforting" champagne and burgundy in abundance. The principal characters were a gentleman in a petticoat, Lady Barrymore dressed as a vestal virgin, and a noisy gentleman impersonating a native of Tahiti. "The greatest part of the nobility", including Mrs Damer, were in dominoes.

In July 1775, to celebrate this social whirl, Daniel Gardner was commissioned, most probably by Anne, to paint pictures of the Duchess of Devonshire, Lady Melbourne, and herself as the witches in Macbeth, dancing around a cauldron. There was possibly a picture for each of the three dancers. Instead of the Shakespearean contents, "eye of newt and toe of frog", the witches are casting roses and carnations into the pot. Lady Mary Coke remarked "I daresay they think their charmes more irresistible than all the magick of the witches." Daniel Gardner's notebook records the following verse to accompany the painting:

> *Tales of Old Witches are no longer heard,*
> *Fictitious legends once receiv'd for truth.*
> *And wisely here the Artist has transferr'd*
> *The pow'rs of sorcery from age to youth.*
> *Beware, ye Mortals, who those comforts prize,*
> *Which flow from peace from liberty, and ease,*
> *Th' Enchanter's wand, and magick spells despise,*
> *But shun the witchcraft of such eyes as these.*

In October 1775 HW, once more in Paris, wrote to Harry asking him to "tell Mrs D that the fashion now is to erect the *toupée* into a high detached tuft of hair, like a cockatoo's crest". Caroline and Anne had brought back from Paris headdresses made of tall feathers, which were very much *à la mode*. To their chagrin, the Duchess of Devonshire had obtained even taller feathers. Not to be outdone, they obtained horses' funeral plumes from their local undertaker. A chart of *"bon ton"* hostesses, published in the *Morning Post*, gave Anne high marks for her figure, elegance, wit, sense, grace, and expression, lower marks for beauty and sensibility, and an extremely low score for principles. Overall she was somewhere in the middle division with 96 points, well in front of the Countess of Jersey with 48 points, but far behind the Countess of Barrymore with 165. In July 1776 Lady Mary observed that the *bon ton* were still in town and that "the Duchess of Devonshire, Lady Melbourne, and Mrs Damer have dinners and suppers and live much together." In real life, the cauldron dance was spinning ever faster. Anne can have had no idea how soon, and how completely, her life was about to change.

On 4th July 1776 the American colonies declared independence. On 13th July Harry, having got himself into a sweat playing skittles at Park Place, was exposed to a cold and unseasonable wind. As a result he suffered a small paralytic stroke to one side of his face. The effects did not last long and by 24th July it had become clear that the only parts of the body affected were facial muscles. By 3rd August Hertford wrote to HW saying that Harry's health was improving daily, that his speech was now nearly perfect, and his head perfectly clear, he was in good spirits and in great heart. He was obediently following the doctor's instructions, and a proposed journey to Mount Edgecumbe was almost certain to be cancelled on health grounds.

This attack may also have been brought on by worry. Harry was deeply concerned over the rumours circulating about John Damer's debts. Although the married couple were separated, Anne might well have had some legal liability. John's brothers had also run into similar trouble as a result of gambling, and they were preparing to take the standard 18th century remedy of leaving the country and going to France where creditors would not pursue them. On 11th August 1776 HW wrote to Sir Horace Mann that Harry was "uneasy, himself, with reason, about his daughter. Her husband and his two brothers have contracted a debt – one can scarcely expect to be believed out of England – of seventy thousand pounds! Who but must think himself happy to marry a daughter with only ten thousand pounds to a young man with five thousand pounds a year rent-charge in present, and twenty-two thousand a year settled? And yet this daughter at present is ruined! Her behaviour is such as her father's would be; she does not only not complain, but desires her very own jewels may be sold. The young men of this age seem to have made a law among themselves for declaring their fathers superannuated at fifty, and then dispose of their estates as if already their own. How culpable to society was Lord Holland for setting an example of paying such enormous, such gigantic debts! Can you believe that Lord Foley's two sons have borrowed money so extravagantly, that the interest they have contracted to pay amounts to eighteen thousand pounds a year? I write the sum at length, lest you think I should have mistaken, and set down two or three figures too much. The legislature sits quiet, and says it cannot put a stop to such outrageous doings; but thus it is punished for winking at the plunder of the Indies, which cannot suffice. Our Jews and usurers contrive to lounge at home and commit as much rapine as Lord Clive!'"

It is not clear what caused John Damer's parlous financial situation. Horace said that he didn't gamble; he was supposed to have spent heavily on clothing. He may also have made some unfortunate investments. His connection with George Colebrooke has already been noted in connection with membership of parliament for the rotten Borough of Gatton. Colebrooke was a speculator – first in the East India Company of which he was a director from 1767 to 1771 and from 1772 to 1773, and in commodities, such as hemp, flax, and alum. In all of these his losses were substantial. His bank stopped making payments in 1776, and he himself was declared bankrupt in 1777. It might well have been that Damer had either been a party to Colebrooke's banking activities, or had suffered similar losses in commodity speculation. Since his separation from Anne there had been two households to maintain, Anne in Tilney Street, and he himself in very substantial premises in Cookham. Horace's correspondent, the Reverend Mr Cole, had heard from Dr Ewin, a Cambridge neighbour, that in the previous week John Damer had lost £20,000 in one night of gambling, the last throw of a desperate man. This seems to have been second- or third-hand gossip, but may contain a grain of truth.

Anne, whose expenditure as a society hostess and lavish entertainer in her house in Tilney Street had also been considerable, and an additional burden on John Damer's funds, was preparing to escape their creditors and leave England in company with her equally indebted brothers-in-law. On Thursday 15th August she went to Park Place to tell her parents that this was her intention, and to take her leave of them. She intended to return to London on the following day.

At 10pm on 14th August John Damer, in a state of some excitement, arrived at a public house, the Bedford Arms in Covent Garden, London. The publican, John Robinson, had received a note from him between 7-8pm asking for supper to be ready at 10pm. He requested that his meal be accompanied by Burnet, who was a blind fiddler, and some young ladies, specially a Miss Richmond who sang. John arrived at a little after 11 o'clock, and had taken supper in a room on the first floor in company with four women and Burnet. The latter said that John had eaten very little. After supper the women sang and stayed till about 3am, when John told Robinson to take the women away and give them a guinea each. Burnet remained in the supper room. After a few minutes he came downstairs saying that John would send for him again in a quarter of an hour. Having heard nothing after 20 minutes, the blind Burnet went upstairs and soon returned. He had opened the door and stood there for a couple of minutes, but heard nothing: he said that there was a disagreeable smell and that he imagined a candle must have fallen down. Robinson immediately went upstairs to investigate and found a strong smell of powder and one of the window sashes open. John Damer was sitting in a chair bleeding from a hole on the right side of his head; his clothes were covered in blood and there was much blood on the floor. Robinson had felt his hand, which was not cold, but he could see no sign of life. Robinson believed that he had shot himself with a pistol that he found between Damer's feet, and which appeared to have been discharged, with the lock down. Burnet informed the coroner's inquest, which met at 6pm that evening at the Bedford Arms, that he had heard no noise above stairs, nor had anybody gone up stairs from the time that he had left Mr Damer alone. He believed that the deceased had shot himself, but he had not heard the report of a pistol. Robinson said that John Damer had been a customer for some years, and that his behaviour on the night of his death had been unusual. He had made Robinson put John's hat upon the fiddler's head, which Burnet confirmed, adding that he had not been as cheerful as usual. Both agreed that Damer was not drunk.

Only one additional witness to Robinson and Burnet was called by the coroner of the inquest into John Damer's death. This was John Armitage, Damer's house steward. He gave evidence that he had worked for John Damer for the past nine years. During this time he had frequently had to ask for money; the last occasion had been two days before Damer's death, when he had given him £26 and five shillings for household use. He added that for some time the deceased had been uneasy and disturbed in his mind, and that he had been depressed, though Armitage had no idea of the reason for this.

The coroner's jury had no hesitation in declaring that John Damer had taken his own life in an act of lunacy. At that time, in cases of suicide, lunacy at the time of dispatch was an essential verdict to be able to obtain Christian burial on consecrated ground. The alternative verdict of felonious suicide, intentional self-killing whilst in a rational state, was a crime, for which the punishment was interment on common unconsecrated ground, and just as importantly, forfeiture of all the deceased's possessions to the Crown.

Horace related in a letter to Sir Horace Mann written on 20th August, that on the morning of Friday 16th Anne was returning to London from Park Place, having told her parents that she was going to France with her brothers-in-law, a move of which they had sadly approved. Lady Mary Coke heard from Lady Harrington the circumstances in which Anne heard of her husband's death. Lady Harrington and Lady Harriot were in their coach, with Mr Foley leaning upon the carriage door, when Anne drove up. None of them had the courage to tell her what had happened, and Anne drove on. Shortly afterwards Charles James Fox passed them on his horse, and they confessed that they had been unable to face up to informing Anne of events. Fox said he would do what he could, and riding on, caught up with Anne and told her enough for her to guess what had happened. However, he was unable to stop her from going home, where she was met by her brother-in-law George Damer, who told her that his brother had killed himself. Anne was beside herself, and insisted on seeing his corpse, until someone had to tell her that the fatal deed had taken place in a low tavern in Covent Garden.

HW went on to relate the circumstances of John Damer's death to Sir Horace Mann and to add some additional information that had not been revealed to the coroner's jury. Horace said that the landlord Robinson "came up, and found Mr Damer sitting in his chair, dead, with a pistol by him, and another in his pocket! The ball had not gone through his head, nor made any report. On the table lay a scrap of paper with these words: 'The people of the house are not to blame for what has happened, which was my own act.' This was the sole tribute he paid to justice and decency! We are persuaded lunacy, not distress, was the sole cause of his fate. He has often, and even at supper that night, hinted at such an exploit – the very reason why one should not expect it. His brothers have gamed – he never did. He was grave, cool, reasonable and reserved; but passed his life as he died, with troops of women and the blind fiddler – an odd companion in such scenes!"

Lady Mary Coke's diary noted in addition that suicide was suspected because the act seemed premeditated, if somewhat incompetent. The balls he had bought had been too large for his pistol, "upon which, as it was found afterwards, he had sat down and pared them with a penknife till he had made them fit".

Horace went on to say that the one good thing to emerge from this catastrophe was that the moneylenders, "the leeches, the Jews and extortioners", would lose very considerably. Lord Milton, whose great-uncle had been a moneylender himself, knew the rules of the game, and had refused either to see or to bail out any of his sons. A man "whom anything can petrify and nothing soften", he had blamed Anne for her husband's death and had insisted on selling her jewels to pay off those debts which did need to be settled. Horace continued that "this is all the hurt he can do her; she must have her jointure of £2500 a year". The real value of such a jointure to a young widow in uncertain times, and the wisdom of including it in the pre-nuptial marriage settlement, had become clear.

It is worth reflecting on what had driven this man who was "grave, cool, reasonable and reserved" to such a measure. Was Lord Milton right to blame Anne? He believed that his son's behaviour was very much influenced by Anne's frequent absences during their married life, and by inference from the marital bed. Was her frigidity, her icy disposition, to blame for the lack both of love and of children? Did her expenditure as an active partying member of *le ton* add to John's financial straits? Or was John, weak, spendthrift and self-centred, the cause of the marriage's failure? It is probable that the discordant personalities of both husband and wife had a part to play.

For John Damer it was certainly the end of the road. Or was it? While researching the Milton family in Dorset, the author came across a small book entitled *Ten Dorset Mysteries,* by Roger Guttridge. Mystery number four was entitled *The Coffin in the Crypt*. Guttridge tells the tale of Damer's suicide and the subsequent inquest. He notes that the inquest only examined three witnesses, the landlord, the fiddler and John Damer's steward. There was no recorded identification of the corpse, and no sound of a shot was heard by either Robinson or the fiddler, the latter of whom, like most blind people, might have been expected to have acute hearing. There was no mention of a suicide note, nor of the fact mentioned later by HW that the ball had not gone through his head. Guttridge fails to mention in addition the open sash window.

Suicide was the ultimate way of avoiding your creditors; a fake suicide would have the same effect without the attendant mortal consequences. The witnesses had noticed that the deceased seemed disturbed; that could have been the case, whether he was planning to end his life, or to carry out an elaborate deception. The latter would have required the collusion of the landlord Robinson, and the steward, Armitage. The blind fiddler would not have seen the body; there is no reason for any of the jury to have recognised the corpse. It would not have been difficult in the 18th century to borrow a body, bring it up a ladder through the open window, place it in the chair, and make an escape down the ladder. Taken by itself this is no more than idle speculation; however Guttridge had approached the subject from the Dorset perspective, and in particular from Milton Abbey.

Joseph Damer, the first Lord Milton, had not been popular among his immediate neighbours around Milton Abbey. Change is seldom welcome and the demolition of the buildings around the Abbey, and their replacement by the model and much healthier village of Milton Abbas attracted opprobrium; the gist of any contemporary village gossip was likely to have been derogatory to the Milton family. However this particular story seems to have lived on for a considerable time.

Around the year 1873, Mr Frederick Fane was staying at Milton Abbey when he heard the tale of John Damer's death. Over 20 years later, at a meeting of the Dorset Natural History and Antiquarian Field Club, he recalled his visit. At the time repairs were being carried out on the North transept of the Abbey Church. One morning before breakfast he had walked into the Abbey and talked to the clerk of works in charge of repairs. The latter spoke of an old tale of a bogus funeral in the village of Milton which dated back about 100 years to when the village was still on the ground adjacent to the Abbey. One of the young Damers, a son of the unpopular Lord Milton, had run up a series of debts, and was sought by the bailiffs for repayment. Shortly afterwards news arrived, stating that the young man had died on the continent and was being brought home for burial. The funeral had taken place, and the corpse was interred in the family vault below the north transept. Subsequently, however, the villagers, a naturally suspicious bunch, claimed to have seen the recently-buried young Damer in the flesh, in and around the Abbey, on many occasions.

During this conversation, the clerk of works mentioned that owing to the current repair work, the Milton family vault was open, and that if Fane cared to descend into it, he would see something that might make the village legend appear more credible. On descending Fane found, as far as he could recollect, either two or three large open vaults with several coffins resting on trestles. In the furthest vault was a coffin with the brass nameplate formerly attached to the now-decomposed wooden outer case resting on the internal lead one. It was inscribed with the name of a Damer who had died in his 20s, around 1770. The clerk of works suggested that Fane should lift the coffin, which he found impossible owing to its weight. He then invited Fane to lift a neighbouring coffin, which he did without a problem. The clerk dourly explained that the latter had contained a body, now turned to dust, but that the former was filled with stones which were more impermeable. At the end of the repair work the vaults were re-sealed with the contents intact. They remain sealed.

Chapter 5

GOING SOLO: STRINGENCY
AND STATUARY

To the outer world, Anne accepted John's death with composure. Although she had been shocked by the news broken to her by George Damer, she soon recovered her equilibrium. Her friends stood by her. Elizabeth Melbourne wrote to Georgiana that she had been in London again with Anne, who was now better and had gone to Park Place. The Duke of Richmond had also come to her aid and stayed a week with her in London, which had been of enormous assistance. Left to herself, Anne could let her brave face slip. Elizabeth Melbourne reported that "if ever I found her alone. I was certain to find her crying; but I hope she will be better now as she has changed the scene, for her own house was certainly ye worst place she could be at."

However it was perforce the end of her flirtation with the *ton*. She may well have had enough of that sort of life, and indeed this was always her subsequent claim. From now on she made a firm decision to lead a simpler life, and to set out on a new career as a sculptor. She was not the only one to change course. Georgiana Devonshire had also turned over a new leaf. In April 1778 she wrote an autobiographical novel, *The Sylph*, in which a young maiden, Julia, fresh from the country and unsuspectingly married to an adulterous rake, Sir William Stanley, enters London society. She is guided by two elder women, Lady Besford, clearly modelled on Elizabeth Melbourne, and Lady Anne Parker, drawn from Anne Damer. By the time the book was written, Georgiana's interests had moved on to a new friend, Mary Graham, and to the fascination of Charles James Fox. Elizabeth and Anne are unkindly portrayed, the first entirely amoral, the second a sarcastic gossip. "If I dislike Lady Besford, I think I have more reason to be displeased with Lady Anne Parker – she has more artifice and is consequently a more dangerous companion." As the book nears its end, Sir William Stanley takes his life in a public house. It was time to move on.

On 26th August Harry received a letter from Anne, telling her parents that Lord Milton refused to pay any of his late son's debts, and that she would need to set aside part of her own income for a year while she paid off those creditors who needed to be paid. In the meantime, she would come and live with them for at least a year. This proposal came as a huge relief to Harry and Caroline, who welcomed her to Park Place. Harry immediately wrote to Horace Walpole inviting him to join them there.

John Damer's death certainly caused a stir amongst friends and neighbours. According to Lady Mary Coke: "Damer's debt alone, according to his father, was £60,000", and "Lord Milton looks upon Mrs Damer as the cause of all. He insists on selling her jewels, which are magnificent, for discharge of just debts". Lady Louisa Conolly wrote to the Duchess of Leinster on 17th September, confirming that Anne had given up £1500 a year of her jointure to pay John's debts, and intended to live with her father and mother on the remaining £1000.

Lady Sarah Lennox, in a letter to Lady Susan O'Brien dated 19th September 1776, summed up the situation perceptively: "Was not you surprised at poor Mr Damer's death? I had no idea that he was maddish even, and in my mind he has proved that he was quite mad, for I cannot account for his death and the manner of it any other way. I am provoked at Lord Milton, for I was throwing away my pity for him, and behold! Not even the death of his son has softened him about his family in general, or taught him generosity. He has been very shabby about Lionel Damer, very unkind to George Damer, and quite brutal to Mrs Damer, who, by the way, behaves with all propriety in the world; when one commends a widow for behaving well, it is allowing that love was out of the question, which is to be sure in her case. I think one has no right to blame her more than him; he had no more business to marry a girl he did not like, than she had to accept of a man she was totally indifferent to, and he was as much to blame in giving her the example of never being at home, as she was to make all her way of life opposite to his. In short, I cannot think it fair to blame one more than t'other, but as it's evident love was out of the question I must give her credit for her present conduct. Lord Milton has taken her diamonds, furniture, carriages, and everything away to pay the debts with, and he abused her for staying in another man's house (for she stayed a few days there before she went to the country, and the house is another's, being seiz'd). Upon hearing this she left it and chose to go in a hackney coach taking only her inkstand and few books, her dog, and her maid with her, out of that fine house. I think it was spirited and noble in her; she had but three guineas in her pocket, which was to last her till Michaelmas, for Lord Milton did not offer her any assistance. Her sister, as you may imagine, attended her and gave her money and she went to Mr Conway's house; she is to live with him for a year in order to save one year's income which she gives towards the payment of Mr Damer's just debts, which cannot be quite paid by the sale of everything even. The poor servants are ow'd 14 months wages, which I think is one of the most melancholy reflections, for you see that they are in absolute want of bread if they are unlucky in not getting a place immediately. She paid (out of the Duchess's money) those servants who were in immediate want, the rest were too generous to take any, and refused absolutely to take more than would serve them for immediate use; they are all fond of her and cried bitterly at her leaving the house, in such a way too, but the Dss tells me she walk'd through the house amidst them all, into her hackney coach, with a firmness that is quite heroic, for though she may be accused of not loving her husband, she cannot be accused of not loving her house and all her grandeur."

The house in Tilney Street was advertised for sale on 17th December 1776, to be sold by auction by Mr Christie on the premises and after the Christmas holidays. It was described as "a capital and elegant mansion, with suitable offices etc of the Hon John Damer, deceased, desirably situate in Tilney Street, Mayfair, with a full view of Hyde Park. The principal apartments are noble and splendid, and the domestic ones abound with conveniencies. The household furniture and effects would be sold at the same time, and dates for viewing and for the sale would be "timely given".

The actual sale took place over an eleven-day period from 3rd – 13th February 1777. The house was sold at 1pm on the first day, for 4300 guineas to Lord Francis Stanhope. Messrs Christie and Ansell's catalogue listed "the superb household furniture, magnificent jewels, embellished watches and snuff boxes and … an extensive wardrobe of rich, elegant and fashionable wearing apparel". Days 1, 2 and 3 dealt mainly with furniture, china, glass and kitchen equipment, including 6 claret coloured and 6 pea-green glass beakers. A superb Dresden dinner service was bought in by Anne, her only purchase in the whole course of the sale. A turbot pan sold for 2 guineas. The fifth day featured Anne's jewellery. The star of the sale was sold to Mr Duvall: "A pair of magnificent Brilliant Ear-rings the drops particularly superb, delicately shaped of the finest water, and of matchless beauty and perfection", and made £2800 – 40% of the whole sale. Were these the earrings that Anne's mother had boasted cost £4000, the ones that she could not wear immediately after her wedding, as the court was in mourning? In all Anne's jewellery fetched just under £5000. On this day too the auctioneers disposed of three fowling pieces, several pairs of pistols, various swords and canes. The entire seventh and eighth days of the sale were devoted to John Damer's clothes and a relatively modest quantity of linen, which together sold for £846.10s. There were over eighty fine frock coats and waistcoats. These included "a fine rose coloured striped silk coat and breeches with gold shell embroidered border lined with Astrican lamb fur, and white satin embroidered waistcoat, with a border correspondingly elegant" which sold for sixteen guineas. "A green striped velvet coat and breeches lined with rose coloured satin, and a gold striped waistcoat with gold embroidered and coloured border and green shag lining" went for 10 guineas. John Damer had evidently ordered his glassware to match his coats.

In Christie's archives the last two days of the sale – John Damer's library, which included Adam Smith's *Enquiry into the Wealth of Nations* – are separated from the earlier days by the commencement of another sale in bankruptcy, that of John Damer's erstwhile parliamentary colleague, Sir George Colebrooke. Whether or not the two men had been connected in their business ventures, they were united by Mr Christie in their dissolution. The gross total for the Damer sale, excluding the house itself, was £7,042 2s, which after commission and bills came to £6,464 17s.

This was not the end of the dissolutions. A further advertisement in *The Sun*, dated 6th May 1777, announced under the heading "To be lett", "a mansion house, elegantly finished in the modern taste, situated in an exceeding good neighbourhood, at Cookham, in Berkshire on the banks of the Thames, three miles from Maidenhead and the Bath road, and about twenty-nine from London; with beautiful gardens and pleasure ground, of near four acres adjoining to the house, well laid out, open to the Thames … and with the most delightful prospects of the adjacent country. The house is very dry, has good cellars, and consists on the first floor of a hall, parlour, and drawing room, housekeeper's room, servants hall, kitchen, butler's pantry, larder, servery, and other useful offices. On the second, six good bed chambers with closets, and a large dressing room, besides servants' rooms. There is a detached building which has been used as a laundry, with seven bedrooms, a coach house for three carriages, and stabling for eight horses, with hay lofts and two bed chambers for servants, and a close of meadowland about six acres with two acres more in a common meadow near the house. Also included to be let, at the same time or separately, another very good house, furnished or unfurnished, situated near the above-mentioned, which has been well fitted up, and consists of a hall, large parlour and drawing room, servants' hall, kitchen, housekeeper's room, butler's pantry, and other useful and convenient offices, seller, wine vaults and bins. On the second floor, eight good bed chambers; also a detached building, used as a laundry, with a bedchamber over it, double coachhouse, stabling for four horses, with hay lofts and another bedchamber for servants.

"All the above mentioned premises are in good repair and lately occupied by the Honourable John Damer, deceased, whose elegant goods and furniture are advertised to be sold by auction by Mr Christie very soon, and of which public notice will be given."

Sadly there appears to be no record of a second sale of furniture and effects in Christie's archives. Communications even between Cookham and London could be slow and by the time that Mr James King of Cookham, attending the premises, Mr Payn, attorney at law, of Maidenhead, and Messrs Baxter of Furnivall Street London, had agreed the details and arranged for their publication, the advertised sale could well have been the one that had already taken place in February. John Damer would hardly have kept his eighty suits of clothing in Tilney Street, whilst living in Cookham.

Although some of the details of contemporary correspondence are contradictory, their general purport is clear. Anne had had to give up her personal possessions and £1000 of her £2500 jointure for a year. Her father-in-law had blamed her entirely for her husband's death, but others felt that both parties had contributed. To make ends meet, she would go to Park Place, and live with her parents for a year. In future she would of necessity adopt a simpler and less costly lifestyle, while at the same time developing her skills in sculpture. Subsequently she would still be well provided for by her jointure.

Life at Park Place would have seemed quiet after recent events. But it would have been comfortable and, for a time, what Anne needed whilst she took stock of the situation. After retiring from his role as Secretary of State in 1768, Harry had turned to enjoying and developing his estate. The bridge over the Henley Road and the Gothick cottage overlooking the Thames had been completed earlier; by the time of John Damer's death in 1776 much more had been done. Harry's taste in embellishing his grounds was generally appreciated, and by common consent Park Place was the finest estate along that stretch of the Thames. It was substantial, with 275 acres of ornamental grounds, 130 acres of parkland, and 500 acres of farmland. It included shrubberies, a landscaped valley with views down to the Thames through the Lesser Arch, and the cottage and road bridge already referred to. Two very special features were the subterranean passage, some 275 yards long, and the viewing terrace, some three quarters of a mile long, both designed by Harry. There were extensive views across Berkshire to the New Forest in Hampshire, and on a fine day to the South Downs in Sussex.

The landscaper's vision was complemented by utility within the garden. There was a walled kitchen garden with espaliered fruit trees, a hot wall with internal flues heated by boilers, a poultry place and a pheasantry. Nearby was a half-acre flower garden with alley walks, flanked by flowerbeds; it contained a little pool with gold and silver fish, a present from HW, and small statues and vases with foliage wreathed in festoons.

Harry was also something of an inventor. This was the age of Turnip Townsend and the agricultural revolution, which developed concurrently with its industrial counterpart. Amongst more or less financially rewarding experiments, Harry supervised the growing of six acres of cabbages for seed, the crop being sold in the London market. Two acres of caraway were grown for seed, and two for distillation and sale as oil. Eight acres of lavender were distilled and sold as oil for £170 to Messrs Smith of Bond Street. This was a yield of over £20 an acre on ground which had hitherto proved barren. A further 23 acres of potatoes were grown and distilled into a poteen whisky-type spirit. The distilled potatoes provided excellent fodder for the pigs; history does not relate who got to drink the poteen, or whether the pigs remained sober.

The central point in this experimentation was the distillery, which itself cost £4000. Its primary object was to turn coal into coke, used by maltsters who malted the barley used in brewing beer. The rationale was that coal's bulk increases after coking, 12 sacks of coal producing 16 to 18 sacks of slower burning coke. A simultaneous objective was to flux copper and iron, though this did not always work successfully. In addition to the cost of the still and the materials, Harry employed a salaried chemistry professor, who occupied a fine four-bedroom house on the estate. Harry took out a patent on the distillation process, but in the end nothing came of it.

However the experimentation was typical of the age, which produced a revolution in agricultural practice and in food production. In the midst of this idyllic classical landscape, in England's green and pleasant land, Harry had been able to build his own dark satanic mill. He was fortunate that planning permission was not a requisite.

Landscape improvement for Harry was an ongoing enterprise. The results he achieved were remarkable, and the grounds must have been an ideal place for the widowed Anne to walk and regain her composure. She would not have been so fortunate indoors. In October 1776 HW hoped that Anne's cough had departed and that her health had improved. It was unlikely to do so in Park Place, which was cold and desolate in winter. The new bow window room was the least draughty, but little else had been done to the house. As late as 1787 there were still 100,000 bricks on site, waiting for a builder to bring the accommodation up to the standard of its surroundings.

As well as winter frigidity, Park Place lacked the company of people of Anne's own age. She did however make one friend in Miss Freeman, from Fawley Court on the other side of the River Thames. She was possibly the daughter of Sambrooke Freeman, a prosperous merchant, who had employed Wyatt both to decorate his house and to build a temple on a nearby island in the middle of the Thames. Capability Brown had been commissioned to improve the landscape. Miss Freeman was to be Anne's model for Isis, the budding Thames, on Henley bridge, and also for her early bust of the Egyptian goddess Isis. Anne is also said to have worked the *palmetto*-inlaid friezes on the bookcases at Fawley Court. It is easy to imagine Anne, stuck in the cold discomfort of winter at Park Place, making a daily journey to Fawley Court, better built and probably warmer, to model both Miss Freeman and the library friezes as a welcome distraction to her self-imposed incarceration at Park Place.

In August 1777 HW proposed spending a couple of days at Goodwood, the country home of the Duke of Richmond and his wife, Anne's half-sister Mary. The Conway family, including Anne, also stayed there on their way to a seaside sojourn at the delightful Mount Edgecumbe, just outside Plymouth. There they arrived to meet Edward Jerningham, the rather curious poet, with whom any daughter would be safe, henceforth to be known by the Conway family as "the charming man". He was very happy to meet them: "We have a very agreeable family here, General Conway, Lady Ailesbury, and Mrs Damer. Upon being acquainted with Mrs Damer I find her uncommonly agreeable and clever. She has withdrawn herself from the world since her husband's unhappy death." It was during this visit that the young Lord Valletort, Lord Mount Edgecumbe's heir, was sufficiently impressed by Anne to commission the carving of the following acronym, based on her name, in gilt letters on a stone bench:

> ***D**'avid ne'er played the harp like thee,*
> ***A**'nson ne'er found thy like at sea,*
> ***M**'ara had not a melody like thine,*
> ***E**'dgecumbe, who thinks thee all divine*
> ***R**'ecords thy worth in every line.*

Sadly, he was no more competent in life than in his verse. He composed another ode on the death of Cupid, a pet pig, which was placed on its monument. George III was found by Queen Charlotte observing this oddity, and on her enquiry as to what he was examining, replied: "The family vault, Charly, the family vault".

In September Horace invited the Conway family to join him at Strawberry Hill: "I have got a delightful plaything, if I had time for play. It is a new sort of *camera-obscura* for drawing the portraits of persons, or prospects, or insides of rooms, and does not depend on the sun or anything. … Had you better not come and see it? … Remember that neither Lady A, nor you, nor Mrs D have seen my new divine closet [The Beauclerk Tower, completed July 1777], nor the billiard sticks with which the Countess of Pembroke and Arcadia used to play with her brother in law Sir Philip, nor the portrait of La Belle Jennings in the state bedchamber. I go to town this day… and as to be sure, Mount Edgecumbe has put you out of humour with Park Place, you may deign to leave it for a moment." In early October he invited them again: "To ensure Mrs D, beg I may expect you on Saturday next, the eleventh. If Lord and Lady William Campbell will do me the honour of accompanying you, I shall be most happy to see them, and expect Miss Caroline." The last named was their daughter, Caroline Campbell.

By November 1777 Anne had left her parents to set up on her own. Lady Sarah Lennox wrote: "Mrs Damer is improved, I think; she is vastly less of a fine lady, and appears to have more sensibility than I ever saw in her manner before. She has behaved very properly in every respect as a widow; she did everything in regard to his servants that show'd respect and regard for his memory for she paid all she could ……. She now acts sensibly on her own account, for she has taken a small house, and lives with propriety without affecting splendour, and says that, having shown she knew how to live well when she thought she had money, she is resolved to show she knows how to live prudently, now she has it not; for tho' her income is good, it will not do for shew and the comforts of life too, without outrunning it, and she prefers the comforts, and not being in debt, to shew. She also means to travel, I believe. I have been running on about these people as if you cared about them, which I daresay you do not, for whenever one is caught an inch out of the great circle one becomes a looker on, and in doing so one acquires an excess of indifference about it all, which one easily loses the moment one returns among them again."

The new house was in Sackville Street, which runs north from Piccadilly, and was adjacent to the new mansion, Melbourne House, fronting on to Piccadilly. It was rented from her great friend Lady Melbourne, and had access through a garden gate to Melbourne House.

Widowhood had come at a difficult time on the national front. The American War of Independence had begun. In 1778 France and Spain were to take advantage of England's involvement in America to declare war. Peace was not to return until 1782, and the fall of the North government. During the latter years there was a perceived threat of a French invasion, and general despondency as things went wrong. At home the Gordon Riots in 1780 were to be followed by the Siege of Gibraltar abroad, and by a French attempt to capture Jersey, where Harry was Governor. He visited the island frequently, ensuring that its fortifications were sufficient to withstand a French onslaught. On 17th June 1778 he had been present at a sitting of the island's Parliament, the Estates, which expressed their appreciation of his visiting the island at this critical time and thanked him for everything that he had already done for the defence of the island. In July 1778 hostilities in the Channel commenced. In May 1779 Harry visited the island again, shortly after a French invasion force had been repelled by Lord Seaforth's Regiment of Foot and 6000 Jersey militia, aided by artillery.

In the meantime the 1778 London season proceeded as usual. In one week there were three masquerades, an installation, and the Ball of the Knights at the Haymarket. In addition there had been a "*festino*" at Almacks, a reception at Lady Spencer's, Ranelagh and Vauxhall Gardens open, operas and plays. The Season ended in mid-June with a subscription fête at the Pantheon, where those attending were led into a subterranean room laid with earth, planted with trees and crammed with nosegays; the stench and moisture were suffocating, and on returning upstairs, they were poisoned by the chicken and ham. HW commented that he supposed there would be no more balls unless the French landed, and then they would have to recommence to show that the British were unconcerned by the invasion.

In the summer of 1778 Anne went to fashionable Spa, in neutral Belgium, to take the waters and enjoy the company. Here she met the Vicomte du Barry and his wife Hélène. Adolphe du Barry was the nephew of Louis XV's mistress, Mme du Barry. At the height of her influence, in 1772 and 1773, Mme du Barry had provided her nephew with an allowance, a position at court as equerry to Louis XV, and a bride. His marriage to the seventeen-year-old, extremely beautiful Hélène de Tournon, had taken place in the private chapel at Versailles, the bride in a magnificent dress of silver lace given to her by her new aunt. Louis XV had himself seemed most taken by Hélène's attractions. Unfortunately, when this was remarked upon to her aunt, she produced the pert reply that any interest from that quarter would still be keeping His Majesty in the family. These words had been relayed to Marie Antoinette, the Dauphine, and confirmed her intense dislike of the aunt, to which the niece was now added. The young du Barrys were excluded from the social life of the young court-in-waiting, and confined to the company of their aunt and her elderly friends. Hélène, lonely and discontented, hated both her husband and her provider, and sought a separation. On 10th May 1774 Louis XV died. Three days previously he had made his final confession, asked for his sins to be forgiven, and instructed that his mistress, Mme du Barry, should be sent to a convent. Her influence and much of her family's fortunes perished with the King. Adolphe, an attractive, amiable but aimless young man was left with time on his hands, unemployed, and forbidden to appear at court.

Eventually the young du Barrys effected a reconciliation. The Vicomte helped to provide a commission for his brother-in-law and an education for his sister-in-law, Marie-Sophie. In 1777 final proof of the reconciliation appeared in the birth of a baby son. Tragically, the infant did not survive. Heartbroken by their loss, the parents sought other distractions. Adolphe reverted to gambling, Hélène threw herself headlong into a life of hedonism. Comte Jean, father of Adolphe recorded sadly that "my daughter-in-law, governed by her taste in everything brilliant and expensive, her vanity and her love of spending, led my son, good but feeble, into expenses which were beyond him. … He had the misfortune to believe that he could pay off his debts by gambling."

On 8th July 1778 the du Barrys, accompanied by Helene's sister Marie-Sophie, arrived in Spa. Here they met up with a former colleague, James Louis Rice, an Irish adventurer raised to the rank of Count of the Holy Roman Empire by Joseph II for his service in the Austrian army. HW was later to describe him as "this friend, alias toad-eater, is a sharper, not of the first order." Their style of life in Spa was beyond their means. The Comte Jean reproached his daughter-in-law for her excessive expenditure: she had a score of dresses, two vehicles, and kept a sumptuous table. Hélène replied that Spa was a lot cheaper than Paris. On 24th July Anne also reached Spa. She soon met up and made friends with the du Barrys and Rice, and it was at her instigation that they crossed the Channel in late October to accompany Anne to Bath. If Spa had been expensive, life in Bath was still more costly. Bath was then a rendezvous for rich travellers from many countries, with "no occupation other than that of passing time, the most laborious of all. Half the inhabitants do nothing, and the other half furnish the means of doing nothing." The Vicomte's role in this pleasurable existence was to set up and operate a Faro gambling operation, with his wife and sister-in-law acting as hostesses. Rice, also attached to the party, was there as a friend, and in the case of Hélène, when her husband was occupied at the green baize table, rather too close a friend.

The du Barrys took a house in the most fashionable area of the city, at No 8 Royal Crescent, and Anne, having settled them in, returned to London. The gambling room opened and they entertained nightly. Among the guests was Louis Dutens, an anglicised Frenchman and tutor to the younger son of the Duke of Northumberland, who had found No 8 "so agreeable that I couldn't spend a day without going there." On 10th November he noticed that the Vicomtesse appeared worried, and, in response to his asking the reason, she replied that she had a headache. There was no sign of the Vicomte. Somebody said that he was indisposed, and that the Comte de Rice was keeping him company. The Vicomtesse left the room some twenty times, on the pretext of wanting fresh air, and eventually disappeared altogether, leaving her sister as hostess. The following morning, Dutens heard that there had been a duel at dawn that morning between du Barry and Rice. The former was dead, the latter severely wounded.

Dutens, as a fellow French citizen in England, was immediately aware that "the situation of the Vicomtesse suddenly presented itself to me in all its complexity. Deprived in this moment of her husband and her friends (for Mr Toole had been one of the seconds), young, foreign, and without experience, without knowledge of the country, surrounded by foreign domestics, everything contributed to her distress. I ran to her home to offer my services and demanded to talk to her maid." She said that her mistress knew nothing. She understood that the two friends, du Barry and Rice, had gone out sometime after midnight, leaving her mistress, who had tried to prevent them, in tears. Under the pretext of descending with the Vicomtesse to the dining room, they had run on ahead into the street. She had run after them, but soon lost them in the dark. Her maid had searched for her, and eventually at 2am had found her leaning against a wall, nearly fainting and brought her back to the house.

It transpired that there had been a violent quarrel between du Barry and Rice. Du Barry had contradicted something that Rice had said, sworn at him repeatedly, and called him a liar. Rice had immediately challenged him to a duel, a challenge that was speedily accepted. They had set out for Claverton Downs, high ground to the east of Bath, accompanied by two seconds, Mr Toole and Mr Rogers, and a surgeon. At dawn the following morning, with each combatant armed with two pistols and a sword, a bloody duel took place. Du Barry fired first, winging Rice in the thigh; Rice fired next, mortally wounding his opponent with a shot to his chest. Both contestants had time to get off a second shot, both missing, and had then advanced on each other with drawn swords before du Barry, vomiting blood, collapsed, asking Rice to spare his life. The request was granted but it was too late. Du Barry died shortly afterwards. Rice was left on the ground, unable to stand, while the surgeon bound his wound. He was then carried in some pain to lodgings in Bath.

Dutens discovered that though rumours of the Vicomte's death had reached them, the servants had chosen not to tell the Vicomtesse until the details became clearer. He took it upon himself to visit Rice, who had seemed pleased to see him and offered a garbled explanation of the causes of the duel, followed by its outcome. On leaving

Rice, Dutens had found the Vicomtesse's steward looking for him. His mistress was determined to find out what had happened, and he was at a loss as to what to do. Dutens, feeling that the news would be better delivered by a lady, ran to Mrs McCartney, a friend in whom the Vicomtesse could trust, and begged her to come with him. She had then informed Hélène that Dutens had discovered that her husband had been mortally wounded in a duel with Rice. Dutens, to give the Vicomtesse time to recover had allowed a quarter of an hour to elapse, entered "and found her in such affliction as may be more easily imagined than described". Gradually he had described to her the events of the previous night, and as he did so, she gave way to tears and grief which Dutens considered profound and real.

After she had composed herself, the Vicomtesse sat down and wrote a note for Rice. As the latter was in no condition to reply in writing, Dutens offered to carry the note to the wounded man and return with a verbal reply. He told Rice that he was unaware of the contents of the note, and asked him to reply in general terms that only the Vicomtesse might understand. Rice requested him to say that he had already given orders for what she had requested, and that he would like her *valet de chambre* to be sent to him, as he had something to tell him. When this man arrived, Rice penned him a note to his mistress. This opening of a correspondence between Hélène and the killer of her husband caused some surprise to those who observed it.

Dutens spent the rest of the day consoling the Vicomtesse. An urgent message was sent to Anne Damer in London, requesting her to return immediately to her friends. Arrangements were put in hand to make ready for the departure of the Vicomtesse to France, as soon as Anne had arrived. Dutens returned to Rice and learned from him that the exchange of correspondence had been to do with the Vicomte's business affairs, which fortunately were in good order; he had made the necessary provisions for all debts to be paid in the event of his death, and provided the cash to do so. His second, Mr Toole, had been entrusted with 350 guineas for the purpose. However, Mr Toole, fearing that he might be incriminated in any ensuing coroner's inquest, had gone unavoidably absent, taking the cash with him. The seconds had apparently agreed with the duellists before the contest that it should be a fight to the death, with no quarter given. Under English law there was a chance that this might be construed as murder and aiding and abetting murder. Mr Toole was taking no chances.

Twenty-four hours later, Anne arrived in Bath. Dutens told her that Rice wished to see her, and advised her not to do anything that might increase public suspicion with regard to the Vicomtesse. Anne therefore sent a message to Rice saying that unless he had anything to say to Hélène's benefit, she would not come, and that if she did come, he should give his word of honour that he would abide by this condition. Rice replied that he would do nothing that would implicate the Vicomtesse, and that he would write shortly. Dutens then advised Anne that he would take care of the funeral arrangements, and that it was imperative that she and Hélène should leave Bath immediately. Before the coroner's jury sat on the following day, they were gone. The result of the inquest was a verdict of homicide in the heat of passion, which fell short of murder. Although a subsequent trial would be required, Rice and his seconds could breathe again. Dutens saw Rice again, and the latter told him "everything that it was necessary for the Vicomtesse to know." Dutens immediately left for London, to see and inform Hélène, before she and Anne departed for France. Despite the fact that England and France were at war with each other, Hélène was back in Paris before her husband was buried in Bathampton churchyard.

A few days later Dutens met up with Mr Toole, who confirmed to him that he had been able to return the 350 guineas to the Vicomtesse before she departed from London. He said that when he had been called as a second, the argument had gone too far for a reconciliation to be possible. He believed that the real reason had been the Vicomte's jealousy of Rice, though he would say nothing derogatory about the Vicomtesse. In subsequent talks with Rice, Dutens was told that the real reason was that Rice had discovered a plot by the Vicomte to poison him. Dutens advised him to keep his suspicions to himself, as they would only serve to cast aspersions on a friend who was no longer able to defend himself.

On 29th November Mme du Deffand wrote to HW telling him she had heard that two days earlier the Vicomtesse du Barry had arrived in Paris, accompanied by Mme Damer, but that yesterday Mme de Cambis, a great friend of Mme Damer, knew nothing about it. Nearly a year later, in another letter to Horace dated October 1779, she asked, *inter alia*, for news of Anne and her family. She said that Paris was expecting the return of the Vicomtesse du Barry, who had rented an apartment. "It was she whom Mme Damer accompanied on her return from England." Shortly after her return, the Vicomtesse requested that she be permitted to return to her maiden name of de Tournon. By the spring of 1780 the new Comtesse de Tournon had been accepted at Versailles, and her public links with the du Barry family finally cut, though privately she continued to draw income from the marriage settlement that her aunt by marriage had made her. Rice was tried at Taunton Assizes on 31st March 1779. The judge recommended that the jury bring in a verdict of manslaughter, but the members of the jury, not being Francophiles, preferred to bring in a plea of not guilty, and Rice was acquitted.

The local and national papers were full of the story. English friends, including General Smith, came forward to pay any outstanding bills, and in due course were repaid. Anne, to whom the violent loss of a gambling and unloved husband must have brought back familiar memories, had been at the centre of events. At best it could be said that she had combined courage and kindness in aiding a friend in desperate need. At worst, she had made a doubtful choice of friends, and been implicated, if only at a distance, in a death with dark and murky undertones. Her prompt removal of one of the principal participants to a foreign country at war with England raised several questions. If she wished to avoid the strictures of gossip columnists and scandalmongers, she had not acted in her own best interests.

In November 1778 Lady Sarah Lennox wrote to Lady Susan O'Brien, saying that du Barry's death had reminded her of John and Anne Damer. The latter was now trying hard to adopt a more prudent lifestyle. To her credit, she was quite prepared to admit that "she had been rich and was now poor". Her income was sufficient for all reasonable comforts of life, though not for magnificence. Nowadays, travelling, books and a comfortable home had taken the place of fine clothes and carriages. How long the situation would last was questionable, as "she is vain and likes to be at the head of the great world, and is easily led into that style of life. Upon the whole, I think she is a sensible woman without sensibility, a pretty one without pleasing, a prudent one without conduct, and I believe nobody will have a right to tax her with any fault, yet she will be abused, which I take to be owing to a want of sweetness in her disposition; she is too strictly right ever to be beloved. As for the abuse she has met with, I must put such nonsense out of the question, and in everything else her conduct is very proper."

War with France led to more excitement for Anne in July 1779. She set off again, *en route* to the fashionable waters of Spa in neutral Belgium, accompanied by her aunt, Lady William Campbell. They sailed aboard the mail packet boat *Prince Frederick*, travelling from Dover to Ostend. Also on board were the Dowager Duchess of Leinster and her husband, the Reverend Mr Ogilvy, and Mr Tickel, author of *Anticipation*. Midway across the Channel, they were chased by a French privateer. A four-hour sailing match took place, during which time two broadsides were fired by the privateer. Anne stood on the deck, enjoying the spectacle. She insisted on hauling up the tackle to help launch a boat to sink the mail. However, becoming unbalanced on the slippery and sloping deck, she slipped into the hold into the middle of a pack of hounds. She quickly extricated herself from the surprised canines without damage and resumed position on deck. Eventually the packet, which was unarmed and much smaller, surrendered and struck its colours.

When the Captain of the French cutter boarded the English packet, he was surprised to find Anne on deck, and addressing himself to her politely, hoped she was "recovered from those fears which the action must have unavoidably occasioned". Anne, after thanking him for his civility, replied "I believe, Sir, you will find paler cheeks among some of the gentlemen below." The French captain wanted only his prize of the ship itself, and was very happy to land the passengers, bid them farewell without charge, and a good journey on to Spa.

In September 1779 Anne returned from the continent, this time without new friends and without incident. Horace was relieved that she had not gone on to Naples, where she might have witnessed the eruption of Mount Vesuvius. "How poor Lady Hamilton's nerves stood it I do not conceive". The rest of 1779 and 1780 was spent in England, as the war with France and Spain made travel abroad difficult. Harry spent a considerable time in the island of Jersey, seeking to strengthen its fortifications against possible French attack. However he had returned to the mainland in May 1781, when Horace recorded him attending a comedy called *The Miniature Picture* at Drury Lane. His party had included, among others, Lord Craven, the husband of the playwright, Anne and her half-sister Mary, and a military friend of Harry's, Colonel O'Hara.

Anne busied herself with her sculpture, and it was around 1780 that she produced her neo-classical busts of Lady Melbourne and the Duchess of Devonshire. All three remained firm friends, albeit the wilder excesses of *macaronis* and masquerades that had characterised 1775 to 1776 were now a thing of the past.

On 6th January 1781 the possible French invasion of Jersey became a reality. Whilst the sentries were asleep, about 800 French troops landed; a further 200 were drowned in the attempt, while their accompanying artillery was lost on the rocks. They entered the marketplace of St Helier and captured the Lieutenant-Governor, Moses Corbet. Their triumph was short lived; the following day a combined force of the 78th and 95th regiments, supported by the local militia and a field piece, counter-attacked and swiftly retrieved the situation. The French general, who insisted that Moses Corbet stand with him to resist the attack, received three wounds; Corbet received two balls through the top of his hat, but was otherwise unscathed. 500 prisoners were taken and swiftly dispatched to England. It was subsequently found that the French had put to sea on 24th December and had been afloat in the Channel without being spotted until they landed on 6th January. There had been no English naval or coastal patrols sent out. The French had also planned, if successful, to light a beacon, to summon a further 4000 troops waiting in France as reinforcements. Harry, who had been celebrating the Christmas holiday at Park Place, whilst recovering from a broken arm, received the news at 11am on 8th January. General Amherst had written a note to Lt-General Monckton saying "the intelligence has been sent to Gen Conway, his health has been bad lately, what he may do on this occasion I do not know". Harry was ordered to proceed immediately to Jersey. He reached London by 3pm that day, and set out again for Portsmouth the same evening. He spoke to the Secretary of State, Lord Hillsborough, before leaving and wrote him a note from Portsmouth the following day. There he had found only the frigate *Emeralde*, on which he embarked at 9am hoping to sail by 10.30am. By 11th January Harry was again in Portsmouth, having been driven back by contrary winds and bad weather. He sent a letter to Lord Hillsborough, stating that the captain had done his best, and that since news of the invasion's failure had now reached Portsmouth, he proposed to return to London.

Although disaster had been averted, Harry realised that this was not due to him, and was apprehensive as to the outcome of any enquiry. Matters were made worse as he was taken ill whilst returning, with a violent pain in his broken arm, fever and rheumatic pains all over his body. The rigours of the storm-bound sea voyage had obviously taken their toll, and he did not begin to get up again until 21st January. It was not till 10th February that he was able to write to Lord Hillsborough, saying that he was now strong enough to leave Park Place and come to London. In the event he stayed in London until 18th March, finally embarking for Jersey on the 24th and arriving there on the 26th. He was still there in May when HW wrote to him with news of his new acquisition, Tonton, a small dog, the gift of Mme Deffand. Immediately on arrival the dog had been in a fight with one of Horace's, and come out of it with a bleeding paw. Horace had called his housekeeper, Margaret, to dress it. She had exclaimed "poor little thing, he does not understand my language!" Horace hoped that Harry would soon come and "enjoy a quiet summer under the laurels of your own conscience."

Despite her good intentions, Anne had not been able entirely to give up the world of masquerades. The *Morning Herald* in its column, *Masquerade Intelligence*, reported that at a masquerade at the Kings Theatre, Haymarket, all in masks, "the Duchess of Devonshire with a smart cocked hat, scarlet riding habit and man's domino, looked divinely, and was followed in imitation by the Ladies Melbourne, Jersey, Sefton, Buckinghamshire, and Hon. Mrs Damer *à la militaire*…". It was quite a party: "The refreshments ….consisted of various sorts of French wines, ices, jellies, sweetmeats, fruits, and of the best quality. The company did not break up till near five the next morning."

In the meantime Anne continued with her education in sculpture and planned to travel to the continent, both for health reasons and to soak in the delights of classical antique statuary in Italy. In August 1781 HW wrote to the Earl of Strafford, telling him that Mrs Damer was, for her good and to his regret, going abroad for health reasons. In September he wrote to Sir Horace Mann in Florence, to inform him that "General Conway's daughter is going abroad to confirm a very delicate constitution – I believe at Naples. I will say very few words on her, after telling you, that besides being his daughter, I love her as my own child. It is not from wanting matter, but from having too much. She has one of the most solid understandings I ever knew, astonishingly improved, but with so much reserve and modesty that I have often told Mr Conway that he does not know the extent of her capacity and the solidity of her reason. We have by accident discovered that she writes Latin like Pliny, and is learning Greek. In Italy she will be a prodigy. She models like Bernini, has excelled the moderns in the similitudes of her busts, and has lately begun one in marble. You must keep all knowledge of these talents and acquisitions to yourself; she would never forgive my mentioning them, at least her mental qualities. You may just hint that I have talked of her statuary, as you may assist her if she has a mind to borrow anything to copy from the Great Duke's collection. Lady William Campbell, her uncle's widow, accompanies her, who is a very reasonable woman too, and equally shy. If they return through Florence, pray give them a parcel of my letters. I had been told your nephew would make you a visit this autumn, but I have heard nothing of him. If you should see him, pray give him the parcel, for he will return sooner than they." Here is another example of Horace collecting and preserving his correspondence for posterity.

By November HW was writing to Sir Horace Mann, congratulating him on getting on so well with Mrs Damer. In December the party moved on from Florence to Rome, and thence to Naples. Whilst in Naples Anne spent most days sculpting in a studio. She completed a model of Ceres in terracotta which she presented to the British ambassador, Sir William Hamilton, who, in addition to acting as her host, had become a friend and correspondent. Hamilton expressed himself to Horace as "astonished at what she did here; from a profile on a Sicilian medal of a Ceres, she made a bust considerably bigger than life, and in my opinion there is not an artist now in Italy that could have done it with so much of the true sublime, and which none but the first artists of Greece seem to have understood." He went on to say that for all its sublimity, the work did have some faults in technique. He finished by asking Horace to "kiss the fair hand for me that is capable of such wonder working."

In March Horace wrote again to Sir Horace Mann, saying that he had heard from General Conway that Lady William Campbell had fallen sick in Rome, and that Anne was returning to Florence, where it was hoped that Sir Horace might be able to find them a good physician and assist in getting a sea passage home from Leghorn for the ailing aunt. In June 1782 a further letter from Horace thanked Sir Horace Mann profusely for his help with Lady William Campbell, and said that Mrs Damer was expected home at any moment. On 14th June he wrote again to say that she had now arrived, how delighted she was by Sir Horace, and by his gift to her of an antique sculpture of a foot. She had been away for nine months and her journey had taken her through Florence and Rome to Naples, and back home again through France, despite the fact that the country was still at war.

Whilst in Italy, she had met and made friends with the Princess Dashkova, who was making a prolonged tour of the countries of Western Europe; during her time in Italy Anne completed a terracotta medallion of Princess Dashkova's daughter. This returned with the Princess to Russia, and does not appear to have survived to the present day. Princess Dashkova writes of Anne as "so justly celebrated for her skill in sculpture and no less to be admired for her profound information and good sense, which under the veil of a peculiar modesty sought rather the disguise than the display of her acquisitions." Anne seems to have made quite a hit with the Princess. Both believed that women could play an equal part to men in the corridors of power and art. The Princess, according to her memoirs, had been instrumental in elevating another woman, Catherine the Great, to the Russian throne, and following her return to Russia, became head of its Academy of Arts and editor of the first Russian dictionary. She followed Anne's party to Naples, where she wrote: "Our morning pursuits were usually concluded in the studio of Mrs Damer. There we generally found her employed with her chisel; but this was a sanctum in which she received only her particular friends; for her character was as devoid as possible of ostentation, and she made so little parade of her talents and learning that I remember one morning she was extremely disconcerted at my having observed a Greek work lying in her room, full of marginal annotations in her own handwriting."

On 15th June 1782 the *Public Advertiser* reported that "yesterday the Hon Mrs Damer and Lady Augusta Campbell arrived in town from the south of France". She had thoroughly enjoyed her continental sojourn. HW wrote to Sir Horace Mann: "Mrs Damer arrived last night. She looks in better health than when she went, but I cannot say, any plumper. She said 'Pray tell Sir Horace how much obliged to him I am; and do you know', she added, 'that he is not only one of the most amiable men in the world, but the most agreeable?' I see that you understand her as well as she does you, for you have given her an antique foot that is the perfection of sculpture."

A few months later, in February 1783, Anne received a long letter from Sir William Hamilton, a postscript to her Italian journey. He reported that he was taking great care of her masterly bust of Ceres, that he had had a copy cast and sent to the Princess d'Ascon, and that he would send the mould on to England so that she could give a copy "to the worthy, of which there are very few, even in England, where all pretend to be connoisseurs".

"Since I had the pleasure of seeing you here we have had a chain of melancholy events." Lady Hamilton, who had been in poor health for a very long time, had died peacefully. This would not have come as a great shock to Anne, who had seen her so recently, but there was still no escape from Sir William's description of the post-mortem. Following "the inspection of her inside, which was in a thorough decay, she never could have enjoy'd a moment's ease, nay it is wonderfull she was able to act the way she did latterly, one lobe of her lungs had certainly been consumed some years and the other was affected, besides many other strange phenomena that were observed within her breast."

In addition, their mutual friend, Mr Drummond had fractured his skull in a fall from one of Mr Beckford's horses. At the beginning of August, Hamilton's dinner table had comprised, in addition to himself and Lady Hamilton, Beckford, Drummond, and Burton the organist. By the end of the month, only Beckford and Hamilton remained alive, the former at death's door with a malignant fever.

In addition, Anne's friend Princess Grimaldi had been entombed alive on 5th February by a dreadful earthquake in Calabria, which had destroyed more or less every town and village in southern Calabria, spreading as far as the city of Messina in Sicily. "The shocks were still continuing when the last accounts came away on the 15th inst, and many thousands of lives are lost, but I fear more will suffer hereafter from famine and sickness. Our poor Princess with every soul in the house was buried in the ruins and what is worse, when digging her out some days after, it is evident that she had received no hurt, but was starved to death. If I did not know the firmness of your mind I would not have ventured to inform you of so many many melancholy events – but it is good to reflect on what we poor mortals are subject to."

On a happier note, Hamilton, who had requested a spell of leave, was preparing to return to England. He was looking forward to renewing his friendship with Anne, and perhaps, now that he was again single, something more: "I feel already happy with the thoughts of seeing you soon." Enclosing an etching of himself, lean and fit from continual hunting parties with the King of Naples, he ended the letter: "Adieu my Dear Mrs Damer, with a most sincere regard and esteem, Yr most obedient and humble servant, William Hamilton."

Chapter 6

ANTIQUES AND ANIMALS

John Damer's death was the catalyst for Anne to turn to life as a sculptor. HW, in his Book of Visitors at Strawberry Hill, gives a list of Anne's works and remembers that (as we have seen) she showed "the first symptoms of her talent for statuary when she was about 10 years. She was reading Spenser, and with bits of wax candle and silk and feathers and tinsel picked out of silks, she made a knight and his esquire not so long as a finger" in costumes as described by Spenser.

In 1763 Horace had mentioned "the Infanta, whose progress in waxen statuary I hope advances", and around 1765 he mentioned further progress in the form of a small wax portrait of a shock-dog, followed by portrait medallions in wax of her mother, her cousin Caroline Campbell, Voltaire, and the Emperor Augustus. Walpole described the wax medallions as being in the manner of Isaac Gosset, who was a regular exhibitor at the Society of Artists from 1760 to 1778. He was probably the best of several professional wax sculptors working at that time, and both Harry and Caroline had sat for him. Wax was malleable, and considered a material suitable for a ladylike leisure activity, a suitable alternative to sketching, or to the needlework at which Caroline was so adept.

There is a tale about Anne and the philosopher David Hume, who was employed as secretary by Harry when Secretary of State from 1766 to 68. During the early months of his appointment, they had been out walking together, when a gypsy lad appeared with a tray of models which he had made; he had tried to sell his wares, and Hume had engaged him in conversation. When Anne had berated him for wasting their time with a tinker, the philosopher had taken her to task, saying that the young man was skilful, and that she should not criticise if she could do no better. The improbable tale goes that Anne worked through the night, produced a model for Hume the following morning, and thus launched her career as a sculptress. In reality, whether or not Hume knew of her precocious modelling talent, he had taken the opportunity to deliver a much needed lesson in good manners.

Anne is said to have received training in sculpture from Giuseppe Ceracchi and John Bacon the Elder, and in anatomical drawing from William Cruikshank. Ceracchi, who was Italian, arrived in England in 1773 and left in 1779. It is reasonable to suppose that Anne's tuition took place between these dates. He worked under, and lodged with Agostino Carlini, another Italian resident in England and a founding member of the Royal Academy. In 1775 Lord Milton chose Carlini to produce a magnificent marble memorial to his wife Caroline, in which the widowed lord bends over the recumbent figure of his departed wife. This fine work still stands in the north transept of Milton Abbey. The introduction to Carlini might well have come through Anne and Ceracchi, notwithstanding the fact that by that time she and John Damer were separated. Ceracchi is credited with teaching Anne to model in clay; he also produced an excellent life-size marble figure, *Anne Damer as the Muse of Sculpture*, with her tools at her feet. This work is now in the British Museum. Horace stated that Ceracchi was so charmed "with her talents and graceful figure that he desired to do a statue of her". He goes on to relate that Harry had subsequently purchased the statue, and so both beauty and sufficiency were satisfied.

Anne would probably have learned to produce a preliminary sketch of her subject, and then do a small model in a soft material such as clay or wax. These preliminary models were known as *bozzetti* (or *bozzetto* in the singular). Some of Anne's earlier *bozzetti* still exist in a private collection – two small wax heads of ladies, and three small clay designs, one of the goddess Isis, as later displayed in Anne's large figure on Henley bridge, one of a gentleman in a periwig tied with a ribbon, and the third of a young lady. In addition Ceracchi would have taught Anne to use her tools and hands to form a clay model of the desired size. The finished clay model would then have been sent out for firing, to be returned later as a finished terracotta model. It is perhaps stating the obvious that in Italian "*terracotta*" means "baked earth".

The move from terracotta to marble was made as a result of her training in the studio of John Bacon. Bacon was born in 1740 in Southwark, the son of a cloth-worker from Somerset. At 14 he was apprenticed to a porcelain manufacturer in Lambeth, first as a painter, and then, after promotion, as a modeller. In 1768 he entered the Royal Academy Schools in the year in which they were established. By 1769 he was helping the Coade Artificial Stone Manufactory, where he improved methods of working with artificial stone. His carving skills gained him many prizes, including in 1769 the first gold medal for sculpture awarded by the Royal Academy. He invented an instrument to transform the shape of the model to the marble more exactly, and set up his own studio and workshop, using his self-taught skills to great effect. He had not had the advantage of, nor possibly felt the need for fashionable training on the continent, and produced much fine and successful work without it. He employed a number of statuaries, the 18th century term for sculptors, and delegated much of the carving to them. In 1777 he is recorded as having worked on some marble figures for the Duke of Richmond, Anne's brother-in-law, and perhaps it was he who effected the introduction.

Bacon's workshop studio would have been a far cry from the surroundings with which Anne was familiar. There would have been dirt, dust, naked models, workmen trundling in with marble blocks, and hewers chipping away at the marble to produce a rudimentary likeness which the sculptor would take on, to turn into a work of art. It would not have been a place suitable for a leading lady of *le ton* to be seen or heard. However it was typical of Anne to select what suited her, even if outside the socially acceptable norm. It might not be a traditional occupation of the English lady, but it was what was required to become a successful statuary.

Working with marble was not a skill to be learnt in a few hours. A number of techniques needed to be mastered. Firstly the block of stone had to be selected, and drawn upon; roughing-out was done with a punch and mallet; features were defined with a chisel and hair with a drill; files, rasps and abrasives were used to smooth the surface. It was usual for the sculptor to employ less-skilled and cheaper colleagues to do the roughing-out. Anne, despite her protestations to the contrary, as recorded by Horace, may well have done likewise.

The third tutor mentioned by contemporaries in connection with Anne's artistic education was Dr William Cumberland Cruikshank, who is said to have taught her anatomical drawing. Cruikshank was a senior assistant to Dr William Hunter, Professor of Anatomy to the Royal Academy, and the leading obstetrician of his day. Anatomical research through the dissection of recently deceased bodies was a facet of 18th century scientific enquiry; it advanced medical knowledge, and to a lesser extent gave artists an insight into what made the human frames and muscles that they were portraying. Notoriously George Stubbs, the equestrian artist, kept dead horses in his studio until the continuing stench drove his neighbours to prevent him. Nevertheless he still produced his seminal work, *The Anatomy of the Horse*, an absolute necessity to give him the knowledge to paint the muscles rippling under the well-groomed coat of Whistlejacket. Human dissection lessons were given to groups of aspiring professionals, whether medical or artistic; it is unlikely that Anne, a woman and an amateur, would have participated. There still exists a small notebook with marbled covers, written in Anne's handwriting: "*X Libris Anna Seymour Damer sculptrice et statuaria qui delineavit*". It contains some 17 pages of anatomical drawings, somewhat water-stained, but clearly and accurately executed. There are several blank pages at the rear of the book, and no tutor's comments. It is possible that this was the total extent of Anne's anatomical education.

The previous paragraphs cover our knowledge and presumptions about Anne's technical training as a sculptress. In order to convert technical skills into the ability to produce a memorable work of art, clear vision, inspiration, stamina and discipline are also required. Anne had no doubts as to the direction her work would take; a manuscript written in about 1815 either by Anne, or at her bidding, sums up her feelings. "This lady exhibited from childhood proofs of the talent which has since distinguished her, and having later been widowed, and therefore less given to society, whose genius led her to follow that taste which had long since occupied her mind, not as a Dilettante, but as an Artist. Mrs Damer received her first lessons from the celebrated sculptor Ceracchi, who at that time found himself in London, learned the technique of carving marble in the studio of Mr Bacon of the Royal Academy, studied the elements of anatomy under the auspices of Professor Cruikshank, and travelled often to Italy to study the works of art which are to be found there in order to perfect her knowledge of the true and simple style of the Greeks she has always tried to emulate." This brief summary contains two essentials pertinent to Anne's credo. Firstly, she was an artist, somebody who put their life and soul into their work, whether or not for payment. Secondly, she had travelled to Italy to find inspiration in the "antique" classical sculptures displayed in the private collections and public galleries. Never mind that most new sources of inspiration were Roman, and not, as Anne believed, Greek; they were still classical, and she was a neo-classical enthusiast.

As an artist, she was considered by her peers to produce work of sufficient quality to exhibit at the annual exhibition of the Royal Academy in most years from 1784 to 1818, though from 1790 her output reduced, and from 1810 it was only intermittent. As a member of the Whig aristocracy, she could not stoop to charging for her work, and, in so doing, becoming a professional. Nowadays the social distinction between gentleman and player has disappeared entirely from the world of art, and almost entirely from that of sport with the notable exceptions of jockeys. In the 18th century it was a bridge that you did not cross. The fact that she was a female artist, and especially a sculptress, was something of which she was extremely proud. However the prevailing feeling of the day was that ladies should be encouraged to take up activities such as needlework, painting and drawing, dancing or playing a musical instrument. By all means they should be proficient, even brilliant, at their chosen pastimes, but they should indeed only be pastimes, or part-time occupations, and certainly unpaid. The role of sculptress was a little *outré,* beyond the pale of recognised ladies' activities; a hammer and chisel lacked the soft touch of a paint brush, or the rhythmic flow of the embroiderer's needle. The number of successful European sculptresses since the Renaissance could be counted on the fingers of one hand.

Anne, a widow at 28, was a proficient modeller, training in the skills of the sculptor's art, a full-time artist, and yet still an amateur, regarded by her social peers with a curiosity which ranged between idle and malignant, and by some of her fellow artists as something of an intruder into their closed professional circle. She did not conform to the current standards of her sex and station, and this, in a gossip-ridden society, was bound to end in criticism, or, as Anne described it "abuse". She herself had determined to be "less given to society"; she might not have realised the aggravation that this decision was to cause her.

She was an artist who studied the "antique". From childhood she had had access to the libraries of her father and HW, and it is certain that they would have encouraged her both to read the Latin classic texts and to study such works as Montfaucon's *L'Antiquité Expliquée et Representée en Figures*. This volume contained what was then the most complete account of classical sculpture available. At the start of her sculpting career Anne's belief, arising from her studies of classical sculpted heads, was that the form should be as near perfect as possible and expressionless; features should give a likeness, but that was subordinated to the quest for perfection. The happy smile, the sparkling eye, the tousled hair would not be shown. The critic might say that this recipe disguised the fact that the sculptress was unable to produce a greater likeness, and there may be some truth in this. However the format of classical expressionless perfection was certainly something that Anne aimed for in her earlier work.

The strict neo-classical period began in the early 1780s, and the sitters to this new and untried sculptress were mainly her friends and their children. After some early experimentation with wax models, among the first of her friends to sit for her was Georgiana Devonshire. The sculpture in terracotta would have been done around 1779-80. Elizabeth Melbourne, whose bust was described by Dallaway in *Anecdotes of the Arts in England*, published in 1800, "as of admirable resemblance and grace," was next, followed by Anne's cousin Caroline Campbell, and a statue of the Melbourne heir, Peniston Lamb, as the infant Mercury. Sadly all these early terracotta models are now lost. In 1781 her first marble bust of a niobid, an idealised classical nymph, was completed, closely following on the heels of a terracotta model of the same subject. This marble bust, now in a private collection, is inscribed with the date, and the words *primum opus* (first work). From then onwards a marble bust was a natural follow-on to the terracotta model. Thus her marble bust of Lady Melbourne, following on from the earlier terracotta model, was exhibited at the Royal Academy in 1784. Marble was less fragile and more likely to stand the test of time than terracotta, an attribute noted in verse by Erasmus Darwin, in the Botanic Garden, published in 1791. Here Anne's bust of Lady Melbourne is linked with a later one of Lady Elizabeth Foster:

> *"Long with soft touch shall Damer's chisel charm,*
> *With grace delight us and with beauty warm.*
> *Fosters fine form shall hearts unborn engage.*
> *And Melbourn's smile enchant another age."*

Judging by exhibits at the Royal Academy, the years 1784-1789 marked the peak output of Anne's sculpting career. All entries were made on an honorary basis, distinguishing them from the already sold, or the "for sale" works of other artists. Other portraits in the antique fashion modelled first in terracotta, followed by marble versions, all of which survive, were made of Anne's friend from Fawley Court, Miss Freeman, as the Egyptian goddess Isis; of Miss Farren the comic actress, as Thalia; of

Anne's mother, Caroline Ailesbury, and of Anne's dear friend, Mary Berry. Works solely in terracotta, none of which remain, included Harry Conway in a helmet, Anne's brother-in-law the Duke of Richmond, and the model of Lady Elizabeth Foster referred to previously.

Bess Foster was another of Anne's friends. They had met previously in Italy where Anne had made a wax profile of her around 1785-6. Born Elizabeth Hervey, daughter of the Earl-Bishop of Bristol, Bess had married John Foster, an Irish MP, separated from him, and in 1782 had joined up with the Duke and Duchess of Devonshire in a *menage à trois*. She had been sent to Italy by the Duke of Devonshire, as she was pregnant by him, and her illegitimate daughter, Caroline, was to be born there. Whilst on the same visit to Italy, Anne completed both terracotta and marble self portraits, again in the antique style, the latter of which she presented to the Accademia di San Luca, and which is now in the Uffizi gallery.

There is another part of Anne's work which owes nothing to the antique tradition and everything to real life. It coexisted with her neo-classical period from around 1782-1790, and centred on the portrayal of family pets. Anne and her family were dog-owners and dog-lovers; dogs were her constant companions throughout her life and she directed in her will that she be buried with "the bones of her favourite dog that died before her." Her animal sculpture started with dogs and proceeded to include cats and kittens. HW tells us that one of her first wax models was a small "Shock Dog". By "shock", he meant a shock of hair, and Anne's shock dogs certainly have the most wonderful coats. In 1780 she completed another shock dog, this time in terracotta. The original model, said by Horace to belong to Harry, combines the size and appearance of a Cavalier King Charles spaniel with the hairiness of an unclipped Norfolk terrier. These were days before the inbreeding of canine varieties, and the dog itself may have looked the spitting image of the sculpture. Certainly, especially when finished in terracotta, Anne's dogs have a liveliness, reality and lightness of touch. You would not be surprised if their tails began to wag. Again all the models of dogs and cats were made for friends or family.

Other models include a greyhound of 1783, now missing, which may indeed have been her own pet, Fidele, variously described as a terrier or greyhound, and probably more approximate to a whippet. This dog may also have been the model for a terracotta sculpture in 1787, followed by a marble version in 1789, described by Walpole as "her own terrier, very like a greyhound, in terracotta, size of life, lying down, but as if listening eagerly, and ready to rise." If this was Fidele, she was to die in 1791, having been taken by Anne to Portugal. Her bones were lovingly brought back to England, and Anne would request that they be buried with her after her death. Sadly the current whereabouts of these three models of Fidele are unknown. A pair of terracotta sleeping dogs are now at Knowsley, in the possession of the Earl of Derby, and a marble version at Goodwood house in Sussex. These dogs have enchanted visitors for many years; the dogs are very different; one is smaller and more easily recognisable, the other fast asleep, lost under the tangle of his curly coat.

Her most celebrated cats were a pair of marble kittens, probably sculpted around 1789 and recorded as being at Strawberry Hill. Following the death of his dog Tonton, HW wrote to the Countess of Ossory: "My resource is in two marble kittens that Mrs Damer has given me, of her own work, and which are so much alive that I talk to them, as I did to poor Tonton." These are now in a private collection.

It is unfortunate that so many of these earlier sculptures have been lost. The early busts of Anne herself, and her friends as Isis and Thalia, are very pleasing pieces, if not great sculptures. Their neo-classical simplicity and purity are charming. They may lack vitality, but that is intended. Her models of dogs, on the other hand, are full of life; much loved domestic pets are portrayed as she saw them, seeming as much alive today as when they were modelled. As Anne got older and her sculpting matured, so did her style of depicting humans, and her choice of models was to alter – but her later sculptures are for a subsequent chapter.

Chapter 7

ABUSED

Following her return to England in June 1782, Anne found herself concerned with the problems of what she referred to as "abuse". During the 18th century, the laws governing libel were at best uncertain, and in general favoured the libeller. Anonymous scribblers and pamphleteers were free to pursue their scurrilous trade with little fear of prosecution. Leading members of the social and political ruling classes, most often the Whig aristocracy and their adherents, were pilloried in print and in cartoons.

In Anne's case, the abuse was to take two forms. The first, to which she took the strongest objections, either inferred that she was, or directly accused her of being, a lesbian. The second form insinuated that her sculpture was not her own. The abuse began after her husband's suicide, and it started because she was a member of the Seymour Conway family. The initial abuser was a penurious gossip columnist, an old Etonian contemporary of John Damer, William Combe. In 1777 Combe had married a discarded mistress of Viscount Beauchamp, Harry's nephew, the heir to Lord Hertford, and Anne's first cousin. The marriage service between Combe and the ex mistress, Maria Foster, commonly called Miss Harley, had taken place quietly at St George's, Hanover Square. The departure of the mistress had freed Beauchamp to marry Lady Isabella Shepheard, a considerable heiress. Combe thought that marriage would provide an end to his financial problems, as in return for his taking Maria as wife, Beauchamp had promised them an annuity. If indeed this had been promised, Beauchamp reneged, incurring Combe's wrath for the whole Hertford family, including Anne Damer.

Combe's satiric poem *The First of April; Or, the Triumphs of Folly* appeared later in 1777. The setting is a masquerade ball at the court of the Queen of Folly. The courtiers are largely Hertford relations. In the poem Anne is portrayed as the sorrowing widow, lamenting not for her husband, but for the loss of a future title.

> *"And lo! The sorrowing D..... then succeeds,*
> *In all the mournful pomp of Widow's weeds.*
> *I heard a loud lament and bitter moan,*
> *Not for a Husband, but a Title gone.*
> *Close by her side, I saw the illustrious Dame,*

Whom Wits the Modern Messalina name;
Who whisper'd comfort to the mourning Fair,
And told of joys which blooming Widows share;
Whose easy life no haughty ruler knows;
Who, when th' awakened passion wanton grows,
May, where her fancy leads, allay the flame,
Nor fear a husband's threats or ruin'd fame."

Anne, as a young and attractive widow with no marital ties, is informed by Messalina that the field is now wide open, wherever "her fancy leads". Messalina, the wife of the Emperor Claudius, was portrayed by classical authors as having a prodigious sexual appetite. The reference to the "joys which blooming Widows share" might be construed as sharing them together; however, it could equally mean that all 18th century aristocratic widows could enjoy playing the field.

Any mild inference contained in Combe's poem, was followed by a more direct attack in 1779 in James Perry's *Mimosa; Or, The Sensitive Plant*. This poem was dedicated to Sir Joseph Banks, who had introduced mimosa to England following his 1771 voyage with Captain Cook to the new lands of Australia and New Zealand. However, the content had little to do with botany. The Sensitive Plant in Perry's verse is a synonym for the penis, and its varying uses.

"Can Botanists find out the cause,
That contrary to nature's laws,
Some people can abuse it?
ST-T claps it in his valet's b-m;
H-LL fingers it, and some
Like DAM-R never use it."

Damer is the only woman of the three to whom the writer refers. A footnote refers readers to his meaning: "This lady's late elopement with the Countess du B—e will explain this." Readers, with the late duel in Bath fresh in their minds, were left to draw their own conclusions.

In the next scurrilous pamphlet, "*A Sapphick Elegy*", published possibly around 1782 under the pen-name Jack Cavendish, the allusions brooked no misinterpretation. Anne was specifically mentioned as "D" or "Dame":

"Like D(amer) I had scorned the youth,
Kissed every female's lovely mouth"

and:

"Or if report is right,
The maids of warm Italia's Land,
Have felt the pressure of your hand,
The pressure of delight."

Cavendish was of course the family name of the Dukes of Devonshire, and the pen-name was undoubtedly used to associate the poem with the family. Anne was a close friend of the Duchess of Devonshire, and a member of the Devonshire House set. The actual identity of the writer remains a mystery.

Anne was a good-looking 34-year-old childless widow. Like her mother, her name had neither been involved in any marital scandal, nor mentioned in connection with any lover, either during her marriage or during the first years of her widowhood. In an era when the tittle-tattle of servants, acquaintances and indeed friends, noised abroad the wildest gossip, Anne's name was free of conventional scandal rumours. Her greatest friend, Elizabeth Melbourne, was well known to be having an affair with Lord Egremont. As soon as she had borne her husband a son and heir, Georgiana Duchess of Devonshire would take Lord Grey as her lover. As Sheridan had put it in *School for Scandal:* "women of fashion in London are accountable to nobody after they are married." But Anne had been an exception to that rule.

As a widow she had turned to the traditionally masculine art of sculpture. She was also well known to favour the company and habits of French high society, of which the death of the Comte du Barry had been a notorious example, close to home. The national sport of Frog-bashing found a popular outlet in the gutter press, which insinuated a more than close relationship between Queen Marie Antoinette and the Duchesse de Polignac. The name of Anne's friend Georgiana Devonshire had been linked not only with the Queen of France but also with the beautiful Mary Graham. In the summer of 1782 Georgiana was to meet and befriend Bess Foster, probably introduced to her by Mary Graham, and their relationship, too, was to be the subject of scurrilous speculation. There is no doubt that such friendships were intense, and the language of their letters is equally direct. Georgiana wrote to Anne saying "It is impossible for me, my Dearest Mrs Damer, to thank you as much as I wish for your charming letter. I love you so sincerely that you must judge how happy evr'y mark of your goodself makes me. You are quite charming to write me such delightful letters. Pray let me have a great many to comfort me for not seeing you … I saw Lady Harriet (Stanhope) last night. She look'd beautiful … Poor Lord Stormont seemed to know it very well – you cannot conceive how delighted he seemed whilst he was playing, to peep at her now and then, I fancy he must always lose for what he was about seem'd much the farthest from his thoughts – I believe this to be a very strange letter but I have been writing whilst my hair was drying and am just going to set out. Adieu my dearest

Mrs Damer, I shall write to you very soon to tell you a thousand times how much I love you. GD."

However no one was ever to link the names of Georgiana and Anne in any sort of relationship. This overblown sentimentality was the language of *le ton* at that time. It had been predicated to them by Rousseau in *La Nouvelle Héloise*: "I imagined two women friends, rather than two of my own sex, since although examples of such friendships are rarer, they are also more beautiful. I endowed them with analogous but different characters; with features if not perfect, yet to my taste, and radiant with kindliness and sensibility. I made one dark, the other fair; one lively, the other gentle; one sensible, the other weak, but so touching in her weakness that virtue itself seemed to gain by it. I gave one of them a lover to whom the other was a tender friend and even something more; but I allowed of no rivalry or quarrels or jealousy because I find it hard to imagine any painful feelings, and I did not wish to discolour my charming picture with anything degrading to Nature." These were friendships based as much on literary Romanticism as on physical attraction. It was a language that was probably peculiar to that clique at that time; even Lady Jersey, that inveterate seducer of her friends' husbands, was to write to Georgiana, after receiving various protestations of love, that "some part of your letter frightened me." Nevertheless it provided a fertile background for the invention of scandal.

In many ways Anne had unwittingly set herself up as a target for the scandalmongers. As a sculptor, she was practising in what was normally a man's domain. Unlike her contemporary colleagues, she had not taken a lover. She, like several of her friends, was fond of cross-dressing at masquerades. However she was also attracted by men. She was to receive two proposals of marriage: one from Sir William Hamilton, the second from William Augustus Fawkener, with whom she was to have an affair. Other friendships with both men and women were warm and close. Sometimes with women they were intense, but their meeting place was more likely to have been in a study with a book or pen, or a studio with a chisel, rather than in a bed. No one would dispute that she clasped her female friends fondly to her bosom, and that she talked long into the night with them. If physical relationships did go further, it was a private matter, and not one for this book.

Some years later Mrs Hester Thrale, later Mme Piozzi, had worked herself into a fury on the subject of Sapphism in general, and rumours from the French court in particular. In April 1789, on the eve of the French Revolution, she was lamenting that "The Queen of France is at the Head of a Set of Monsters call'd by each other Sapphists, who boast her Example, and deserve to be thrown with the He Demons that haunt each other likewise, into Mount Vesuvius." A year later, in 1790, she wrote in her diary that Mrs Damer, "a Lady much suspected for liking her own Sex in a criminal Way, had Miss Farren, the fine comic Actress, often about her last Year; and Mrs Siddon's Husband made the following verses on them:

"Her little Stock of private Fame
Will fall a Wreck to public Clamour,
If Farren leagues with one whose Name
Comes near – Aye very near – to Damn her."

It is worth noting that well before this time Mrs Thrale, the keen supporter and acolyte of Doctor Johnson, was disliked by the Conway family, in the same way that Horace Walpole and Doctor Johnson were not on speaking terms. Doctor Johnson might not have been a very active Tory; he was certainly an admirer of the Highland Scots, the bitter enemies of the Whig clan Campbell, and no lover of the Whig establishment. However Mrs Piozzi, as Mrs Thrale became in 1784, continued to wax strongly and madly on the subject, latterly suspecting many of her friends of being lesbians, and proclaiming that "it is a joke in London now to say such a one visits Mrs Damer."

It was, of course, extremely likely that Anne and Elizabeth Farren should be around together, as Elizabeth was Anne's theatrical mentor and director during the Richmond House plays. The actress was also ardently admired by Lord Derby, another member of the Richmond House set, whom she kept at a suitable distance. As early as 1782 the *Morning Post,* reporting on a farce of the *bon ton* in which "that very deserving young actress Miss Farren supported the sprightly character of Miss Lucretia Titup with astonishing humour and ability: a passage in this entertainment spoken by Lucretia, threw the peerers into what is called the broad grin: 'My Lord loves me, and I love my Lord ... but not so well as he may imagine; his Lordship shall find that I can play about the flame without burning my wings.' This was considered by the knowing part of the audience as a case in point."

The same insinuation concerning Anne Damer and Elizabeth Farren was produced again four years later, in a work called *The Whig Club or A Sketch of Modern Patriotism*, by Charles Piggott, published in 1794. Again this was a political publication aimed at discrediting the Whig establishment. In this case the physically short and rotund Whig, Lord Derby, wished to marry her, but was warned that there was competition for Miss Farren's affections. "Her amorous passions are far from being awakened by the idea (of marriage). Superior to the influence of men, she is supposed to feel more exquisite delight from the touch of the cheek of Mrs D...r, than from the fancy of any novelties which the wedding night can promise with such a partner as his Lordship."

In the event Lord Derby did marry Elizabeth Farren, as soon as decently possible after the death of his first wife in 1797. This event was also accompanied by an anonymous political pamphlet entitled *Memoirs of the Present Countess of Derby (late Miss Farren)*, in which much was made of her humble origins and various affairs with men, but no mention at all of Mrs Damer. If indeed there had been any relationship, it would surely have been included.

The second source of abuse to which Anne was subjected was the accusation that her sculpture was not her own, and that she paid somebody else to carry out the work. She worried less about this criticism than about references to her private life. Alan Cunningham, who included Anne in his *Lives of Eminent Artists Sculptors and Architects,* a history of British sculptors published in 1838 shortly after her death, was critical of her abilities. He also inferred that with regard to the early marble neo-classical busts she had had the assistance of helpers. He did not doubt that the terracotta models were her own work, and that she had chipped away at the marble versions. However he felt that the smooth finish of these earlier models, contrasted with the rather rougher work on those completed in the later more realistic style, had been assisted. Cunningham quotes a Mr Smith, who had claimed that "I carved most of her busts for her."

There seems to be no dispute that Anne modelled in terracotta. It was not unusual for sculptors to employ others to help rough-out and even finish marble busts. Marble carvers, or statuaries, carved and copied for a living in the same way as engravers copied paintings. To make a marble copy of a terracotta sculpture was to ensure that it would probably have a much longer life. Indeed an ideal head sculpture now in the Rhode Island School of Design Museum is inscribed "Nollekens Ft. (Nollekens fecit or Nollekens made it) from a model by the Hon. Mrs. Damer", in exactly the same way as an engraving by Bartolozzi of a Reynolds painting. Anne may well have had assistance with her early marble work, but if so, it was finished to her original design and subject to her approval. Some of the differences between the smoothness of the early neo-classical work and the rougher finish of the later more lifelike representations can be attributed directly to a change in the spirit and design of the sculptures themselves.

Anne certainly finished her later work herself. Visitors came daily to her studio to watch her at work, and to marvel at the way she chiselled hard marble from a raised platform. Horace Walpole advised her not to employ a statuary, and to make sure that she was seen sculpting the figures of Thames and Isis for Henley bridge, lest anyone who wished her ill might infer that they had been done by somebody else. Whilst carving the more than life-size statue of George III, again frequently in the public gaze, she managed to slip off the platform and damage her leg.

Newspaper commentary also delighted in more or less facetious digs at Anne's expense. One of her more unusual commissions, undertaken at the request of the Duke of Cambridge, the future William IV, was to make a plaster replica of one of the celebrated legs of his mistress, the actress Mrs Jordan. The theatrical correspondent of the *Morning Post* particularly liked to rile Anne. A report of 27th February 1789 appeared under the heading "SCULPTURE EXTRAORDINARY". "The Hon Mrs Damer, so universally and justly celebrated for leg modelling, more adroit however in single members than the *tout ensemble*, is about to immortalise separately all the parts of both male and female. These will be rich *morceaux* for posterity from the hands of our female Praxiteles. Some of the rarest productions of British Nature have already been sitting to this fair and elegant artist for their likenesses; amongst these were Lord Brudenell's high cheekbones, the Chancellor's eyebrows, Sir Pepper Arden's nose, Lord Mount Edgecumbe's chin, and Lady Mary Duncan's beard."

And again in January 1793 the *Morning Post* ran an article entitled "Mr Burke and his Dagger": "Mrs Damer, wishing to exhibit the figure of a gladiator, offers Mr Burke a suitable reward if he will stand for half an hour, in the same attitude that he was in when he threw down the dagger on Friday last. Mrs Burke's reply: Mrs Burke hopes that Mrs Damer will not press Mr Burke to stand for half an hour, as she thinks that he has sufficiently exposed himself already."

A cartoon dated 1st July 1789, entitled *The Damerian Apollo*, includes allusions to both strains of abuse. It shows Mrs Damer at work on a giant statue of Apollo, actually destined to be placed above the portico over the entrance to the new Apollo Theatre. (Both theatre and statue were destroyed by fire in 1791.) Mrs Damer sits facing the statue's back. In her left hand a chisel is aimed at the statue's genitals, in her right hand, a raised hammer foretells a mighty thwack likely to result in Apollo's emasculation. To the front of the statue another lady looks on in trepidation at Apollo's spear, held erect and phallic in front of him. The humans are surrounded by sculptures of the human figure, on the one side a satyr and a child's head, inscribed "A model to make a boy from", and on the other naked figures of a boy and girl, modestly covering themselves, entitled "Studies from Nature".

In summary, it was well recognised during her lifetime that she was a serious sculptor, dedicated to her work, and acknowledged by friends and contemporaries as competent at her art. If she did have assistance, it was not to a much greater extent than others. However, by publicly entering into what was viewed as a man's world, she had also laid herself open to ridicule and criticism, whether or not, justified.

Chapter 8

THE 1784 ELECTION

The beginning of the year 1783 saw the end of war with both America and France. The Prime Minister, Lord Shelburne, took the enlightened view that a new and prosperous United States would be a strongly expanding market for free trade British goods. He therefore negotiated a generous peace which recognised the independence of the United States and left the new nation free to expand westwards. Florida was ceded to Spain, ensuring that future relationships with the United States here would be a problem for the Spanish, rather than the British, government.

For France, Spain and Holland, who had entered the war in support of America and in hope of some rich colonial pickings, there was little to show for their efforts. Admiral Rodney in the Caribbean and Warren Hastings in India successfully upheld British imperial supremacy. Britain retained Gibraltar which she had defended against Spanish attack, whilst giving up any claims to Minorca. France gained Tobago, and St Lucia was restored to her, whilst Britain got back Grenada, the Grenadines, Dominica, Nevis, St Christopher's and Montserrat. In short the outcome was to restore the situation to pretty much what it had been before the commencement of the war. The USA had been successfully established. Thanks to Shelburne's diplomacy, the first action of the new nation had been leave her allies in the lurch.

Unfortunately Parliament did not appreciate Shelburne's skills. Members grumbled that the terms of the peace treaty were too generous to the United States. They would have preferred protection to free trade. On 24th February 1783 Charles James Fox and Lord North, the reformer and the unreformed, combined forces in an unlikely combination, only brought about as the other alternatives were even less likely, to defeat and bring down Shelburne. The new coalition was to be led nominally by the Duke of Portland, whom King George, incensed by the removal of Shelburne, refused to recognise for six weeks. The advent of the coalition marked the end of Harry Conway's position as Commander-in-Chief of the Army, a position he had held since the start of the second Rockingham administration in 1782.

The new government was to stumble straight into the problems of India. Many investors in the East India Company were dissatisfied with its financial performance. The Company had successfully fought the nation's wars in India, but at a substantial cost to its balance sheet. On the other hand the executive, headed by Warren Hastings, had clearly enriched itself; the nabobs continued to return home far wealthier than they had left. The system encouraged corruption, which accordingly flourished. Reform was required, and Edmund Burke provided for the coalition, a new scheme of governance based on the totally impractical proposal of control from England of a subcontinent to which instructions took three months to arrive.

As the debate in Parliament rumbled on, some of North's supporters began to detach themselves, and to look for a new leader, unbesmirched by the factional shenanigans of the recent past. It was time for a change. Lord Dundas was able to persuade the 24-year-old William Pitt that his moment had arrived. With the support and direct intervention of the King, the India Bill was defeated in the House of Lords; on 18th December 1783 the existing ministers were dismissed and Pitt became the new First Lord of the Treasury, with a Cabinet drawn entirely from the House of Lords and containing Anne Damer's brother-in-law, the Duke of Richmond. Not unnaturally, the Commons were upset at the assertion of the Royal Prerogative through the House of Lords; they voted to postpone the second reading of the Mutiny Bill until February. Fox proclaimed himself the champion of the independence of the House of Commons, though at the same time negotiating with Pitt to form another coalition. Throughout March the stand-off between Pitt's Government and the House of Commons continued, although the coalition's majority lessened with every division. On 10th March the Foxites voted with the Government to allow the passage of the Mutiny Bill, and it became clear to Pitt that electoral opinion was swinging his way. On 25th March Parliament was dissolved and the 1784 general election declared.

During the political events leading up to the general election in 1784, Anne had been a spectator. Since returning from Italy in June 1782, she had continued in the quieter style of life which she had embraced with widowhood, concentrating on her sculpture and visiting family and friends, in particular Lady Melbourne. In July 1783 she wrote to HW informing him that accompanied by Lady Melbourne and Madame de Cambis, she was coming to Strawberry Hill on the following day to dine with him. In customary style Walpole pointed out to her father that he should be "vastly pleased with the party, but it puts Philip and Margaret to their wits' end to get them a dinner: nothing is to be had here; we must send to Richmond, and Kingston, and Brentford. I must borrow Mr Ellis's cook, and somebody's confectioner, and beg somebody's fruit, for I have none of these of my own, nor know anything of the matter; but that is Philip and Margaret's affair, not mine; and the worse the dinner is, the more Gothic Madame de Cambis will think it." He went on to say that he had drained his pool at Strawberry Hill and saved 15 small goldfish for Caroline and Anne, and that Harry would have to work out a way of transporting them to Park Place.

In September Horace visited Anne and her parents at Park Place. He was able to report to Lord Strafford that Anne was engaged in sculpting two giant masks for the keystones of the new bridge across the Thames at Henley. Sir William Hamilton had obviously been to see them during his period of leave in England and had remarked that they were "in her true antique style".

Anne had also completed and given to Horace two sleeping dogs modelled in terracotta, and had asked his permission to model them again in the more durable medium of marble for her brother-in-law the Duke of Richmond's house at Goodwood. He was totally happy with this suggestion, remarking that he would certainly hang on to the terracotta models himself, as they were sharper and more alive. He reported that the architect, Mister Wyatt (James Wyatt), had seen the dogs and "was sure that if the idea was given to the best statuary in Europe, he would not produce so perfect a group."

However as the election got nearer, so the general interest, and Anne's attention in particular, increased. With the exception of her brother-in-law, the Duke of Richmond, who had joined Pitt's Administration in January 1784 as Master General of the Ordnance, the Walpole-Seymour Whig family phalanx remained loyal to Fox. However they were in a minority; as Horace put it: "The church, the old women, and the country gentlemen (who, as I have often heard you say justly, would like despotism, provided they could be ensured of a low land tax, a good price for corn, and the Game Act) are all running headlong to support ... the immaculate Master Billy (William Pitt)." By the beginning of March excitement was reaching fever pitch. Writing to Sir Horace Mann, HW complains: "Politics have engrossed all conversation ... Our ladies who used to contribute to enliven correspondence, are become politicians and, as Lady Townley says, 'squeeze a little too much lemon to conversation'."

The 1784 election was a political watershed. Pitt and the King had been correct in their assessment that the country had grown tired of a series of factional Whig governments. Burke's attempt to rein in the East India Company had alienated powerful and influential city interests. Even in an era of restricted voting rights, as so often in elections, it was not so much what Pitt and the King promised, but a general sense that it was time for a change which was to win the day. William Pitt was a fresh face from a tried and tested family stable.

Although contested elections swung heavily in favour of Pitt, there were no more contested elections than usual. In the uncontested elections, the same swings also took place. The Court party had busied itself in making the usual deals with local interests that would ensure the return of candidates favourable to the government; sometimes this resulted in the same member with a change of heart, sometimes in a new member, as the previous occupant quietly retired. In Yorkshire Fox's great friends, the Cavendishs and the Fitzwilliams, saw that the young William Wilberforce was so popular that they did not even attempt the expense of a poll. In the event 160 of Fox's

Henry Seymour Conway and Caroline Countess of Ailesbury with the young Anne by Jacob Ecchardt circa 1753. From a private collection.

Combe Bank 1787, F. Wheatley.

Strawberry Hill by Johann Heinrich Muntz c.1755-59. Courtesy of The Lewis Walpole Library, Yale University.

Strawberry Hill The Hall 1788, John Carter. Courtesy of The Lewis Walpole Library, Yale University.

Park Place. Crown copyright. UK Government Art Collection.

Anne Seymour-Conway by Angelica Kauffman 1766. From a private collection.

Horace Walpole as a young man by Sir Joshua Reynolds 1756-57. © National Portrait Gallery.

John Damer in academic gown by Sir Joshua Reynolds 1762. Reproduced by permission of the Provost and Fellows of Eton College.

Elizabeth Viscountess Melbourne (l), Georgiana, the Duchess of Devonshire (c) and Anne Damer (r) as the Witches in Macbeth by Daniel Gardner 1775. © National Portrait Gallery.

Mrs Damer and an unknown man, probably John Damer, against a stormy background, circa 1770. Artist unknown, possibly George Dance. From a private collection.

Head of a girl (Miss Caroline Campbell?) in wax.
From a private collection.

Anne Damer sculpted as The Muse of Sculpture by
Guiseppi Cerrachi 1778. British Museum.
© Trustees of the British Museum.

Model of Isis for Henley Bridge in clay. From a
private collection.

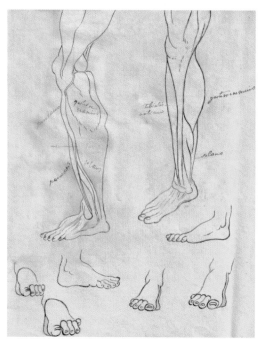

Drawing of feet from ASD's anatomy exercise book. From a private collection.

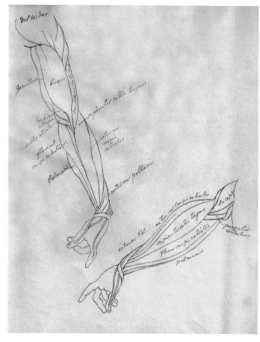

Drawing of left arm from ASD's anatomy exercise book. From a private collection.

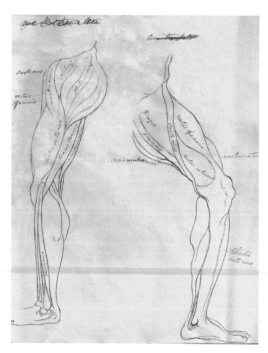

Drawing of left leg bent from ASD's anatomy exercise book. From a private collection.

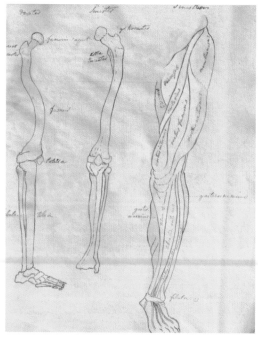

Drawing of straight leg from ASD's anatomy exercise book. From a private collection.

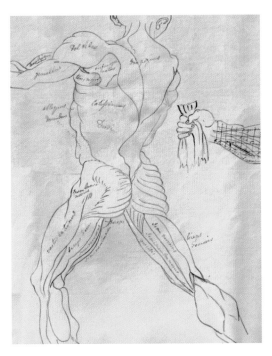

Drawing of legs and back from ASD's anatomy exercise book. From a private collection.

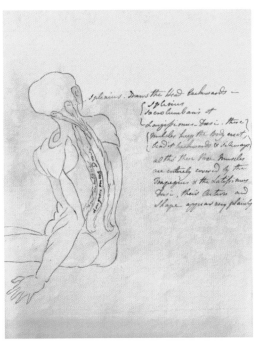

Drawing rear view seated from ASD's anatomy exercise book. From a private collection.

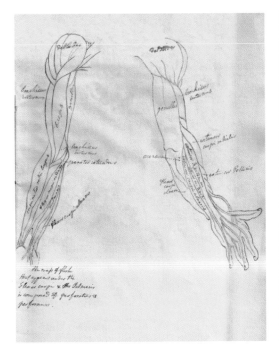

Drawing of right rear arm from ASD's anatomy exercise book. From a private collection.

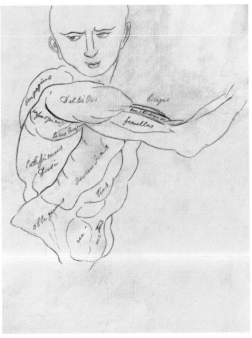

Drawing of upper torso from ASD's anatomy exercise book. From a private collection.

Shock Dog terracotta 1780. From a private collection.

Sleeping puppies terracotta 1784. By permission of the Rt.Hon. Earl of Derby.

Kittens marble 1789. From a private collection.

ΑΝΝΑ.ΣΕΙΜΟΡΙΣ
ΔΑΜΕΡ
Η.ΕΚ.ΤΗΣ.ΒΡΕΤΤΑΝΙΚΗΣ.
ΑΥΤΗ.ΑΥΤΗΝ.ΕΠΟΙΕΙ.

Self portrait in marble, 1785-6, given by Anne Damer to Uffizi Gallery, Florence.

XIV

Anne Damer's self portrait bust in the Vasari Corridor Uffizi Gallery adjacent to self portraits of her friends Angelica Kauffman and Maria Cosway.

Niobid "my first" marble. From a private collection.

Elizabeth Farren marble, 1789. © National Portrait Gallery.

Miss Freeman as Isis marble, 1789. © Victoria and Albert Museum, London.

Henley Bridge. Author's photo.

Isis on Henley Bridge. Author's photo.

Father Thames on Henley bridge. Author's photo.

colleagues were not returned to the Commons. The old Whig powerbase was excluded, and subsequent reforms which whittled away at rotten boroughs and at the place system were to ensure that it never returned. Pitt was to govern for the next 17 years, until 1801, into the beginning of a new century. Harry Conway, who saw which way the wind was blowing, decided not to seek re-election. He had sat as an MP continuously for 43 years, and by this time relished the opportunity of retirement to the pleasures of Park Place.

The more the Foxites saw that they were losing in the country, the more they determined to return Charles Fox as Member of Parliament for Westminster. The King, through William Pitt, was adamant that Fox should be excluded. There were three candidates for two seats: the cause of King and Pitt was represented by the naval hero, Admiral Lord Hood, and by Sir Cecil Wray, whilst Fox stood for Liberty and the supremacy of the Commons over the Royal Prerogative. Many of Fox's male supporters were absent from London, defending their own seats in the country, and a large part of the task of organising canvassing fell to the ladies of the Devonshire House set, led by Georgiana and ably assisted, among others, by Anne Damer. The polling booths which opened in Covent Garden on 1st April were not to close for 6 weeks.

Fox's supporters divided their canvassers into three teams, one led by Georgiana, another by Mrs Crewe, and the third by Anne. By 5th April they had been joined by the Duchess of Portland, Lady Jersey, Lady Carlisle and the three Waldegrave sisters. They all wore the blue and buff colours of Fox, and sported foxes' brushes wound around their hat brims. They visited those entitled to vote in their shops, in their homes, or wherever they could find them. In return for a vote for Fox and Liberty, the ladies offered shopkeepers the promise of future purchases, whilst Georgiana was particularly singled out by the *Morning Post*, controlled by the Pitt interest, as offering sexual favours to electors. Ribald cartoons depicted her and the Duchess of Portland kissing butchers, while at the same time placing money in their back pockets.

Although physically exhausted by the canvassing, in which she had to retire midway, returning after a short respite, Georgiana loved the rowdy cut and thrust of the hustings. The thrill of leadership got her adrenalin moving, and though she resented the abuse and innuendos, the calls of her mother to behave in a more ladylike manner went unanswered. In a world where ladies were brought up to be demure, the Spencer family and society at large were horrified by Georgiana's activities.

Anne Damer's part in canvassing goes unrecorded after the first day, and it is likely that having retired from public life following John Damer's death, she did not find the same satisfaction as her friend in showing herself off to the public.

After the first day of the polls Fox had secured 302 votes and led both Lord Hood and Wray. But this happy state of affairs was only temporary, and in the next days the

Court candidates, following the national pattern, surged ahead. However with a total electorate of 18,000, Westminster, the home of Parliament, the constituency of John Wilkes, had a hard core of voters to whom an appeal to the flag of liberty was a welcome call. Georgiana's active canvas and Fox's rousing speeches gradually took positive effect. As the election progressed and the Court party's stock rose through the country, in Westminster it faltered. After six weeks the election was declared over; Lord Hood had received 6694 votes, Charles Fox 6234, and Sir Cecil Wray 5998.

As the poll closed, a triumphal march took place, starting at St Paul's, running down the Strand, taking in the residence of the Prince of Wales, Carlton House, and continuing down Piccadilly to Devonshire House. The procession was led by 24 horsemen in blue and buff with foxes' brushes attached to their hats. Behind marched a brass band playing Whig tunes, followed by Fox himself, born aloft on a triumphal chair. A motley crew of supporters walked behind carrying placards supporting Fox and Liberty, and acknowledging the help of Georgiana and her assistants with a banner emblazoned "Sacred to Female Patriotism". The Prince of Wales rounded off the celebrations with a week of dinners and balls at Carlton House. As was traditional with Hanoverian heirs to the throne, Prinny was in permanent opposition to his father and was delighted to see him furious and discomfited at Fox's election.

The King and Pitt attempted to delay Charles Fox's entry into Parliament on the grounds of electoral malpractice, and demanded a scrutiny of the Westminster election. After a few months however the Commons grew tired of this delaying tactic and voted Fox back. He was consoled by suing the Bailiff of Westminster and receiving £2000 in damages. However, it had been a Pyrrhic victory; the old Whig powerbase had failed to stop a government supported by the Crown and public opinion. It was not so much the failure of Liberty as the end of the Whig monopoly of power. To Anne Damer, Horace Walpole and Harry Conway, it was significant as the demise of a way of government that had been introduced by their forebear, Sir Robert Walpole.

Harry Conway was able to look forward to retirement both from Parliament and from his role as Commander-in-Chief of the Army, although he retained the governorship of Jersey. In future he would be based at his beloved Park Place, improving the landscape and making scientific experiments. Horace wrote to him on 5th May 1784: "Your cherries, for aught I know, may, like Mr Pitt, be half-ripe before others are in blossom ... In truth, I think you will be much happier for being out of Parliament. You could do no good there; again you have no views of ambition to satisfy ... and when neither duty nor ambition calls (I do not condescend to name avarice, which never is to be satisfied, nor deserves to be reasoned with, nor has any place in your breast) I cannot conceive what satisfaction an elderly man can have in listening to the passions or follies of others: nor is eloquence such a banquet, when one knows that, whoever the cooks are, whatever the sauces, one has eaten as good beef or mutton before … and, perhaps, as well dressed. It is surely time to live for oneself, when one has not a vast while to live; and you, I am persuaded, will live the longer for leading a country life. How much better to be planting, nay, making experiments on smoke (if not too dear), than reading application forms from officers, a quarter of whom you could not serve, nor content three-quarters! You had not time for necessary exercise; and, I believe, would have blinded yourself. In short, if you will live in the air all day, be totally idle, and not read or write a line by candlelight, and re-trench your suppers, I shall rejoice in your having nothing to do but that dreadful punishment, pleasing yourself." Caroline and Anne also were able to take advantage of this new domestic bliss. There would now be more time for house parties of interesting and varied guests, not only from the immediate circle of family and politics, but also from the world of the arts, from literature, from painting, from the theatre and music.

It was possibly during the summer of 1784 that Anne received a proposal of marriage from Sir William Hamilton. Following his affectionate letter at the end of the previous chapter, he had returned to England on leave. He had visited Park Place, and two years later he wrote to his niece Mary, after Anne had been to stay with him, stating: "The fact is I am neither nor ever was in love with her. I do believe that if I had chosen the part of the dying lover, but I never could act a part in my life, and consented to live at home in England, I might have succeeded. If she had consented to take me as I am and live chiefly here, I certainly wou'd have married her, for having lived 22 years *en famille* it is most terrible to live chiefly alone." The significant words in this passage are "nor ever was", as it is unlikely that he would have wished to propose to her in the spring of 1786, for reasons which will become clear in due course. However much Anne had loved Naples and its winter climate, she clearly had no intention of making it a permanent home in the role of the Minister's wife and hostess. Equally Sir William had no intention of retiring as yet from his "kingdom of cinders", where his studies of volcanoes and collection of classical antiques still had time to run. It would have been more a marriage of convenience, than for love, and in the event, its potential inconveniences for both parties rendered it a nonstarter.

Chapter 9

SCULPTURE AND THE THEATRE

Summer of 1784 started "as cold as Christmas", according to HW. It was marked by the illness both of Caroline and of her niece Caroline Campbell, who since her father Lord William Campbell's death in 1778 had lived as a member of the family at Park Place. On 30th June Horace wrote to Harry: "Instead of coming to you, I am thinking of packing up and going to town for winter, so desperate is the weather!". In the same letter he remarked on the sudden death of Lady Harrington, of whom, before his marriage, Harry had been an ardent admirer. "Have not you felt a little twinge in a remote corner of your heart on Lady Harrington's death? She dreaded death so extremely that I am glad she had not a moment to be sensible of it. I have a great affection for sudden deaths; they save oneself and everybody else a deal of ceremony." Horace also expressed a wish to visit Park Place when summer had come, and did actually stay from 18th to 20th July. He was one of a succession of friends who came as well-wishers to the convalescing Caroline. As Harry wrote to his brother, Lord Hertford, "the Harrowbys, Campbells, Richmonds, and just now the Churchills, Mrs Hervey, and Mister Walpole, left us this morning." Caroline's health continued to give cause for concern and on 15th October Horace wrote to Harry from Strawberry Hill: "As I have heard nothing from you I flatter myself that Lady A mends, or I think you would have brought her again to the physicians: you will, I conclude, next week, as towards the end of it the ten days they named will be expired."

References to health are commonplace in 18th century literature and would have been equally so in daily conversation. Poor health, sickness, and accompanying deaths were part and parcel of 18th century life. Families were larger than today; Anne Damer's aunt, Lady Hertford, had thirteen children in a marriage lasting 41 years and died at the age of 56. Longevity was much less certain, infant mortality common and medicine not greatly advanced. The Scottish brothers, William and John Hunter, the latter of whom was surgeon to George III, improved knowledge of anatomy and surgery during the middle years of the 18th century. However it was not until 1796 that Edward Jenner discovered that inoculating children with cowpox offered immunisation against the dreaded scourge of the disfiguring and often fatal smallpox. There were no chemical drugs, and herbal remedies had advanced little from the potions prepared in mediaeval monasteries. HW suffered continually from either gout or rheumatic arthritis. Anne Damer's ills, especially in winter, gave her a reputation for being delicate and a reason to travel to warmer climates. She also suffered from headaches, depression, and undefined problems with her leg, which may have been exacerbated by her fall from her sculpture platform when working on a giant figure of George III.

Health was therefore a general topic of conversation, and methods of improvement of great interest. The wealthy believed that the various waters available from differing spas would be efficacious. The new spa towns were noted for their fine buildings, crescents and terraces; they had their own mini-seasons with assembly rooms, theatres and concerts for the *cognoscenti* who arrived to take the waters. Bath was the pre-eminent city, but Cheltenham, Tunbridge Wells and Buxton were also fashionable, and each of them contains a fine legacy of Regency building. Nor was the seaside neglected. Horace Walpole expressed his opinion that "though I am too indolent ever to try, I have the highest opinion of sea air, and always in every illness determine to go to the coast; and as constantly neglect it when I am better". The seaside resorts of Bognor Regis, Brighton, and Margate all thrived and were visited for health reasons at various times by Anne Damer.

It would be reasonable to suppose that Anne would have spent a large part of the time during the summer of 1784 helping to care for her mother at Park Place. It seems equally likely that she would have set up a studio there for her sculpting. The weather that summer eventually changed for the better in early September. Horace's spirits brightened, and on 5th September he dined with Mrs Garrick along with Sir William Hamilton, who was returning to "the kingdom of cinders". Sir William had seen and admired the two giant masks Anne was modelling for the bridge at Henley. These two model masks were of Isis and Thames, in terracotta, probably exhibited at the Royal Academy in the following year. The final full-size masks in Portland stone were completed in the year 1785-6, and again it would seem probable that the actual stonework was completed at Park Place, close by their eventual destination and near to Fawley Court, the home of Miss Freeman, the model and inspiration for Isis. The bridge had been designed by William Hayward in 1781, with five arches and a balustraded parapet. General Conway claimed to have had a hand in its design, in particular the number and shape of the arches. It is of course also possible that he was instrumental in securing the commission for the giant masks for Anne. The mask of Thames, facing downstream towards London and the sea, was put in place in 1785, and Isis, facing upstream towards Oxford, in 1786.

In May 1785 Horace, writing to Sir Horace Mann, tells him that "Mrs Damer … is engaged on an extraordinary work. There is just built a new bridge of stone over the Thames at Henley, which is close to Park Place. Mrs Damer offered to make two gigantic masks of the Thame and Isis for the keystones, and actually modelled them:

and a statuary was to execute them. I said 'Oh it will be imagined that you had little hand in them: you must perform them yourself.' She consented. The Thame is an old Marine God, is finished and put up; and, they say, has prodigious effect. She is now at work on the Isis; a most beautiful nymph's face, simple as the antique, but quite a new beauty. The idea was taken from Mrs Freeman of Fawley Court, a neighbour of General Conway. The keystones of a county bridge carved by a young lady is an unparalleled curiosity." In the same letter, Horace hoped that Anne would pay another visit to Florence, as "she is very delicate, and often out of order; and certainly was better for her Italian journey."

The Conways' neighbour, the Rev Thomas Powys, composed the following lines upon the new bridge:

> *"Through this fair arch henceforth with conscious pride,*
> *Let Thames and Isis roll their mingled tides,*
> *Hastening to swirl old Ocean's watery stores,*
> *And sound their triumphs to his farthest shores.*
> *Tho' Tiber's classic waves distinguish'd flow,*
> *Our English rivers claim superior praise,*
> *From Damer's sculpture, and from Denham's lays."*

By August Horace had visited Park Place and actually seen the bridge. Writing to Lady Ossory, he recorded that "I was just getting into my chaise with Mr Jerningham to go to Park Place on Friday when I received the honour of your Ladyship's letter, and consequently could not answer it as punctually as I generally do. We saw the new bridge at Henley which is complete on one side, and is most beautiful; the bend of the arch was regulated by General Conway himself, on three centres, and for grace does not veil the bonnet to the Ponte di Trinita at Florence. His daughter's head of the Thame is placed, and has charming effect. The Isis is fixed too, but not yet uncovered. They are going, not the Thame and Isis, but the father and daughter, with the Duke of Richmond to Jersey, and I hope the sea air will be of service to her, for I think her far from well."

Indeed for reasons of health, Anne set out for the continent in the autumn. She wished to avoid the English winter, which Horace related had already "begun severely; we have had snow twice. Till last year, I never knew snow in October since I can remember; which is no short time". On this occasion she was accompanied by her cousin Caroline Campbell, the daughter of Lord William Campbell and of his wife, Anne's former travelling companion, who had sadly died the previous year. Caroline was a great family favourite and, according to Horace, a "sensible girl". He was using the word "sensible" in its 18th century meaning of being sensible to the niceties of civilisation, rather than in its current usage of level-headed. He told Sir Horace Mann that if they came to Florence he should persuade Anne to give the Grand Duke one of her sculptures, which would be "a greater curiosity than anything in his chamber of painters." The Grand Duke might not have agreed.

Anne was not the only English lady in Italy for her health that winter. Bess Foster, painfully thin, had been sent to Paris for the winter of 1784/5, with her expenses paid by the Duke and Duchess of Devonshire. Here she speedily became the mistress of the British ambassador, the Duke of Dorset. The reason for her exile was soon clear; both Georgiana and Bess were pregnant by the Duke of Devonshire, the future children having been conceived within days of each other. Georgiana's second child, Harriet, was born on 29th August 1785 in the luxury and comfort of Devonshire House. Bess's daughter, Caroline, was born on 16th August in a squalid hostel in the small town of Vietro, on the Gulf of Salerno. The baby was lodged with the family of Louis, a family servant, and Bess rejoined her brother Lord Hervey in Naples where, having acquired a taste for the diplomatic corps, she began a flirtation with the Russian ambassador. She was to remain in Italy for nearly a year, and during that time she met up with Anne Damer who produced a wax profile medallion of her. It may also have been at this time that Anne produced a marble self-portrait bust of herself, perhaps taking up HW's suggestion to Sir Horace Mann. Signed in Greek, it is in her strict neo-classical style. Now in the Uffizi gallery, it is handsomely displayed in the Vasari corridor between self portraits of Anne's friends, a large picture of Angelica Kauffman to the left and a smaller one of Maria Cosway to the right. Another Italian connection, sculpted by Anne, was the daughter of Princess Dashkova, who had been a visitor to Italy at the same time.

Anne and Caroline's continental trip seems to have been a long one. In February 1786 HW reported that the travellers had sent Lady Ailesbury a letter reporting on Horace Mann's excellent health, at the same time saying how they were indebted to his nephew for his kindness to them. On the 8th or 9th March Anne arrived in Naples as a guest of Sir William Hamilton. She was accommodated in the Palazzo Sessa. On 26th April they were joined by another guest, arriving on her 21st birthday, Emma Hart. She had been dispatched by her lover, Charles Greville, to give pleasure to his uncle, Sir William Hamilton, and to get her out of the way in England, thus freeing him to marry an heiress. Emma's effect on Sir William was instantaneous. She remarked in a letter to Charles Greville: "He is never out of my sight. He breakfasts, dines, supes, and is constantly by me, looking in my face. He does nothing all day but look at me and sigh. I can't stir a hand, leg or foot; but he is marking it as graceful and fine." On 1st May he had made some sort of proposition to her which she had turned down angrily. Anne Damer was probably equally annoyed. By 30th May, Sir William was writing to his niece, Mary, to say "Mrs Damer has been here, lodged in my house and has gone home." Whatever Anne's chances of marriage might have been, the arrival of Emma had put paid to them.

By May Sir Horace Mann's health had deteriorated, and HW expressed himself as impatient for Mrs Damer's return from Rome to report on the progress of his convalescence. However Anne had decided to travel to Venice with Bess Foster, arriving there in June. It was during this visit that she would have experienced the scenes that she was later to portray so vividly in her novel *Belmour*.

In June, Horace longed for Anne to return to carve him a bust of his recently-purchased Jupiter Serapis, sadly described by him as the last purchase in his Strawberry Hill collection. "And here my collection winds up; I will not purchase trumpery after such jewels. Besides everything is much dearer in old age, as one has less time to enjoy it."

Finally, on 22nd July Horace wrote to say that Mrs Damer was now expected from Paris the following week. At the end of August he stayed for a few days at Park Place to join a family party with Lord and Lady Frederick Campbell and Anne. They had ventured on to the Thames to see the new bridge at Henley and its colossal masks. Horace, in his usual manner, over-egged the qualities of a family venture: "There is not a sight in the island more worthy of being visited. The bridge is as perfect as if bridges were natural productions, and as beautiful as if it had been built for Wentworth Castle; and the masks as if the Romans had left them here."

In September Anne stayed with her half-sister at Goodwood, where she was recorded in the house weighing book as being 8 stone 13ozs before dinner. Three years later, she had put on a little condition, weighing 9 stone 5ozs before dinner, and 9 stone 5½ozs after dinner. The food at Goodwood was obviously satisfactory.

Once back in England, Anne took up her chisel again. She produced a marble bust of one of Lady Melbourne's sons as the infant Mercury, and shortly afterwards, demonstrating her continuing link with Lady Melbourne, she modelled a terracotta figure of an osprey which had been trapped at Brocket Park. HW later reported that Anne had given him her sea eagle modelled life-size in terracotta. During its capture the bird's wing had been severely damaged. Anna had portrayed her eagle in "that momentary rage" of the moment of capture, and Horace was delighted with the gift. He wrote to Lady Ossory "I hope your Ladyship will approve of the motto I design for it. Do you remember the statue at Milan with this legend: 'Non me Praxitiles, sed Marcus finxit Agrati'? Mine is to be this pentameter: 'Non me Praxitiles finxit, at Anna Damer'."

As usual, he was puffing up the reputation of his beloved goddaughter. It is a great pity that this eagle has vanished, and that we are unable to see, assess, or comment upon it. A print of the bird published in 1790, shows what appears to be a half-grown fledgling. If the sculpture resembled the print, Horace had indeed been over-generous in his assessment.

Sculpture was one occupation at Brocket Park. Love affairs were another. It was a house whose corridors creaked with the sounds of creeping. Elizabeth Melbourne was never happier than when arranging her house parties, with amateur theatricals, masked balls, and *fêtes champêtres*. Opportunities for dalliance hung like the peaches in the walled garden, ripe and ready to be picked. In the arts of marital misbehaviour, the guests took their cue from their hostess. During the autumn of 1786 and the spring of 1787 Anne succumbed to the custom of the house and took a lover. He would appear to have been a Mr Fawkener, most likely William Augustus Fawkener, a regular member of the Brocket Hall set; less likely his brother. He was the son of Sir Everard Fawkener, a wealthy merchant, member of the Levant company, who had made his fortune in Aleppo, and had subsequently been appointed ambassador to the Sublime Porte in Constantinople. Everard had married Harriot, daughter of the Walpoles' old family friend Lieutenant-General Charles Churchill. He had been a friend of Voltaire, who idolised him as the "*marchand anglais*", the cosmopolitan trader and diplomat, appointed for his skills and not for his birth.

William Fawkener was some two years younger than Anne, a capable diplomat, with a ready if supercilious wit. He was well connected, and a *protégé* of William Pitt, which HW, a Whig of the old school, regarded as being detrimental. He had appeared previously in the annals of Strawberry Hill. In 1776 Horace mentioned that Fawkener had just returned from Italy through France, where he believed that Choiseul would be replaced. He had been appointed a clerk to the Privy Council in 1779, and was to head government missions, to Florence in late spring 1787, and to Lisbon in October 1787.

Fawkener's dalliances with the opposite sex had not as yet been blessed with marked success. In 1779 his attentions to Lady Laura Waldegrave had been terminated by her mother, the Duchess of Gloucester. In 1783 Horace reported in a letter that "Mr Fawkener has just abandoned a daughter of Lord Ashburnham with worse circumstances if possible than Lord Egremont did my niece. You will not wonder when you reflect who was his patron (Wm Pitt)". In November 1784 he had eventually married Georgiana Poyntz, a niece, without prospects, of Lady Spencer. The marriage, like Anne's was "arranged", probably by Fawkener himself, as his parents were both dead. Like Anne's it was not a success.

While the newly-married couple were staying at Brocket Hall in the autumn of 1785, Georgiana Fawkener had met and fallen in love with the Hon John Townshend. By November the liaison was common knowledge among *le ton*. In early 1786 Fawkener received an anonymous letter telling him of the affair, but his wife denied it. In May Fawkener was told of a lovers' tryst that was to take place in Ranelagh Gardens, and on going there he found Townshend and his wife in deep conversation. Fawkener told them never to meet again. A few days later he found Townshend on horseback, lurking outside his house. He told him to go away, but Townshend "being a young man of spirit warmly replied, and a few words passed: the consequence of which was an appointment the next morning in Hyde Park."

Hyde Park was popular for walking, riding and taking a carriage drive. It was a daytime meeting place for *le ton* and the place for dawn assignations for duellists. Fawkener arrived, with his brother as second. Pistols were produced and the duellists faced each other. Fawkener fired first and missed. Townshend discharged his pistol in the air, and the matter was over. Georgiana left Fawkener's house in South Street Grosvenor Square, to go to her aunt, Lady Spencer. A few days later she departed with Townshend.

By July Fawkener had brought an action against Townshend for criminal conversation, the 18th century term for adultery. The defence offered only a plea of poverty for John Townshend, it being well known that peers' younger sons were generally impoverished. Fawkener was awarded £500 in damages and in April 1787 obtained a divorce by Act of Parliament.

The evidence for Anne's affair with Fawkener comes entirely from Anne's later correspondence with Mary Berry, when Fawkener's name crops up again. Possibly in connection with the affair, Anne's best-friend relationship with Elizabeth Melbourne had also come to an abrupt end. Anne's hostess had done or said something which had caused Anne suddenly to lose all trust in her old friend. Certainly in late 1786 Fawkener and Anne were free parties, *de facto*, if not in law. They had failed arranged marriages and family friends in common. They were welcome guests of the Melbournes – and also of the Devonshires. The Duke had given evidence at Townshend's trial and described him as a frequent visitor to his house. How long the affair continued is unclear. Both lovers spent considerable parts of the year abroad, and perhaps love was rekindled when they re-met – perhaps not.

As Fawkener disappeared on diplomatic errands to Tuscany and Portugal, Anne turned to a new occupation – amateur theatricals. Private plays in private houses for invited audiences had become increasingly fashionable during the 1770s. Sir Watkin Williams Wynn at Wynnstay on the Welsh border, Oldfield Bowles at North Aston in Oxfordshire, and Mrs Hobart at Ham Common, were but a few who became patrons of the amateur stage. Anne had previously shown a talent for acting at Brocket Park, and with the arrival of the new fashion for amateur plays staged by the aristocracy for the aristocracy, she found an intellectual niche to which she was particularly fitted.

The first occasion on which she took a leading role was on 20th April 1787 at her brother-in-law the Duke of Richmond's private theatre at his London home, Richmond House. The Duke's own family made up a large part of the cast, and it was probably family connections rather than theatrical talent or experience that gave Anne her chance. She played Mrs Lovemore in *The Way to Keep Him*. This was a five act farce, by Arthur Murphy, originally produced by David Garrick in 1760, on the theme of marital infidelity, in which the unfaithful Lovemore, also posing as Lord Etheridge, tries to seduce the young widow Belmour, and others. Mrs Lovemore meets up with the widow Belmour and agrees to cast off her role as a dutiful, conscientious and gloomy housewife to return to the bright and beautiful young girl that Lovemore married. Husbands and wives are reconciled and all ends happily.

The epilogue, delivered after the final curtain had come down, was written by General Burgoyne, another man like Harry who was both soldier and playwright. It was spoken by Anne, and it included a kind allusion to her sculpture:

> *"Oh, cou'd my humble skill, which often strove*
> *In mimic Stone to copy forms I love,*
> *By soft gradation reach a higher art*
> *And bring to view a sculpture of the heart."*

The theatre at Richmond House at which the performances were to take place consisted of two rooms especially converted for the purpose by James Wyatt. Guests were first shown to a salon from which temporary steps rose to large folding doors. When the play was due to start, the doors were opened and the audience entered into the back of the theatre. Below them the seats were arranged in tiered rows down to the stage. There was a gallery to one side, and on the other a box for the Royal family. The stage itself was said to be "elegant and lively, corresponding with the furniture of the room." The sort of furniture that you might find in a ducal drawing room was that used on stage. There was seating for a select audience of around 120.

The Richmonds took great pains to ensure that the audience was indeed select, and that there was no "intrusion of improper company". Tickets were limited, twenty being reserved for the Duke, twelve for the Duchess and lady actresses, six for each actor and the two generals, Conway and Burgoyne, who had written the prologue and epilogue, two for the Earl of Abingdon who had contributed a song, and one for the director, Miss Farren. Those to whom tickets were distributed were charged with writing the name of their guest upon the ticket and of sealing it with their personal seal. Lists of guests so invited were required to be returned to Richmond House on the day before the performance to ensure that they were approved by the owners. Performances began at 8pm, and no admittance was permitted to the salon after 7.30pm. To ensure a clear view of the stage, ladies were not permitted to wear headdresses of any description.

The theatrical sets were remarkable. Thomas Greenwood, the scene painter at Drury Lane Theatre, together with the gentleman portrait painter, John Downman, designed and executed the three scenes. The latter painted portraits of Anne's friends to hang on the walls; these included the Duchess of Richmond, the Duchess of Devonshire, together with her sister Lady Duncannon, Lady Bess Foster, Mrs Siddons and Miss Farren. The last named's picture, as befitted the most recent newcomer to the coterie, remained on the floor against the wall, as if, just purchased. For the final performance on 17th May, attended by the King and Queen, the scenery was yet more lavish, and representations of busts by Anne of her mother Lady Ailesbury and of Lady Melbourne were added.

Rehearsals had started in February 1787, alternating between Harry and Anne's homes. The first open rehearsal at Richmond House, to which sixty friends were invited, took place on 12th April. Mrs Bruce as Muslin the chambermaid was so convincing that a friend subsequently remarked "My dear, if I did not know you to be a gentlewoman I should swear you were born a chambermaid." The final rehearsal was on 18th April, the first night on the 19th, with subsequent performances on 20th and 30th, and on the 5th, 12th, 16th and 17th of May.

Rehearsals and production were directed by the comic actress Elizabeth Farren, assisted by another even better known thespian, Sarah Siddons. The cast included, in addition to Anne as Mrs Lovemore, Lord Derby, who was eventually to marry Miss Farren, as Lovemore, and the Hon Mrs Hobart, as the widow Belmour, this stage name being the title Anne would later use as an author in her one and only novel. Other players included Mr Edgecumbe, he who had inscribed the bench at Mount Edgecumbe, and Sir Harry Englefield, Mr and Miss Campbell, and Mrs Bruce, all relations of Anne and her half-sister the Duchess of Richmond, and Major Arabin. All the non-family members were experienced amateur thespians, the family, novices.

The Gentleman's Magazine described Mrs Damer's costume as "morning habit, a plain white robe; when dressed, embroidered gauze on a white background, a diamond necklace of prodigious value, wheat-sheaf of ornaments of diamonds in her hair, a girdle of diamonds and stars of the same festoons as on her dress." There was a band of 16 performers clad in scarlet tunics, composed of a mixture of members of the Sussex militia, of whom the Duke was Colonel, and of professional musicians. After the performance a fine feast was supervised by the Duke of Richmond. Toasts were drunk, songs sung, and the party broke up at 4am.

The dramatic critics in the papers remained largely silent, probably because they were not invited and had not seen it. Lord Ailesbury, who did have a ticket, wrote in his diary that "Mrs Damer in the epilogue had monotony of voice, and she did not speak the epilogue well; there was little or no applause." However it had undoubtedly been a place to see and be seen, and seems to have been generally enjoyed with not a spare seat in the house. The first production of the Richmond House players can be rated an outstanding success.

HW, writing to the Countess of Upper Ossory in June 1787, had his own idiosyncratic take on *The Way to Keep Him*: "I am very far from tired, Madam, of encomiums on the performance at Richmond House, but I by no means agree with the criticism on it that you quote, and which, I conclude, was written by some player from envy. Who should act genteel comedy perfectly but people of fashion that have sense? Actors and actresses can only guess at the tone of high life, and cannot be inspired with it. Why are there so few genteel comedies, but because most comedies are written by men not of that sphere? Etherege, Congreve, Vanbrugh and Cibber wrote genteel comedy because they lived in the best company; and Mrs Oldfield played it so well because she not only followed, but often set, the fashion. General Burgoyne has written the best modern comedy for the same reason; and Miss Farren is as excellent as Mrs Oldfield because she has lived with the best style of men in England: whereas Mrs Abington can never go beyond Lady Teazle, which is a second-rate character, and that rank of women are always aping women of fashion, without arriving at the style … The Richmond Theatre, I imagine will take root. I supped with the Duke at Mrs Damer's the night before I left London, and they were talking of improvements on the *locale* as the French would say."

The theatre did indeed take root, tickets were keenly sought, and the fashionable world embraced the Richmond House Theatre. The improvements on the *locale* would next be seen in a play called *The Wonder*, written in 1715 by Susannah Centlivre, like Anne, an advocate of womens' rights in a man's world. It is a comedy, set in Portugal, in which lovers get muddled in a complex plot; there is much disguise, hiding, misunderstandings, and all the contents of a traditional farce. Anne was cast in the role of Donna Violante. Rehearsals took place during December 1787, again under the supervision of Elizabeth Farren.

HW watched rehearsals closely. "The play at Richmond house is to be *The Wonder*, with *The Guardian*. The new performers are Lord Henry Fitzgerald, who never played in comedy before, but is good in tragedy; a Miss Hamilton, niece of Lord Abercorn, and a Captain Merry," he wrote to the Countess of Upper Ossory, requesting at the same time that she send him details of her theatre at Ampthill; for she too had subscribed to the popular craze of amateur theatricals. Two days later Horace continued: "I was at the rehearsal last night and amazed. Lord Henry is a prodigy, a perfection – all passion, nature, and ease; you never saw so genuine a lover. Garrick was a monkey to him in Don Felix; and then he is so much the man of fashion and so genteel. In short, when people of quality can act, they must act their own parts so much better than others can mimic them. Mister Merry is an excellent Lissardo too."

In January Horace congratulated Lady Ossory on her own theatrical successes, regretting that Ampthill was a step too far for him to be part of the audience. He wrote that he had not been to any more rehearsals at Richmond House, but that "if the young actress who played Kitty so admirably in *High Life Below Stairs* is not engaged at either of the theatres at Blenheim or Wynnstay, I believe she might have a large salary and free benefit at Richmond House, where they are in sad want of an Ines in *The Wonder.*"

On 29th December a rehearsal took place at Mrs Damer's house for a select audience. The opening night was on 7th February 1788, still at Richmond House, but in a newly constructed theatre in an adjacent building purchased for the purpose by the Duke of Richmond, capable of holding 260 guests. The theatre was designed by Wyatt and again the decorations were by Greenwood. The seats all had pea-green backs, to a standard of comfort unknown in public theatres; however it was slightly cramped, poorly ventilated, and very hot in the summer months. Guests on the first night included the Prince of Wales, the Dukes of York, Gloucester and Devonshire and Horace Walpole. Lord Henry Fitzgerald was generally acknowledged as having acted superbly; Mrs Damer was described as bringing fashionable grace and elegance to the part of Violante, and liveliness and familiarity, in a very different role, as a maid in *The Guardian*. On 9th February the Gazeteer reported that she gave it "all the fine touches that the most finished art of acting could produce." However this acclaim was not unanimous. The Earl of Ailesbury noted in his diary that Mrs Damer was "very indifferent". Lady Eleanor Butler, one of the ladies of Llangollen, who had left her Welsh home to see the play, was more forthright. "Performance at the Theatre, Richmond House execrable, except Lord Henry Fitzgerald, his Don Felix equal to Garrick. Ogilvie as if heaven and Earth were coming together. Mrs Damer detestable. Mrs Hobart well in some, indifferent in others, horrid in many parts." Whatever the standards of acting, the evening was enlivened by the London mob which for undisclosed reasons gathered outside and threw stones which broke some windows. There were seven performances of the two plays. On 14th February Horace wrote that he had got a cold last week at the play at Richmond House, and that "Mrs Damer is ill, and the play is postponed till Monday (the 18th), if Lord Henry is not run away with in the meantime, for he has raised a thousand passions." It was apparently at this performance that the opposing political leaders, William Pitt and Charles James Fox, had both been present. The admission tickets bore the legend: "No one admitted after half-past seven". Pitt realised that he would not be in time, owing to a debate in the Commons, and obtained special permission from the Duke of Richmond to be late. Fox, who had also received an invitation, typically did nothing, but having heard of the concession to Pitt arrived at the same time. The doorkeeper refused admission, saying that he had instructions to admit only one. Fox replied "I know that; but tonight I am a 'rider' on Mister Pitt". He was allowed in and reportedly was much impressed by Anne's performance. On 1st March the King and Queen headed the audience, prior to which an outhouse had been erected for constables and guards to ensure no repetition of the stone throwing.

At the same time the Richmond House players had already started rehearsing another play, *The Jealous Wife*, by George Colman, chosen by Mrs Hobart, who played the leading role of Mrs Oakley. Anne played the smaller part of Lady Freelove, a role which had been played in the opening Garrick production of 1764 by Horace's neighbour at Little Strawberry Hill, the comic actress Kitty Clive. This ran for five performances during March and April 1788; during one of these Mrs Hobart who was rather stout got stuck between the wall and a side wing from which she had to be extricated by "the extra ordinary exertions of Major Fury", another of the actors. A royal party, headed by the King and Queen, was present at the performance on 29th March.

Following this, the players decided to turn to tragic verse and selected the play *Theodosius*. This was a shortened version of Nathaniel Lee's restoration tragedy set in Constantinople with singers, orchestra and chorus, in which Lord Henry Fitzgerald had previously starred in an Irish production in 1786. The final rehearsal took place on 24th April, and the play opened on the 26th. Again Lord Henry Fitzgerald took the plaudits for his playing of Varanes, and Anne Damer was excellent as Athenaïs. The scene between them which ends with Varanes falling on his sword was so full of drama that Miss Harriet Hobart and Lady Ann Wesley had to be carried from the theatre in a faint. It may be that the lack of ventilation within the theatre was a more potent cause of their discomfort. The dresses and scenery were again exemplary, and much better than any to be seen in the public theatres. Anne's imperial robe in the last act was of purple, decorated with silver and ermine, and was the one that she wore for the Reynolds portrait which appears as the front cover of this book. Five performances were given, and the King and Queen attended the last of these on 6th May.

There was to be only one more play from Richmond House during 1788. This was a new production, *False Appearances*, translated by Harry Conway from the French of *Les Dehors Trompeurs ou l'Homme du Jour* by Boissy. The principal characters were the Earl of Derby and Mrs Damer, well supported by Miss Hamilton, Mrs Bruce, Miss Campbell, and Captains Merry and Howarth. On 28th May 1788 Mrs Libby Powys reported that she had been at the first night of *False Appearances*: "The prologue and epilogue were both very clever, wrote by General Conway, and spoken with great spirit by Lord Derby and Mrs Damer. The whole was amazingly well acted. The house filled with all the fine people in town."

HW had his take on this performance as well, writing to the Earl of Strafford on 17th June 1788: "Mr Conway's play, of which your lordship has seen some account in the papers, has succeeded delightfully both in representation and applause. The language is most genteel, though translated from verse; and both prologue and epilogue are charming. The former was delivered most justly and admirably by Lord Derby, and the latter with inimitable spirit and grace by Mrs Damer. Mr Merry and Mrs Bruce played excellently too. But General Conway, Mrs Damer, and everyone else are drowned by Mr Sheridan, whose renown has engrossed all fame's tongues and trumpets." Lest the reader should think that Sheridan too had a part in the play, it must be pointed out that Horace is alluding to Sheridan's acclaimed speech, made during the impeachment of Warren Hastings. There were five other performances of *False Appearances*. The last, on 14th June, was preceded by a petition from the musicians to the Duke of Richmond, complaining of their monotonous diet and asking for liquid refreshment to counteract the intense heat of the theatre. The Duke refused all requests, and perhaps the combination of a stone-throwing mob and a striking band quenched his enthusiasm for the amateur theatre; for *False Appearances* was to be the last production of the Richmond House Theatre. In December 1791 Richmond House was burned to the ground, never to be rebuilt. In 1792 the Duke of Richmond presided over the building of a new theatre in Chichester, on the doorstep of his Goodwood estate, and safe from the mob. He subsequently generously provided furniture and scenery. Perhaps without Richmond's assistance in 1792 the modern Chichester Festival might never have existed.

The Richmond House players had produced five productions in a little over a year. Each had been a sell-out, and each had had a Royal presence. The costumes and sets had far outstripped those of the public theatres, where funds were tighter. Great attention was paid to the detail of every set and every costume, and the guiding hand in the project seems to have been Anne Damer, ably assisted by Elizabeth Farren, Lord Derby's intended wife. From a standing start, with no experience save a few charades, frequent visits to the theatre as a spectator and a wide reading list, it had been a remarkable achievement. Although Anne's acting was not to everybody's satisfaction, the plays which she had masterminded certainly were.

During these active theatrical years from 1787 to 1791, Anne made it her business to befriend and write to leading members of the professional stage, and to various fellow-members of the theatregoing gentry who acted as host and rest house for exhausted actors, either on tour or resting from the London Season. These included the Greatheeds at Guys Cliff near Leamington, Lord and Lady Harcourt at Nuneham Courtenay, Sir Charles Hotham at Dalton in Yorkshire, and Anne's parents and herself at Park Place.

Anne and Sir Charles Hotham corresponded regularly. Born in 1729 and some 20 years older than Anne, he was a Yorkshire baronet who had been a friend of her parents. He was a keen and knowledgeable theatregoer, happily married to Lady Dorothy, with a single daughter, Henrietta, born in 1753. He retained Anne's letters to him during this period, and these are now in the archives of Hull University.

In June 1787 Anne wrote to Sir Charles enquiring how his journey to the North had gone, and telling him that Miss Farren, who had not been well yet continued her stage performances, was expecting a letter from Lady Dorothy. Anne herself intended to go to Park Place, and promised to pass on Sir Charles's best wishes to her parents.

On 21st August Anne wrote again, this time from London. She had been busy at Park Place, modelling her dog. She apologised for not writing, with the excuse that "you who are so good as not to disdain the company of an artist, know that a model must not be left in its wet state, unfinished. Since I came to town, I have been very uneasy about our friend, dear Miss Farren. She has had terrible returns of the pain in her head and has looked so ill, your heart would have ached for her, I am sure. Her doctor absolutely forbade her writing, which is the reason that you have not heard from her at Dalton, and it has caused her much anxiety, I assure you; today I promised to tell you this, for, tho' she plays tonight, she would have written as she could not bear deferring it any longer. But I was certain that you would have desired her not yourself – I think her better, and have tried to persuade her to give herself a little air and quiet which would recover her before the fatigues of the winter. I hope she will listen, but you know how careless she is of her health – how I wished for you the night she played Beatrice! Her glory was great, I assure you, a house as full as it could hold, and very great applause." Anne continued that she looked forward to seeing the play again, together with Sir Charles, during the winter. She ended the letter by concluding that the actor Henry Keane was still staying at Dalton, and hoped that newspaper reports of an improvement in Keane's health were correct.

On 21st October Anne wrote from Park Place, saying that she was about to return to London in November, where rehearsals for *The Wonder* were due to begin, under the direction of Miss Farren.

In May 1788, a further letter from Anne to Sir Charles gave her reactions to the first night of *False Appearances*. "It was beyond all expectation – a crowded house, containing everything London now produces most worthy of the ambition of authors and actors to please – the applause was far greater than any we have ever had and keeped up with so much spirit that it could but be sincere, everything was so well understood – not a word or look lost, and so much laughing, so much attention when it was required, that the actors were inspired from the beginning of the performance. I need not tell you the effect that has – what I felt before I began, and till the very flattering turn I saw things take, I cannot express – yet I do firmly believe that our friend, dear Miss Farren suffered still more, I never shall forget the anxiety of her fine expressive countenance, which I only saw at a distance, for she would not venture to come near us till the play was over – the author has every reason to be flattered and where the play was most doubtful, its success seems secure, I mean in want of life and spirit – this clearly shows how impossible it is to judge of the effect of a performance till it actually is on the boards – Kemble, I hear was charmed with it. He said he never heard such language and pronounced that it would do for a public theatre.

"You will probably have heard from poor Mrs Siddons, as her journey has been deferred by the illness of her son, but I flatter myself that he is now recovering as Mr Greatheed has just told me that she means to go in a day or two. What a persecution she has gone through this winter. Justice certainly, in these affairs, is not always clear to our poor mortal eyes."

The correspondence between Anne and Sir Charles continued fitfully until 1791. All of the letters mention actors and actresses and their health – Mrs Siddons is better, though her father is unwell, while Miss Farren's constitution is too delicate for the "foggs and boggs of this sad world". The last letter, dated 29th May 1791, is written from London, following Anne's return from travels in Portugal and Spain. She tells Sir Charles that she is hard at work with her sculpture of King George III, but hopes to go to the country at the end of the month "for green trees and flowers and fine prospects." She does not intend to stay long. "Having no taste for snow and foxhunting, I shall return early to town, and I hope this time to finish my statue." She looked forward to seeing Sir Charles again in "Our House" – the London theatre.

The Hotham correspondence shows how actors and actressess were welcomed as friends by those members of the landed gentry who were also theatrical *aficionados*. They were appreciated for their style, their wit and intellect, and doubtless, even if not in the best of health, made a welcome change from more stolid country neighbours. Their hosts found it a pleasant duty to care for their guests while they recharged their acting batteries.

There was still time between theatricals for sculpture. After completing the plaques of the water gods on Henley bridge, Anne was asked by the Duke of Devonshire to provide a bas-relief for the new well house, named St Anne's Well, the fount of the healing spa waters at Buxton, the new "Bath of the North". Horace described it as a "small bas-relief of nymph and urn for fountain at Buxton". In 1979 Christie's sold a rectangular plaster maquette, about 20 x 25 cm, signed Anne Damer, and described as "the goddess Hygeia, kneeling and pouring from a vase with a serpent touching its lip". Hygeia was the Greek goddess of health, and obviously a suitable choice for a spa. Whether this model was ever worked up to full-scale completion is unclear. Much of the fine building work carried out by the architect John Carr of York, including St Anne's Well, was demolished in Victorian times to make way for buildings designed by Joseph Paxton. Fortunately Carr's great Crescent still remains.

Further and larger bas-relief work followed. John Boydell, an engraver and publisher of prints, and sufficiently celebrated to become Lord Mayor of London in 1790, conceived the idea of a gallery of works of art connected with the plays of William Shakespeare. From the paintings on show engravings would be made and sold as prints to a burgeoning market. Almost all the leading painters of the day contributed work: Fuseli, Reynolds, Opie, Angelica Kaufmann, Joseph Wright of Derby, Romney and many others painted for the gallery. Only two sculptors were chosen, Thomas Banks, whose model of Shakespeare Attended by Painting and Poetry adorned the entrance to the gallery, and Anne Damer who was commissioned to produce two bas-reliefs of Antony & Cleopatra and Coriolanus. Anne, as befitted her position as an amateur sculptor, was the only artist not to be paid by Boydell. From the publicity-conscious Boydell's point of view, he obtained both a free exhibit and a name that should attract visitors, a compelling business case and good reason not to invite more experienced contemporary professional sculptors.

The gallery opened in 1789 with 34 pictures; by 1802, the year in which Boydell's Shakespeare prints were published, the number had risen to 170. Anne's sculptures were probably completed fairly early on, though no record of this exists. Large numbers of visitors came to the gallery itself, but unfortunately they failed to buy the prints as well. By 1804 Boydell was in financial trouble; he had to abandon his plan to bequeath the contents of the gallery to the nation and obtained permission from Parliament to dispose of it by public lottery. The winner arranged for Christie's to auction the gallery and its contents in May 1805. Boydell had died, a broken man, in the previous year.

Anne's bas-relief sculptures now exist only in the form of prints made for sale by Boydell. They both depict scenes of classical antiquity and are portrayed in Anne's neo-classical style. The Antony & Cleopatra picture is taken from Act V, sc. ii of Shakespeare's play: a doleful Cleopatra is shown seated in her Monument, with an asp around her wrist; her attendant Iras lies dead at her feet, having kissed Cleopatra farewell: "Have I the aspic in my lips?". Her other attendant, Charmian, kneels sorrowfully at her side. In the next instant she will apply the asp to her breast. The Coriolanus model is taken from Act II, sc. I of the play. Coriolanus, his brow clad with a wreath of oak leaves, stands in the centre with his mother, Volumnia, weeping, and his wife, Virgilia, to the right; the two ladies are balanced by Cominius, Titus Lartius, and Valeria to the left:

> *"My gracious silence, hail!*
> *Wouldst thou have laugh'd had I come coffin'd home,*
> *That weep'st to see me triumph? Ah! my dear,*
> *Such eyes the widows in Corioli wear,*
> *And mothers that lack sons."*

On 28th April 1790 *The World* reported that Mrs Siddons and Mr Kemble had sat for Anne as Volumnia and Coriolanus. A week later it again mentioned this bas-relief as being "in the chaste simplicity of the Greek style".

Both of the bas-reliefs seem flat and stilted in design. However this may owe more to the engraver's translation of the scenes than to the originals, which are now lost. Both scenes portray the fashionable air of melancholy to which Anne Damer was beginning to succumb. It would not be long before it immersed her, as she deprecated its depressing effects whilst at the same time welcoming it as her natural habitat.

If money equates to quality, Cleopatra was better than Coriolanus. The print of the former sold for one guinea, the latter for five shillings. When the originals were sold by auction following the breakup of the gallery, they were both purchased by a Mr Bacon, possibly another sculptor, John Bacon the Younger. He paid four guineas for Cleopatra, but only had to stump up three guineas for Coriolanus.

By this time Anne had mastered the techniques required for working in marble, and in general whenever a terracotta model was made, it was followed by one in marble. In 1787 she completed a terracotta bust of the young Polish Prince Lubomirski in the character of Bacchus. The prince was nephew to the Princess Czartoriski, who conducted him round Europe for a series of artists to record his youthful good looks. The following year this bust was repeated in marble, and given by Anne to Oxford University. It is currently in the Ashmolean Museum. It features a rather effeminate youth, with head inclined forwards, much in the style of her self portrait in the Uffizi. Possibly her busts were intended to stand on high chimneypieces, at or above eye level, and the downward inclination would have made them easier to view. About the same time she also completed terracotta and marble versions of the son of Rossi, the dancer, as Paris, a handsome youth with a Phrygian cap perched on top of a curly head. Again both versions are missing today. Both these statues were completed in neo-classical style, though with slightly more life in the figures than in her earlier neo-classical busts.

In 1787 Anne began her *magnum opus*, which was to take seven years to complete and instal. This was to be a giant eight-foot statue of King George III, undertaken at the request of her uncle, Lord Frederick Campbell, the Lord Clerk Registrar and Chief Legal Officer for Scotland. It was destined to be finished in marble and to be placed in the new Adam-designed General Register House in Edinburgh. It had to be fitted in between travel and theatricals. The terracotta model took from 1787 to 1790. Work on the marble version lasted from 1790 to 1794. Anne described it as "my overgrown child", and worked on it from a raised platform, from which she experienced at least one tumble, damaging her leg. *The World* reported on 9th June 1787 that "when the King and Queen saw Mrs Damer at work on her colossal statue, and necessarily clambering about in unaccustomed positions, they equally complimented her on the steadiness of her hand and of her feet". A later royal visit saw the work completed. *Lloyds Evening Post* of 21st August 1793 reported that "yesterday Her Majesty and the four elder princesses honoured the Leverian Museum with their presence and after inspecting the statue of His Majesty, done by Mrs Damer, expressed their opinion of it in the most flattering terms". A two hour visit had taken place, following which the royal party were treated by Mrs Damer to a cold collation. They were attended by Lord Frederick Campbell, Anne's uncle, and by Harry, her father. It was not to be until August 1795 that the statue eventually arrived at Leith docks after a journey by sea. It was placed in prime position under the central dome of the building, to be viewed from all sides. Today it is still in the same room, but positioned to one side of the dome, framed by a passageway.

The finished statue shows a youngish-looking King displaying a rather too shapely calf, which peeps through full-length coronation robes. The left hand grasps a sword, the right, with elbow raised and arm at right angles across his body, holds the sceptre with the cross. On his head rests a copy of King Edward's crown. The crown and sceptre are made of gilt metal, a late addition by Anne and the result of collaboration with Benjamin Vulliamy, the royal clockmaker. It is the only one of Anne's works which combines coloured metal with white marble. The king's facial features are in Anne's ideal classical style, his clothing a faithful reproduction of his coronation attire. The robes are well carved, their folds both from the front and back flow with style and exude authority. For a sculptor inexperienced in portraying a human figure, the robes also provide a convenient hiding place. It is a halfway house in her sculpting career, combining neo-classical features with modern dress. Sir Joshua Reynolds would not have approved, but the world was changing.

It has been said that it is not one of Anne's more successful works. The radical pamphleteer Charles Pigott lampooned it as:

> *"Lord! What a lumpish, senseless thing!*
> *And yet 'tis very like the king!"*

Seen close up, it certainly has its faults. The idealised head is far from ideal; the calf lacks muscle; calf and foot meet seemingly without an ankle, and the royal shoe resembles a plump sausage tied with a bow. Anatomical inexperience shows. However from a short distance it is impressive. In its current position, well-lit and framed against the dark background of the passage way, the white marble glows in contrast with the gilt regalia. The dark shadow between the robe's folds adds depth. It is a figure of majesty, and not by size alone, carved to secure the loyalty of Scottish subjects to a Hanoverian king.

A second large sculpture was attributed to Anne at around this time. This was another giant, a naked figure of the Roman god Apollo, intended to stand upon the roof of the new Apollo Theatre. It is uncertain whether this was ever completed. Contemporary prints of the theatre show a large figure above the entrance portico, but the theatre was burnt to the ground shortly after it opened. The time taken to produce King George, and her lack of anatomical expertise, would seem to rule out any sculpting activity by Anne for this venture.

Sculpture and the theatre would have left Anne little time for rest and recreation. However the joys of Park Place were still very much available, and she made good use of them when time permitted. On 29th July 1790 *The World* reported that "Mrs Damer at present suffers her chisel to repose, and is with Lady Ailesbury and General Conway at their paradise in Berkshire." A year later, on 13th July 1791, *The World* reported that the chisel had again been "laid aside, to participate in the festivals of Park Place"; while in November the *Gazetteer* reported that Mrs Damer had resumed her chisel on a bust of Venus.

Harry was enjoying a life of retirement and making full use of available time further to improve his country home. Caroline, though suffering from periods of poor health, continued in her role of hostess to old friends and relations, combining them with a delightful mixture of authors, actors and artists. HW reported in September 1788 that he had been "to Park Place on a pilgrimage to Little Master Stonehenge, alias the Druids' temple from Jersey". This was an ancient stone circle, which had previously stood on the island of Jersey. The islanders, knowing of Harry's penchant for beautifying the landscape of Park Place, had made a present of it to him, as a gesture of thanks for his work as Lieutenant-Governor of the island. The gift was accepted with alacrity, and after much debate the circle was re-sited on an eminent hill, flanked by groves of fir trees, to be seen from the garden above a long ridge of firs. The original site in Jersey had been carefully charted and each stone was meticulously restored to its original position on the new site. Horace described it thus: "Though the whole is diminutive, yet being seen on the horizon it looks very high-priestly, and in that broken country may easily be taken for respectable ruins of an ancient castle or Caractus's own summer residence." Horace admitted that both he and Anne had suggested that the circle be placed closer to the house, and that Harry had been right, and they wrong in their suggestions. He went on to say that "Park Place is now one of the spots the most deserving to be visited in our island; for, besides the variety of the ground, the diversity of the landscapes and prospects, all glittering with meanders of the Thames at a distance, or washed by it as it borders the shores, what singular objects are to be seen there! – the rocky bridge, the Druidic temple, Lady Ailesbury's worked pictures, and Henley Bridge with Mrs Damer's colossal heads of the Thames and Isis." Anne, happy to play her part in entertaining guests and helping to care for her mother, was always welcome at home.

Chapter 10

MY STRAW BERRYS

In October 1788 HW wrote to the Countess of Upper Ossory: "I have made....the acquaintance of two young ladies of the name of Berry, whom I first saw last winter, and who accidentally took a house here with their father for this season. Their story is singular enough to entertain you. The grandfather [actually great-uncle], a Scot, had a large estate in his own country – £5000 a year, it is said – and a circumstance I shall tell you makes it probable. The eldest son married for love a woman with no fortune. The old man was enraged, and would not see him. The wife died, and left these two young ladies. The grandfather wished for an heir-male, and pressed the widower to remarry, but could not prevail, the son declaring he would consecrate himself to his daughters and their education. The old man did not break with him again, but much worse, disinherited him, and left all to his second son, who very handsomely gave up £800 a year to his elder brother. Mr Berry has since carried his daughters for two or three years to France and Italy, and they are returned the best-informed and the most perfect creatures I ever saw at their age. They are extremely sensible, entirely natural and unaffected, frank, and, being qualified to talk on any subject, nothing is so easy and agreeable as their conversation, nor more apposite than their answers and observations. The eldest, I discovered by chance, understands Latin, and is a perfect Frenchwoman in her language. The younger draws charmingly, and has copied admirably Lady Di's Gypsies, which I lent, though for the first time of her attempting colours. They are of pleasing figures. Mary, the eldest, sweet, with fine dark eyes that are very lively when she speaks, with a symmetry of face that is the more interesting from being pale; Agnes, the younger, has an agreeable sensible countenance, hardly to be called handsome, but almost. She is less animated than Mary, but seems, out of deference to her sister, to speak seldomer, for they dote on each other, and Mary is always praising her sister's talents. I must even tell you they dress within the bounds of fashion, though fashionably, but without the excrescences and balconies with which modern hoydens overwhelm and barricade their persons – in short, good sense, information, simplicity, and ease characterise the Berrys. And this is not particularly mine, who am apt to be prejudiced, but the universal voice of all who know them. The first night I met them I would not be acquainted with them, having heard so much in their praise that I concluded they would be all pretension.

The second time, in a very small company, I sat next to Mary and found her an angel both inside and out. Now, I do not know which I like best; except Mary's face which is framed for a sentimental novel, but it is ten times better for a fifty times better thing – genteel comedy."

Horace's eulogy on the two sisters was not universally shared. All agreed that Agnes was charming, sweet tempered, somewhat unworldly, and an adequate sketcher. Mary was described as striking in appearance, but to Lord Glenbervie, meeting her early in the 1790s, she had a more forbidding appearance: "The eldest (Miss Berry) with her eagle eyes and manner – if not to threaten, to command; Agnes more mild, if less beautiful". Later in the same meeting he had listened to Mary giving her forthright views on *Les letters écrites de Lausanne,* by Mme de Charrière. He described her as "the elder Miss Berry, whose words would announce the wisdom of Minerva, if a sense of her own beauty did not to nice observers mingle some emulation of the attributes of a less awful goddess". On the same occasion, Glenbervie met Anne for the first time: "She is handsome I think and agreeable".

Horace was aged 71, Mary and Agnes, 25 and 24 respectively. The two girls, and Mary in particular, were to become close friends of both Horace and Anne, and because they will feature so prominently in the coming chapters, it is worthwhile to look more closely at their lives hitherto. Horace was almost but not quite right in the description given above. Mary Berry herself wrote her *Notes of Early Life* which were found among her papers following her death. Curiously, there is no mention of any grandparent. Mary simply stated that "my father was the maternal nephew of an old Scottish merchant of the name of Ferguson". Mary's great-uncle had come to London at the beginning the 18th century. His business prospered, and although he either acquired or inherited an estate at Raith in Fifeshire, he did not return to his Scottish roots, and was eventually to die, childless, in his home situated above his office. His natural heirs were the two sons of his sister, who had married a Mr Berry. Robert, the eldest, was trained as a barrister but never got round to practising, preferring continental travel and literary society to work. Financially he was entirely dependent for his allowance of £300 a year on his uncle, a hardheaded businessman with whom he had little in common. In 1762 Robert married a Miss Seton, a distant cousin, who was to give birth to two daughters, Mary in 1763 and Agnes in 1764. In 1767 their mother died in childbirth, the baby also being stillborn, thus leaving no male heir. Mary related that uncle Ferguson had attempted to persuade Robert to marry again, in the hope that he would produce the requisite son, but that he had refused, saying that he wished to concentrate on bringing up his two daughters. In the meantime, in contrast, William Berry, the younger brother, had proved himself a successful businessman, and had married a well-dowered wife who had produced two sons in the first two years of his marriage.

In 1769 Robert Berry and his daughters moved to a rented house in Chiswick. Here a governess was employed, but when she left to get married after five years, she was not replaced and the girls were left to fend for their own education. In 1781 the Ferguson uncle expired at the age of 93. He left Robert a capital sum of £10,000 whilst William, who had inherited the rest of his estate, generously made over an annuity of £1000 a year to his brother. Mary continued to complain firstly that this amount was too small, and secondly that it was for her father's life only and would not be extended to his daughters. However Robert Berry was, on an income of £1500 a year, reasonably well off. Leaving his mother-in-law, Mrs Seton, to live with another daughter, he went with his girls on a tour of the West Country. In 1782 they extended their travels to Holland, thence to Switzerland and to Italy, and remained abroad until June 1785. For the next three years they remained in England, living in London, visiting relations in the country and widening their circle of friends. It was during the winter of 1787/8, at the house of the banker Sir Robert Herries, that the Berrys first met Horace Walpole. They made an immediate impression on each other, and it was probably due to this acquaintance, which rapidly blossomed into friendship, that the Berrys rented a house in Twickenham, close to Strawberry Hill, for the summer of 1788. By then Mary had come to realise that without a mother, and with a totally unworldly father, it was up to her to control the family's destiny: "I soon found that I had to lead those who ought to have led me; that I must be a protecting mother, instead of a gay companion to my sister; and to my father a guide and monitor, instead of finding in him a tutor and protector." In addition to Robert's innate weakness of character, she would also have to make decisions on behalf of the "less animated" Agnes, who was happier sketching and in following where her sister led. Responsibility had come early, and fortunately she had the ability to deal with it, though at the cost of missing out, in her words, on "the thoughtless gaiety and lightheartedness of youth". By the time she met Horace, at the age of 24, the burden of looking after her father and sister had produced a woman whose natural intelligence and vivacity was tempered by a seriousness of mind, which led easily to periods of introspective melancholy.

To the septuagenarian Horace, the two girls were the find of a lifetime, and they arrived at a particularly convenient time for him. Shortly after their first meeting Horace invited the girls to Strawberry Hill to come and see his printing press. He had hurriedly prepared the following verses for them, set upon the press.

> *To Mary's lips has ancient Rome*
> *Her purest language taught*
> *And from the modern city home*
> *Agnes its pencil brought.*

Rome's ancient Horace sweetly chants
Such maids with lyric fire
Albion's old Horace ne'er sings nor paints
He only can admire.

Still would his press their fame record,
So amiable the pair is!
But, ah! How vain to think his word
Can add a straw to Berrys!

The following day he was delighted to receive a reply from his "Latin nymph":

Had Rome's famed Horace thus addrest
His Lydia or his Lyce
He had ne'er so oft complained their breast
To him was cold and icy.

But had they sought their joy to explain
Or praise their generous bard,
Perhaps, like me, they had tried in vain,
And felt the task too hard.

No matter that the scansion and grammar showed a lack of polish, not surprising from someone self educated since her governess had left her at the age of 12, the reply showed originality and enterprise and Horace, the elderly man, was much pleased by it. For he was well aware that old age was galloping on at an increasing pace. In relaying the verses above to the Countess of Upper Ossory, Horace asked "that they may go no farther, for trifles that *egayent* a little private society, are ridiculous if they get abroad, especially from a septuagenary rhymer".

With increasing age came the threat of mortality. In February 1789 Horace wrote following the death of Mme du Deffand's dog, Tonton, left to him in her will: "I have had the satisfaction, for my dear old friend's sake and his own, of having nursed him up, by constant attention, to the age of sixteen, yet always afraid of his surviving me. ...... I sent him to Strawberry, and went thither to see him buried behind the chapel, near Rosette. I shall miss him greatly, and must not have another dog; I am too old, and should only breed it up to be unhappy when I am gone. My resource is in two marble kittens that Mrs Damer has given me, of her own work, and which are so much alive that I talk to them as I did to poor Tonton!" Horace believed that he was not long for this world, but knew that to secure his place in posterity, there was work still to be done, to collect and edit his life's literary works. In Mary Berry, who was industrious, intelligent, adaptable and eager to learn, he had found the ideal person. The fact that she was not financially independent but that he could help her to become so, was a further advantage. From Mary's point of view, to be connected to the great man of letters and to bask in his literary glory was reward enough. They needed each other for business purposes, and though this necessity may never have been mentioned – to do so would surely be bad taste – it must have become apparent fairly early on in their relationship. They were also remarkably fond of each other, both sisters avid listeners to the most interesting of men, Horace appreciating their direct and unsullied approach, so different from the backbiting conversations of his day-to-day neighbours. To the two girls and the world in which he lived, Horace would continue the light-hearted approach of an elderly gentleman, infatuated by not one but two young beauties, referring to his "twin-wives", to Mary as "*suavissima Maria*", and to Agnes as "my sweet lamb", or signing himself "Horace Fondlewives". However he lost no time in involving the sisters in the literary life of Strawberry Hill. He began his *Reminiscences of the Courts of George I and George II* very shortly after meeting the Berrys and completed it by January 1789, dedicating it to the sisters, and following it up with the *Catalogue of Strawberry Hill*, again dedicated to the Berrys and published at the end of 1789.

It was natural that he should want to introduce his newly-found friends, both in his letters to his various correspondents and in person, to those close friends and relations who were regular visitors to Strawberry Hill. First among these were his favourite cousin Harry, Caroline his wife, and Anne their daughter and his goddaughter. The introduction was made on 20th March 1789 and seems to have been an instant success, for Horace constantly alludes to Anne in his letters to the Berrys, who departed for Yorkshire and a visit to their cousins from June to September. Horace was left to care for their dog and look for suitable accommodation for them near to Strawberry Hill. He did not care much for the dog: "He is not beautiful … especially as I have had him clipped. The shearing has brought to light a nose an ell long." In July he missed securing Lady Dudley's house, "in my own lane … and for a song! '*Pazienza, mie care!*' … And who, of all the birds in the air, do you think has got it? Only the Pepys's … Why, there is poor Mrs Pepys with not a rag of linen but the shift on her back. They sent their whole history by water. It was a most tempestuous night; the boatmen, dreading a shipwreck, cast anchor in Chelsea Reach, intending to put to sea the next morning – but before daybreak pirates had carried off the whole cargo, to the value, Mr Cambridge says, of some three hundred pounds."

A week later Horace, writing to give news of the storming of the Bastille, bemoaned that he had not heard from Yorkshire, but revealed that Anne had received a letter. "Such unwriting wives I never knew! And a shame it is for an author, and what is more, for a printer, to have a couple so unletteral. ... Mrs Damer dined here yesterday, and had just heard from you."

By August Horace lamented that he had heard that the Berrys were now going to stay on in Yorkshire until the end of September, having previously arranged with Anne and her parents that he should bring them to visit and stay at Park Place. However he went on to reveal that he had come to terms with the dog, who seemed now to be named after the recently deceased relict of Mme du Deffand. "The personage that will gain most by your delay will be Tonton, whose long nose begins to recover its curled rotundity. It is the best tempered quiet animal alive, which is candid in me to own, as he, as long as it is light, prefers my footboy, or a bone on the lawn, to my company. In the evening, as I allow him to lie on every couch and chair, he thinks me agreeable enough. I must celebrate the sense of Fidele, Mrs Damer's terrier. Without making the slightest gesture, her mistress only said to her: 'Now, Fidele, you may here jump on any chair you please.' She instantly jumped on the settee; and so she did in every room for the whole two days she stayed. This is another demonstration that dogs understand even language, as far as it relates to their own affairs." Again Anne is mentioned as having become by now very much part of a Berry, Walpole, Damer triangle.

By the end of August Horace had secured a house at Teddington, where "you may shake hands with Mister Pepys out of the window", at twenty pounds for two months. He suggested that on their return Mr Berry and his daughters should all stay with him at Strawberry Hill, to view the accommodation. The Berrys returned from Yorkshire in early October 1789 and seem to have stayed at Teddington till after Christmas. By February 1790 mail was being sent to Somerset Street in London. Mary's entry for 1790 in her memorandum book reads: "Summer for three weeks in Montpelier Row. Go abroad in October; winter in Florence and Pisa." There was also time during the summer of 1790 to visit Park Place in late June. On 25th June Horace, writing to Harry, said: "I hope my wives were not at Park Place in your absence: the loss of them is irreparable to me, and I tremble to think how much more I shall feel it in three months, when I have to part with them for .... who can tell how long?" They obviously did stay there, for on 2nd July Horace wrote to Mary Berry in Lymington: "I am glad you staid long enough at Park Place to see all its beauties. The cottage and all its purlieus is delicious, so is the bridge and Isis, and the Druids' Temple seems to have been born and bred on the spot where it stands." Presumably Anne would have been in attendance as host. A day later he wrote again to Mary in Lymington: "Mrs Damer tells me in a letter today that Lady Ailesbury was charmed with you both (which did not surprise either of us); and says she never saw two persons have so much taste of the country, who have no place of their own. It may be so; but begging her Ladyship's pardon and yours, I think that people who have a place of their own are mighty apt not to like any other." By early August the Berrys had returned to Somerset Street, dividing their time between there and temporary accommodation in Montpelier Row, Twickenham, close to Strawberry Hill.

Mary also wished to get to know Anne better, and at some date in late July or in August, asked Horace "Do tell me where Mrs Damer lives; though we are not to have the pleasure of being admitted till next week, we wish no longer to delay leaving our name at her door." During the two months of August and September she must have met Anne a considerable number of times, as it was during this period that their relationship changed from pleasant acquaintance to an intense and extremely close friendship. It was to result in an almost daily correspondence from the moment that the sisters and their father set sail on 10th October.

Throughout the summer the sisters had received a torrent of letters from HW, largely dedicated to tales of the horrors of the French Revolution across the Channel. Each letter contained the strongest advice that they should not carry out their intended plan to travel to the continent to spend the winter in the warmer climes, thereby endangering themselves and depriving Horace of the enjoyment of their company. His advice was not taken and on Sunday 10th October, the day of their departure for the continent, he wrote: "Is it possible to write to my beloved friends and refrain from speaking of my grief for losing you; though it is but the continuation of what I have felt ever since I was stunned by your intention of going abroad this autumn? Still I will not tire you with it often. In happy days I smiled and called you my dear wives, now I can only think on you as darling children of whom I am bereaved! As such I have loved and do love you; and charming as you both are, I have had no occasion to remind myself that I am past seventy-three. Your hearts, your understandings, your virtues, and the cruel injustice of your fate, have interested me in everything that concerns you; and so far from having occasion to blush for any unbecoming weakness, I am proud of my affection for you, and very proud of your condescending to pass so many hours with a very old man."

Chapter 11

TRAVELS ON THE CONTINENT

On 10th October 1790 the Berry family left North Audley Street at 11.30am, arriving at the Old Ship at Brighthelmstone at 8.30pm in the evening. The following day they sailed at 6.00pm on board the *Speedwell,* a 40-ton sloop commanded by Captain Lyn, at a cost of 8½ guineas, inclusive of carriage and baggage. It was to be a journey in which there was an exchange of letters between Mary Berry on the one hand, and Horace and Anne, separately and privately, on the other. When Anne died in 1828, she directed in her will that all her correspondence be burned. Sadly for us, her executor faithfully carried out her instructions to the best of his ability. Little remains, apart from Anne's letters to Mary Berry. These begin on the family's departure to France, continue in a constant flow till 1797, and then become less frequent in the following years. Mary must have been aware of Anne's wishes, but even so retained many of these letters, about which she wrote in 1842: "These letters, selected from a hundred others, I cannot bring myself to destroy. I cannot for my soul obliterate all memory of the truest, the most faithful and the most generous friendship that ever animated two Human beings.

"I am aware that when I am gone these letters can interest nobody. I am aware that they are almost entirely expressions of character and of affection. But I cannot ask my own hands to destroy the flattering proofs of having been the object of such affection, of such constant, unwearied, unselfish Friendship. Would that the conscious pride with which I look back to these recollections was entirely unsullied by my not having borne with sufficient patience in later years some weaknesses and peculiarities which I felt indignant at creeping over such a character as *Hers*!

"O noble, elevated, and tender spirit! If, from some higher state of existence, thou canst read my inmost Soul, as thou ever didst in this, read then my self reproaches. Read the just punishment of such impatience, in the entirely widowed Soul that has thus long survived Thee, wandering through the world – 'without a second and without a judge'."

Though Mary could not destroy the letters, she could indeed edit the correspondence, with the ability to select "from a hundred others". Those concerning life in Lisbon and her travels through Portugal, Spain, and revolutionary France, read as excellent memoirs of 18th century travel, and contain fascinating observations as to people and places. However the emotional expressions of friendship, and something more, in the extracts from Mary Berry's letters, which are contained in *Anne's Notebooks*, a discussion of which follows, must have been in response to, and in the certainty of receiving, something more personal.

Mary may have kept Anne's letters to her, but there is no similar source of letters from Mary to Anne. However there are four hand-written volumes entitled *Anne Seymour Damer's Notebooks*, and described as "these four vols found among Mrs Damer's papers in her own handwriting" and commencing 12th January 1791 at Lisbon. These seem to be excerpts from letters between Anne and Mary. In the first volume especially, there are, in addition, a number of classical quotations in Greek and Latin, mostly concerning the virtues of friendship. A close study of the letters' content shows that nearly all, if not all of them, are extracts from Mary's letters to Anne. If this is indeed the case, why should Anne not have kept the complete letters? It may be that she feared they might get into the wrong hands, or be used in some way to resurrect gossip about her supposed lesbian tendencies. Equally, they may have contained frank and sometimes derogatory comment about people and places within the Berrys' ambit. They seem to be very much in datal order, though at times references to dates are few and far between. Volume One seems to cover the period from October 1790, when the Berrys left England, to their return in November 1791.

In the intervening period Anne, too, arranged to travel on the continent, leaving about a month after the Berrys and returning before them in May 1791. Both sets of travellers were going ostensibly for the good of their health, to avoid the rigours of the English winter and to gain the warming benefits of South European sun. It is pertinent to ask why, if such a friendship had arisen between them, they did not make a journey together. As Anne's departure for Portugal had come nearer, Mary, already arrived in Italy, wrote: "I could not help thinking much, of your longer and more unpleasant voyage, the sad necessity for it." What was this "sad necessity"? One might imagine that it was sad that they were not going on the voyage together, to Anne's beloved and civilised Italy, rather than to the wilder shores of Portugal. Possibly both were apprehensive that they might be abused as lesbians if they travelled together. Perhaps they did not wish to incur Horace's jealousy, displeased that his goddaughter might be taking over his proprietorship of at least one of his beloved Berrys.

Why then did Anne have to travel at all? Certainly she liked to avoid English winters for health reasons, and perhaps it was her health that had caused the "sad necessity." Perhaps she really wanted to be alone, to concentrate not on her established professional sculpture, but on a new pastime, the writing of a novel. And this necessity would seem sad, at least to Mary Berry.

One further, if remote, possibility occurs. It was extremely unusual for a lady to travel alone at this period. Both the dangers of the journey and a sense of propriety dictated that a lady should always take a companion. Indeed, on her previous journeys

Anne had always taken her Campbell cousins. Solo travel was an exception and therefore taken for exceptional reasons, such as Bess Foster's trip to Italy to give birth away from the eyes of the world. Could Anne have had similar reasons?

She was aged over 40, and childless. History does not relate whether she had ever become pregnant and suffered a miscarriage during her marriage to John Damer. However, prior to befriending Mary Berry, she had been involved in a romantic relationship. As a widow, it would be socially inconceivable for her to conceive; as a woman, she might have feared the dangers and stigma of abortion. The only practical alternative might have been to endure pregnancy and birth away from the eyes of the world, abroad, in a quiet and selected spot. William Fawkener had previously visited Lisbon on a diplomatic mission in 1787, and would have had helpful contacts. The Casa Pia in Lisbon was perhaps the most celebrated orphanage of its time.

Whatever the reason, they went their separate ways. The Berrys had set out to go to Italy via revolutionary France, while Anne sailed directly to Lisbon and thence by land through Portugal and Spain, returning to England via France. Evidently the terrors of the revolution held little fear for either party. Almost every day Mary and Anne wrote effusive messages of friendship from different corners of Europe.

Their relationship had changed swiftly, dramatically and deeply, from Mary's request two months previously to have Mrs Damer's address, so that she might call upon her. The following quotation from Mary Berry, recorded in *Anne's Notebooks*, charmingly describes the new situation: "You left your fan here last night, a sentiment of honesty at once prompted me to return it, but another sentiment, not so easily defined, prompts me to keep it – farewell, we are just setting off and I am as melancholy as a cat – but I have been happy, and I shall be happy … can we ever say more? … remember all your kind promises last night … farewell, farewell."

Their recorded correspondence begins with Anne writing on the day of the Berrys' departure: "I have been for some time with my paper, pens, and ink before me, wishing to write you a few lines, but quite unable. Do not, from this beginning, fear the style of some former letters. No, no, my gratitude to you, setting all other considerations apart, will shew itself by unremitting attention to everything you have said to me. I have not, it is true, been accustomed to the charm of real friendship, but my own heart has taught me its value. Rest assured that, could you know to what degree you contribute to the comfort, even the repose, of my mind, your utmost good nature would be more than satisfied. My heart is full, yet I may comparatively say that I am composed. I have at least spoken to you on one miserable subject. I felt every day more and more that I owed this to you, every day more and more that I owed to you that you should know me, see me not only as I am, but as I have been, and then judge for yourself. From you, as from a superior being, I was sure of candour and mercy, but unequal to explain thoroughly those circumstances, which tend to excuse, tho' nothing can defend, me. You are sensible what I must suffer, with everything that most interests me, everything that most deserves to interest me, at stake."

"I have at least spoken to you on one miserable subject". Here Anne seems to be unburdening herself of some past action which she perhaps regretted, though unable to explain fully to Mary the circumstances that might have excused it. The final "nothing can defend it" seems to indicate that, whatever might have occurred was in her eyes serious. There were two subjects upon which Anne suffered "abuse". Firstly, that she was not the author of her sculptures, secondly, that she was actively lesbian. Whether "the miserable subject" concerned either of these charges it is impossible to say. Later in her correspondence it appears that she had made several enemies during her adult life, and the undisclosed subject might well have been to do with one of these. Pregnancy remains a possibility.

She ended the letter: "And indeed I want a little time to arrange my melancholy thoughts into a lasting order. For the present, farewell." She commenced the next on the following day with the words "I could not write any longer to you last night. My spirits were oppressed and my head grew confused. I took a few drops of laudanum, possibly without necessity, and slept quietly."

The Berrys arrived in Paris on 15th October and after a visit to the National Assembly, ("such a set of shabby, ill dressed, strange looking people I hardly ever saw together. Our House of Commons is not half so bad"), they set out again, reaching Lyon on 22nd October and Turin by 2nd November. At this stage they had received no post from England, as it had been sent on a longer route through Germany to avoid the disturbances in France. A considerable amount of correspondence was due. HW had written on 12th October with regard to negotiations for the purchase of Little Strawberry Hill, for the Berrys' benefit, positioned on the edge of the garden at Strawberry Hill. This was the property that had belonged to the actress Kitty Clive and was familiarly known to Horace as Cliveden. By December he was able to write that he had formally secured it for them in their names.

On 13th October Horace wrote thanking Mary for her letter sent before boarding the trans-Channel boat, and telling her that he would inform Mrs D that "yr being summoned on board suddenly prevented yr writing to her." Horace was already getting competitive in his desire for Mary's letters and favours, and from now on seldom missed a chance to score points off Anne if he should receive a piece of information withheld from her. Equally he would be piqued by Anne's receipt of letters from Mary, and would feign lack of interest if she tried to read them to him. He would of course lose no time in reading to Anne correspondence addressed to him from Mary. He also expressed concern that the miniaturist painter, Miss Foldson, whom he had commissioned to paint the two sisters, had not yet produced the expected portraits. Her excuse had been that she was at Windsor, drawing the Queen and Princesses; as

Horace put it: "not the work of a moment". On 15th October Anne wrote to Mary telling her that her friend General O'Hara had been recalled; that he had no new command, and some questions to answer. Anne promised to try and ascertain further details from her brother-in-law, the Duke of Richmond.

On 30th October Anne wrote: "This day three weeks I was still with you, and still saw you not only in my mind's eye. When will that day come again?" Her own travel arrangements had been put in place: "my spirits are not equal to a winter in England." She had also made arrangements with her lawyer cousin, Lord John Campbell, instructing him in writing, in the strongest terms, to deal with any "abuse" during her absence. She had left him with sufficient money at his disposal, should it be needed, and told him that more would be available for any reasonable requirement. On Friday 3rd November, Anne wrote from London, shortly before departing for Portugal: "What I am, you know, and that you shall find me. You have received me with all my faults, and it shall be my first care, where it is possible, that you shall not suffer from them."

On 14th November, the Berrys arrived in Florence, where they did not stay long, moving on for the winter to better-priced and warmer accommodation in Pisa. The sisters had also expressed a wish to avoid the society of certain unnamed lady compatriots, who were wintering in Florence. The Berrys arrived in Pisa at around the same time that Anne, accompanied by her dog Fidele, sailed on the boat for Lisbon. Before departing she had enjoyed a family farewell supper at Richmond House with her parents, Horace, and the Richmonds.

Anne arrived in Portugal sometime in November 1790. She soon addressed a letter to Mary Berry in Pisa bemoaning the insolence and indifference of Portuguese workmen. "When I came, I found two panes of glass broken, and for five days, tho' the master of the house and mine own servants went twenty times a day after the people, I could not have them put in." She wished to see something of Portuguese life in Lisbon, not easy for a foreigner and a woman. However she was fortunate that the English Minister, Mr Walpole, was Horace's first cousin and therefore related to her by marriage. She was very soon invited to dinner, which took place in the late afternoon. Her fellow guests included a variety of English men and women, "of that sort no foreign town is free from, fat vulgar women, and scowling unknown men, consuls, and some of the Factory." The Factory in Lisbon was in fact not a factory at all: it was the headquarters of the English commercial community, including offices and warehouses for a variety of trades and undertakings, and was the centre from which cargoes were assembled and shipping instructions given. In the evening following the dinner Anne attended a *soirée* for the French Ambassadress (Madame de Chalons) and all the *Corps Diplomatique*.

At first Anne was unable to receive letters from Mary, as Horace had forgotten to give her a forwarding address. However on 16th December he wrote to Mary giving her

Anne's Lisbon contacts. "*Aux soins de Messieurs Mellish et de Visme à Lisbon,*" saying that he had already heard from her and that her voyage had been only seven days. It is doubtful whether Anne would have heard from Mary much before the New Year.

It did not take long for Anne to make further acquaintances. A social round was available, should she choose to make use of it. On Mondays it would be an evening visit to one of the Factory wives; on Wednesdays to the Portuguese house of the Marquis D'Abrantes; on Thursdays Mrs Walpole; on Fridays an assembly and ball in the long room; on Saturdays the French Ambassadress, and on Sundays the Opera or a Portuguese play. "The hours are early; sometimes they begin to make visits at five o'clock, and everything ends, at latest, unless it be some *fête*, by eleven." On one occasion she accompanied the Minister to a grand *fête* at a Portuguese house, given on the wedding of a great heiress, "who has married her uncle, as she could find no one great enough to marry" outside her own family. If Anne did take to the social round, in Lisbon, there is not much evidence of it from the letters that survive. These contain generalised descriptions of Portuguese lifestyle and places, rather than personal anecdotes with actual people.

For a lady of fashion, getting about in Lisbon would have been something of a problem. There were in general only two wheeled chaises, open to the elements in front, with only minimal weather protection from drawing leather curtains. These vehicles, pulled by two mules, nodded their way over rough pavements and up and down the steep hills upon which Lisbon stands. Though pretty good in daytime, chaises were difficult to "scramble up into … in rainy weather with a gauze petticoat and a dressed head." Anne was a tall woman, and her coiffure could have added another 12 inches to her height.

She lived simply in rented accommodation, spending most of her time in a small, whitewashed study. It had a sort of farmhouse chimney occupying one half of it, high, and formed with large rough stones; there were some shelves, two tables, and many chairs. Anne was surrounded by her books and much occupied in her "writing". Obviously this occupation would include a regular letter routine, though from time to time both Horace and Mary complained that her letters were not as frequent as they would have liked. Writing also included a new project: a novel. Anne would only produce one during her lifetime: *Belmour*, eventually published in 1801, was started here in the small whitewashed room. Writing was less physically demanding than sculpture, and so much easier to do whilst in transit. Pens and a supply of paper were easier companions than hammer and chisel, and she did not feel the transition too difficult: "My ideas are not at least outwardly frozen". If she was pregnant, this secluded existence would have been as she wished.

Anne was an observant commentator on the appearance, customs and habits of the citizens of Lisbon. She much admired the native costume of large cloaks worn very gracefully by both men and women. "They are eternally wrapped up in them, riding, walking, hanging over a balcony, when the sun shines…. I like to see them, as I have, sitting cross-legged in numbers in the churches, with their nets and their fine hair combed partly over their faces, and the men, with their cloaks thrown gracefully over their shoulders, leaning against the walls, or standing by them. Coming to Portugal is really instructive to one who sees things with the eye of an artist or an observer." Anne found the Portuguese way of life very much behind the standards of the rest of Europe. Women in particular were treated in a way that echoed the past Moorish occupation. "To this day the ladies of the *vieille cour* plump down on the floor and sit with their legs crossed without a chair in their rooms. I saw a woman of the first rank, who from misfortune did not choose to appear among the company, sitting in deep mourning on the floor, just within the door of the next room with the maids," and she noted that the custom was for the Portuguese "to live quite shut up with their own families, and the women separately from the men, even near relations must not go into their rooms, nor speak to them."

In the great houses of the capital, there were large retinues of maids and attendants, "like retainers bred in the families from father to son", with whom the proprietor's family sat and played. Here there was no shortage of food: "Cold fowls and hams in the morning, not forgetting the *mirenda* in the evening, which with the addition of dinner and supper, helps to make the day pass." All the young ladies grew fat in their early twenties, and seemed good-natured, if idle: "a state to which they seem to have a great propensity, by what I hear and by the little I have seen." Having delivered this verdict, a *sine qua non* of any English man or woman abroad in the 18th century, Anne went on to say that she disapproved of the manner in which the Portuguese attempted to ape the manners of other nations "I wish they had not begun to improve, they would be much more entertaining…. I would have nations polish, but I wish the polish could be given to their own national customs and manners, and not the manners of other nations always attempted."

As an 18th century tourist guide, Anne's description of Lisbon's sights lacks substance. She admired a giant aqueduct and a colossal bronze statue of King Joseph I; otherwise her verdict was that "though there are not many things to see at Lisbon, there are some … some respectable Gothic churches in particular … which will bear seeing more than once". The Lisbon earthquake of 1755 had left a terrible footprint. One of the oldest churches was totally ruined, with nothing but its outer walls still standing, and the Castle, formerly a Moorish Palace, was practically destroyed: "Here and there a bit of column etc stuck in little better than a mud wall." The Queen had put her rebuilding energies into a new church, called the Convento Nuevo, or the Coracao de Jesu (the Heart of Jesus), in the worst taste, adorned by many colossal statues "in the style of Bernini exaggerated."

At the end of January Horace wrote to Mary: "I wonder you have not heard oftener from Lisbon. She seems perfectly well, and to have settled her return, which is to be through Spain: after the 20th February our letters are to be directed to Madrid. She is in great distress, and I heartily pity her, about Fidele, which seems dying." The death had actually taken place on 2nd January. On that day she wrote to Mary: "You do not know how much I am grieved. I have lost my poor dog. I know that you will feel for me." The following day she was still miserable: "When I am by myself, I do nothing but cry." She gave some details of Fidele's last hours. She had tried to save her by administering James's powders, usually prescribed for human beings. Anne and her maid had spent the time with the patient, in Anne's bedroom, taking it in turns to sleep and to care for Fidele, but all to no avail.

After consideration Anne had decided to follow Mary's advice, from experience with a favourite cat, to cremate the corpse and retain the ashes. It was arranged that the cremation would take place shortly after dark in a small field nearby. Anne's servant and the owner of the lodging house had gone out, lit the fire, and commenced the cremation when they were surrounded by 30 armed guards. At first they had claimed they were burning some old clothes belonging to Anne, but eventually they told them the real cause of the blaze. The guards had been satisfied by the provision of beer from the house and departed, bearing with them the unused logs from the fire. The ashes were returned to Anne, who was to retain them until her own death in 1828, when they would be buried with her.

This distressing incident had its effect on Anne, and an echo of it appears in her novel *Belmour*, where the friar, whom the hero meets in Portugal, reveals that the small cenotaph in memory of his dead sweetheart Rosaura, before which he daily prays, is in the shape of an urn. "Death here," said he to himself, "has surely been accompanied by some unusually aggravating circumstance."

If there were ever any truth in the theory of an unwanted pregnancy, the reality could have been a horror more than worthy of a Gothic novel. Was the death of Fidele, as described to Mary, a coded message which only she would understand? Did it actually mean that the baby had been stillborn, that the cremation had not been that of a dog, and that the ashes which Anne carried to her grave were those of her dead baby? Cremation was not approved of by the Catholic Church. The penalty could be death, and the visit of the guards might have had fatal consequences.

Anne's one real complaint about Lisbon was the cold. "Everyone complains, and no one attempts a remedy." To walk in the sunshine was pleasant, but it was impossible to go out and be certain of walking back to the warmth of a welcoming fire. The houses were cold, the Atlantic sea breezes damp, and open hearths and roaring flames were non-existent. It was no consolation that inland the roads would have been impassable and the weather even colder. Anne was stuck with Lisbon for the winter. However spring comes early in Iberia, and on 17th February, she was able to write to Mary that "my mules are on the road, and will be ready on Monday next, and that evening or Tuesday I shall probably cross the water and begin my journey, and from the time I leave Lisbon, till I arrive at Madrid, I shall not have a single letter."

Before she left Lisbon Anne may have had an unexpected visit from an old friend of the family. General O'Hara, was *en route* to England from Gibraltar, where he was Commandant. According to HW he had persuaded the captain of *The Assistance*, Lord Cranstoun, to anchor at Lisbon, so that he could meet up again with Anne. However there is no mention in Anne's correspondence with Mary of an actual meeting taking place. His ship left Lisbon on 31st January 1791, docking in England on the 12th February. News of O'Hara's arrival was relayed to Mary by HW on 18th February with the observation that "you will love him better than ever."

Around the same time Anne received a letter from Jerningham saying that Horace was unwell. She wrote to Mary, hoping fervently that the Berrys would agree to return to England in the autumn of 1791: "The thoughts of that will support him. If you can, I know that you will." She went on to outline her intended journey to Seville and Granada, and thence to Cordova and Toledo, the Escurial and St Ildefonso. She ended by congratulating Mary on keeping up with her Latin. "How very few ever read the books most worth reading, except at an age when they are not capable of receiving any real satisfaction from them. Many construe Homer, Virgil, Plato and Cicero, but few read them. With your taste, this will be a constant source to you."

Anne set off around 21st February 1791. On the first night she stopped at sunset at a small village on the coast. "The inn being bad, I was recommended to a private house. No house ever deserved the epithet less, for my own room was full, from the moment I came till I got away, of the whole family, the *padrone* (a little shop-keeper), the *padrona de casa*, all the children, and all the maids, talking to me, staring at me, or kissing my hand. As I turned them out of their room, and everything they wanted was in that room, even when they would consent to leave me there was every instant something to be fetched out of a drawer, or a closet."

The following day, riding in a carriage drawn by seven mules, she traversed a large sandy plain, "sometimes through woods of the most beautiful pines, always shrubs and plants that only really grow in fine climates. I am now settled in a room where (to be sure) there is not much furniture; but I think rather upon the whole better than one often finds in Italy."

By the end of February Anne arrived at the Portuguese border at the frontier town of Elvas. Because there was a customs post through which she would have to pass, she had been given a letter to the Governor, "that my baggage might not be stopped." The Governor was a brother of "old Mello's". He had been a friend of Harry's in England, and had written to announce Anne's imminent arrival. For Anne, who was travelling

alone and enjoying the solitude and peace, there was to be a rude awakening. The
Governor had ordered that this distinguished traveller should be "received with the
honours of war." She was escorted into the city by a guard of thirty horsemen with
drums beating, trumpets sounding, and cannon firing. Anne "was dragged to the
Governor's house instead of going quietly to my inn, and sat down almost
instantaneously to a great dinner with a dozen or fourteen officers." The whole
company then set out to see the sights of the town, and Anne had to extricate herself
with great difficulty by insisting that, "what was too true", she was quite exhausted.

On the following day, 1st March, she arrived at Badajoz, the first town over the
border. She compared it unfavourably with Elvas, which had been pretty, neat and tidy.
Its Spanish counterpart was a dismal place, its walls neglected and the Moorish
fortifications in ruins. Its only redeeming feature was a fine Roman bridge of twenty-
nine arches over the Guadiana. "I wonder this does not make the Spaniards a little
ashamed of this place, for these two towns are looking at each other, and not above
eight or nine miles distant."

By 6th March Anne had reached Seville. Her journey had not been without incident,
and she was feeling extremely tired. "The real truth is, that I did not know the roads
were impassable for a carriage with four wheels." However they had made it with the
help of the *calessiere,* "the best driver, without exception, I ever saw", who drove with
a mixture of Spanish dexterity, and, with regard to the carriage, English care. Their
journey had taken them through the Sierra Morena (part of the present day
Extremadura), a wild tract of untamed landscape. Anne had seen some of the most
beautiful wild scenery imaginable. The mountains were not very high, but strewn with
rocks interspersed with native shrubs, heathers, and wildflowers, in the first flush of
spring flower and growth. Clear streams rolled among the rocks and stones. At lower
levels forests of the evergreen ilex and of untended cork oaks provided contrasts of light
and shade. "It gives one the idea of an eternal spring." Much of it had to be seen on foot,
and Anne found that her walking pace could just about keep up with the mules. There
she was, a forty-two-year-old lone Englishwoman, of uncertain health and with a poor
grasp of Spanish, tackling some of the roughest terrain in Spain, and probably in
unsuitable shoes; Anne was certainly no wimp. She had enjoyed it. "If there are
moments in my life when I breathe freely, without the oppression of painful reflections
– when the world seems nothing to me, and the idea of those I love everything – it is in
walks when I can undisturbed enjoy what is grand, beautiful, and awful in nature." As
she ruefully reflected, it was her own choice: "*Tu l'as voulu, Georges Dandin.*"
(Georges Dandin was the Molière husband who had married a more upmarket wife and
never ceased to regret it: "you brought it on yourself, Georges Dandin.")

On her first day at Seville Anne went out to walk dressed in the Portuguese fashion
and bare headed. She was immediately mobbed by the local children who followed her

chanting *'francese'*, which, despite her liking for all things French, she found infuriating. To ensure no repetition she was forced from then on, when going out, to wear "one of their vile *mantillas*, a piece of silk or linen thrown over the head and then crossed and twisted round the waist, and let to hang down". She noted that in Spain no woman could go into a church or walk about a town without a *mantilla*. She found it a particularly frustrating garment, restricting vision to either side. Nor could she look upwards without immediately been identified as a foreigner: Spanish ladies apparently kept their eyes cast down. Once identified, a foreign lady became a matter of great interest to the locals who "follow you, get before you, pursue and persecute you in a manner that far exceeds anything of the sort that I have ever seen in any other country".

To recover from the ardours of the Sierra Morena, Anne stayed in Seville a day longer than she had intended. She considered the city to be charming and the climate mild. As a true pupil of Horace, she appreciated the simple Gothic gloom of the Cathedral, from which she could look outwards through magnificent painted glass windows. She was also pleased with the Alcàzar, and especially with the Moorish section of it. She was less pleased with Mr Swinburne, whose *Travels through Spain*, published in 1775 and illustrated from drawings on the spot by the author, had been a major factor in her choice of itinerary. Anne found that Granada and the Alhambra bore little resemblance to the book's description. Though still marvellous, they were in a ruinous condition. From Swinburne's description she had expected "that I was to have seen a great part of it as if the Moorish kings and their queens had, hand in hand, just walked out of their palace." She might have reflected that the author had visited more than 20 years before, and that ants and other natural causes lead to swift deterioration. She also found that the climate of Granada was cooler than Seville, "with a sharpness in the air to which I am always sensible." She attributed this to the closeness of the Sierra Nevada mountain range, from which the snow never departed.

By this stage of her journey the roads had much improved, but if she was hoping for a more restful time she was to be disappointed, for she found the Spanish very noisy at night. On one occasion, after she gone to bed hoping for a quiet night's sleep, "the Corregidor de Granada, his wife, I know not how many *signoras*, and a dozen servants, as many little dogs with bells, and four or five carriages", arrived in time for their supper. "The talking, screaming and scolding was beyond imagination." The next morning, after a restless night, Anne descended the stairs to go to her carriage, only to find the Corregidor and his wife waiting at the door and expecting her to "make them a compliment, hope that they had slept well, and wish them a good journey," which she did as well as her command of the language would allow her. She noted that everybody in Spain from the highest to the lowest expected to be spoken to; a polite bow which might have been acceptable in England, here was not enough. Anne, perhaps surprisingly for someone who professed shyness, found these greetings appealing. She liked to hear them "say to me, *Condios*, which I translate, God bless you; and then they seem so pleased" when she replied.

Not only did Anne find the customs of the Spanish appealing, she was also drawn to their appearance, or at any rate to that of the men who were "uncommonly genteel" and good-looking with their Montero caps and cloaks. She was less complimentary about the women remarking only that they wore a black or white piece of silk over their heads, "much as they do at Venice".

Anne, her carriage, mules and driver left Granada on 17th March, heading north by way of Cordoba, and made for Madrid. They arrived at Aranjuez, a day's journey from their destination, on 29th March. This part of their travels had been unremarkable; dragging the coach along a road sometimes hewn out of the rock, sometimes sandy, and at other times stony. In the last four days, travelling through La Mancha, the country was particularly "odious", with vast dusty treeless plains. Aranjuez was something of a relief; in the neglected gardens of the palace Anne discovered a number of charming antique statues; one that especially caught her attention was a small Etruscan bronze figure positioned in the middle of a marble water basin. The subject was not unusual, a boy taking a thorn out of his foot, but the modelling was better than she had seen anywhere else. In another basin was a statue of Venus, whilst another contained a fountain of Apollo. Sadly, here as elsewhere in Spain, there was nobody to give any information to the passing traveller; as a tourist, she had to fend for herself.

By 1st April she had arrived in Madrid and collected the letters that were awaiting her, mainly from Mary, but also one from Horace, written in his own hand and not dictated to his faithful secretary, Thomas Kirgate. This gave her a measure of relief that his health must have improved. A letter from Mary had also arrived, praising a picture by Andrea, to which Anne replied agreeing with Mary's assessment. At the same time she advised her to read the letters on friendship from Cicero to Atticus. It may also have been here that she received a later letter with worrying news from Mary: she had fallen down a bank near Pisa and sustained a deep cut on her nose (which would eventually scar her for life). The stay in Madrid extended above a week; she was visited by the English Minister to Madrid, Lord St Helens, and by the British Consul. She found the *ton* of the society in the capital to be "very grateful to my ears: this perhaps struck me the more as (to you I may say it) there was scarcely anything where I passed the winter that had not a tinge of vulgarity or barbarism."

By 10th April she had moved on to the Escurial, which at that time was a monastery, full of good pictures. On 16th April she had reached Valladolid, having visited *en route* the royal summer palace at St Ildefonso, close to Segovia, where she appreciated the extent of statuary in the garden, and the whole ambience of an "enchanted castle". By this time she was getting weary of her travels: "I am really now tired of seeing, which I cannot help doing with attention, and should to the last, and tired of travelling: I wish for quiet." Also she was missing Mary: "Had you crossed Spain in my carriage you would have been pleased, and I do believe have thought little of inconveniences: I think I could make such a journey with you…"

From Valladolid Anne travelled to Burgos, and then on to Vittoria, eventually entering France at Bayonne on 24th April. She had perfected her own method of entering Spanish monasteries: at Valladolid she had got into a Dominican monastery, whose Gothic architecture she had admired, by the simple expedient of smiling. However at Burgos she took greater precautions. She entered the Cathedral cloisters "in Lady Spencer's fashion", avoiding writing her name in the visitor's book and dressed in a large cloak and boots, to which "the bench of bishops could not object". She passed unnoticed, and talked of "the ring of Gyges, which, if I mistake not, made the wearer invisible".

Burgos Cathedral she found particularly impressive and, to a sculptor, educational. The Gothic stonework was carved with particular sharpness and spirit, in particular two heads and a very large quantity of foliage. "Many things in the carvings in wood, and in stone, that one sees in all old Gothic, are incomprehensibly strange and impossible to describe."

Anne was anxious also to see something of revolutionary France. The Berrys had written with their impressions whilst travelling through the country in the previous autumn, and Anne wished to compare notes. Her first experience of the new régime was at Bayonne.

"I was interrupted by the most ridiculous personage that can be imagined, a sort of Ragotin in figure, round, fat, with the tightest silk dress, not a tooth, a mouth that went every way, and the voice of a frog. '*Madame, je suis le banquier, je m'appelle de Broc, Maire de la ville*'. *Maire de la ville* and *Ipse Rex*, for without this creature I could neither have money, passport, horses, nor permission to go out of the town. I saw how it was, from his manner of announcing himself, and immediately knew beforehand all his power and consequence. Before the visit was over we were such friends that he gave me some of his verses on C Fox, and if there is a corner in this letter, I must send them to you, for I was delighted and desired to have them:

> *A L'ORATEUR FOX*
> *Tel qu'un aérostat occupant l'horizon*
> *Fox occupe au Sénat la barre de Polymnée;*
> *L'un captive le feu, dans le char de Uranie*
> *Et l'autre le reprend dans la belle oraison.*

My little Ragotin I cannot think of without an inclination to laugh. Among other things he told me that he had some very fine tea, some of which he should send me; then looking up, and considering a moment, quite gravely added, '*Mais du ponche je n'en ai pas, je ne sais pas comment nous ferons*'. I assured him that I never drank punch, and was remarkably fond of tea, which, however, luckily he never sent, nor a national cockade which he offered. In the evening he returned, and brought one of his clerks to read the gazette to me, who read through his nose in the most ridiculous manner and he kept screaming at him '*Plus haut, monsieur, plus haut*'. Quite a mistake I thought."

Anne's attentions to the mayor secured her a speedy pass towards Paris. On 24th April she reached Bordeaux, where she found everything quiet. She arrived in Paris on Tuesday 3rd May to find correspondence awaiting her from both Mary and Horace. Letters from Mary describing her recovery from the deep gash on her nose brought relief; these were echoed by Horace: "Even the scar on the sweetest of all earthly noses (I never saw the houris) will scarce be discernible by the 1st November, by which day they have vowed their return."

She lost no time in getting out and about, and found things essentially quiet. Effigies of the Pope had been burnt by the mob two days previously, and the Spanish ambassador, passing by, desired to make a contribution towards the conflagration, "which he generously did and passed on." Anne called on Mme de Balbi, a friend from previous visits and, as mistress of the Comte De Provence, later to become Louis XVIII, a source of useful contacts. Anne found her busy, surrounded by the world, *à sa toilette*, and extracted from her a promise to take Anne to the National Assembly the following day. She thought Paris much as usual; people could move about freely without harm at any hour of the day or night. Though she admitted that many people were leaving, or had already left the city, Anne could see nothing for foreigners to fear. A short while later she would have a rude awakening. She was sitting with her letters in her room, in an undressed state, attended by her hairdresser, when she was alerted by a loud and violent altercation outside. Her maid rushed in, in a state of alarm, blurting out that *les Poissardes*, that notorious sisterhood of Parisian fishwives, were at the door and insisting on entering. Indeed they had bought a bouquet to present to Anne. Her hairdresser confirmed that financial recompense would be required in return for the bouquet, and so Anne went straight out of her room to meet them, reasoning that it would be easier afterwards to retreat into that room than to have to get the fishwives to leave it. She admitted to feeling "much discomposed; however I thought, I must put on a good face upon the occasion." She gave them six francs, which they immediately asked her to double. She paid up and headed for a successful retreat; however the ladies had still not finished. One of them proposed to embrace her, which she did not dare refuse; fortunately the other six or seven in the room did not follow suit, and nor did the large number in the court below. Apparently this behaviour was commonplace; the fishwives went wherever they pleased and neither porters nor servants dared stop them, dreading the fury of the fishwives rather more than the blade of the guillotine. Anne had actually been quite fortunate, for a short time before around forty fishwives had visited the King and Queen, seeking assurances that they were not about to leave Paris, and on having been assured of this, had all insisted on embracing both monarchs.

That evening Mme de Balbi escorted Anne to the National Assembly, which she found very much as described to her by Mary Berry the previous autumn. Anne accepted an invitation to return to dinner, following which a man whom Anne recognised as the Comte de Provence, but who was not introduced, came into the room. He was obliging and gentle, and Anne was overwhelmed with sadness at the thought that the Parisian society which she knew and loved had changed so much. She had found that almost all her friends had departed, and that if Paris was as full as ever, it was not with those that she had come to know and like on previous visits. While Mme de Balbi's *appartement* reflected the perfection of taste of the Paris that Anne had known, a solitary drive afterwards past the ruins of the Bastille gave her cause for very different reflection. The French cry of *"Liberté!"* of 1789, so enthusiastically espoused by Charles Fox and his followers, Anne not least among them, had already a very different meaning. She would be glad to get home.

Even in the 18th century tourism had its travel problems, caused by the intransigence of the transporters. On the road to Boulogne, Anne had heard that there was a dispute between the English and French captains of the packets, and that no sailings were taking place. She therefore went on to Calais, and after a day's waiting secured passage, eventually arriving in London between 10 and 11pm on the night of Thursday, 12th May 1791. She went first to her father's house, where she expected to find them either at home or shortly returning for supper. She let her thoughts wander and dreamt that perhaps she might find "dear Mr Walpole alone, sitting by the fire, as I often have, waiting their arrival". She was greeted by her mother's maid, who emerged to say that the house was empty, that the whole family had gone to her uncle Lord Frederick Campbell's for the evening, and that their carriage had been ordered to take them home at midnight. Anne still felt that she had to see them, and being "in a state when no fatigue is felt", ordered the coachman to drive on to her uncle's home in Arlington Street, where, outside the house, she found many coaches waiting, and a party in full swing. This was not the homecoming she had planned; whilst in a quandary as to whether to go in or turn around and go home, her mind was made up for her by her servant who, unbidden, knocked on the door. Her aunt came down immediately, followed by her parents; Anne flew from her carriage to embrace them. At the top of the stairs Horace was waiting, seemingly as well as ever, "not thinner, less lively, or less all that you left him, or all that you can wish – so at least he appeared to me last night".

Horace himself recorded Anne's arrival in a similar vein, though he claimed to have descended at least some of the stairs: "Last night we were at Lady Fred.

Campbell's – the usual cribbage party, Conways, Mount Edgecumbes, Johnstones. At past ten Mrs Damer was announced! Her parents ran down into the hall, and I scrambled down some of the stairs. She looks vastly well, was in great spirits, and not at all fatigued, though she came from Dover, had been twelve hours at sea from Calais, and had rested but four days at Paris from Madrid. We supped and stayed till one o'clock; and I shall go to her as soon as I am dressed. Madrid and the Escurial, she owns, have gained her a proselyte to painting, which her statuarism had totally engrossed – in her no wonder. Of Titian she had no idea, nor have I a just one, though great faith, as at Venice all his works are now coal-black; but Rubens, she says, amazed her, and that in Spain he has even grace."

Travelling solo, she had braved winter in Lisbon, the toughest of journeys through Portugal and Spain, and finished with the fishwives of revolutionary France. She had recorded a courageous journey with accuracy, wit, and genuine interest to the reader, who must be thankful to Mary Berry that she did save Anne's letters, even if on a selective basis. The balance of probability is that the "sad reason" for the journey was to separate herself from Mary and the lesbian rumour factory, and that the baby for which she had set out and with which she had returned was her novel, *Belmour,* mewling and puking in its infancy. The ashes in the casket were indeed the mortal remains of Fidele.

Chapter 12

LETTERS TO AND FROM ITALY
AND LIFE IN ENGLAND

Anne returned to England in May 1791. It was to be another six months before the Berrys did likewise. Their correspondence with Horace continued as before, with weekly letters, and many of his are preserved, although none of Mary's. With Anne, now back at home and a reasonably certain recipient, the flow of letters between herself and Mary was probably greater than whilst Anne was travelling. As previously noted, some of Anne's letters to Mary remain, saved by the latter, but only extracts of Mary's letters to Anne, meticulously copied in the first volume of *Anne's Notebooks*. Sadly there are no records at all of the correspondence between Horace and Anne. In addition Mary kept a detailed journal of her family's travels, describing the places visited and the people they had met. As a travel correspondent she was much more meticulous than Anne, though her narrative lacks the latter's talent for anecdotes.

The frustrations of this three-way correspondence were summed up by Horace. Writing on 31st March 1791, he says: "I feel every week the disagreeableness of the distance between us: each letter is generally three weeks on its passage, and we receive answers to what one must often forget one has said; and cannot under six weeks learn what one is anxious to know. Balloons, had they succeeded, would have prodigiously abridged delays." The general tenor of Horace's correspondence was to the effect that he greatly missed both sisters, that he was constantly worried by the dangers of travel, especially in revolutionary Europe, and that he was old and sick and wished them to return at the earliest opportunity. He was particularly concerned by a letter from Anne suggesting that the Berrys were planning to stay on the continent until spring 1792, some eighteen months after they had set out. His remonstrances did produce an assurance of a return in autumn 1791, which went some way to satisfy him and produced a typically-phrased response: "It wounds my heart, as I find I have hurt two of the persons I love the best upon earth ... The truth, as you may have perceived, tho' no excuse, was that I had thought myself dying and should never see you more; that I was extremely weak and low when Mrs. D.'s letter arrived, and mentioned her supposing I should not see you till spring twelvemonth ... I thought it unfriendly to let me learn from others what interested me so deeply. Yet I do not in the least excuse my conduct. No, I condemn it in every light, and shall never forgive myself if you do not promise me to be guided entirely by your own convenience and inclinations about your return." This apology continued for two full pages, and was followed the next week by another in similar vein. However Horace had made his point: he had provided Little Strawberry Hill for the Berrys' return, and he expected to welcome them there.

The Berrys had originally left England in October 1790, travelling via France to Italy, arriving in Turin on 1st November after an uneventful passage. Here they collected their first consignment of letters, including several from Horace. By Sunday 14th November they had arrived in Florence, going on to spend the winter in the warmer climate of Pisa and arriving there on 11th December. A torrent of correspondence from Horace awaited them, or arrived after them, at their various destinations, largely complaining about the slowness of the post, blaming the revolutionary French for holding it up, and imploring the family to return to England at the earliest possible moment, avoiding travel through France. In January 1791 Horace wrote complaining about the gout in his hand and rheumatism in his arm and shoulder. By the end of the month the body had improved but the spirits were low, as the rollercoaster of the date of the Berrys' return had caused them to take a dive after Anne's news that this was likely to be in spring 1792. A denial of this rapidly improved his spirits.

It was in March 1791 that Mary suffered her unfortunate accident; falling down a steep bank in the vicinity of Pisa and suffering a deep cut on her nose. Horace only heard the news on 3rd April: "How I hate a party of pleasure! It never turns out well; fools fall out, and sensible people fall down!" He had lost no time in conveying news of the fall to their friends: "My sad news seemed like throwing a bomb into the room. You would have been flattered at the grief it occasioned; there were Mrs Lockhart, the Pepys's, Mrs Buller, Lady Herries......and some who scarce know you, who yet found they wd be very unfashionable if they did not join in the concern for you and in yr panegyric...".

A fortnight later Horace wrote to both sisters, jokingly rebuking Agnes for lack of attention to her drawing, but at the same time praising her painting of the *Death of Wolsey*, and reminding her that it was due to be hung in the Little Parlour at Strawberry Hill, where it would join Lady Di Beauclerk's picture of gypsies and Anne's sculpture of dogs. He finished with a typical flourish: "I defy your favourite Italy to produce three such monuments of female genius."

Writing on the 4th May, Horace recorded, besides the usual tittle tattle, that Harry had had a lucky escape. He had been supervising a practice review of his regiment, the Blues, prior to a review by the King. His horse had slipped, fallen and rolled on him, bruising his arm and leg. The bruising had swelled, causing him to miss the Royal review. In the same letter Horace reported on the excesses of the Parisian mob, and worried that Tom Paine, an American, was trying to fan the flames of revolution in England. A week later, in the letter announcing Anne's return, Horace added that her father's fall had now been diagnosed by Doctor Hunter as a broken collarbone, and that his arm was in a sling.

Anne had returned to England bringing with her the unfinished copy of her novel *Belmour*, and either a sheaf of letters from Mary, or the first volume of her *Notebooks*, into which she would already have copied excerpts from those letters. These notebooks paint a picture of a passionate relationship, certainly on Mary Berry's part: "Indeed my letters deceive you horribly if they do not <u>all</u> seem written from my heart, aye from my heart of hearts". It is a relationship that develops in print, though slowly, owing in large part to the restraints imposed by long periods between receiving and replying to correspondence. At the outset, Mary appears somewhat nervous, and feeling her way. Before they left England she was writing "Thank heavens we seem now to understand one another; you enter, I think, into my ideas and feelings, and I begin now to write to you with real confidence in your character and real comfort to myself". However she was still nervous of making a mistake: "I can procure you so few satisfactions I would not for the world be the means of depriving you of any", and again: "I have no reason upon Earth for not wishing to see you, and a thousand for being always desirous of your company – if one silly word therefore said I hardly know why, should prevent your coming and derange your plan, I shall have a new reason for being thoroughly out of humour with myself".

As the correspondence progressed, so Mary's confidence grew, and she was able to write: "Your absence and our correspondence have had exactly the effect I supposed – it has given the degree of knowledge of, and confidence in, your character, which in the circumstances we stand, I might have been years in acquiring, and instead of being estranged in any degree, I shall meet you feeling ten times more intimate with you than when we parted".

At the start of the correspondence Mary asked Anne to tell her everything about herself and to take her entirely into her confidence: "Be well assured that if <u>you</u> have a 'satisfaction in keeping nothing from me', <u>I</u> have a still greater in hearing every thing that either does, or ever has concerned you". Anne, as we have seen, had experienced something in her past of which she had been ashamed, and which seems to have been the basis of the abuse she had suffered. During the correspondence the details of this misdemeanour seem to have been revealed to Mary, but to no one else: "You desire me not to forget my promise of <u>suspending my judgement</u>. I know not upon what particular subject that promise was made and I have certainly broke it already, for I can be in no <u>suspense</u> about anybody who I think of, write to, and esteem as I do you … we are no longer new acquaintances … I have already given you such convincing proofs that I cannot now entertain doubts or suspense without supposing myself the most imprudent and you the most deceitful of human beings … and we're neither the one nor the other … the more I know of your <u>character</u> the more I love, esteem, and admire it, but it never <u>has</u>, never <u>will</u>, alter my <u>opinion</u> (tho' it has totally changed my sentiments) with respect to your <u>conduct</u> … I trust I shall ever therefore think of you as I do now."

Mary seems to have been prepared to forgive and forget, because of her confidence in Anne's essential goodness, honour, and strength of character. Anne, for her part, seems to have doubted whether this would ever be possible. Both writer and reader agreed that the harsh verdict of an unfeeling world on what had gone before was vile and unmerited, but would not affect their relationship: "As a correspondent you have taken me for better for worse".

Mary was confident in writing, and enjoyed it: "To you I shall write as often as possible because the unrestrained confidence with which I feel sure I may express myself to you makes it a real pleasure to me". She expected replies: "And let me hear from you always as often as you possibly can, it will be but too seldom". She found it easier to marshal her thoughts on paper than in face-to-face encounters. She wrote to Anne: "My heart was so oppressed, and my head so confused… when I last saw you, that I know not what I said … I know what I <u>meant</u> to say was not condemning you, or likely to give you any uneasiness"; and again: "My letters, too, unlike those of the generality of the world, give a much more faithful picture of myself than my conversation; in the last I am often so ridiculously confused, embarrassed and agitated, that I am sure I must often be terribly misunderstood, while my letters express much more clearly, and consequently more exactly, my real feelings and sentiments". In this judgment Mary was undoubtedly correct; the heat of the moment in a face-to-face encounter, especially between lovers, will often result in pain as well as pleasure; the following quotation is just one of several where the previous evening's meeting had not gone as smoothly as might be wished: "The faults and errors of those one loves or has loved must ever give one most melancholy feelings and in this respect only, I hope, you felt yourself agitated last night. With respect to me you need not have a regret." Letters from abroad, which might take six weeks from writing to receiving a reply, gave tempers more time to cool and provided the opportunity for a more measured response.

Through the long litany of Mary's opinions, the melancholic side of her character predominates. Whereas Agnes is gay and fun loving, Mary is more serious, weighed down by the cares of the world and by poor health, whether of herself, Horace, Anne or Agnes. Melancholy, especially when shared with kindred spirits, was very much in vogue with *le ton*. Horace extolled the gloomth of Strawberry Hill; Belmour, the hero of Anne's novel, is always full of melancholy thoughts. It is true that the human spirit can be as easily plunged to deeper levels of awareness by melancholy, as it can be lifted to more exalted feelings by joy. Mary refers to her 'Blue Devils' of depression, but it was a state for discussion and reflection, rather than for the medication of today. "I set out enduring a sort of calm melancholy with which such a scene always inspires me till it was quite dark." This was a melancholy to be savoured and appreciated. Anne too found inspiration in melancholy and, in all probability, this shared bond, so different from the "Insipids" who in Mary's eyes made up the greater part of society, was one of the main constituents drawing them together.

Of the other items referred to in the first hundred pages of *Anne's Notebooks*, it is worth recording that Mary had been delighted that the newly-returned Anne had met up with her old friend, Mrs Cholmeley, and that this had been a success. Mary had also requested Anne to model a self-portrait in wax as a coming home present for her.

Mary had promised Horace that she would be back in England at Little Strawberry Hill by the autumn of 1791, and she stuck to her promise. She told Anne that her health and spirits required communication with kindred minds, "to enable me to get on with the rest of the world." These she could only find in England, and whether it was Anne, or Horace, or her friend Mrs Cholmeley, or possibly even General O'Hara, she looked forward to returning. Typically she listed the downsides of return: change of scene and climate, a less easy life and "a thousand other plagues", but had convinced herself that being with those she really loved was all that mattered. Agnes saw matters in a different light. She liked the Italian climate and her health had improved under Italian suns. She enjoyed the gaiety of life in Pisa and dreaded the return to England. Mr Berry's views were not recorded, and in the event, as usual, both he and Agnes did as they were told. The family left Pisa on the 18th April 1791, *en route* to Florence, where they remained until September. Their return journey took them to Venice, thence through Austria and Switzerland, arriving in revolutionary France on 24th October, and in Paris on the 28th. After a brief stay, they departed on 7th November, eventually arriving in North Audley St on 11th November.

During the summer and autumn of 1791, whilst the Berry family were slowly making their way back to England, Louis XVI, Marie Antoinette, and their family, attempting to escape from Paris, had been discovered at Varennes, and brought back under guard. At the same time, as part of government policy dedicated to *egalité* and humanitarianism, a new form of execution, suitable for all, was being devised. Previously decapitation had been reserved only for the nobility, now it was to be available to everybody. During 1791 Tobias Schmidt, an engineer and harpsichord maker, designed the guillotine. Across the Channel, England remained peacefully unchanged. Anne had returned to an unruffled mix of sculpture and socialising with family and friends, whilst keeping up a ceaseless correspondence with Mary, mixing gossip with endearments and frustrations, real or imagined.

Her first letter from England to Mary, dated 16th May, complained that she was "teased and tired to death with the number of persons coming to see me." She found it difficult to accept the combination of her public popularity, of people queuing to see her sculpting on her scaffold, with the private "abuse" which accompanied it. On 14th May 1791 she went with her mother to the Pantheon Opera. No sooner had she got to her box, than she saw, close to her right shoulder, Mrs Cholmeley, the great friend and confidante of Mary Berry. "In an instant a thousand ideas crowded into my mind, or rather one, sufficient to occupy both my head and my heart. I cannot express the feeling this gave me. My teeth, I assure you, were but auxiliaries." The two had immediately begun talking of Mary, worrying about the scar on her nose. The conversation turned to HW, and Mrs Cholmeley said that Mary had suggested that she visit him and introduce herself, but that she had felt too shy. Anne had agreed to bring Horace to meet Mrs Cholmeley. But before that Anne was to take Horace to dine with her mother and the "charming man", Edward Jerningham. The latter had apologised to Anne that no sooner had she got home than he was leaving London for a fortnight. She had also seen Livie, her classics tutor, anxious to restart her Greek lessons; "when or if at all constantly he will come to me, I know not. I shall go out of the world without knowing it, I fear. … I rather lose ground, and what is worse spirit."

On 24th May Anne, in order to write "particularly" of what "I am sure you like to know", stopped her sculpture early at 11am, and went to see Horace. She found him concerned by news of a letter from Agnes saying that Mary was not in the best of health. Anne went on to complain about the weather and the vagaries of the post, and ended the letter: "You will perhaps one day thoroughly know me, but it will be a day too late. Do not think I doubt your kindness, or your opinion of me, without which that kindness could not exist."

Three days later Anne apologized for her last letter: "I was not in spirits when I ended my letter to you last. … When I complain, it refers to anything on earth but yourself". She had been impressed by Mrs Cholmeley's common sense and intended to take her up on an offer to "come and sit with me" at home one evening. She was now concentrating on her sculpture, working most mornings and sometimes, during the long hours of daylight, in the evening. The initial stream of visitors had somewhat diminished. She wrote to Mary: "I did not tell you that the first thing I saw when I flew into my rooms on my arrival, was the Muff I had so much regretted." She had found her study relatively undisturbed; only one small terracotta figure was broken, of which she had collected most of the pieces.

On 31st May Anne replied to a letter from Mary written on the 17th and received the previous day. She had been out early to view a selection of Richard Cosway's paintings, which he was selling, and afterwards had gone to Berkeley Square armed with Mary's letter, which she had intended to read to Horace. She had found him in a great tizzy, claiming that he had to be away to Caroline's before the crowd got there. Anne remarked that though Horace was only too keen to read Mary's letters to him, or to read them aloud to whoever cared to listen, he showed a marked indifference to hearing Mary's letters to others read to him. Mrs Cholmeley had undergone a similar experience. She said that he "despised her intelligence, and with all the insolence of a lover, boasted of three letters which he had himself received".

Anne congratulated Mary on her perception of Cicero's letters, which she had previously advised her to read. She confirmed Mary's views as being: "so exactly after my own heart. Little did I think when I read them, when I wrote them in my poor dictionary, that I should ever find a being that would read and see as I did." If by "my poor dictionary" Anne is referring to her notebooks, which seems only too likely, it shows that at least the classical quotations are her own, and not transcripts from Mary's letters.

At the beginning of June Anne caught an unsummery cold and retired to bed with a fever. By the 8th she had recovered, and on the 16th was at Mrs Buller's with Horace and Mrs Cholmeley, whom Horace had met and commented upon favourably. The following day Anne was due at Strawberry Hill to repair Horace's Roman eagle, whose bill had been broken by a visitor who, adding insult to injury, had pocketed the broken piece to avoid discovery.

Writing to Mary Berry on 20th June, Anne made no mention of her recent ill health. She apologised for not writing, excusing herself by saying that she had been busy looking after her mother, arranging small excursion parties in the daytime, and sitting with her in the evening. She had consequently gone to bed later, and risen the following morning later than usual. This had eaten into the early morning, time which she normally reserved for letter writing and reading, before taking up her hammer and chisel. She described a fall from her sculpting scaffold, which had shaken her. Before she had properly recovered, her mother had arrived accompanied by Dumby, an unidentified companion, possibly her lady's maid. Anne had continued to work, though diverted by "a sort of comedy". Dumby's whole conversation was "Lord! What a charming scaffold! What a delightful scaffold! So clever, so well contrived!" and Lady A's: "Look at her figure, what a good figure; well, I do admire her figure, and how well she does look". The figure in question was Anne's own; neither mother nor maid had noticed the sculpture. While this conversation was taking place, the pain had become more intense and Anne, feeling faint and not wishing to show it, had been forced to drag herself upstairs where her faithful lady's maid, Mary, had revived her with a "good glass of hartshorn and water", remarking at the same time that she looked very ill. Hartshorn was the standard pick-me-up of the time: distilled from the carbonated horn and hooves of deer, it formed a *sal volatile*, the basis of 19th century smelling salts. Anne remarked that she meant to join her parents at Park Place in about a fortnight's time; even in June she dreaded the coldness of the house. She finished by apologising to Mary for some undisclosed action that had caused her pain.

This letter was immediately followed by another, dated 21st to 24th June. Anne related that she had been talking to Jerningham "on my unfortunate subject" (presumably lesbian abuse). He, hesitant as usual, had needed Anne to insist on being told what he was trying to say. Apparently William Combe, author of *The First of April*, now believed his previous denigration of Anne to be untrue. He wished to make amends by republishing his work, without any reference to Anne, and with an apology to her. "As to all others mentioned, he said that it was what they deserved, and he should not retract." Jerningham had advised Combe that if he did reprint, he should not apologise, as this would only serve to relight a dying flame. Anne, unusually for her, was unable to judge the right course of action, though she confessed that recently she had received a good press from Combe. She had accused Jerningham of bringing the subject up with Combe; however he had insisted that this was not the case and that Combe was genuinely repentant. Anne was not so easily persuaded; she remarked that it might assist in discovering the original perpetrator of the rumours, but on the other hand if Combe did issue an apology, the reader might assume that she had bought him off. Jerningham had also mentioned that "a certain fiend, *'scio quam dicam'*," (I know of whom I am talking), possibly Anne's niece Lady Charlotte Campbell, had tried to abuse Anne whilst in conversation with Lady Mount Edgecumbe, "who received what she said with scorn and contempt".

The next day Anne had received Mary's letter of 10th June after working all day on her statue of George III, followed by an evening's relaxation working in the garden, which she aptly described as "not a very large field for fame". This letter is accompanied by similar expressions to those used by Mary in *Anne's Notebooks:* "To see you long with a doubtful opinion of my character, or to be seen by you with indifference, would be, to me, insupportable. Never spare me in anything that concerns you. Our interests cannot be separated. In everything that regards a world I have so ill understood, let your better head and better judgement direct. Your decrees will never appear harsh to me while accompanied with that tenderness and kindness I have ever experienced from you." She went on to say that she made a point of mentioning Mrs Cholmeley and her kindnesses to Mary, as firstly she thought it would please her, and secondly because she had seemed unwell. Anne confirmed that Mrs Cholmeley had now returned safely to her country home, Brandsby Hall in Yorkshire.

On 28th June Anne, in a rare moment, turned from an introspective examination of personal feelings, to the wider world. She wrote to Mary that everyone in London was concerned about the future fate of the French royal family, apprehended at Varennes, though she herself had little to say about it. It was, she admitted, a sad tragedy which might have concerned her more if she had been remotely interested in the human beings involved. "But no matter; as miserable individuals, I do from my soul pity them." Other than in this announcement, despite London being filled with aristocratic French refugees whom she would have met on a daily basis, she showed little interest in political events across the Channel. Horace's letters were full of concerns that the revolutionary fervour could cross to English shores, led by such as Horn Tooke and Tom Paine. Anne was possibly embarrassed by the way that the brave new liberties of French politics had descended into mob rule and mentioned these events only in relation to their direct impact on her personal life, in this case the Berrys' impending return journey from Italy.

She next visited Strawberry Hill, where she carried out emergency repairs to Horace's recuperating eagle, replacing the damaged beak with a wax one, "so that he can again receive company." A marble replacement was promised in the near future. Whilst there, she had breakfast with Madame d'Albany, the widow of Bonnie Prince Charlie, the Young Pretender. He had died in Rome in 1788, although he and his wife had separated in 1780. She had become attached to an Italian poet called Alfieri, was in England with her attachment, and had asked to view Strawberry Hill. She had previously met the Berry family on the continent and did not endear herself to Horace by failing to recall their name on being shown Agnes's picture of the *Death of Wolsey*, "with which Mrs D. is anew enchanted." Eventually it transpired that she had remembered them as the Miss Barrys. "I cannot say that whitewashed her very much in my eyes", was Horace's comment. Later in the week Anne gave a supper party in London for Madame d'Albany, attended also by Horace, the Richmonds, the Mount Edgecumbes, Mrs Buller, and Edward Jerningham, her perpetual charming and spare man.

A week later she moved on to Park Place, writing to Mary: "From the Sierra Morena and the plains of Andalusia to the chickens of Park Place is a falling off". She had seen General O'Hara before leaving London and was able to tell Mary that "You seem pretty safe as to his remembrance. He talked of you in a way that pleased even me, and I think would not hesitate in remembering your name, however pronounced. He is, in my opinion, not only a most agreeable and most entertaining but a most valuable creature."

Back with her mother at Park Place, Anne was in Campbell country. She wrote to Mary with some fairly forceful views on her Campbell cousins. She related that much of the family were then at Inveraray, where her uncle, now fourth Duke of Argyll, was unwell. Her cousin Augusta, who had eloped with General Henry Clavering, was described by Anne as "most indifferent", whilst Augusta's younger sister Charlotte, "carving some name on some tree and lolling on the arm of a *confidante* in the form of Miss Campbell" came in for special criticism. "To be serious, believe me, I much regret the unfortunate education of this cousin and the dangers that now surround her".

Anne continued the Campbell theme with a letter to Mary on 3rd August. She speaks of Charlotte, not by name, but by the title of "foul fiend". Another cousin, Caroline, orphaned daughter of Anne's uncle William and aunt Sarah who died respectively in 1778 and 1784, had been largely brought up following her parents' death by Harry and Caroline. It was she who had appeared in the Richmond House theatricals in 1788, as Lady Constant in *The Way to Keep Him*, where on the occasion of the King's attendance her solo on the harp had included a special version of *God Save Great George the King*. She had followed this up as Harriet in *The Wonder*, rather nervously portraying "the tender anxieties of chaste passion". Sadly, a year later she had died. She was probably no great beauty, as Anne related sadly that, like so many "of her unfortunate figure", she had frequently imagined herself in love and been in need of someone in whom to confide. Initially this had been a lady's maid, a girl of her own age, provided by the Conways. Anne had disapproved of this choice, to whom the young Caroline had confided everything, and in due course she departed.

The role of confidante had then been assumed by Charlotte, who tried to persuade her cousin that her guardian Harry was seriously in love with her. At first it seemed a joke, but gradually Caroline, persuaded by her cousin's invented stories, had come to believe it, which had made her miserable. Anne had tried to talk to her and tell her that Charlotte made up stories and was not to be trusted. After young Caroline's death, Anne's mother had given her her cousin's letters and papers, "to look over, preserve, or destroy, as I thought fit." Among them she had found a letter of her own warning her in strong terms against Charlotte's wiles. Anne surmised that possibly Caroline had shown Charlotte this letter, and that in revenge she might have concocted some fiction about Caroline and Anne. Edward Jerningham had reported that Charlotte had become acquainted with William Combe, and Anne hoped that he would not be influenced by her lies. Mary had obviously told Anne not to worry about the newspapers, but she had still asked Jerningham to talk to Topham, the proprietor of *The World*, about some foolish remark which had appeared in his paper. In 1787 there had been a query as to whether General Burgoyne, like Mrs Damer, had had a view of Mrs Jordan's legs. In February 1789 Anne had been abused again in *The World* as being universally and justly celebrated for leg modelling. Topham had apologised that he had been out of the country at the time, and said that he would ensure no re-occurrence. But, as Anne said, "there is in all this a persecution that too often quite sinks my spirits. Think of their putting into another of the newspapers that I was modelling Lady Cadogan's arm!"

Among Caroline's letters, there had been several from Charlotte, which she would like to have read. "But a certain thing called Honour made me seal them up immediately, and thus seal'd I sent them to her, as I did to all those whose letters I found among her papers." Anne continued that she had known Charlotte from infancy and that her "bad qualities" had increased over the years. She knew two eminent people who refused to have anything to do with her, and she herself was rapidly coming to the same conclusion. In Charlotte's defence, it must be said that she went on to become a celebrated beauty and a successful author, writing several novels and a diary illustrative of the times of George IV. She was later to become much closer to Anne, especially during the period in which she was lady-in-waiting to Caroline Princess of Wales. Nevertheless it is clear that she was a gossip, and sometimes a malicious one.

Others to incur the sting of Anne's pen in her gossip columns with Mary included the "*materfamilias*" identifiable as her old friend Elizabeth Melbourne. Anne's house in Sackville Street adjoined Melbourne House and they saw each other on a very frequent basis as friends and neighbours. However something that had occurred six years before, which Anne would never be able to forgive, meant that in 1791 Anne could never again look on her as a bosom companion. Elizabeth, if she had ever realised or remembered this misdemeanour, had soon forgotten it. Anne had taken pleasure in declining an invitation to supper at Melbourne House, preferring "to pass my evening alone, more to my satisfaction, ideally with you (Mary Berry), than really with others."

That "fine coat gentleman" the Duke of Buccleuch, whose behaviour towards Anne when she was launched on society in 1767 had been somewhat short on good manners, deserved "the censures of the world, as usual, on the score of avarice … You perhaps will think that I have a pleasure in saying that, and so I have, but I should have none if I did not think it strictly true." Nevertheless she had still found time to see an archery match that he had laid on – though not to stay to supper.

By the beginning of August Anne was suffering both from her leg, injured in the fall from her scaffold, and also from a lump in her throat. Her doctor, Fordyce, had suggested that she try sea-bathing as a palliative, and she set forth, by way of her half-sister at Goodwood, to Felpham, a small hamlet, on the Sussex coast, close to Bognor Regis, "a stupid place where there is no company and where I can be quiet". A contemporary description of Felpham as a bathing venue mentions the village as "at once rural and marine, having a dry and healthy soil and a genteel clientele." In addition to bathing, sea-born excursions could be made to Selsey Bill or the Owers lightship.

On 15th August Anne wrote to Mary from Felpham, where she had received Mary's letter of 30th July. Mary, possibly fed up with Horace's ceaseless pleas for her return, had remarked to Anne that to get him out of his "fears, fusses and jellies", he needed something to do. Anne agreed but said it was not so easy to think of anything acceptably enjoyable to him. She said that Horace's ward was mad and mischievous and likely to do something that would make him miserable.

Anne thoroughly enjoyed a solitary life at Felpham. She bathed probably, even in that isolated spot, from a bathing machine, the first of which had been introduced in 1781, trundled into the water for her. She then walked along the beach to sit "like King Canute, till the waves washed my feet, but thank Heaven! without his crown, or his courtiers." She could grow quite fond of the place: "The day was so fine, the sun so bright, and the sea so smooth, and so divinely beautiful", that she had wished that "those good spirits which hover round your *dulce caput*, would gently transport you, *per aerem*, to me, for one half hour..."

She wrote to Mary with further gossip. Lady Duncannon, whose husband had passed on to her some disease caught from "the vile company he kept", had given her "terrible medicines", and kept her from knowing the cause of her illness, endangering her life in so doing, by preventing her from having proper medical advice. However she had now gone to Bath and was somewhat better. Also taking the waters was Anne's great friend Sir William Hamilton, accompanied by Emma Hart, whose talents were generally admired there. Anne believed that he meant to marry her and that perhaps that was for the best. "One great folly often swallows up little ones, and he does, by all I hear, make himself completely ridiculous in his present state." This was the man who, having recently buried his first wife, had returned from Naples to London to see that eligible widow Mrs Damer, who had sculpted so prettily in Italy. There is surely a touch of sour grapes in those remarks, as in the catty follow-up that the Duke of Buccleuch was also in Bath with a Lady "'*scis quam dicam*' – a very pretty society you will say. Say what you please." Lady Charlotte Campbell also came in for renewed criticism: "What you say of Lady Charlotte puts me in mind (tho' I know not if justly) of Miss Boyle, now Lady Henry Fitzgerald. Would to God! that half the instruction which has been lavished on her, and seems now jumbling, jolting, and filtering away in rides, drives, balls and a round of idle, empty amusements, had been bestowed on my poor cousin. I think she would have profited by it, and now in a worldly way, the best thing one can hope for her is some hurried marriage, with a thousand chances, even in that, against her..."

A few days later Anne was visited at Felpham by the Duke of Richmond and Miss Le Clerc, his natural daughter. He arrived in a phaeton, and after dinner they drove and walked. The Duke displayed an expert knowledge of the Sussex coast: he knew the name of every hill giving onto the beach, and how and where they drained into the sea. He showed Anne the rocks and sandbanks which made this an inhospitable coast and pointed out the lighthouse just visible in the distance, inshore of which no boat of any size could venture.

By the 21st August Anne was tiring of her "stupid quiet" bathing place. She determined to get through her prescribed bathing regime as quickly as possible and then to go to Goodwood for a few days. She planned a visit to Strawberry Hill for the end of September, when she hoped to persuade Horace to come and stay for a time at Park Place. She was also thinking of the Berrys' impending return. All things being equal, she would go London about the end of October. However she told Mary that if, for any reason, she should wish Anne to be absent from London at the time of the

Berrys' return, she could easily arrange either to stay on at Park Place, or to visit the Melbournes at Brocket Hall. Four days later she wrote to Mary saying that it had been blowing a gale for the last two days again, and that though she found bathing agreeable, it did not seem to have made her feel any better. Solitary walks by the sea, she found, led to "serious and sad reflections". She had determined to leave for Goodwood the next day.

There Anne described the lifestyle she preferred: that of a grand English establishment in the 1790s. The Duke of Richmond was extremely wealthy; he had financed the Richmond players, including the cost of the extravagant settings and players' costumes. He was Lord-Lieutenant of Sussex, and Colonel-in-Chief of the Sussex militia, in whose wellbeing he was particularly interested. If the French were to invade England, the Sussex militia would be part of the first line of national defence. Goodwood was the central hub of Richmond's regional world. Anne described the house as "the easiest of all houses and every one may do what thing they please." There was always something to learn at Goodwood; on this visit she was attracted by the Duke's laboratory. There a young scientist employed by the Duke arranged a course of lectures for Anne. She was accompanied somewhat unwillingly by the only other guest staying at the time, Mme de Cambis, described by Anne as cross and acidic. It could be hoped that her temper would be improved by the Duke's band, part of the Sussex militia. This fine group of men, who also played at the Richmond House theatricals in London, played nightly at Goodwood, in a room adjoining that in which the guests sat. Anne would have been welcomed at Goodwood by her own sculpture of marble dogs asleep.

Anne felt that her duty was to be with Horace, believing that in the absence of the returning Berry family, "I am the only one to whom he can, or will, tell his anxieties, and numberless they will be". By 25th September Horace had reported that Anne had arrived at Strawberry Hill, stayed a night, and then gone on to London. Care was only short term. She had found the old man in good spirits. She arrived between 6 and 7pm and found him making his tea, dressed in his best wig and preparing to go out. She had also brought with her a young cousin, Louisa Campbell, the younger daughter of Lady William Campbell and sister of the recently deceased Caroline. Anne's mother had decided that Louisa should be sent to a nameless school. She went early to bed and Anne was left to calm Horace's nerves about the Berrys' travels north. She arranged to return for one night the following week with Mme de Cambis, before they both went on to Park Place, where Horace was due to follow them the next day. On 9th October Horace, who had already arrived, wrote to Mary Berry from Park Place that his only fellow guests were Anne and Mme de Cambis, and that he was glad of it.

Meanwhile Anne, too, had been worrying as the day of the Berrys' return got nearer. Mary considered that the solitude at Felpham had been bad for Anne, though

Anne's reply had shown that she did not totally agree: "That solitude prolonged too long struck me nearly in the same light as you. Its charms are powerful and may be pernicious, but to be sometimes alone is surely not an 'excess'. What can I do when depression of spirits, anxiety, or ill health, renders me unfit at times, for society? You will not coldly say, do not be depressed, do not be anxious. It would be to me, as if you said, do not be ill. Your anger against poor Felpham diverts me." She was also annoyed by Mary's suggestion that she had wilfully spoiled the little wax head of herself, prepared as a present at Mary's request. She said that if Mary didn't like the head when she saw it, it would be altered, or another modelled. She recorded that she had been to the theatre, but that most evenings had been spent with Lady Melbourne, who was staying at home, deeply concerned about the future of her son, young Peniston, ill with consumption; the result, according to Anne, "of the folly and dissipation that so much prevails." She again referred Mary to the mysterious Melbourne event of six years before, "I mean, with regard to me. It will seem strange that I should allow any person concerned to make me this sort of confidence, but circumstances, on which so often hang the rights and wrongs of this world, will, I think, justify my conduct. If I did not follow in this the strict laws of friendship and honour, I have erred most unknowingly. Your 'penetration' will show you, from what I have said, and from what I now say, that a character I had looked up to, and admired for a thousand, thousand valuable qualities, was in one instant, sunk below reproach, and the comforts and satisfactions friendship alone can give, and to which I looked forward with so much pleasure, as but increasing with time, suddenly destroyed."

Whilst Anne was staying at Park Place, Harry and Horace made a joint visit to Windsor. Both were delighted with what they saw, especially the Gothic glories of St George's Chapel, in process of being cleaned to give "a scene of lightness and graces." They also admired the excellent new choir screen. Encouraged by their descriptions, Anne, too, visited Windsor, on her way from Park Place to London, where work on her Colossus called, "or it will never be finished."

Back in London, Anne again spent time with her neighbours, the Melbournes. Whatever her reservations, she still maintained their friendship. She also suffered from an unpleasant bout of toothache, to relieve which she administered laudanum to herself. She was trying desperately to get Horace to agree to come up to London, away from the cold and damp of Strawberry Hill in winter. She could keep an eye on him if they were both in London, and soothe his fears about the dangers which he imagined the Berrys faced. However she was not very successful: "I wish to God Mr W would come. It would, I am sure, be better for him and I should then know always when he heard, at least, how far you were on your journey … I hope that you will continue not to tell him all." He was certainly not intended to know that the return route was planned by Paris.

Towards the end of October Horace found two further items to add to his fusses. His eighteen-year-old footman, John, had got into debt, pawned a silver strainer and spoon taken from Horace's London house in Berkeley Square, and then disappeared. At the same time Horace was suffering from a "very troublesome erysipelas" on his left arm; Mr Gilchrist, his apothecary at Twickenham, was dangerously ill, and there was no one to treat him near Strawberry Hill. This ailment was then compounded by another attack of gout. A visit to London, to see his trusted doctor Mr Watson, to check whether anything else was missing from Berkeley Square, and to set about finding a replacement footman had been urgently arranged. Sadly he was soon to discover that Philip, his valet, and Kirgate, his secretary, had told John to confess. But he had not done so, had crept out of the house at night and hanged himself in the garden from a tree close to the chapel. After the event Horace claimed that if John had owned up, he would have both pardoned and retained him.

With the help of Mr Watson, Horace recovered to be ready to meet his beloved Berrys. After some discussion it was agreed that they should go first to their home in North Audley Street, where they should settle themselves, and thence to Strawberry Hill for a night or two, before Horace ceremoniously welcomed them to their new country home at Little Strawberry Hill.

Horace's respite and peace of mind were to be short lived. On 5th December 1791 his nephew, George third Earl of Orford, died without heirs, leaving the title first bestowed on his father Sir Robert Walpole, to Horace. Their relationship had not been close, and despite Horace's efforts to assist him in two bouts of illness verging on lunacy, the third Earl had restricted any contact to an annual gift of two boxes of plovers' eggs, with an accompanying note identifying the donor. The elevation was not unexpected, but it was unwelcome. Horace, writing to John Pinkerton on Boxing Day 1791, describes it as "A source of lawsuits amongst my near relations, endless conversations with lawyers and packets of letters to read every day, and answer – all this weight of new business is too much for the rag of life that yet hangs about me." He went on to tell Hannah More on New Year's Day 1792 that "I am little disposed to cheerfulness now, I am overwhelmed with troubles, and with business – and business that I do not understand; law, and the management of a ruined estate, are subjects ill-suited to a head that never studied anything that in a worldly language is called useful." The business with which Horace was overwhelmed related almost exclusively to his duties and responsibilities in administering the estate of the third Earl. The troubles which equally overwhelmed him were largely to do with Mary Berry.

Horace had purchased the house known locally as Little Strawberry Hill, and familiarly by those at Strawberry Hill, as Cliveden, after its former owner, the comedy actress Kitty Clive. Horace had composed an ode in memory of her, inscribed on an urn in the Cliveden garden:

"Ye smiles and jests still hover round;
This is mirth's consecrated ground:
Here liv'd the laughter loving dame,
A matchless actress, Clive her name,
The comic muse with her retir'd
And shed a tear when she expir'd."

Cliveden was a substantial dwelling, two small meadows distant from Strawberry Hill, with a fine garden with paths bordered by trellis work. The house had been bought by Horace as a country home for the Berrys, enabling his new and dear "wives" to be close to him in old age. During their absence abroad, he had quietly groomed Mary in the art of letter writing, and of ordering and storing letters. Each of their letters to each other were numbered, and it was Horace's intention that each was to be saved for posterity, together with those of his other correspondents, Sir Horace Mann, Lady Ossory, George Selwyn, and the rest. Mary Berry was intended to be the person who would do this.

Horace had arranged that the Berrys should occupy Cliveden rent-free. This arrangement seems to have come to the notice of the popular press. In early December an article had appeared suggesting that there was more to the rent-free arrangement than met the eye. The exact imputation is not clear, but was certainly worrying enough to Mary Berry to cause her to threaten to give up the family's occupation of the house. Mary wrote: "I did not like to show you, nor did I myself feel while with you, how much I was hurt by the newspaper. To be long honoured with your friendship and remain unnoticed, I knew was impossible, and laid my account with, but to have it imagined, implied, or even hinted, that the purest friendship that ever actuated human bosoms should have any possible foundation in, or view to interested motives; and that we, whose hereditary neglect of fortune has deprived us of what might, and ought to have been our own, that we should ever afterwards be supposed to have it in view, or be described in a situation, which must mislead the world both as to our sentiments and our conduct, while our principles they cannot know, and if they could, would not enter into – all this I confess I cannot bear – not even your society can make up to me for it.

"Would to God we had remained abroad, where we might still have enjoyed as much of your confidence and friendship, as ignorance and impertinence seem likely to allow us here...... If our seeking your society is supposed by those ignorant of its value, to be with some view beyond its enjoyment, and our situation represented as one which will aid the belief of this to a mean and interested world, I shall think we shall have perpetual reason to regret the only circumstance in our lives that could be called fortunate."

Horace replied that he was burdened with his new responsibilities, that the erysipelas on his arm had again needed the attention of Mr Watson, and that gout was giving him pain. The last thing that he required was this outburst from Mary. "Is all your felicity to be in the power of a newspaper? Are your virtue and purity, and my innocence about you; are our consciences no shield against anonymous folly or envy? Would you only condescend to be my friend if I were a beggar? ... For your own sake, for poor mine, combat such extravagant delicacy, and do not poison the few days of a life, which you and you only can sweeten." In the event, the charms of Cliveden overcame the sisters' agitation, and in his letter to Hannah More, already referred to, Horace alluded to them: "My pretty wives, I kindly thank you, are returned better than they went, and I hope not only as constant as they were, but that they will remain so, though become Countesses."

Chapter 13

PROPOSALS

Both Anne and Mary were in raptures to be reunited. The volume of letters increased and they wrote to each other daily, Anne writing in the mornings, and Mary in the evenings. Volume 2 of *Anne's Notebooks* contains copious excerpts from Mary's letters to her. They wrote to each other whether or not they had seen each other on the same day or the previous evening. The excerpts, as in Volume 1, are repetitive; they talk of friendship and love, and of depression and melancholy, of poor and worse health, and sometimes of lovers' tiffs. The following extracts give a flavour of the tone of the whole volume. "Hearts and feelings so exactly consonant as ours were, I am convinced, made for each others' comfort, support, and consolation in what ever circumstances they may be placed". "However, you will take me I know for better or for worse and would to heaven that my better was more worthy of you, and my worse less oppressive to myself". "I feel sure that you would never follow the ridiculous maxims of the rest of the world about concealing things that give pain. No pain on Earth would to me be equal to any sort of concealment, or your having one idea on the subject that you would not share with me".

Some facts gradually emerge from the mists of morose yet affectionate prose. Firstly, Anne took good care that meetings were not too frequent. Mary continually sought to see her more often, but Anne had no wish for the old lesbian rumours to revive. The two ladies did not appear to the outside world at this time as being an inseparable pairing. Indeed during 1792 Anne had received a proposal of marriage, probably from her old admirer William Augustus Fawkener, Clerk to the Privy Council, diplomatic envoy, and *protégé* of the younger Pitt.

Fawkener's diplomatic career had prospered, and in 1791 he had been sent on an important diplomatic mission to Catherine the Great in St Petersburg. In July Horace referred to her as "Catherine Slay-Czar", a suitable nickname for an empress who had disposed of her husband before seizing the throne for herself. He had heard that Catherine had asked Fawkener to obtain a bust of Charles Fox for her, "for his eloquence has saved two great nations from a war – by his opposition to it." Horace remarked that she couldn't have asked a more unsuitable person than Fawkener, who had been sent by Fox's arch rival, William Pitt. History does not relate whether Fawkener asked Anne to model a bust of Fox; if he did, she was a long time in completing it, as her first known bust of him dates from around 1802.

Fawkener's private life may also have progressed. The marriage register of St George's Hanover Square records the marriage on 20th April 1789 of a William Fawkener to Elizabeth White. Either this was another William Fawkener, or the Fawkener who was Anne's lover was not William but his brother, or William Fawkener in proposing to Anne was laying himself open to a future charge of bigamy. If indeed the husband was William Augustus Fawkener, he kept the marriage quiet. Possibly he was confident that Anne would refuse him, and the proposal was a cynical ploy, perhaps with Elizabeth Melbourne's connivance, to test Anne's relationship with Mary. His track record of promises to ladies was not good. There is little reason to suppose that this time it would have been any better.

It is certain that William Augustus Fawkener did marry a second time and his wife is recorded as having been Elizabeth Wright, which sounds very similar to White. They had two daughters, Mary and Sarah, born a year apart around 1788 and 1789, who may or may not have been born in wedlock. Both these daughters were to marry well, Mary to her cousin Horatio Walpole.

As a man, Fawkener seems to have been something of a cold fish. He was undoubtedly clever, competent as Clerk to the Privy Council, a discreet diplomat, and possessed of an acerbic wit. Anne and Mary had invented the nickname "Dorimont" for him, a name stemming from Sir George Etherege's restoration comedy *Sir Fopling Flutter or The Man of Mode*, and used frequently thereafter to describe would-be gentlemen adventurers of a less than martial nature. When not employed in diplomatic duties abroad, he was a member of the same social circle as Anne. Mary mentions him by his nickname several times in *Anne's Notebooks*, though the lack of dates makes the references difficult to follow. "His exact and perfect civility does not inspire me," commented Mary, "that that being should have been, in a greater degree, the arbiter of your fate – so cold, so *composé*, so apparently unlike yourself! And yet I am convinced that these great differences of character are in some cases the luckiest thing that could happen, and preserve you from more lasting and wide spreading evils."

The proposal seems to have been made in the autumn of 1792, and its reverberations rambled and rumbled on late into November. Mary's comments in the Notebooks included: "I am sure whatever you determine on will be right," and: "I thoroughly believe you when you say that were any change to take place…. you should feel for me still more than for yourself." A little later she wrote: "You will see by the comments I made in my last letter upon Dorimont's visit to us, how much I enter into your sense of his character."

In a letter to Anne, Mary, always confident in the power of reason, suggested that Anne had to consider the simple proposition that marriage might make a positive contribution to her future peace and happiness. She argued that Anne was unlikely to find anybody else. Her exact wording bears scrutiny: "the delicacy of your own mind, the remains which you own of an unextinguished passion, and a thousand other circumstances will prevent, as have done, your ever forming such a friendship or connection, for I would wish to speak as I think, unromantically with any other person." Does Mary here mean that she wishes to speak as she thinks, unromantically, the triumph of reason over passion, or does she mean that the friendship or connection might be unromantic? The sense seems to suggest the former, in which case the unextinguished passion must be for Fawkener.

Mary went on to point out that marriage would put an end to any future accusation of lesbianism, and ended by pointing out: "If you do not think him absolutely unworthy of your sentiments for him, and his very errors may probably make him otherwise," a marriage in which the heart was occupied rather than satisfied would at least mean that she was no longer on her own, unconnected with and insulated from a closer form of human relationship. She finished by pointing out that their own friendship might fail, if only by reason of her ill health and possible mortality.

Anne replied that Mary did not really know the character of the man "to whom, by so many arguments, you would dispose of your friend." Even through the mists of passion her "more sober sense" had been able to see that their differing personalities would make happiness impossible. She was indeed aware that Mary thought that Fawkener's return to her, Anne, no longer young and censured by the world, when he could still have captivated the "young, beautiful and gay", showed constancy. Anne's view was that in an engagement she risked all, while he risked little, though her logic is somewhat difficult to follow. She was certain that if, at some time in the past, Fawkener had only shown her "but the shadow of true affection", she would have jumped at it, but that it was now too late. She doubted whether marriage would make much difference to the innuendos of past behaviour, and believed that the advantages of companionship must be allowed to develop, and not be forced upon her. She firmly believed that she was not "foolishly throwing away proffered good, when I am avoiding misery."

Two days later Anne wrote to Mary making the point that they both wished to hear. She could not bear the thought that marriage might deprive her of the comforts of passing evenings alone together. That alone, even if she were inclined to debate the subject, would convince her that her decision to refuse the proposal was correct. The following day they again discussed the matter, during which Mary had turned the conversation to her own problems, presumably in the context of a lonelier existence if Anne married Fawkener. She talked gloomily of a short and miserable future, of an excess of expenditure over income, and proposed getting rid of North Audley Street and living totally in the country at Little Strawberry Hill. Anne replied to her letter the next day telling her to brace up, and "I will show you that I can speak in plain terms, call '*un chat un chat*'." She pointed out that Twickenham in winter would be cold and lonely, and that if she were to spend all her time there, the world would probably renew its innuendos concerning Horace and Mary's relationship. The monetary shortfall which had concerned Mary was quite easily manageable during her father's lifetime, and should he perchance die, thus losing the allowance paid by his brother, Anne was sure that Mary would not refuse "to share the fortune of a being so truly devoted to you, and one with whom, great or small, you would feel the first of comforts in sharing your own."

By Sunday evening, 11th November 1792, the final decision had been made. Anne had returned from a weekend at Brocket Hall. The weather had been mild and pleasant, though she had not enjoyed the company and suffered from a dreadful cold. She wrote to Mary, resentful that she had not come round to spend an hour or two by candlelight "to add a few words of Dorimont". Anne had made up her mind, but her feelings still remained confused. "Sensations from the loss of one would not be much felt engaged in a serious and long connection with another". Over the past year Fawkener had given no sign of the affection for her which he now displayed, and she could not think of any event which might have changed his feelings. "And in all this what I may feel never seems thought of." Despite her complaints, Anne was still attracted to him: "I was now grown (I will confess it) often to wish still more than to fear seeing him." A final note from Fawkener was simple and contained but one word, "Farewell". In the *Notebooks* Mary's comment was also recorded: "Oh! Dorimont, Dorimont, thou <u>very</u> Dorimont! I could not help thinking when I read over again his note, and yet you do not know how much I feel for you, and how much I enter into your feelings".

However Mary, as always practical, continued in an admonitory tone: "I cannot help regretting since you have recommenced seeing him at all, that you do not seem to think his character sufficiently sure and ingenuous to be able to form with it that sort of friendship (the exact limits of which it were perhaps difficult to trace) which always <u>should</u> and I think often <u>may</u> exist when another passion ceases – and which I feel can <u>alone</u> satisfy and tranquillise your mind on this subject." This was followed a few days later by: "I do not at all like the footing you are upon with Dor. It is uncomfortable and unsatisfactory in every respect." In fact Fawkener was to continue to play a role in Anne's life, if only a minor one.

The year 1793 saw the Reign of Terror in France in full swing. The horrific scenes taking place in France kept both *émigrés* and English in England. Horace's diaries record vividly at second hand the rumble of the tumbrils and the swish of the guillotine. On 21st January 1793 Louis XVI was executed, to be followed nine months later on 16th October by Marie Antoinette. Extracts of letters from Mary in *Anne's Notebooks* contain no mention of extraneous events; those from Horace to Mary, only an occasional reference compared to other correspondents, and from Anne to Mary, again nothing. Anne passed the year in London and at Park Place, with journeys to Strawberry Hill and other friends and relations. From time to time during spring and early summer their paths would cross, and both Anne and Mary looked forward to such meetings with avid expectations. Sometimes the meetings were happy, and at others less so. Both took good care to ensure that their names were not coupled together in the public eye. They wrote on an almost daily basis, and if letters were not forthcoming they scolded each other. Whilst the Berrys were at Little Strawberry Hill from January to September little exists of their correspondence, other than the snippets contained in *Anne's Notebooks*. From September to December the Berrys went on their annual peregrination. Unable to go abroad, owing to the war with France, they went instead to Yorkshire, to their maternal Seton grandmother and to Mrs Cholmeley at Brandsby Hall. Correspondence increased, and Anne's letters preserved by Mary contain a fuller record of her activities.

The following quotations from Mary Berry's letters, contained in *Anne's Notebooks,* go some way to describing their relationship. Firstly, there is the mutual comfort that each of them got from writing and receiving letters: "If you will be dreaming of me, let your ideas of me tonight, recovered and well, soothe (as I ever would) and not disturb your rest." Or: "Writing this letter has relieved me, do not let it oppress you." This is a typical Mary Berry "on the one hand – on the other hand" expression. The first half of the sentence talks about relief, the second half contrasts it with oppression.

Then there are the arrangements to meet: "I look forward with real pleasure to having more frequent opportunities of enjoying your society in town, and, heaven knows, it is <u>almost</u> my only <u>real</u> pleasure, and that is accompanied as you know, like all the pleasures of this miserable existence with a thousand regrets, and a thousand tantalising circumstances." Again regrets contrast with tantalising circumstances.

Sometimes the meetings took place, on other occasions they did not: "I felt sure that you would call tonight … I am alone, in pain, low, and longing to see you", or: "How unlucky that you did not come last night! I could have spent an hour or two with you so quietly, so uninterruptedly! And I know not when I can again". And sometimes history does not record the outcome: "But I want to see you come here tomorrow for no reason but that I want to see you".

Most often the meetings could be regarded as successful: "Thank heaven that we have found a home for our hearts in each other's bosom", or: "I know that there is but one relief, which is the sympathising bosom of some kindred being." Occasionally there are tiffs: "I am quite cross about it and so I will endeavour to hold my tongue."

There are many references to what today would be called depression, but which was then the desirable state of melancholy, the need to be quiet and alone to digest the misfortunes that life brings. This, of course, is easier when the melancholic does not have to get up, go out to work, and be sociable with colleagues. "My spirits are, I think subject to more frequent and overcoming attacks than they used, and for them I believe there is but one cure, and that you will not allow me even to wish for...."

In August a letter from Mary Berry in Yorkshire to an unnamed friend, which was preserved in her correspondence, set out quite succinctly the practical problems which seemed to her insuperable. While Mary's father was alive, the Berry family enjoyed an annuity of £1000 per annum, gifted to him by his brother. In addition they had further income of £750 per annum. On Mr Berry's death the annuity would cease, and the sisters' income would be reduced to £750 or, if one sister married, to £325 for the one remaining unmarried. Mary was acutely aware of "how little can be done with such a sum". Although she went on to say that money was less important in life than honour and integrity, when one or two special friends would always welcome them, her words had an empty ring.

She was also worried that rumours were circulating that she was attempting to ensnare the septuagenarian Horace. The previous winter he had spoken frequently of his "wives", and though this had been spoken in jest, its reverberations had echoed back as a possible reality. As Mary noted: "Why should he? When without the ridicule or the trouble of a marriage, he enjoys almost as much of my society, and every comfort from it, that he could in the nearest connection? As the willing offering of a grateful and affectionate heart, the time and attentions I bestow upon him have hitherto given me pleasure. Were they to become a duty, and a duty to which the world would attribute interested motives, they would become irksome."

Mary had made Horace aware of such rumours, which amused rather than disturbed him. On 17th September 1793 he wrote jointly to both Mary and Agnes, who had just departed for Yorkshire: "I have been three score years and ten looking for a society that I perfectly like......I soon found the charming Berrys, though young enough to be my great-granddaughters, lovely enough to turn the heads of all our youths, and sensible enough, if said youths have any brains, to set all their heads to rights again – yes, sweet damsels, I have found that you can bear to pass half your time with an ante-diluvian without discovering any *ennui* or disgust, tho' his greatest merit towards you is that he is not one of those old fools who fancy they are in love in their dotage. I have no such vagary, tho' I am not sorry that some folks think I am so absurd, since it frets their selfishness." By the end of September he was continuing in a similar vein: "The Post Office, I believe, will think it our honeymoon still: you have been gone but five days and I have written to you on three of them running. As you know I am not partial to the moon, I shall desire to christen the era of my double marriage our honey sun."

Anne was more considerate to her friends. She had made a wax self-portrait as a present for Mary: "Your wax head is the prettiest thing that ever was seen by daylight and excessively like." In September 1793 she left her coat with Mary, who described it as "my hope stay and comfort. Give up all idea of ever possessing it again … I fancy it looks somehow like you and delight in wearing it, and would not part with it for the world."

Mary added that she had much enjoyed the last four days spent with Anne in town. Especially memorable, in keeping with the pleasures of Gothick melancholy, had been a visit to the tombs in Westminster Abbey: "alive or dead among tombs, may we only go together is all I pray! They all think that I look remarkably well so take care of yourself for heaven's sake! That you may not go first".

In October Anne sent to Cliveden a gift of some lavender plants from Park Place, where Harry's lavender oil distillery had ensured no shortage of these fashionable additions to the garden. The plants would arrive complete with cultural instructions, in case Mary had forgotten to give these before leaving for Yorkshire. Anne's letter, announcing the plants' despatch and written in the morning, was followed by another in the evening, as her usual morning writing routine had been disturbed by plasterers "singing and splattering" around her window. Unable to make up her mind whether the plasterers gazing in at her were more or less desirable than the room being in Stygian gloom, she had given up writing and gone out. Horace reported the arrival of the plants on 18th October and sent his gardener to "distribute them about Cliveden, which I hope next summer will be as odoriferous as Mount Carmel."

Park Place meanwhile remained a congenial base for letter writing. On 12th October 1793 there was a family success to celebrate. At the age of 72, the time when most generals would happily have thought of retirement, Harry was created Field Marshal. It was in fact an honorary appointment, without the anticipation of military action, and Horace noted in a letter to Mary that "next week Mr Conway must go and kiss hands for his idle Truncheon". From Yorkshire, parted from Anne by 200 miles, Mary asked her whether she was going to Goodwood or to Brocket Hall; she complained of Agnes's behaviour, or lay in bed waiting for the post. "This morning I knew you [your letter] would be coming and so lay still quietly expecting you – you was more entertaining than usual but don't mistake me you was more interesting the time before … however your visit today was a longer one and God Bless you for it."

She dreamt of Anne sharing her beloved Yorkshire, of walking in York Minster together, or of a shared journey to Beverley. Sometimes her spirits were low, and on one such occasion she was grateful to her grandmother who had given her a book in which she had transcribed poems and letters from friends and relations sent on the occasion of her mother's early and unexpected death at the age of 22, and containing a drawing of her monument and epitaph.

By the beginning of November Anne returned to London and was writing to Mary using their pet nicknames for their acquaintances. Anne's mother was fretting about the Bee, their name for Mrs Buller, while poor Mrs C (Mrs Cholmeley), persistent and down to earth, continued to counsel Mary in Yorkshire. The exact tenor of her advice is never clear; it seems to have started in warning Mary about Anne's reputation, followed by a change of mind and acceptance of her. Shortly afterwards, Mrs Cholmeley herself was plunged into depression on the death of one of her children, which caused all advice to be shrouded in melancholy. Nevertheless Mary was able to record that "she thinks nothing so beautiful, nothing so agreeable, nothing the least like us – poor soul". To cheer her up, Mrs C had been given some scenes from a comedy that Mary had started to write. Mary, impatient to be back in London, had left her "much affected and far from well". Anne noted that "poor Mrs C" was likely to come to town for the winter; she hoped that the change from Yorkshire to London might effect a change from melancholia for both Mary and Mrs Cholmeley.

Another nickname, the wildcat, was applied to Anne's friend Mrs Hervey. On the first Saturday night following Anne's return to town, they had gone together to the Haymarket Theatre. At some stage, Anne had found herself "*en tiers*", literally one of three, when two is company and three a crowd. The new arrival was a gentleman whom Anne felt that neither of them had expected. He had bowed in the very oddest manner, first to Mrs Hervey, and then to Anne, exclaiming "I came for the pleasure of your company, and yours". The effect on Anne's senses, whether or not she showed it, was traumatic. "Oh! defend me, but that is too late, defend therefore what is more dear to me than myself from caprice! At times, cross and distant, formal or reserved, at others how different, yet never seeming to act, or speak *ex imo corde*: completely a gentleman it is true, but a modern one. Oh! What a contrast with a character full of romantic impudence (if I may be allowed the expression) but with still far more depth than violence of passion, saved from farther or greater miseries, perhaps from the excess of its feelings." The unnamed gentleman who had produced this outburst was indeed William Fawkener, alias Dorimont.

After the theatre, the party had gone on to Renard's, and then back to Mrs Hervey's. She had not been expected home; a servant stoked the fire, and brought in tea, followed by cold meat. Anne believed that Mr Hervey was out of town, and feeling uneasy made her excuses and left as soon as possible. "I hate such scenes, tho' I sometimes can go tolerably thro' the acting. I excused myself as having been up rather late the night before, and we parted. During my short journey home I reflected on the wonderful licence some enjoy, guessing how they lead one to a chaos."

Anne and Mary continued to correspond on a regular basis, although most of the letters have been lost or destroyed. Horace's letters to Mary, which are preserved, have frequent reference to Anne and her activities. He was annoyed that Anne had told the sisters that he had been unwell; in future any minor disorders would be concealed from her. At the beginning of November Anne stayed the night at Strawberry Hill, returning thence to London and the winter season. There was a pre-Christmas round of theatres and supper parties. She had gone to the theatre with her father, and on afterwards to supper with Horace in Berkeley Square. The following evening she had arranged another supper party there, this time including his niece Sophia, the Buller family, and Edward Jerningham, whose play *The Siege of Berwick* had just received favourable reviews. On 29th November Anne had given a supper party which included Horace, her half-sister Mary, Lord Derby with Elizabeth Farren and her mother, and Edward Jerningham again. At the beginning of December she had gone with Horace to the Little Haymarket to see *The Children in the Wood*, starring John Bannister, described by Horace as one of the most admirable performances he had ever seen. Two days later they saw *The Siege of Berwick*, in a box organised by Anne. After the play her guests, who included Horace, Harry, Anne's half-sister, Mary with her pretty friend, Mrs Stanhope, and George Colman, manager of the Drury Lane Theatre and his wife, were given supper by Anne. Horace had found the play "much superior to my expectation". On the day following *The Siege of Berwick*, Anne had a quiet day, a brief visit from 'the Charming Man' during the morning, and a short supper with the Bullers.

Afterwards she wrote to Mary giving a thoughtful, if wistful, account of herself. "Tis certain that in the course of my life I cannot recollect wishing for gaiety or amusement, tho' I have taken both when they came in my way, and been pleased with both. I neither deny or wish to deny that I want to be taken from my melancholy self, but for the world, we can never now be upon more than civil terms, but while I have another and a dearer interest than my own to consider, I will, with scrupulous care, attend even to that world, and to the best of my judgement do all it requires. ... Of all plagues, the greatest are intimate acquaintance, 'tis so difficult to make them remain where you intend, they persecute you with their company when you do not want them, and are a bar to all rational employment of time, and if, when you are ill and unhappy, or in distress, it might be possible for them to relieve you in some degree, they are too much affected, the sight is too over-coming, and they must avoid you".

She also took the opportunity to warn Mary about her feelings for an unnamed relation, probably her Ferguson cousin, and about men in general. "How plainly what you tell me of him proves that all real sentiments and affections of the mind, and I fear even real passions, remain, the first I am convinced unaltered by time or absence, and the latter ever dangerous and apt to be renewed. Therefore don't make too long visits or the piece of 'cold elegance' will stand a bad chance, but men have an advantage, if it may so be termed, they gallop-away, and drive by-away, and game-away, and I know not what away; many an infant passion weakens it before it comes to its growth, or has power seriously to contend with them, while a poor helpless woman nourishes with care a future tyrant that may destroy her".

Anne went on to add that Mary's bust had returned from being fired. However the oven had been too hot, resulting in small cracks and a blemish on the right cheek "which, *soit dit en passant*, to a face without a blemish does not add to the likeness".

As the Berrys travelled towards London and reunion with Anne and Horace, there was a further exchange on the matter of William Combe's proposed apology, which must again have reared its head. This time Mary advised Anne not to have anything to do with a man who had published without any enquiry into the truth of the matter. She believed "his praise would be as indiscriminate and hardly less disagreeable than his abuse." In a letter dated 18th December 1793 Anne agreed to follow this advice. She thanked Mary for writing about the matter, as she would prefer that their reunion after a long absence was not taken up with "that cruel subject". On 20th December each wrote the other a last letter before they met again, after three months' separation. Mary promised Anne that the first time that they were alone together, "which I trust in heaven will be soon", she should see some verses which she had written. She ended the letter: "Farewell, tell me that your head don't want my shoulder to night – mine I know would be the better for yours." Anne's missive, telling Mary that Horace had not been overdone by seeing two plays in a week, ended: "I say nothing of my near hope of seeing you, need I? How and what I feel you know. This I think, will be for this time my last letter to you ... you may not have it long before you set out. Heaven preserve and bless you. Farewell, farewell."

On 14th December 1793 the current session of correspondence between Horace and Mary had also come to an end. As the Berrys were returning from Yorkshire to London, they had written to him: "You need not leave a card; we shall be at home."

During the spring of 1794 they were all much in each others' company, and the need for and frequency of letters decreased. Indeed Mary noted that she lost much in writing less frequently, because although they saw each other more often, it was only for a few hurried moments. In fact these two determined women, guided by reason, may have found it easier to carry on their relationship on paper, than in person. Anne certainly needed to ensure that there would be no further abuse and therefore to keep Mary at a distance. Mary writes: "You are very un-easy about me I know – as I am low in spirits with a heavy cold," and again: "Without unbounded confidence there can be no friendship like yours, and without your friendship, your affection, I feel so certain that I could not live, that my only reliance is whatever may destroy the one, will inevitably put an end to the other."

However by April the friendship seems to have been restored to a more normal and less romantic footing. If absence had made the heart grow fond, reality had cooled the ardour. Also, by April the London winter season was coming to an end. Horace wrote to Mary from Berkeley Square: "delighted that you have such good weather for your *villeggiatura*. ... All my evening customers are gone, except Mrs Damer, and she is at home tonight with the Greatheeds and Mrs Siddons, and a few more......". He added a jibe at his old enemy Mrs Piozzi (Hester Thrale) who had just published her *Synonyme*: "I have picked out a motto for her work in her own words, and written it on the title page: 'Simplicity cannot please without elegance!'. The advent of spring took Horace to Strawberry Hill to join the Berrys at next door Cliveden.

On 19th April Mary wrote from Cliveden that the weather had been so fine and the country so pleasant that she had never once thought of Anne – though she had gone on to say: "if you believe this, why you are welcome." She finished her letter "Good night; may the many good nights your consoling friendship has procured me sweeten your own slumbers." Another extract from the *Notebooks* referred to the fear that "I do not always make you uneasy." Despite the weather, and true to form, Mary talked of solitary walks and melancholy musings; a dark and heavy cloud of depression formed as she sensed that they were gradually moving apart.

On 23rd April Anne looked forward to meeting Mary "without a regret" next day. She had been bidden to Mrs Hervey's at any time. She would therefore go there for dinner, and as long afterwards as was polite, and then go on to Horace's house in Berkeley Square. She arranged that Mary should go in the early evening to Horace, in his carriage, which Anne would arrange. Anne would then scoop up Mary and deliver her home. "I believe this is what you would prefer, things being as they are." Anne would tell Horace to have his transport ready for them.

In response to a remark of Mary's concerning somebody whose name is purposely erased from the letter, Anne gave vent to a tirade on "the commonplace *jeu* of modern gallantry". She hated gentlemen (by inference) who permitted cool calculating self-interest, with scarcely a shadow of passion, "to cause suffering to virtuous minds, unable at all times to stem the dreadful tide of passion." The spectre of Dorimont had risen again.

On a lighter note, in reply to Mary, who had doubtless been thinking of a joint holiday, she wrote that her ideal "Castle (in the air)" would be "a few, a very few rooms in a good farmer's house near the sea, a fine coast, some trees, and in no town". There seemed to be no question of her actually finding this castle, or arranging to share it with Mary. Her letter ended: "Rest assured that the greatest comfort I can receive on Earth is from the idea of ever being a consolation to you. Once more, Heaven bless you." Consolation, not castles, was all that was on offer. Mary was also practical: if an offer from Anne was not forthcoming, she could always fall back on Broadstairs with Agnes and her father.

By May Day Horace was back at Strawberry Hill and the Berrys elsewhere, causing him to lament: "as I have bushels of may, though no milkmaids as you are not at Cliveden, I shall make a garland for myself; and as I cannot yet dance, shall sit and hear the nightingale sing its country-dance, as I did last night".

In the early summer Anne decided to move from her house in Sackville Street. In 1792 the Melbournes had left Melbourne House next door, to which Anne had enjoyed a private entrance through the garden. The new owner, Frederick Duke of York, had allowed Anne's private entrance door to continue. However this was an insufficient attraction and during the late summer she moved to a new house, No 9 Upper Brook Street, on the Park side of Grosvenor Square. She had been in Sackville Street since shortly after her husband's death in 1776, and so leaving was something of a wrench. Mary advised her to "have a degree of pleasure in your house, and not be dwelling on the 'hows' and 'wheres'."

As summer progressed into late July, Agnes, whose romances either imagined or real had become a worry to her sister, went to Cheltenham with Mrs Lockhart, while Mary and her father went to stay at Park Place. They can have stayed little more than a week. On 31st July Horace wrote to Agnes in Cheltenham saying: "Your father and sister arrived soon after seven yesterday evening. I did not, though that was the time they had fixed, expect them so soon, concluding they would be pressed to stay longer at Park Place, and would be frail. They have found the alterations to the house advanced rapidly."

During their stay at Park Place, Anne and Mary had taken time off to visit Oxford, where they had purchased Greek exercise books. They had then gone on to Blenheim, returning by way of Nuneham Courtenay, the seat of Horace's great friend Lord Harcourt. For Mary, this visit had been of very special importance, and a year later she was to look back on it with affectionate memory: "This day 12 month (29th July) we left Oxford together – it is quite foolish to say how much the anniversary of all I afterwards suffered recalls in my mind."

Following the return from Oxford a quarrel took place, "sitting on the bench in the garden" at Park Place. Neither the beauty of the scenery nor the magical tones of Cynthia Johnstone's singing could lift Anne's spirits. The cause of the disagreement is not clear, but it seems to have been connected with the closeness of their relationship and the frequency of their meetings, and may have been as a result of a chance meeting with someone who might "abuse" them. Mary was "almost convinced that his vile, dark, capriciously wicked mind conceived and executed this plan of destroying satisfaction he could not enter into and of which my open, straight forward and unconcealing manner, made him perhaps doubly envious." At any rate the stay at Park Place was not extended, and on 1st August Mary was writing from Cliveden to Anne: "Oh God, you will know my real situation". Anne's friendship, she wrote, was her only real comfort: "For God's sake let me have it on such terms as I can give." She added that she felt better for a good cry, and that her father was talking of removing her to the seaside, where perhaps he felt that she would recover and he might have some peace.

Mary did not intend that they were to be separated from each other, but she thought it wise that they should meet less frequently. This was effectively achieved by Anne visiting Goodwood in August, while Mr Berry took his daughters to Prospect House at Broadstairs for a holiday commencing at the beginning of September and lasting until October. This period seen from the *Notebooks* seems to have been one of continuous letter writing, while Anne and Mary tried to sort out a new *modus vivendi*. Mary remembered "that whole Oxford party, connected in my mind with what immediately followed, as something infinitely melancholy." She sat looking at a picture of Anne in her black gown, noticing that in the portrait Anne appeared "all life and cheerfulness", doubting whether she now looked the same and wishing that she might see her. However she realised the perceived danger that "the same malicious being who has so wantonly aimed one blow at all my comfort and happiness, should follow it up by another, of which, it seems they so well know my horror". She added that nothing could make her more miserable than the idea that anything untoward should appear in the papers, especially if she did not know about it.

Some sort of relief was provided to Mary in the form of a letter from the ever-solicitous Mrs Cholmeley, which she sent on to Anne, saying that it had done her good and that she hoped it would have the same effect on Anne. Mrs Cholmeley's advice seems to have been not to worry unduly about printed abuse and to continue their friendship, but in a more sober and mature manner, seeing more of other people, and being less dependent on each other. Over a period of years the world would come to see that their relationship was founded on mutual respect and similar cultural interests, and not on "the baseness of vice, or the weakness of '*engouement*'." Anne's reaction, if any, to Mrs Cholmeley's advice is unrecorded. She was busy arranging to move house to Upper Brook Street. Anne and Mary did meet at least once in London before the Berrys departed for Broadstairs, and perhaps more often. Mary wistfully noted: "I shall give a melancholy look to the corner of the street, but remember that I shall be happy for you being really settled there". At the end of a long and a dismal month Anne, back with her elderly parents at Park Place, received a letter from Mary: "It is the finest moonlight; I long to be sharing it with you at Park Place. This month must have an end, and September a beginning".

By the end of September Horace had visited Anne's new house. He wrote to Mary Berry in Broadstairs that "I went yesterday evening to Mrs Damer, and had a glimpse of her new house; literally a glimpse, for I saw but one room on the first floor, where she had lighted a fire, that I might not mount two flights: and as it was eight o'clock, and quite dark, she only opened a door or two, and gave me a cats-eye view into them. One blemish I had descried at first: the house has a corner arrival, like her father's." He had had the opportunity to see her recently-completed bust of Mrs Siddons, which he described as "a very mistressly performance". From Anne's house Horace had gone on to his sister's, where he had found "Sophia, Lady Englefield, Mrs and Miss Egerton, and Mr Fawkener." Dorimont was still about.

On 27th September Horace noted that Anne was surprised by his saying that he expected to see Mary again in a week's time. Anne had not thought that the Berrys were returning so soon, and in keeping with their new format of friendship, fervently hoped that she would not see them too soon. Conveniently for Anne, news came from Goodwood that her sister was ill, and in the first week of October she removed herself thither. In the event she was right about the length of the Berrys' stay in Broadstairs, for they remained there until at least 19th October. Anne, still at Goodwood and helping to care for her sister, wrote to Mary saying that she was not at all sorry the Berrys were now leaving: "Storms and dark nights at this season in such a place really grow serious considerations." She went on to say that as Mary did not "much care" about seeing her at present in London, she was deferring her departure from Goodwood for a further three days; if both arrived in London on the same day, tongues might start to wag. She expected to arrive in London on Thursday to find the comfort and consolation of a letter, but not of Mary in person.

In the meantime she remained at Goodwood, which was full of officers, military reviews, and long dinners at which she had to be polite. She also had to act as a companion to Todle, who was awaiting "with the loquacious fidget of a very moderate understanding, the arrival of Mr Lennox after eight months' absence in the West Indies – and when he came he looked so like a bear led to the stake!". Todle was the family nickname for Lady Charlotte Lennox, who had married Colonel Edward Lennox in 1789. She was the daughter of the Duke of Gordon, and he was the nephew and heir to the Duke of Richmond. He had been serving with his regiment in Dominica and the Leeward Islands, where a bout of yellow fever had resulted in the death of four officers and 600 soldiers. In 1815 it was to be Todle who, as fourth Duchess of Richmond, was the hostess at the famous ball in Brussels on the eve of Waterloo.

In the same letter Anne said that she was not sending to Mary Horace's letters to herself, but was keeping them carefully for Mary to deliver them to him in due course. She asked Mary to let her know when she would require them again. Perhaps Horace had already started to groom Mary in the methods required to collect, collate, and maintain his correspondence for posterity.

During October Mary started to practice Mrs Cholmeley's advice. She saw less of Anne and started to write weekly rather than daily. She said that although her prospects had never been rosy, and were probably now less so than at any other time, nevertheless she found comfort, support and consolation. She reported that people said that she looked better, and that she was proud of the fact that she was now able to write less often. She encouraged Anne to go out more often and not live alone, and pointed out that "the more you live with other people, the more I can live with you." In early December Mary reported she felt better during the winter than she had for many years past, while Anne seemed to have won the approval of Mrs Cholmeley who, according to Mary, wrote of Anne: "just as I would have her feel. *C'est beaucoup dire.*"

Little correspondence between Anne, Horace and Mary remains from the first half of 1795. Presumably Horace and Mary were seeing each other at Twickenham too frequently to require letters. Mary and Anne were trying to restrict themselves to a weekly letter on Mondays, though few of these are recorded in the extracts in the *Notebooks*. Their meetings also seem to have been restricted, in keeping with the Cholmeley doctrine; the tone of the *Notebooks* extracts reduces from passionate to fond, and Mrs Cholmeley seems to have added the role of occasional duenna to that of adviser. Mary wrote: "We have no engagement in the evening. I have told Mrs Cholmeley I will do what she likes, but I shall take this *cum grano salis* if you are at liberty to do what you like." And again: "I wish you had never said a word about having a second place at the play for I am low and should have liked going alone with you" (and without Mrs C).

Anne had also resumed normal activities; she sculpted and exhibited a bust in the 1795 Academy exhibition. This was the first work she had done since the terracotta of Mary executed in 1793. Sadly no record remains of the identity or sex of the sitter, nor of its current whereabouts. She was also seen occasionally at Court, Mary admonishing her "from my own chair in your own room, six o'clock – and you not returned from your drawing room!" (the Queen's *levée*).

On 9th May Mary wrote from Cliveden, fondly rather than passionately: "When one says one will write on Monday is it breaking our promise to write on Saturday? I longed for you on Thursday when we came down here! It was the finest warmest quietest evening and everything looking and smelling so fresh and so green and so peaceable it must have done you good … I sat out enjoying the sort of calm melancholy with which such a scene always inspires me till it was quite dark. I have a room so full of roses that I felt quite vexed you do not see us and yet to ask you to come down for one day just to go back in the evening appears to me inflicting a sort of mortification upon ourselves."

The second half of 1795 brought unexpected grief. On 7th July Horace, who had the previous day received a visit to Strawberry Hill by the Queen and eight princesses, six of them English, the Duchess of York and the Princess of Orange, wrote to Harry that "I am not dead of fatigue with my Royal visitors, as I expected to be, though I was on my poor lame feet three whole hours. Your daughter, who kindly assisted me in doing the honours, will tell you the particulars." She was never able to do so. It was Harry who was to die, not of fatigue, but of a sudden attack of cramp in the stomach, in the early morning of 9th July. The doctors said that this had been brought on by exposing himself to cold. He was 74 years old, had been in good health, and his death was entirely unexpected.

Anne was in London at the time of her father's death. His servant from Park Place had arrived at 9.30 in the morning with the news. She just had time to dash off a note to Mary before departing for Park Place, asking her to break the news to Horace. She did not know when she would return but would need Mary to comfort her when she did. Mary, returning to Cliveden from Strawberry Hill, needed a few moments to recover from the shock of Anne's note.

By that evening Anne was at Park Place. She found her mother more composed than she had expected, but unable to deal with the practicalities of the situation. Anne immediately sent for her cousin John Campbell, the lawyer, who would know what was required. She had found Elizabeth Farren and her mother staying at Park Place. They had been on the point of leaving, but Anne had asked them to stay on. They had been a great help to Anne's mother at the time of her niece Caroline's death, and they would be company again for her now.

A few days later Anne received a letter from Mary to comfort her in the melancholy duties in which she was engaged. Harry Conway, Field Marshal of His Majesty's Forces, Colonel of the Royal Regiment of Horse Guards Blue, Governor of the Island of Jersey, one of the Lords of His Majesty's Most Honourable Privy Council, Caroline's husband and Anne's father, was buried on 20th July in the Ragley Old Vault in the small church at Arrow in Warwickshire. The church lies at the bottom of the hill, opposite the main entrance gates to Ragley Hall, the family seat of the Conway Seymour family and the home of Harry's elder brother, created Marquis of Hertford in 1793. Horace arrived to join the family funeral party and returned afterwards to Park Place, where he stayed on till 1st August.

Anne wrote to Mary saying that she needed rest. She had really appreciated Horace's presence, but was not sorry that he had now gone as, though in good humour, his outlook had been depressed, and there was little extra that he could have done. She was pleased that he had seen her mother gentle and composed. Mary, practical as ever, had given Anne some advice as to her mother's future. Anne replied that "at present my mother seems perfectly disposed to enter into every reasonable arrangement, and not at all objects to my solicitude to find her a house in our neighbourhood. She seems also to have entirely made up her mind to parting with this place, and these are the two great objects of my solicitude for her, as unless she does part with this place, the remainder of her life will be a scene of uncomfort and derangement. Never did you see a creature so unused and so unequal to business."

Anne was also suffering from a knee complaint. This was possibly a legacy from a few years back, when she had tumbled off her sculpting scaffold; at any event, after the strains of the past three weeks, it was causing her severe problems. On 1st August she had forgotten to bandage it, and it was so bad that she could hardly get upstairs. She had since put on a bandage, and found that if she limped about with great care, the pain was much less.

Two days later, Anne woke up at Park Place to find a gale battering her window. She thought that in many ways it would be good to be rid of the estate. Neither she nor her mother would be able to attend to its management and cultivation, and, using her ample stock of common sense, she could see no good reason why a solitary stroll could not be taken with as much pleasure over somebody else's land. Yet, at the same time, when she thought of the pride and pleasure that her father had got from Park Place, of the landscape that he had made, and of the enterprises that he put in place, now all destined to go to an unknown buyer, she felt that common sense might have its limitations.

The next day Anne wrote to Mary, still insisting that despite the current sad circumstances, correspondence should be ordered and not on the spur of the moment. She told her not to go on so much about death, which was common to everybody, and not to complain that she was surrounded by barbarians. "Do not take up things for others so much more seriously than they do for themselves, nor think that every clouded brow proves a broken heart." She also advised her not to worry too much about Agnes, whose latest dalliance had come to nothing. Mrs Cholmeley again came in for the rough edge of Anne's tongue: "I am downrightly angry with her, and quite provoked at what you tell me, the beginning of which I saw, as I told you, the evening she passed with me … there is not a doubt but the parson will lean towards the softest cushion." What her misdemeanour had been on this occasion is unclear.

Anne's letter continued, hoping that Mary's planned visit to Cheltenham in late August, where she would join Agnes and Mrs Lockhart, already there, would be successful. Mary's health in her own words was "nothing either good or bad", but Horace, the self appointed medical adviser, had counselled her to make the journey for health reasons, telling her that he had high hopes that the waters, a change of air, and a variety of amusements without late nights would prove effective. He had also prescribed for her a diet of "much fruit, and currant tarts, especially at night; her stomach, alas, is rather weaker than that of an ostrich!"

At the same time Horace was also prescribing for Anne. He feared that the cause of the problem in her knee was attributable to a blood condition, and suggested that perhaps the Harrogate waters might cure her. In the meantime he recommended that she took magnesia, her late father's favourite medicine, for which Horace himself claimed to be a satisfied customer. "I take it every morning, and am convinced of the benefit I receive from it." He also recommended sea-bathing for Anne, provided that her doctor would sanction it.

By 28th August Horace had heard from Mary that Cheltenham agreed with her. She wrote that she had been joined there by General O'Hara, and on 8th September Horace replied, delighted that "she had chained her General to her car." Perhaps he was not really as delighted as he stated, and sensed that O'Hara might be a threat. His correspondence accelerated; he wrote to Mary on an almost daily basis, telling her of Twickenham gossip, of his numerous social activities, and reminding her of his generosity at Cliveden, where he was paying for two new bedrooms with closets, along with a giant ice house. He reported that he had also offered to make up the pay of the Cliveden gardener, who had given notice as his wages were too low.

On 15th September Horace wrote that Anne had spent an agreeable day with him, the first time he had seen her since Mary had gone to Cheltenham. Her knee was much improved and her lameness scarcely noticeable. He had agreed with her that he would come to Park Place at her mother's request, and that they would all meet up there with the Berrys on their return from Cheltenham, towards the end of the month. What he did not know was that his beloved "wife", Mary, had received a proposal of marriage from General O'Hara, sometime on the 30th or 31st August.

Chapter 14

A DIFFICULT CHOICE

In Mary Berry's notes of early life she mentioned that in 1779, when she was 16 years old, she conceived a girlish passion for a Mr Bowman, which, owing to the wise intervention of her relatives, was nipped in the bud. The one serious heterosexual love affair of her life, however, did not occur until 1795, when she was 31. Then she lost her heart to Charles O'Hara.

O'Hara, who was born about 1740, was among the younger of around fourteen illegitimate children of James O'Hara, second Lord Tyrawley. His father, a professional soldier, had been Colonel of the Coldstream Guards under the Duke of Marlborough, a member of the Privy Council and envoy to Russia and Portugal. Horace described him as "singularly licentious, even for the courts of Russia and Portugal", and on his return from Portugal in 1741, wrote that "my Lord Tyrawley is come from Portugal and has brought three wives and 14 children; one of the former is a Portuguese with long black hair plaited down to the bottom of her back". This was Charles's mother, Dona Anna. The boy was educated at Westminster School, leaving early, in 1752, to take up a cornetcy in the third Dragoons. In January 1756 he was a lieutenant in his father's regiment, the Coldstream Guards, and became *aide-de-camp* to his father in Gibraltar, a role he continued in Germany with Lord Granby after the battle of Minden. In 1762 he acted as quartermaster-general to his father in an expeditionary force to Portugal, sent to repel a threatened Spanish invasion, which never occurred.

Following the Treaty of Paris in 1763, he went to Africa as governor of the newly formed African province of Senegambia, the primary East Atlantic base for the lucrative slave trade. He commanded His Majesty's African Corps of Foot, a British forerunner of the French Foreign Legion, being a penal detachment of military delinquents pardoned on condition that they served in Africa. Here he antagonised slave traders, lost most of his troops from disease, and was negligent in his civil duties. The latter led to a Board of Trade investigation, resulting in his dismissal in 1776.

The following year, still with a commission in the Coldstream Guards, he quickly transferred to America and The War of Independence. He was made responsible for the defence, first of Sandy Hook and then of Manhattan, where he was noticed more as a plausible talker than as a successful organizer. Eventually, after a spell in charge of prisoner exchanges, he returned to England on leave in 1779. At about this time his military engineering capabilities had brought him to the attention of Harry, and HW recorded that Colonel O'Hara had been present in May 1780, along with the Duchess of Richmond, Lady Ailesbury, Mrs Damer, and others, at a play by Lady Craven.

By October 1780 he had returned to America in command of the Brigade of Guards, and distinguished himself at the battle of Guilford Courthouse, where he was severely wounded. His commander Lord Cornwallis wrote: "The zeal and spirit of General O'Hara merit my highest commendations; for after receiving two dangerous wounds he continued in the field whilst the action lasted." In October 1781, when Cornwallis surrendered at Yorktown, it was O'Hara who offered the formal surrender to George Washington and the French Comte de Rochambeau. After Yorktown, he remained on parole in New York until he was exchanged in February 1782. Later that year he returned to England to take up command of his new regiment, the 22nd Foot.

Once back home he soon succumbed to high living and gambling, and finding that expenditure exceeded income, took the common recourse of departure to the continent, where he was safe from English creditors. Whilst there he took the opportunity of a belated Grand Tour, and at the end of March 1784 he was introduced to Mary Berry. He was aged about 44, she 21; they were both on their first visit to Italy. She had gone with him and others, including Harry's nephew, Edward Conway, to view the upper storeys of St Peter's in Rome. They most likely also met on at least two other occasions in Rome, when the English community dined together.

They met again on 21st April, when the Berrys spent the evening at Terni with O'Hara and Mr Conway. The following day they went together to see an idyllic cascade. Mary remembered in her diary that "the banks are well wooded down to the water's edge, or rather into the water, which runs round the roots of many of the trees forming little islands. ... A more beautiful subject for the pencil can hardly be conceived: the froth rises like thick smoke far above the top, and at the waters edge. ... The people had told us it would take three hours to see the cascade; we were much above six." Again on 29th April they had come across O'Hara and a large party returning from Chamonix. These early meetings had left a fond memory for both of them.

With the help of Lord Cornwallis, O'Hara managed to sort out his financial affairs and by 1785 was back in England. It is probable that Mary would have seen him again in the latter half of 1785, or in 1786, though for much of the latter year the Berry family was in Scotland and Yorkshire. In 1787 O'Hara was appointed as commandant of the garrison at Gibraltar, an office which he retained until 1791. A letter from HW to Mary Berry in Turin in October 1790 stated that "Boyd is made Governor of Gibraltar, and somebody, I know not whom, is appointed Lieutenant-Governor in the place of your friend O'Hara – I know not how or why, but shall be sorry if he is mortified, and you consequently."

In early 1791, O'Hara sailed for England, arranging, *en route*, to call on Anne in Lisbon. On 20th February 1791 HW wrote to Mary, in Italy: "O'Hara is come to town, and you will love him better than ever … O'Hara has been shockingly treated."

Two months later in April, HW regretted that he had not yet seen O'Hara as "he is so dispersed … that I have not seen him even at General Conway's. When I do, can you imagine that we shall not talk of you two? Yes, and yr accident I am sure will be the chief topic." By 15th April he was able to write that he had now seen O'Hara "with his face as ruddy and black and his teeth as white as ever, and as fond of you two, and as grieved for your fall as anybody … He has got a better regiment."

In 1792 O'Hara was promoted to the lieutenant-governorship of Gibraltar shortly before war began with France. In 1793 he was given his first independent command as British military governor on French soil at Toulon. This port had surrendered to the English at the end of August 1793. O'Hara took up his new duties on 23rd November, following which Toulon was attacked by the French. O'Hara authorised a sortie under Major General David Dundas to capture the redoubt containing the French artillery trained on the town. This was initially successful; however the French counter-attacked and the English retreated with considerable loss. During this engagement, O'Hara was wounded and forced to surrender to a young French officer named Napoleon Buonaparte, who treated him with the honours of war.

The civilian authority to which he was handed over was less accommodating. There he was classed as a political criminal, forced to watch mass executions by guillotine, and threatened with execution himself. He was sent to Paris where he was paraded through the streets with the insults of the mob ringing in his ears. He was imprisoned in harsh circumstances and great discomfort in the Luxembourg where he remained until being finally released in August 1795 after an exchange of prisoners. It was ironic that the General Rochambeau for whom he was exchanged bore the same name as the general to whom he had given the sword of surrender at Yorktown.

It was now over ten years since O'Hara had first met Mary; he was aged 55, Mary was now 32. During most of those ten years, O'Hara had been stationed overseas, either as commander or prisoner. The couple had had relatively few chances to see each other, yet their friendship is well attested by both HW and Anne. No sooner had he returned to England, than he went swiftly to Park Place to pay his respects to Caroline, in mourning for her husband and his old friend Harry.

At Park Place Caroline had invited some guests. Anne was staying with her mother, and on Friday morning 28th August she was sunning herself on a bench under the orange trees near the greenhouse, whilst reading a play by the Latin author Terence. Earlier that morning the house party had gone for a walk, during which Mrs Hervey had brought up the subject of Dorimont, and whether or not he was already married to the woman to whom he had been so long attached. Anne had tried in vain to avoid this particular conversation by stopping to pick a flower or gather seed. Apparently the lady in question lived in a small villa close to Mrs Hervey's mother, who was addicted to a more than occasional peep through her curtains. Caroline, who disliked Mrs Hervey, shrugged her shoulders and said that she had heard that Dorimont had enquired very particularly about Anne. If this observation had been intended to rile Mrs Hervey and please Anne, it did not have the desired effect. If Dorimont wished to know about her, she exploded, he should ask her himself. She was certainly not going to enquire after him.

On the Friday afternoon, the ladies were sitting at the tea-table. Into their midst, burst O'Hara, totally unexpected. He was to stay two nights and depart early on the 30th August to meet up with Mary Berry in Cheltenham, bearing with him a letter from Anne to Mary. She wished that she had seen more of "Dear O'Hara", but she had succumbed to an extremely painful attack of colic on the morning of the 29th. She had been forced to call for the apothecary, Doctor Harley, who had administered a speedy cure, enabling her to join the house party after dinner.

In the letter, Anne set out her own position with regard to O'Hara. She had been somewhat shocked both by his sudden arrival and his intended precipitate departure, and had wondered whether something must be wrong. However he had looked better than when she had last seen him, and she understood the convention that since he had been formally exchanged as a prisoner, he had to continue on active service. This was to be as governor of Gibraltar, and his appointment there would silence any criticism of his fitness for high command. Anne would have preferred that he had been given a home posting, though she would have seen little of him if he had been in England. Although he was a really good friend, she was neither gay enough "nor many other things enough" for him. She would be quite satisfied with just a taste of him now and then lest she might forget how different he was from other men. Anne was in her late 40s; O'Hara, who had been one of the fourteen children of an admired father, needed a wife who would provide him with children of their own.

O'Hara lost no time in getting from Park Place to Cheltenham. He was equally quick off the mark in proposing to Mary, who appears to have accepted. The post also was no sluggard. On Tuesday 1st September Anne replied to a letter from Mary, received sooner than expected. Mary wrote: "my heart as well as my vanity is highly flattered by the opinion I know he has of me and by his knowing and entering into my character (except where some of his own queer crotchets warp his judgement) more than anybody except yourself."

Anne was anxious to know more details of Mary's conversation with O'Hara. "Had he mentioned me you would have told me, but he may think me a disadvantage to you, and imagine that we live more constantly together than alas! we do. Or he may suppose (for he knows me not) that I endeavour to influence you against marrying, thinking it probable that in other circumstances I might see you less … and that because I have remained single myself, I think it a fine thing so to do in general. Even this second idea would give me much pain, so contrary to what your own heart tells you, and to the anxious wishes I have for your happiness, which would never appear to me too dearly bought by any sacrifice I could make." Anne continued that any such ideas might be entirely without foundation, but that Mary had asked her to think aloud, and this is what she was doing.

Anne continued to write daily from Park Place to Mary, but surprisingly, during that week, there was no further mention either of the proposal or of Mary's response. The contents of her letters cover her day to day activities. There had been a visit from HW, described as "the Grim King", whom she was always glad to see, as his conversation soared above the fatigue of daily chitchat. She had been stung by midges whilst reading in the garden. In her letter of Friday 4th September Anne said that she intended going to London on Monday for a few days, asking Mary to write to her there. She found Park Place dispiriting and wondered how her mother could bear the difficulties and distress of selling her houses. Her London home in Soho had received no offers; the selling agent, Mr Pocock, with the eternal optimism of estate agents, talked of a second potential rich buyer for Park Place. She looked forward to seeing Mary "to comfort and support her". Of O'Hara there was no mention.

Eventually, on 9th September, Anne summoned up the will to write to Mary about the proposal. She started her letter saying, unconvincingly, that writing brought her relief whenever she had anything on her mind, which at the moment she had not. However she felt that Mary was expecting her to write with her reactions to O'Hara's offer, and was uneasy that she had not done so. She apologised that in her letter of 1st September, she had been "under the influence of painful sensations, almost at the moment of a first impression. Yet you would not wish me not to feel, and will allow for all I do feel". The subject was then immediately changed to discussion of Agnes's *amours*, Mrs Cholmeley's selfishness, a dinner at Mrs Hervey's, and an improvement in her gammy leg.

Two days later, on 11th September, Anne told Mary that she was totally pleased and satisfied on the subject of O'Hara, "and there, while we are here, I think it most wise for us to rest." Nevertheless she immediately returned to the subject, not finding it strange that he was puzzled by Mary's character, such a mixture of "tenderness and passion, virtue and resolution". Anne knew very well that one of the things that the plain-talking soldier found strange was her own relationship with Mary.

Meanwhile Mary and O'Hara had been free to enjoy the waters and attractions of Cheltenham together, and would continue to do so for the month of September. They would both have had time to reassess their feelings towards and about each other. In the ten years since they had first met, much had changed. O'Hara had aged with war and imprisonment, which would have left their scar on him; he may have been a little out of touch with a society that had moved on in his absence. He certainly could not get his head round the development of Anne and Mary's relationship. He was mindful of the fact that he would need to take up his command in Gibraltar in the very near future, and wished to marry and take his newly-wed wife with him.

Mary was still the responsible keeper of her sister and father. She had now added both HW and Anne to her life and friendship. A comfortable existence for her family at Cliveden depended on her continuing literary association with HW. She found it hard to separate herself from life with Anne. By the end of the month, both Mary and O'Hara were beginning to have doubts about a future life together. Convention, pride and embarrassment prevented them admitting it. By 21st September Mary was growing impatient to meet up with Anne and begrudged the two days that remained doing nothing at Cheltenham.

Meanwhile HW, who had not been made aware of the proposed engagement, also continued to write daily to Mary. With no mention between them of O'Hara other than, on 15th September, a smile from Horace at "the General's sober advice", probably given in connection with Mary's purchase of a horse, and an observation that another lady, "the noisy personage you wot of", would have taken both the advice and the general. On 19th September he looked forward to meeting up with Mary and O'Hara at Park Place on either Sunday 27th, or Monday 28th, which would be after they had arrived.

History does not relate what took place when Anne and Mary, O'Hara, HW and Caroline met at the end of September at Park Place. Because they were all together, no letters passed between them. Because it was necessary to keep the engagement secret for the present, it would only have been mentioned in confidence in talks between Anne, Mary, and O'Hara. It soon became clear to Anne that the course of true love was not running smoothly.

On 3rd October Anne, still at Park Place, wrote anxiously to Mary, asking for news. She confessed that she really knew little about O'Hara's character. It seemed impossible to believe that he was not seriously attached to Mary; however many years of soldiering and living in the real and sordid world might have clouded his natural good sense and judgment. She believed that at present, instead of being united by indissoluble ties, they were in danger through inability to express themselves, of not understanding how much each loved the other. It was unfortunate that O'Hara would soon be called away on service to Gibraltar; a little more time might have helped to sort out his prejudices and "crotchets". Anne declared that her absence from Mary showed proof of her forbearance whilst Mary came to a decision. "If I loved you but half as well, or thought of you but half as much as I do, I should fly to you."

Anne appreciated Mary's regard for HW, and the need to keep him in the dark until a final decision had been taken. It would be a major blow for him "should all his castles fall to the ground, with what ever degree of absurdity and want of sight they may have been constructed."

By 6th October Anne at Park Place had heard again from Mary. She replied, wondering if O'Hara might be afraid of women, albeit that the woman in question was so very superior to those with whom he had previously been in contact. In addition Mary had been trying to persuade O'Hara to look more kindly on Anne. This was hardly a good tactic at a crucial time. Anne instructed Mary to think of herself and not her friend. Apparently neither Agnes nor her father suspected anything. HW also chose to say nothing, and as Mary said, "none, they say so blind."

Anne again implored Mary to think of her own comfort and happiness. She argued implausibly that HW, when told, would take it with composure, that Agnes would not refuse a suitor to keep a sister, and that her father would only be delighted by the union. She finished the letter by saying that she expected O'Hara soon at Park Place "to tell me all". Her arms would be open to receive him, her heart also. However she sounded a note of caution that his prejudices against her profoundly grieved her and cast a melancholy cloud over future prospects.

She intended to remain at Park Place to help her mother over the sale of the property and its contents, but would be happy to come to Mary at a moment's notice if she should require it. She added a quaint but touching request from her mother concerning a cow. This had been a present from Mary to Caroline; she could not bear her to be sold, nor to leave her behind, and so had requested that Mary dispose of her to a friend. Mary had other things on her mind, and the present of a cow would hardly have been likely to improve matters with O'Hara.

A quotation from Mary in *Anne's Notebooks*, dated 7th October, noted that Anne had probably not yet seen O'Hara, which she very much wished her to do. There had obviously been a rift with O'Hara, and it was to be Anne's task to mend the bridges. Mary wanted to see him once more: "My heart does not so easily separate itself from anything that it believes attached to it". However the affection pendulum was swinging back in Anne's direction: "The longer we live I fancy the more necessary we shall find it to feel for one another what so few other people feel for us".

Two days later, the meeting between Anne and O'Hara had taken place. She described it as an interesting and tender interview. O'Hara had said little at first, and seemed to avoid the subject; gradually he had opened up and repeated to Anne what Mary had already told her, often in the same words. The net outcome had been that he did not wish to see Mary again. He was, Mary considered, "afraid to trust himself". He had told Anne that his embarkation orders had been brought forward, and that he would be setting out the following Tuesday evening, having seen Anne in the morning. He had been unable to tell her if he would see Mary, nor could he see Caroline again, before he left.

Anne recounted that "he said in the course of our conversation many and many so kind things that the reflection at this moment has filled my eyes so full of tears I can scarcely see what I am writing. Strange it might sound to others, but I should have pressed him with still greater tenderness to my bosom had he been taking from it at this moment all that is most dear to me in life. ... Yet as it is, God knows, I felt and, I believe, expressed, enough." Following this meeting Anne had been unable to touch her dinner; now she heard the bell man come to collect the letters. She just had time to tell Mary that she had forgotten to ask O'Hara for the return of her locket and picture, but that she would certainly secure the return of the former by Tuesday. "You will, I need not ask you, come if you can and when you can to me ... what a world! And whither is one to turn!"

The next day, Saturday 10th October, Anne wrote again with more considered yet more convoluted views on the previous day's meeting with O'Hara. She thought that he had avoided her attempts to persuade him in favour of the marriage, preferring to listen to his own fancies and prejudices, whatever they might be. His reluctance to listen to her arguments might have led her to say less than she ought to have done, and she had an awful pang of regret that perhaps she had let a chance of happiness for Mary slip through the net. On the other hand she had been torn the other way by the likelihood of losing Mary so suddenly, the misery of her absence, and the worry of dangers at sea *en route* to Gibraltar. However she was clear that it would be unwise for Mary to use her powers of captivation to persuade O'Hara, as his absurd scruples might return at any time to render their marriage miserable. She remained anxious and she thought it likely that O'Hara would try and see Mary again, and that he might try to rekindle hopes which she believed he would not voluntarily abandon.

On Thursday 15th October another meeting took place, firstly between Mary and O'Hara then, Anne having arrived, between Mary and O'Hara and Anne, and finally, after Mary's departure, between Anne and O'Hara. The first part of this session, a long conversation with O'Hara, was described by Mary in *Anne's Notebooks*. She was flattered and touched to have inspired O'Hara's love, and to have made such a friend, even if he would never be more than that. She trusted that after she had left them O'Hara had been able to explain more fully, and looked forward to filling in Anne at a future date, with the gist "of a more detailed conversation than any we had before, all which will please <u>you,</u> or else I am mistaken, and will <u>not</u> please <u>me</u>".

That night Anne wrote to Mary from Grosvenor Square saying that after she had left, "O'Hara obeyed you and the great coat was laid aside". He had spoken to Anne openly and confidently, with passion softened by concern for Mary, which Anne had found very touching. She considered that this blunt soldier, unused to sentiment and affection, found it difficult to trust what his heart told him. She could not express how much the recollection of what he said concerning Anne and Mary had affected her.

By this time the proposed marriage was effectively over. However Mary, O'Hara and Anne all had problems in admitting it and closing the chapter. Letters continued to flow and meetings to be arranged. Anne would tell Mary that O'Hara "put up his hand to his dark eyes after listening to me and, turning away his head, took hold of my hand, which he pressed with that tenderness of expression that goes directly to my heart". But it was too late. As Mary noted to Anne: "The more I reflect upon all that has passed lately and all it may probably lead to, the more I feel satisfied with the chance of such sort and degree of happiness as you and I may ever hope to attain in this world … I am sure this will give you pleasure and it ought for heaven knows! It is your work … I am not ashamed of not being able to go alone while I have you to lead me … and when I lose you!"

The strains caused by these shenanigans were beginning to tell on Anne. Though she remained surprisingly patient with Mary, others not so involved caught her tongue. Agnes, who had belatedly been made aware of the engagement, was pleased for Mary's sake, but sad to lose her. This not unreasonable attitude had annoyed Anne, who observed that as things stood she was unlikely to lose her, and that during the time she had benefited from Mary's guidance, she had not been content with it. HW who was cross with Mary, possibly because he had got wind of the possible engagement, also came in for a pasting. "I do not feel uneasy at his indisposition, as I rather conclude it over, and I am sure when I think of what his dinners are, and how he eats them, I wonder he and his cat are not sick together every day for their dessert."

By Monday 19th October O'Hara had told Anne that he had heard from the Admiralty that he was to sail very shortly. Anne herself was going early the next morning to Goodwood and intended to return on Tuesday 27th October. She told Mary that if she wrote and requested it, Anne would call at Cliveden on her return journey, before going on to London. On the Tuesday morning O'Hara sent his servant to Cliveden to tell Mary that the fleet was under orders to sail immediately. He asked her to come to town that evening so that he could see her before he left.

Mary wrote to Anne that the intended meeting had taken place. It had not been a success. Miserably, Mary asked Anne whether her absence at Goodwood was designed to show Mary how much she depended on her. If so, it was unnecessary; she had never required to be deprived of a blessing, in order to realise its value. She requested that Anne would return from Goodwood by way of Strawberry Hill, and asked her to arrange this with HW.

On Thursday 22nd October Anne replied from Goodwood that it was difficult for her too, as every day her own affection and attachment for Mary increased, since she was the "only real interest and comfort I have, or ever can have in this wide world." Her own sister Mary looked miserably ill and emaciated; she slept badly, and then only with the help of laudanum; and most alarmingly of all, she suffered from dreadful coughing fits. She was so unwell that Anne doubted whether she could return as planned. Mary's doctor, John Hunter, was due that day and she would await his report. Anne regretted that Hunter only came when he was sent for, from 30 miles away, and she feared that he did not understand the symptoms. However her sister refused to see anybody else, which made it extremely difficult for the Duke of Richmond, who continued his usual routine. Indeed he had just reported a large fleet sailing out from Spit Head. Anne wrote that she was going up the hill to see this fleet for herself, using the glasses and telescopes installed there.

On Saturday 24th October Mary, at Cliveden, woke after only a few hours of broken sleep, in which she had dreamt of seeing O'Hara the next day, to the melancholy reality of a long uncertain and painful absence. She hoped that in future Anne would love her better as a result of the sacrifice that she had made, by not marrying O'Hara immediately as he had wished. There were others including Agnes, her father, and HW, who depended upon her, and whose feelings she had wished to protect. In the meantime he was gone, leaving her with her mind in turmoil. She had asked O'Hara that if he were in danger he would send her some token or assurance that showed he had thought of her till the last. She believed that by this time he would be in Portsmouth and prayed that he would write as soon as possible.

On Tuesday 27th October O'Hara penned his reply: "Dearest Mary ... every moment of my existence proves, too forcibly for my peace, that comfort will be a stranger to my breast when absent from you, for I cannot, like you, from the imperfection of my nature, derive fortitude sufficient to sacrifice my own to the happiness of others ... that I should give you, in the event of illness or danger, some token that my sentiments respecting you continued the same as at present makes too deep an impression for any language to express." However he doubted that he would see her again before he left, as he had seen a note from Admiral Cornwallis saying that even though the wind was in the wrong direction, they would sail as soon as it moderated. He begged her to tell Anne that he hoped to write the next day.

As a result of this series of meetings around the end of October between Mary and O'Hara, as principals, and Anne, and Mary and O'Hara, with Anne acting as intermediary, agreement seems to have been reached that O'Hara would sail unmarried, to return at some unspecified time to wed Mary. In reality, it was a pact that was extremely unlikely to be fulfilled.

On 30th October Anne, back in Brook Street, wrote apologising that she had not had time to write before, and that this letter too was written in a great hurry. She pitied Agnes who had been to see her, worried about what Mary was going through, and about her incapability of comforting her. Anne could see from "her hurry, fidget and confused ideas" that she would not have been a great help. Caroline had sent Mary her very best wishes and was insistent that she come with Anne to Park Place the following

Tuesday 3rd November, where they would spend a few quiet days together. By now almost all Anne's immediate friends seemed to know about the on-off romance, with the possible exception of HW.

The fond farewells were increased beyond reasonable measure by delays in the fleet leaving harbour. On 31st October it was still in Portsmouth, and O'Hara was again writing to Mary, though the message may have been wearing a little thin. "Here I am, my dear, dear soul, and here am determined to remain, for I cannot venture to see you again". He continued: "Let the pleasing reflection that when we meet again it will be for life, comfort and support us through the anxious, tedious hours of our separation."

He went on to advise that she did not inform HW of their engagement until such time as she was about to quit "your father's house for mine", and that she herself, and no one else, should be the messenger. With regard to Mary's father, sister, and her other self, "the dear dear stick" (Anne), they would know that when Mary was his, she would also be as much theirs as ever. They, being independent, might be with the O'Haras as much as they pleased.

Two letters from Mary lay unopened on O'Hara's table. He had just been getting around to opening them when he had been sent for by the Prime Minister, William Pitt, to meet Sir Ralph Abercromby, the senior army general. A postscript announced that he had returned from the meeting with Pitt but that his hand was shaking so much, as a result of his wounded arm, that he was unable to write any more. He exhorted Mary to prepare to be his nurse. Mary was exhausted; she wrote to Anne that she really wanted to get away for a few days, and longed for the quiet that she could only find with her.

Back in the West, the fleet had ventured out as far as Plymouth when a storm arose, and they were blown back to Portsmouth, from where on 9th November, still anchored firmly to the shore, O'Hara wrote to Anne a note of final exasperation. He thanked her for her care of Mary who seemed to wish to remain with Anne for ever, "folded in her arms, her throbbing breast pressed to yours", speaking a language "to you two alone on Earth well understood". He referred to a letter from Anne which had urged him to heal the wound which his groundless apprehensions had inflicted upon Mary. He said that he had attempted to do this in a letter which Mary had received the previous day, and if this was not acceptable to both of them, he believed it better for everyone's sake that he was forgotten. He suggested that Anne get Mary to show her his latest letters. As soon as Anne had received this letter she wrote from Park Place to Mary enclosing O'Hara's letter with the injunction: "It so affected me, it must please you". She had read it three or four times, with tears trickling down her cheeks. She expressed concern about O'Hara's arm, and suggested a trifle facetiously: "Would we were both now going there to coddle him!"

On 9th November Mary wrote to Anne, thanking her for the stay at Park Place and for her advice and comfort: "Nobody but those who have a stick can know, after leaning upon it continually for a whole week, how cruelly one misses it and how helpless one feels without it". Shortly afterwards she received Anne's last letter from Park Place, with its enclosure from O'Hara, to which she replied on 14th November: "You know how I must feel O'Hara's letter to you …. this is indeed writing to my heart and gives me the comfortable conviction that I have not deceived myself or him in supposing that we shall mutually contribute to each other's happiness for <u>such</u> sympathy in <u>such</u> feelings assures us of all that two rational beings can expect in this irrational world". A postscript to this letter shows that the immediate correspondence with O'Hara had come to an end. "Alas! My dear so all our letters are too late. The papers yesterday, which I did not see till late, announced the sailing of the *Barfleur* on Wednesday afternoon."

Mary continued to write, but O'Hara remained stubbornly silent to her letters. The fleet passed Falmouth early in 1796; a week later it was at Lisbon, and by the end of January at Gibraltar. Still there was no communication. In January 1796 Mary wrote a despairing epilogue to O'Hara. Ever practical, she set out a housekeeping account, proving that "as indeed I told you at the time", his imagined lifestyle was unaffordable, but that a sober and ordered establishment might be afforded without having to pinch and scrape. She told O'Hara that she had cut all his extravagances and that were they to live anywhere else than London it would be considerably cheaper, and she would be very happy to go with him where ever he went. She said that her father who was by now aware of the engagement, did not want his daughter to be a financial burden to her new husband and wished to ensure that "everything I can have from him shall belong to you as soon as I do myself." Mary did not elaborate on how little this might be. She had worked out that total living expenses would amount to £1263 per year, and that they would require an additional £800 for him and £200 for her making a total of £2263. Once more O'Hara remained silent.

At last, on 26th April, Mary received two letters from O'Hara, written on 26th February and 30th March, while Anne, a day later, received one written on 7th March. He complained of the extraordinary treatment he had received from both Mary and Anne, and particularly from Anne, whom he loved with the warmest affection, not only for her own sake but because she was the daughter of parents whose affectionate protection had been so very responsible for his own good fortune. Mary replied immediately, and she did not mince her words. "Make yourself perfectly easy", she wrote "your having consented to become my husband, as you are pleased to express yourself to Mrs D, will entail none of the evils you so much dread." O'Hara had presumed that her imaginary apprehensions were put on to disguise the fact that she had changed her mind about marriage; she replied that it was he who had changed his, and kept her waiting three months to tell her so. A gentleman would have told her frankly without delay and by so doing have remained a good friend, if no longer a lover.

Two days later Mary saw Mr Barnes, a friend of O'Hara's who delivered two further letters which received an equally dusty reply. On 2nd May Anne added her own broadside. She claimed that when she had parted from O'Hara on 28th October 1795 the marriage was agreed in everything but the time and date. Nothing had changed from Mary's point of view, and O'Hara's vacillation had cost him her friendship. The scars of bad habits and a bad world had virtually destroyed the natural goodness of his heart. The final letter from O'Hara was dated 20th June, and answered at length by Mary on 16th July, with the final admonition that "I shall cease endeavouring to convince myself that the O'Hara with whom I have been corresponding is the same warm-hearted, rational, affectionate O'Hara with whom I had parted in October."

Mary Berry's romance had come to an inglorious end. The 44-year-old bachelor general whose eye had been taken by a 21-year-old girl in Rome in March 1784, just over 12 years before, had lost his bride. The same girl, now a mature 33-year-old, who had been consistently teased by Horace about her beloved General, would never find a husband. More than 200 years later, far removed from the event, and dependent for evidence on an incomplete correspondence, there is little to be gained by trying to apportion blame.

However this book is about Anne Damer, and it is worth looking at her major role in the affair. Three years earlier in 1792 she too had received a proposal from Dorimont, which from the start, although attracted to the man, she had no intention of accepting, despite Mary's reasoned protestations in favour of the match. In 1795 the tables had turned and it was Anne who was counselling both the intending bride and her groom-to-be. Did she really want to see her dear friend Mary married and separated from her? Did she really believe that O'Hara and Mary would be suited to one another? It is possible to believe that her protestations in favour of O'Hara were not sincere, that she did not wish to lose Mary, and that she thought she only had to wait, with a judicious aside, an innuendo here and there, for the intended match to fall apart, as in fact it did. If so, she was playing a cruel and calculating game for her own advantage, oblivious of the feelings of her friend.

It is difficult to make that scenario fit Anne's character. When the engagement was first announced, Anne had already taken the opportunity physically to distance herself from Mary, apart from planned intellectual outings such as those to Oxford or Westminster Abbey. From this point of view, Mary's engagement to O'Hara was welcome as a potential to reduce the possibility of lesbian abuse; Mary had previously advanced a similar argument in connection with Anne's possible attachment to Dorimont. From Anne's standpoint, the suitability of O'Hara as a husband for Mary might not have been of prime importance. No one had asked her whether John Damer would make an ideal partner. Admittedly her late husband had been a substantial heir, while O'Hara was penurious; however Mary herself was no heiress, nor was she getting any younger. Anne would still have had the comfort of a regular correspondent and the possibility of a winter sojourn in the Governor's House in Gibraltar. Marriage for any young lady was socially desirable, and she seemed genuinely to wish that her friend should benefit from it. She acted continually as adviser and marriage broker; indeed she believed that when O'Hara sailed, the marriage was agreed in everything but the time and the date. She may well have had her doubts as to the reality of this, but it was not in her interest to undermine it.

It is more probable that it was the two would-be partners who both came to recognise that they had not known each other well enough when they became engaged, and that they had both changed over the past ten years. Mary had found it difficult to give up the relative security of her father, sister, Horace, and Anne, and her literary career for a precarious financial future. O'Hara, the seasoned war-scarred soldier was quite unable to fathom Anne and Mary's friendship. Neither had wished openly to acknowledge their mistake and suffer public disapproval as a result, and so the charade of letters across the sea had continued until it finally stuttered to a muddled and unsatisfactory conclusion for all concerned.

O'Hara remained as governor of Gibraltar until his death, six years later, in 1802. By all accounts he was a popular governor, known by his troops as "Old Cock of the Rock". Lacking a wife, he found consolation with two mistresses, by each of whom he had children. A later description of him hints at the qualities which Mary had once found irresistible: "His appearance, indeed, was of that striking cast which, once seen, is not easily forgotten. General O'Hara was the most perfect specimen I ever saw of the soldier and courtier of the last age, and in his youth had fought with Granby and Ligonier ... Notwithstanding the strictness of the discipline which he scrupulously enforced in the garrison which he commanded, no officer could be more universally popular than General O'Hara ... In his own house and, above all, at his own table, he delighted to cast off all distinction of rank and to associate on terms of perfect equality with even the humblest of his guests. The honours of the table were done by his staff, and the general was in nothing distinguished from those around him, except by being undoubtedly the gayest and most agreeable person in the Company..."

Mary bundled up her letters and her memories. Years later, aged over eighty, she opened the packet in which the letters were stored and inserted the following sad note: "This parcel of letters relates to the six happiest months of my long and insignificant existence, although these six months were accompanied by fatiguing and unavoidable uncertainty, and by the absence of everything that could constitute present enjoyment. But I looked forward to a future existence which I felt for the first time would have called out all the powers of my mind and all the warmest feelings of my heart, and should have been supported by one who but for the cruel absence which separated us, would never have for a moment doubted that we should have materially contributed to each other's happiness. These prospects served even to pass cheerfully a long winter of delays and uncertainty, by keeping my mind firmly riveted on their accomplishment. A concatenation of unfortunate circumstances – the political state of Europe making absence a necessity, and even frequent communication impossible, letters lost and delayed, all certainty of meeting more difficult, questions unanswered, doubts unsatisfied – all these circumstances combined in the most unlucky manner, crushed the fair fabric of my happiness, not at one fell swoop, but by the slow mining misery of loss of confidence, of unmerited complaints, of finding by degrees misunderstandings, and the firm rock of mutual confidence crumbling under my feet, while my bosom for long could not banish hope that all might yet be set right. And so it would, had we ever met for twenty-four hours. But he remained at his government at Gibraltar till his death, in 1802. And I, forty-two years afterwards, on opening these papers which had been sealed up ever since, receive the conviction that some feelings in some minds are indelible."

Chapter 15

TWO DEATHS AND A REMOVAL

Mary was exhausted, disillusioned, and depressed as the O'Hara saga came to an end. She wrote to Anne that she looked forward to spending time somewhere with her "as the best and only cure for my wounded spirits. I feel every day more forcibly the absolute necessity of change of air, change of scene and a total change of habits of life to recover my mind from all it has suffered from various causes these last six months." They determined on a seaside holiday in Sussex, alternating between Bognor, where they would go for the sea-bathing, and Goodwood, the home of Anne's half-sister, Mary. At the end of July Horace wrote to Mary, playfully warning her of the dangers of the Bognor rocks; on 5th August he received a letter from Mary, which confirmed that the sea-bathing was doing her good. Among the neighbours at Bognor were the Pepys from Twickenham, and the Prince of Wales's mistress, Lady Jersey. Writing to Edward Jerningham on 16th August, Lady Jersey described Bognor as delightful, quiet, cheerful and clean. The air was delicious and the countryside around beautiful, though a little devoid of kindred spirits. She described her house as much better than any of the Brighton lodgings, and her dining room and drawing room were much the same size as her rooms in the Pavilion. She told Jerningham that Mrs Damer, who was there with "Miss Burny", had called upon her the previous week and had been *"fort aimable"*. They had since met out riding, and greeted each other. However Lady Jersey did not intend to extend the social acquaintanceship as, probably correctly, she thought that her children would not be suited by or suitable for Anne and her friend.

Whilst there, Anne and Mary visited Arundel Castle, and Horace recommended also that they visit Petworth, Standstead, and Uppark. By 24th August Horace was exhorting them to "bathe on, bathe on and wash away all your complaints; the sea air and such an oriental season must cure everything but positive decay and decrepitude." On 29th August Horace told Hannah More that he had sent on a letter from her to Mary, who was still bathing in the sea at Bognor rocks. On 30th August Mary was writing to John Barnes from Bognor refuting his defence of O'Hara's behaviour.

Anne had much else to concern her during the period of Mary's engagement, separation, and convalescence. Her father had died in July 1795, just as he had completed the modernisation of the house at Park Place to be worthy of its surrounding

Anne Damer by Sir Joshua Reynolds RA 1788 dressed as Athenais in the Richmond House Players production of Theodosius. From a private collection.

Mary Berry bronze 1793. © Christies Images Ltd 2013.

Mary and Agnes Berry by Anna Tonelli 1795. From a private collection.

Anne Damer and Mary Berry reading together. Artist unknown. Courtesy of The Lewis Walpole Library, Yale University.

King George III, 1790-93, marble, "my colossus". A 2.9m statue carved for The General Register Office Edinburgh. Crown Copyright 2008, NRS.

Anne Damer by Harriet Carr 1788. © Scottish National Portrait Gallery.

Anne Damer by Richard Cosway RA engraved by L.Schiavonetti 1794. From a private collection.

Anne Damer in old age detail from watercolour by John Downman. From a private collection.

The Honble Anne Damer.

Anne Damer with her bust of Paris by Richard Cosway RA 1790, pencil drawing. From a private collection.

The Damerian Apollo. A cartoon by William Holland 1789. © Trustees of the British Museum.

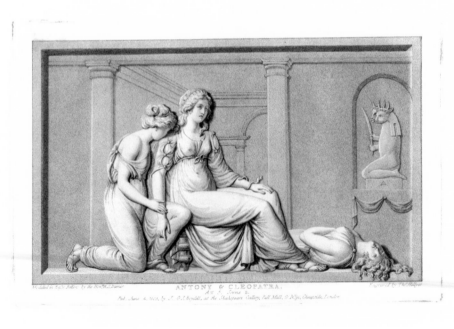

Antony and Cleopatra bas relief from The Shakespeare Gallery. © Trustees of the British Museum.

William Fawkener miniature on ivory, date and artist unknown. From a private collection.

Charles James Fox 1794 by Karl Anton Herkel. © National Portrait Gallery.

Horace Walpole in older age by George Dance, pencil 1793. © National Portrait Gallery.

Sir William Hamilton 1777 by Sir Joshua Reynolds. © National Portrait Gallery.

Caroline Ailesbury marble bust 1789. Courtesy of Sothebys.

Rabbits – detail from a needlework tapestry by Caroline Ailesbury. From a private collection.

Prince Lubormirski. Marble bust 1788. © Ashmolean Museum. University of Oxford.

Sir Joseph Banks bronze 1812-13. © Trustees of the British Museum.

Charles James Fox marble 1812, Château de Malmaison.

Sir Humphrey Davy terracota painted black 1813. Conway Library, The Courtauld Institute of Art, London.

XXVIII

Admiral Nelson bronze 1827-28. Courtauld Institute. © The Royal Collection. Photographic Survey
The Courtauld Institute of Art, London.

Princess Caroline 1814. © English Heritage.

Strawberry Hill 1793, J. Farington. Courtesy of The Lewis Walpole Library, Yale University.

York House 1808 by J.P. Malcolm. Courtesy Twickenham Museum.

Above: Napoleon 1815. Given by Napoleon to Anne Damer, and by her to the British Museum. © Trustees of the British Museum. Left: The coat which Nelson wore during the Battle of the Nile. Presented by Nelson to Anne Damer and by her to the Duke of Clarence (later William IV). © National Maritime Museum Greenwich.

landscape. He had left the property to Caroline, who found the estate far too large to manage, the house too big for an ageing widow and the memories too powerful for her to want to remain there. The property was put on the market, and Anne's assistance in dealing with the estate agent, Mr Taylor, was both valued and essential, for Caroline was no businesswoman. The sale process was protracted and frustrating; in August Anne described Mr Taylor as a serious nuisance, more forward, more troublesome and more vulgar than ever. By the beginning of September 1795 she found Park Place melancholy, with her father missing and her mother unsettled, while a train of prospective and unappreciative purchasers came to view. She had to endure the usual estate agents' hype; there had been a second application to view via another agent, Mr Pocock, from "rich people". By October, to general relief, a suitable purchaser had been found and approved. Lord Malmesbury was a diplomat, and as Horace put it, "no banker, and does not propose to buy the most beautiful villa in England to make money of it." Caroline, with Anne's assistance, continued to live there until 16th December 1795. On 14th December Mrs Lybbe Powys and her husband dined there. She said that Lady Ailesbury had insisted on their going, but that it was a visit they would rather have avoided, as with Caroline on the eve of departure, the house appeared empty and sad. At the same time they were dejected at the loss of a good friend and neighbour.

A similar situation arose with regard to Caroline's London home, Conway House in Soho. This too had to be sold, and again much of the work fell upon Anne's shoulders. By early 1796 Caroline had moved in to Anne's own house in Upper Brook Street, and from then on mother and daughter lived together.

On 5th June 1796 Anne, Mary and Agnes, and their friend Daniel Lysons, chaplain to Horace Walpole, visited the exhibition at the Royal Academy, where they met Joseph Farington, the Secretary, an artist and despiser of women sculptors. Anne, fully occupied in dealing with Mary's romantic problems and with her father's estate, had had little time or inclination for sculpture and did not exhibit in the annual Academy exhibition. Farington noted that "the observations of Mrs Damer did not seem to me to prove that she has any exact knowledge of painting, what ever she may have of Sculpture; and she did not make intelligent remarks on the latter. I think her manner, and particularly her voice very affected and unpleasing." During the afternoon a formal 18th century introduction took place. Sir George and Lady Beaumont arrived and conversed with Mary Berry, whom they knew. Mary extolled Sir George's virtues to Anne, who agreed that she would like to meet him. Farington was requested to inform Sir George, who replied that he wished Mary to introduce him to Anne. The introduction was then effected.

The health of Anne's half-sister, Mary Duchess of Richmond, again gave rise to anxiety. Anne had spent time nursing her in the autumn of 1795, when the O'Hara saga was at its peak. Mary's health had improved subsequently, and in June 1796

Horace recorded that she had visited him in Berkeley Square and that she was much better than when he had last seen her. She had recovered her looks and her spirits: "in short, my joy has made me shed tears!" However her recovery was short lived; Mary Berry, who was spending July and August with Anne, first at Bognor, and then at Goodwood, wrote to Horace in July and again in August, saying that the Duchess was not at all well. Horace replied that he trusted in her slow recovery, though he might not be around to witness it. Sadly it was not to be; Mary died in her bed at Goodwood on 1st November 1796, after a long and painful decline, with the Duke, Anne and Caroline beside her. Horace lamented that "she is gone, and I am still here, though above 20 years older!" *The Gentleman's Magazine* obituary described her as a "woman whom neither titles could dazzle nor pains depress; who bore her honours so modestly upon her, that, while her dignity enforced respect, her gentleness inspired love. Though nursed in all the luxury and splendour which rank and opulence could procure, and gratified with every object of human avidity and ambition, she never forgot the hand of Heaven whence she received them." The Duke of Richmond behaved generously to all Mary's servants, providing them with pensions. He sent Horace a bequest of one of Mary's rings. Sadly he recounted that "I can never put it on my swelled fingers, but I will for ever carry it about me, while there is any for ever for me!"

Horace's for ever was not to be for long. His health had given both him and his friends considerable cause for anxiety, with increasingly frequent attacks of what he described as gout. On 6th November 1796, whilst at Strawberry Hill, he was struck down with a violent vomiting fit, with great pain in both legs. On the next day one of his legs was greatly inflamed and he had lost his voice. He was brought to London, where Berkeley Square was warmer and medical expertise more available than at Strawberry Hill. Anne described him as "lying on a couch in a state of weakness and age, that keeps him from seeing anybody, and makes him incapable of conversing on any subjects, public or private." He made a partial recovery and returned to Strawberry Hill, whence he wrote to Mary on 24th November, telling her that Kirgate would certainly make cases for her in which to store his letters: "How ridiculous for me to be ordering still more great-coats for my own letters!". Mary too was not well during these weeks, and Horace's letters to her show a greater care for her welfare than for his own. By 15th December the Berrys were anxious that he return to Berkeley Square and better doctors. On 4th January 1797, in a letter to the Countess of Upper Ossory, he wrote: "I am quite out of pain and full as well as I am ever likely to be; walk again I never shall, but my invulnerable stomach, my pulse that beats the tattoo as strongly and regularly as a young soldier, and the Governor of my citadel, I mean my Sergeant-Surgeon, Mr Huitson, who watches me incessantly, has removed the inflammation from my leg, and I may last a little longer." One more short letter followed on 15th

January, again to his old friend, the Countess of Upper Ossory, which he signed off in his own inimitable style: "I shall be quite content with a sprig of rosemary thrown after me, when the parson of the parish commits my dust to dust. Till then, pray, Madam, accept the resignation of your ancient servant, Orford."

On 11th February Farington recorded that "Lord Orford is confined to his bed. Mrs Damer and Miss Berrys are with him mornings & evenings. His memory has failed. If they are an hour absent, he thinks they have not been for some time ... The Duchess of Gloucester would see him a few days ago – much jealousy of Miss Berrys among that connection of Lord Orford."

Horace was to live a few more weeks, in a semi-comatose state, sometimes lucid, at others suffering from hallucinations; he would call for those closest to him and then call again, forgetting that he had seen them. At last, exhausted, he died on 2nd March 1797. Farington's diary recorded that "His Lordship's body was opened, & though he was in his 80th year when he died and had been much affected with gout and in the earlier part of his life had been considered as of a consumptive habit, yet the lungs were perfectly sound, the heart and stomach the same, nor any defect in the vitals – the abscess in his throat probably caused his death. He took no sustenance for some days & may be said to have been starved. He died with apparent pain."

Horace had spent much time in preparing and revising his will, which took up 32 pages of closely written handwriting. His Norfolk estates were left to his great-nephew, the Earl of Cholmondeley, and if no Cholmondeley heirs, to the Duke of Richmond and his successors. Strawberry Hill was left in trust for Anne's sole use during her lifetime, the trustees being the Duke of Richmond, Lord George Lennox, and Lord Frederick Campbell. After Anne's death it was to pass to Horace's great-niece, Elizabeth, Dowager Countess of Waldegrave and her heirs. All household goods, furniture, pictures, china, jewels, collections of curiosities, silver, plate, cattle, horses, carts and other carriages were left on trust to the occupant of Strawberry Hill, "to preserve the same intire."

As the *Whitehall Evening Post* reported on the 14th March 1797: "What will give pleasure to the admirers of *virtu* is the knowledge that the noble collection of scarce and valuable articles is to remain absolutely entire, as it was left; and they may be assured that the liberal taste of Mrs Damer will not render it less accessible."

To help pay this considerable maintenance bill, Anne was bequeathed in addition two thousand pounds. This latter bequest might seem hardly generous in view of the potential running costs of Strawberry Hill, and this was also pointed out by the *Whitehall Evening Post*: "Mrs Damer is left in a situation of some difficulty by the late Lord Orford. She is residuary legatee. Her legacy has been wrongly stated; it is £2000 nett, not £2000 per annum. Strawberry Hill is only hers for life; it then reverts to the Waldegrave family, from whom it is not alienable until the young Lord is of age."

This residence of genius, and repository of science and art, is in a very decayed state, and will demand a considerable sum to render it thoroughly habitable; and certainly much more than the interest of the fair possessor's legacy to maintain it in orderly repair."

Happily for Anne, the newspaper had not read the final codicil to Horace's will. Here he increased the amount left to Anne by an additional £4000, and he also left a further £4000, the interest of which was to be for the benefit of Caroline during her lifetime, and thereafter to her daughter Anne. She was therefore left £6000 with an expectation of a further £4000. Presumably Anne and her mother would have enjoyed in addition the benefits of the recent sale of the Conway houses, but the delights of living at Strawberry Hill would come at the considerable price of its renovation and maintenance.

Horace, the great family man, did not forget his relatives. Maria, Duchess of Gloucester was left £10,000 in trust for life, and in addition his four small Poussin landscapes in Berkeley Square. His sister Maria Churchill and her daughters, Maria Lady Cadogan and Sophia Walpole received £500 each, as did his niece, Laura Keppel, and her four children. Laura, Dowager Countess of Waldegrave received £5000 and Horace's house in Berkeley Square and its contents. Further smaller bequests were made to other relations. Horace's old friend and correspondent, Sir Horace Mann, had predeceased him, dying in 1786, but Horace directed that his daughters were to share £5000. Horace's deputy at the Exchequer, Charles Bedford, was bequeathed £2000, and William Harris, clerk to the Exchequer £1500 and an additional £300, the interest on which was to be paid to maintain Mary Rowton, whom Horace had maintained from her infancy. His personal servant, Philip Colomb, was left £1500, all his wearing apparel, and his dwelling, Walnut Tree House. Thomas Kirgate of the Strawberry Hill Press was left £100, as were Martha Tanner, a housemaid; Anne Branson, the housekeeper; the widow of his late footman James Sitley; and James Colomb, a current footman. Other named servants received smaller sums, and all the servants in employment at his death received something. Maria Colomb was left an annuity of £6 per annum with instructions that she be kept on at Strawberry Hill in the same capacity as at Horace's death. Horace has been accused of being penny-pinching with his staff, but these bequests were generous, other than that to Kirgate, who had printed Horace's works and handwritten his letters long into the night for many years. Strangely this faithful servant received no more than a housemaid; Horace may have had reasons which he did not disclose, possibly connected with a suspicion that Kirgate was making money on the side from the printing press. However Kirgate was virulent about his ill-treatment, and what is more, he published it in verse:

THE PRINTER'S FAREWELL TO STRAWBERRY HILL

Adieu! Ye groves and Gothic tow'rs
Where I have spent my youthful hours,
Alas! I find in vain:
Since he who could my age protect,
By some mysterious sad neglect,
Has left me to complain!

For thirty years of labour past,
To meet such slight reward at last,
Has added to my cares:
To quit the quiet scenes of life,
T' encounter bus'ness, bustle, strife,
Hangs heavy on my years.

Farewell! My printing-house, farewell!
Where I no more shall calmly dwell,
Within my peaceful door:
No more in conversation free,
Enjoy my friend and sip my tea;
Ah! No; those days are o'er.

On thee, my fellow-labrer dear,
My Press, I drop the silent tear
Of pity, for thy lot;
For thou, like me, by time are worn,
Like me, too, thou art left forlorn,
Neglected and forgot!

Farington reported in his diary that Lady Englefield, a neighbour, was indignant at the will of Lord Orford – in leaving Lady Mary Churchill an annuity and a reversion, he had treated her more like an upper servant than a sister; she was also shocked at his vanity in leaving the Duchess of Gloucester so much. He also noted that the will contained "no marks of attention to his several friends who were in the habit of seeing him much and who contributed to his amusement. Miss Berrys regret it." He went on to say that Mrs Damer did not believe it in her power to make up any deficiencies in Horace's will by assisting Kirgate or others. His government stocks, which had been valued at £56 at the time of his death, were now lower, and should Anne be forced to sell them at the present time, there might not be sufficient to pay all the legacies.

Whatever their regrets for others, the Berry family fared rather better. Little Strawberry Hill, the Long Meadow and the garden were left for the use of Mary and Agnes Berry during their lifetime. They were instructed not to build anything that would obstruct views from Strawberry Hill, not to let the property for longer than a year, to pay any taxes due and keep it in good repair. They were each to receive £4000. They also received special instructions with regard to a square wooden box marked with an O on the outside. This box contained all Horace's own literary work both published and unpublished. This box was to be delivered to Robert Berry, North Audley Street, immediately following Horace's death. The contents of the box were to be the joint property of Robert, Mary and Agnes. All Horace's literary works were to be published by Robert Berry, and the ensuing profits were to be split equally between father and daughters. The box marked O, coupled with the instructions in his will, marked the consummation of the literary marriage between Horace and Mary, the courtship for which had started in 1788. To save any embarrassment or subsequent "abuse", Mr Berry would be the nominal publisher, though the reality was that Mary would do the work to create the profits which the family would share. Farington confirmed that the work would be left to the Miss Berrys, as Horace had held "a very moderate opinion of Mr Berry, in every respect but that of his being a well-meaning man."

Mary started work at once and described herself as labouring incessantly for nearly 12 months, neglecting other interests and only looking at books connected with the work in hand. This first edition of Walpole's works was published in 1798, in five quarto volumes, without the editor's name. An interesting example of Horace's intention that his letters be recorded for posterity occurred in a letter dated 4th October 1797 from Horace Mann, nephew of Horace's old and faithful Florence correspondent, to the *Sun* newspaper. Two days previously the paper had reported that publication of Horace's works was being held up by a dispute over the copyright of Horace's many letters to Sir Horace Mann. The young Horace Mann replied that the story was entirely without foundation. He had personally brought back to Lord Orford all the letters he had written to his uncle on a frequent and regular basis. They had been sealed in packets; no copies had been made, and they had been the sole property of Lord Orford. For Mary, still recovering from the disappointment of O'Hara, the regular hours and hard work of the editing process came as a numbing relief. Her journal for 1797, in addition to the death of Lord Orford, only mentions "I go to Lady Spencer's at St Albans, and to Brooke Hall to meet Mrs D and Mr Whitbread. See much of the Starhembergs".

Meanwhile, Anne too was working hard on behalf of her deceased godfather. As executrix of Horace's will, she set about carrying out its provisions. Horace's filing system would appear to have been somewhat haphazard. Anne wrote to Lord Hertford on 3rd May 1797: "With regard to the Conway papers, which are innumerable, my uncle Lord Frederick Campbell, with the assistance of Kirgate, has with great attention been endeavouring to separate them from many others, both in Berkeley Square and at Strawberry Hill. ... The Grant which I fancied I had seen, I wish much that it may be found, as Ld. Orford seems to have kept, I cannot say preserved, all papers."

She also had to distribute Horace's 1784 *A Description of the Villa at Strawberry Hill,* with later additions of illustrations. Horace had ordered the printing of 200 copies, and produced a list of 78 names to whom copies should be distributed after his death. As the holders of the names had predeceased him, so Horace had written "dead" against their names upon the list, thus reducing the number to be distributed to 68. Three months after his death in June 1797 Anne, together with her uncle Lord Frederick Campbell, acting as executors, formally delivered the copies, bound in a blue wrapper inscribed to record the gift, and tied with string sealed in black wax with the executors' personal seals.

A letter to Anne from her cousin, the Duchess of Gloucester, dated 4th July 1798, started by congratulating Anne on being "so noble in everything you do." Few compliments in letters stand on their own merits, and this one also had its qualifications. The following sentence began: "I am encouraged to ask you a favour." She wasted no time in coming to the point. The £10,000 that Horace had left her in his will was invested in government securities from which she drew dividends. She wished to receive the whole of the legacy to assist in the building of a new house at Brompton. Sadly, Anne's reply is not recorded.

Anne followed Horace's example of opening Strawberry Hill to the public for conducted tours. She made some alterations both to the house and to the tours, and these are evident in a new guide to the house published in 1800. A later letter addressed to a Mr Bullock says that "if Mr Bullock will say on what day he wishes to see the house at Strawberry Hill, Mrs Damer will, with pleasure, send a ticket, provided the Date named be not previously engaged, as only one company can see the collections on the same day ... the ticket will admit six persons". Mr Bullock was advised to make his request to No 18 Upper Brook Street, "as Mrs Damer is chiefly there just at present".

Anne had known Strawberry Hill since she had been sent there as a small child. She had grown up with the building; they had developed together. By the time of Horace's death in 1797, both were beginning to show their age. When Anne was born in 1748, Horace had just rented Strawberry Hill, prior to purchasing it in 1749. It had originally been built as a small lodging house by the coachman to Lord Bradford, and was known locally as Chopped Straw Hall, as rumour had it that construction had been financed by the substitution of straw for good hay for the horses. The original house was completed in 1698, and improved subsequently; fashionable occupants included the playwright Colley Cibber, the Bishop of Durham, Lord Carnarvon, and Lord John Sackville. Horace's immediate predecessor had been a Mrs Chevenix, who ran a fashionable toy and gift shop in Charing Cross.

The house that Anne would have known as a small child was compact, four or five small rooms on each of two floors, and a further one or two rooms on the third. At first Horace, having made the building habitable, had done little to it, and had concentrated his attentions on the five acres of garden. During the year 1748 he had acquired an additional nine acres of meadowland, further from the house, which he adorned with grazing cattle and sheep.

In 1749 he began alterations to the house, assisted by his 'Committee of Taste', consisting of Richard Bentley, John Chute and himself. The chosen style of alteration was to be Gothick, which took its inspiration from mediaeval architecture, mainly of the later perpendicular style. In essence it had to contrast with the early 18th century fashion for concentric Palladian villas of impeccable geometric proportions; it was to be irregular, fit for purpose, and deliberately quaint. Instead of large, evenly-spaced windows, designed to let in the light, Horace would choose narrow vertical openings, often filled with stained glass to exclude an excess of light, and produce the effect which he described as "gloomth". Where classicists saw columns and pediments, the proponents of Horace's Gothick chose arrow slits and battlements.

At this point of Strawberry Hill's development Horace described the hall and staircase as "the most particular and chief beauty of the Castle". Lit only by "lean windows with rich saints in painted glass", and by four grisaille quatrefoil glass panels set in the roof during the day, and by a single candle in a Gothic lantern by night, the hall glowed grey with gloomth. The visitor's eye, when accustomed to the light, would see a Gothic fretwork balustrade to the staircase, based on a design from Rouen Cathedral. *Trompe l'oeil* fretwork, designed from a print of Prince Arthur's tomb in Worcester Cathedral, covered the walls, providing the background for suits of armour, ancient weapons, and heraldic devices. Shortly afterwards, Horace added two larger rooms: a refectory on the ground floor, with a library above, which was to complete his building works until 1759, when the Holbein chamber was begun.

Anne's childhood memories of Strawberry Hill would therefore have been of a small and, in parts, dark and melancholy house, surrounded by gardens, by young trees and shrubs, by beds of flowers, and lawns and terraces.

The next spell of building work began in 1763 and finished in 1772. During this period the size of Strawberry Hill more than doubled. The Long Gallery and the Cloisters below, the Round Tower at the western end and the Cabinet and Great Bedchamber leading off the Long Gallery, their embellishments, their furnishings, and eclectic mix of contents were all added during these years. The final touch was the tower containing the Beauclerc Closet, added in 1776, to contain Lady Diana Beauclerc's illustrations for Horace's play, *The Mysterious Mother*, published by the Strawberry Hill Press in 1768.

As well as the building works to the main house, Horace also supervised the construction of the printing house, whence the output of the Strawberry Hill Press would flow during his lifetime. In addition, he built in the gardens a *cottage ornée* and a Gothic Chapel. His last construction, between 1790 and 1792, was the New Offices. These provided stabling, coach house and grooms' quarters, laundry and washing facilities, a dairy and steward's room. Rectangular in shape, and situated on two floors, the New Offices were to the west of and separate to the Round Tower. It was intended that they should also provide improved accommodation for the Strawberry Hill Press, but in the event this never happened.

As fast as the buildings were completed Horace filled them with his collections of books, paintings, china, sculpture, coins and bric-a-brac, some items very fine, others only mediocre. Many were connected with the Walpole family, both ancestors and more immediate relations. The library was superb, and with Horace's collection of prints had already spilled over into the top of the Round Tower by the date of his death. Everything was displayed with great taste and fitted to the settings that the Committee of Taste had designed for it. A world-class collection of miniature paintings contrasted with the Cardinal's Hat, which may or may not have been worn by Cardinal Wolsey; a suit of armour belonging to Francis I showed Horace's taste for the magnificent, an earthenware teapot with the head of Lord Chatham his appreciation of the humdrum and droll. The size of the collection was enormous. When it was eventually sold in 1842 it fetched £33,000 and took 32 days to sell.

While building and collecting flourished together, Anne would have been a less frequent visitor than in childhood; she was abroad for long intervals accompanying her parents, and after her marriage in 1767 and during the first few years of wedded life her contact with Horace was increasingly rare. However she must have seen him and Strawberry Hill from time to time, and have been fully aware of the ongoing work there.

It was not until after John Damer's death in 1776 that Anne re-established regular contact with Horace. She had played very little, if any, part in the building of Strawberry Hill, nor in assisting with the creation and display of its collections. Her main contribution during Horace's lifetime was in his addition of her sculptures. The only works by Anne listed in the great 1784 description of the contents of the house were *The Dog,* belonging to Mr Jennings of Shiplake, in the Gallery, and in the Beauclerc Closet, two heads modelled in wax in 1777, one of Augustus, from an antique cameo belonging to Sir William Hamilton, and the other a companion piece, of Voltaire. Later, as Anne grew in sculpting experience and stature, Horace added more of her work. In the Little Parlour he placed the original terracotta model of two sleeping dogs, subsequently executed in marble for the Duke of Richmond. The Beauty Room contained a cast of the bust of Lady Melbourne, the Green Closet a profile of Caroline in wax, and the Armoury a *Head of Isis,* being a small terracotta model for the mask on Henley Bridge. Added later still, from 1786 onwards, were a terracotta model of young Paris in the Breakfast Room, produced as a model for a marble bust of the son of Rossi, the dancer, and two kittens in marble in the Green Closet. The last Damer items to be included were the life-size terracotta fishing eagle, modelled in Autumn 1786 at Brocket Hall, and placed in the Strawberry Hill library, and a marble bust of the young Paris, the whereabouts of which was not specified.

Other of Anne's immediate family memorabilia, which she would have known when she and Caroline took up residence in 1798, included various small gifts of china, plate and candlesticks, from both her parents and herself. There was also the Eckhardt picture of Harry, Caroline and Anne as a small child playing with a dog, another of her, probably as a girl, painted by Hamilton, as well as a much later one of Anne, the sculptress, with the head of young Paris in the background, painted by Richard Cosway. Caroline would have found at least three of her tapestries to welcome her.

It must have been quite an undertaking for Anne to agree to take responsibility for her lifetime for the maintenance of buildings, collections and gardens, and to continue to show Strawberry Hill to visitors. The buildings themselves were not constructed to last; Horace had written to Harry: "My buildings are paper, like my writings, and both will be blown away in 10 years after I am dead". His friend, Gilly Williams, said that Horace had outlived three sets of battlements. When Horace died, it was fifty years since he had arrived at Strawberry Hill; Anne too was in her 50th year. The interior of the house's living quarters, especially in the oldest part, required redecoration. The western end of the building from the Long Gallery to the Round Tower was by then over 20 years old, and showing signs of wear and tear. In his old age the Grim King had allowed his standards to slip. In the garden too there was much work to be done. The collections required care and attention; as part of her responsibilities under the terms of Horace's will, Anne had undertaken to maintain them in good condition. She did not intend to add to them; a letter to John Pinkerton on 17th May 1804 thanked him for offering a portrait of the Comte De Grammont, but declined it, "as I content myself with preserving the collection at Strawberry Hill, left in my care by the Earl of Orford, without attempting further to increase it."

However Anne had much for which to thank Horace in his bequest. Since the sale of Park Place, she and her mother had no country home to which to retire once the London Season was over. Strawberry Hill conveniently filled the gap; house and garden were extremely suitable for entertaining; it was a great honour to have been left in charge of this famous building, its collections, and its happy childhood memories.

Most importantly, the Berry family was only a field away at Cliveden. Anne and her mother moved in with enthusiasm in the first months of 1798.

As Horace before her, Anne seems to have begun with work on the Strawberry Hill garden. Horace had frequently complained about his gardener's idleness; it is probable that it had been allowed to grow wild. In 1770 Horace had written his essay on modern gardening, and this had advocated a natural appearance, with nature assisted rather than subdued by man. The essay had preceded the craze for wilder landscapes, and any wild and unkempt Gothick appearance in the Strawberry Hill garden probably owed more to lack of management than a later change of heart. Anne set out to brighten and tidy it, probably using some of the many plants that were becoming available as a result of international plant-hunting expeditions. On 10th August 1798 *The Star* reported that Anne, to whom Horace had "bequeathed his Strawberry Hill and the unique adjoining cottage of the late Kitty Clive, is despoiling all of the Gothic Graces of the former by a fringed petticoat of smoothly planted shrubs" in place of "the rugged cliff and rushy dell …. so chastely appropriate to these classic grounds."

Anne lost no time in replying. On 12th August *Bells Weekly Messenger* carried the message that "Mrs Damer has not despoiled Strawberry Hill of an atom of its Gothic beauties. It was left to her for lifetime only, and independent of that circumstance, Mrs Damer's taste perfectly corresponded with that of the late Lord Orford, whom she assisted in the decorations of both house and garden." Anne had always been an enthusiastic gardener. Back at her home in Sackville Street, she had complained of the lack of gardening space; at Park Place she had eagerly helped her father in the design and layout of the flower gardens, and argued with him on the positioning of the Druids Circle from Jersey. She was to discuss seeds and plants with both Sir Joseph Banks and Josephine Bonaparte. Her description of the lands of Portugal and Spain through which she travelled contain many references to the local flora, and these are repeated in the text of her novel *Belmour,* along with closely observed descriptions of both well-kept and neglected plots.

Chapter 16

NELSON AND NAPOLEON

According to Anne's earlier biographer, Percy Noble, and the *Dictionary of National Biography*, Anne was not to remain long in the Strawberry Hill garden. In early autumn 1798 poor health and the lure of sunshine and warmer climates called her to Naples and her old friend and mentor, Sir William Hamilton, the resident British minister. They had remained friends since his proposal back in England in 1784, when Anne had refused to spend her life with him in Naples.

She had visited him again in Spring 1786, her stay coinciding and overlapping with the arrival of another, and new, guest at the Palazzo Sessa. Sir William, in his mid-fifties and still lonely, had, not unwillingly, permitted his nephew and heir presumptive Charles Greville to send him on approval a young lady called Emma Hart. She was 21, beautiful and alluring, the favourite model of the painter George Romney, and had arrived in Naples believing that she was going on holiday and that she would be joined later by her lover, Charles Greville.

Emma was unaware that Greville, heavily indebted and consequently in need of marrying an heiress, had decided to divest himself of his mistress before entering the matrimonial stakes. Realising that his uncle was in need of female companionship, Greville had introduced Sir William to Emma, and he, immediately smitten by this "fair tea maker", had been induced by Charles to come to an arrangement whereby, in return for paying his debts and acknowledging Charles as his heir, he would become Emma's protector, and she would join his collection of treasures in Naples. She arrived with her mother on 26th April 1786, her 21st birthday.

Emma, born in Neston in Cheshire, the daughter of a blacksmith, had been christened Amy Lyon. She had entered service, finding her way to London and a position in a troupe of dancers. Her beauty had singled her out for the attentions of Sir Harry Featherstonehaugh, the squire of the handsome Uppark estate, overlooking the eastern Solent in Sussex. She had become his mistress, and caused a stir at Uppark by dancing naked on the dining room table for the amusement of the assembled company. Among the guests present had been Charles Greville, who had immediately fallen for her all-too-visible charms, and in due course made her his mistress. He had gone to considerable trouble to educate her in the manners of polite society, and although Caroline commented on her dreadful taste in dresses, she was generally considered to have graduated with honours. Besides being beautiful, she was also intelligent and able, and could combine all her attributes to her great advantage. She invented an after-dinner game which she called "Attitudes", in which, clothed in loose fitting classical garments, she would strike a pose and invite the audience to guess whom she was portraying. She soon made her mark with Sir William as an organiser and assistant, leaving him free to concentrate on his collections of antiquities. He gradually came to realise that she was honest, brave and loyal to Greville, who had abandoned her. Touched by her despair, and remorseful at his bargain, he proposed marriage to her, and she, with nowhere else to go, accepted.

Sir William and Emma returned to England in the summer of 1791. The marriage took place shortly after a visit they made to the Conways at Park Place. Harry wrote to Sir William on 9th September 1791 to congratulate him on his marriage, which he had seen announced in the newspaper. "After your leaving us here, your departure was so sudden, that I lost not only the pleasure I had promised myself of getting another short sight of you, or even sending you a line with my most cordial wishes for all the happiness that could or would attend the event which had immediately preceded it." The event in question was Sir William's marriage to Emma. He continued: "You have had already a honeymoon of five good years; in other words, five years experience of good humour and attachment." He went on to extol his own happy experience of marriage. The letter finished with a note that "Mrs Damer desires me to tell you she has received your letter from Dover, and will answer it soon." It would be interesting to have known its contents and those of her reply.

Following the marriage Emma was accepted at Court in Naples as Sir William's wife, although not as the consort of the British ambassador. Thenceforward she played a prominent part in the life of the embassy. She and her mother, who had come with her as part of the package, busied themselves around the house and gardens, permitting Sir William to relax with his antiquities, and to assist King Ferdinand in his frequent hunting expeditions. Stags, hinds, wild boar, hares and even owls were slaughtered in quantity, many by the King, far fewer by Sir William, who took part in the sport only as a responsibility of his ambassadorial role.

Emma first met Nelson in 1793, when he was sent from Lord Hood's fleet, of which his ship was a part, with dispatches to Sir William in Naples. Nelson made an immediate impression on the ambassador who described him to Emma as "a little man who cannot boast of being very handsome, but such a man as I believe will one day astonish the world". Nelson, writing to his wife, described Emma as a young woman of amiable manners, who was a credit to the station to which she had been raised, and who had also been kind to his stepson Josiah. The next time that Emma would see Nelson would be five years later, on 22nd September 1798, on his victorious return to Naples from the battle of the Nile.

Nelson's victory destroyed French sea power in the Mediterranean and stopped for ever Napoleon's dreams of a French India. He was created Baron Nelson of the Nile and of Burnham Thorpe, and given a pension of £2000 a year for his life and those of his two successors. He received gifts from the Sultan of Turkey and Czar Paul of Russia. He was the hero of the hour. He was to remain in Naples, fêted and convalescent, until 16th October.

According to Percy Noble, and the *Dictionary of National Biography*, Anne was waiting alongside Emma Hamilton to welcome the returning hero, and it was in Naples that he agreed to sit to Anne, who then produced a bust of him. At first sight this seems a plausible story. The three weeks that Nelson was in Naples was enough time for Anne to make a plaster bust. Wounded at the Battle of the Nile, sick and emaciated, he was being nursed back to health by Emma, and would have had ample time on his hands to sit to Anne.

Nelson returned to Naples again on 31st October. However during November there would not have been much time for sitting; Hamilton and Nelson had both encouraged the Neapolitan army to advance on Rome, and to occupy it before the French arrived. The English naval squadron commanded by Nelson was busy supporting the advance on Rome, by landing 5000 troops at Leghorn. It was a policy doomed to failure. Brief success on land was followed by a humiliating retreat to Naples. The incompetent General Mack and a reluctant Neapolitan army were no match for the advancing French.

Sir William, with remarkable but ill-starred prescience, had started to pack up part of his collection of works of art on 27th October, and some were shipped back towards England on *HMS Colossus*, an arrangement made with the help of Nelson. Both the *Colossus* and Sir William's collection were to be lost a few weeks later, when the ship went aground on a reef in the Scilly Isles and broke up.

By December it became clear that Naples would have to be evacuated and left to the mercy of the French. The Neapolitan Royal Family joined Nelson on the *Vanguard*, followed by English residents and visitors. The wind had turned to the north, which delighted King Ferdinand, who declared that it would bring the woodcock south to Sicily, and proceeded to discuss shooting arrangements with his gamekeeper, who had been brought on board with him. After an appalling gale, the worst that Nelson had ever experienced, the *Vanguard* arrived in Palermo on 24th December. Emma and her mother had excelled themselves during the voyage, caring for the Royal Family and nursing a small Prince, who suffered a seizure on the ship and died in Emma's arms. Nowhere is there any mention of Anne.

If Anne had been present during these dramatic events, surely she would have written about them, and even if her own correspondence had been destroyed, Mary Berry, to whom she was still writing regularly, would have replied asking for more details. Percy Noble does in fact quote a letter from Mary to Anne dated October 1798, by which time news of the victory had arrived in England. The letter was written from Brandsby in Yorkshire, the family home of Mrs Cholmeley, where Mary was evidently staying. "I have not said a word to you of our glorious victory, but you do not suspect me of not feeling it. Do you participate in some other less agreeable feelings which to me accompany this and every other success in that quarter? When I think that under the circumstances, we might have been so much nearer the scene of action, and among the first to receive and congratulate the gallant conquerors! How much more appropriate to our minds, interesting to our feelings, and gratifying to our vanity, in spite of all the privations with which such a situation might seem to have been accompanied, than anything we are or have been doing." Noble concludes from this statement that it would appear that the Berrys, as well as Mrs Damer, had been invited to Naples.

Surely if Anne had been in Naples, Mary would have asked for more information. If on the other hand, she had been in England, and like Mary a recent recipient of news of the victory, the letter would make equal sense. Certainly Anne, if she had accepted Sir William's marriage proposal, of which no doubt she had told Mary, would have been in Naples, and have congratulated the returning Nelson. Equally it is possible that Anne and Mary had discussed a possible visit to Naples, and put it off owing to the uncertain political situation in Italy. There seems to be no other mention of Anne's presence in Naples in the autumn, nor in the records of the evacuation of British nationals to Sicily. Cornelia Knight, another friend of the Hamiltons, was staying with them during this period. She kept a detailed diary, and again there is no mention of Anne among the guests at Palazzo Sessa. Percy Noble himself says that "very few incidents are recorded of Mrs Damer's visit to Naples"; he then goes on to describe the Princess Dashkova's description of Anne's studio in Naples, oblivious of the fact that their meeting in Naples had been in spring 1782, some 16 years earlier.

Following the evacuation to Palermo, Nelson, Sir William and Emma were to spend the next two years as a *ménage à trois*. As their ill-fated venture in support of the Neapolitan monarchy fell apart during the winter of 1798, and Sir William's health continued to decline, Nelson fell more and more under the spell of Emma. After the failure of their policy, both Nelson and Sir William were recalled home, Nelson to be replaced in command of the Mediterranean squadron by Lord Keith, and Hamilton by Sir Arthur Paget. They took their time to return, heading home overland, as Emma had had enough of sea voyages and wished to see the courts of Germany. Eventually, on 9th November 1800, they arrived back in London. Nelson was to remain mostly in London on leave until 13th January 1801, when he left for Plymouth and the Baltic campaign which ended in victory at Copenhagen. During this leave, Nelson sat for about seven artists, and it would probably be during this period that he sat also for Anne. Indeed the *Whitehall Evening Post* reported on 29th November 1800 that Lord Nelson's statue in marble, to be placed in the Guildhall, was being produced by Mrs Damer, and that "Lord Nelson now attends an hour every day on the fair artist". On the 28th January 1801 Emma, now substantially overweight as a result of pregnancy and overindulgence, gave birth to Nelson's daughter, Horatia. The baby was discreetly moved to a place of safekeeping. The mother was not noticeably slimmer.

While Nelson was still in Palermo, Anne had decided that she must sculpt the hero of the Nile for posterity. Although she might have complained in the past about abuse from the press, she certainly knew how to use it to her advantage when she required it. *Lloyds Evening Post* dated 16th to 18th January 1799 ran an article containing the following adulatory passage: "One of the most eminent surprising characters of the day is Mrs Damer, the inhabitant since the death of Horace Walpole, the late Lord Orford, of Strawberry Hill on the banks of the Thames near Twickenham. Though this lady possesses a most genteel and elegant figure, she is inattentive to those personal adornments on which the sex in general bestow so much of their time and thoughts: and she devotes herself, with a scientific enthusiasm to study, and to sculpture, her favourite art. No artist who works for bread is more industrious and indefatigable than this lady of rank, fashion and opulence. Wrapped in a coarse dress for the occasion, she spends whole days in her workshop, and, by the chisel, shapes rude blocks of marble into the most exquisite and enchanting forms which rival in beauty the productions of ancient Grecian art. In the Eat-room at Strawberry Hill there is an eagle standing on a marble slab, so beautifully wrought to resemble life, and exhibiting so much genius and skill, that the late Lord Orford wrote under it in compliment to the fair sculptor (making the eagle speak): *"Non me Praxitiles fecit, at Anna Damer"*.

A week later a letter from Anne to the clerk to the Court of Common Council of the City of London was read out to the Court. She offered to execute a portrait of the hero Nelson, either in bronze or marble as a gift for the City of London. The Court accepted unanimously and asked the Lord Mayor to write and inform her of their decision that the statue should be in marble. There is no hint from the correspondence as to whether she already had a terracotta model completed in Naples in 1798, or whether alternatively she wished to begin work at sometime in the future, following Nelson's return to England. A further twist to the conundrum is contained in the report in the *British Evening Post* of 11th October 1800 that "Mrs Damer has almost completed the bust of Lord Nelson which she intends as a present for the City of London." At this date Nelson had not yet arrived back in England.

Other contemporary sources are not helpful as to Anne's movements during 1798. Mary Berry states in her journal only that Mrs D and Lady Ailesbury moved into

Strawberry Hill during the year. In July Mary Berry had noted to Mr Greatheed that after four years she felt the urge to go abroad again, citing as her reason that life in England gave only a narrow bird's eye view of world affairs. However any such wish was not to be granted and in August and September she was in Malvern and Cheltenham, where she wrote to Anne. On 19th August Joseph Farington recorded in his diary that he had dined at Mr Malone's, and that Harding, the artist, who was now employed at Strawberry Hill, had reported that Anne was becoming eccentric; she had taken to wearing a man's hat, shoes and jacket, and walked about the fields with "a hooking stick". The stick, which Anne had needed for support ever since falling from a sculptor's platform whilst carving George III, is familiar. The change in dress is new; Anne to date had been noted for her fine taste in clothing. The description is, of course, at third hand, and given Farington's known dislike for her, it may well have been a little exaggerated. Harding went on to report that the Berrys had changed the name of their house from Cliveden to Little Strawberry, and that the ecstasies on meeting and the tender leave-taking on separating between Anne, Mary and Agnes were "whimsical". On Mary's recent departure for Cheltenham, the Strawberry Hill servants had described their separation as if it had been parting before death.

By October Mary was in Yorkshire, where she wrote to Anne on three occasions while staying with Mrs Cholmeley at Brandsby, congratulating her on her "latent spark of heroism." By November, Mary had returned to Little Strawberry Hill, where she noted that she was busy in her garden. By the end of the year there is little, if any, information about Anne's activities during the last months of 1798.

Neither is there much evidence of Anne's activities during 1799. After her offer to sculpt a bust of Nelson was accepted by the City of London in January, there is no reference to her until April, when she joined a theatrical party at Brocket Hall. In May she exhibited a fine portrait of a dog at the Royal Academy, which was received with approval. *The Oracle* of 25th May stated that "Mrs Damer's dog in the present exhibition may justly be mentioned as an elegant portrait of fidelity from the hand of taste and beauty." *Lloyds Evening Post* of 31st May announced that "the Hon Mrs Damer's dog, No 1104, executed in Carrara marble is a beautiful specimen of this lady's taste." In September she went to join the Berrys, who were on holiday in Malvern. By November Mary Berry, now back at Little Strawberry Hill, was recording that Anne engaged herself in sculpture for the first half of the morning, and in gardening for the second, whatever the weather conditions. In London in December Mary Berry mentions a comfortable quiet game of whist, with only Mr and Mrs Burn, Jerningham, Mrs Damer and herself, with Mme DeCoigny and Agnes later in the evening looking on. Also during this year Anne found time to go to Astley's Playhouse with Mary, and to a china repository with Sir Henry Englefield, brother of Mrs Cholmeley, his mother and Mary.

Spring and summer of 1800 are also quiet as to news of Anne's activities. She exhibited another model of a dog at the Royal Academy. By autumn she was busy not only with the sculpture of Nelson, but also with theatricals at Strawberry Hill. The chosen site for the private theatre is a matter of conjecture. Since the performance was given in winter, it would have been necessary to use existing covered and warm space. The Gallery would have been very suitable, as would the cloister below, providing that exposure to the elements had been sealed off. Both these rooms have access at one end for the audience and at the other for players, with offstage backup. To a lesser extent the same remarks would apply to the Great Parlour. Neither the new offices completed in 1792, nor the recently redundant printing house would have been suitable for size or access. In November 1800 a double bill was presented. The main play was *The Old Maid*, a comedy in two acts, featuring the whole Berry family, Mr and Mrs Burn and Lord Mount Edgecumbe. This was accompanied by *The Intriguing Chambermaid*, with the same cast supplemented by Mr Hervey, Mr Campbell, and Anne. The prologue was performed by Lord Mount Edgecumbe and the epilogue by Anne. The play begins with noise and argument behind scenes. The prologue speaks:

> *"Hold, hold! What's this? No prologue to our play?*
> *Down with the curtain – let it down, I say and go,*
> *let me go for that I must, I will have way!*

(Prologue enters)

> *"So, I've escaped at length; with much ado,*
> *with threats, entreaties, ay, and wrangling too,*
> *I've forced my passage, ere the curtain rise,*
> *to mark your looks, your thoughts to scrutinise,*
> *and read our doom, beforehand in your eyes.*
> *Long in the green room was the point contested;*
> *scarce to my prayer a half assent I'd wrested."*

The reference to the green room is possibly the green closet where the details of the performance had been discussed. However this passing reference throws no new light on the actual venue.

A year later, in November 1801, the theatricals were repeated; this time the performance was of *Fashionable Friends*, a five-act comedy by Mary Berry, which had been long in gestation but at last made its first appearance. The cast was as in the previous year, with the addition of Mr Brownlow North and Lady Elizabeth Cole. The character of Sir Dudley Dorimant was played by Lord Mount Edgecumbe, Sir

Valentine Vapour by Mr Berry, Lady Selina Vapour by Anne, and Miss Lovell by Mary Berry. Both prologue and epilogue were supplied in verse by Mary's friend, the authoress Joanna Baillie. The epilogue refers to the venue of Strawberry Hill:

> *"But in these walls, once a well-known retreat,*
> *Where taste and learning kept a fav'rite seat;*
> *Where Gothic arches, with a solemn shade,*
> *Should o'er the thoughtful mind their influence spread*
> *Where pictures, vases, busts, and precious things,*
> *Still speak of sieges, poets, heroes, kings,*
> *On which the stranger looks with pensive gaze,*
> *And thinks upon the worth of other days."*

The reference to Gothic arches is repeated with reference to Horace Walpole: "Ah! He who o'er our heads those arches bent" does indeed make the reader think of the cloister, in Horace's day open to the elements, but possibly made weatherproof by Anne. *Fashionable Friends* was welcomed by the select audience who saw it at Strawberry Hill, with the reservation that it was long on good characters, but short in plot and action. Among the spectators was the actor Charles Kemble, who thought enough of the play to put it on with professional actors in Drury Lane. Kemble himself played Sir Dudley Dorimant and Miss du Camp, afterwards Mrs Kemble, Lady Selina Vapour. Sadly the public thought otherwise, and after three days it closed.

No sooner were her own stage productions completed than on Monday 15th December Anne attended that of her neighbour, H.E. Count Starhemberg, the Austrian ambassador, at York House, Twickenham, "before a select party of noble visitors, … amongst whom were the Honourable Mrs. Damer and many of her friends, who lately played at her theatre at Strawberry Hill". The whole Starhemberg family mother, father and children, accompanied by amateur musicians, performed.

Not content with amateur dramatics, Anne was also involved, as a lady patroness, in a new venture to form a theatre which could double up as a nightclub or gaming house. In February 1802 the newspapers reported "a proposal for a Private theatre in Ottoman Street. The number of members are limited to 300; among which shall be 12 Lady Patronesses, one director, five managers, and one sub director. The evening amusements shall commence at 9:30; after the plays, or Proverbs, the Theatre will be converted into a ballroom, and apartments made ready for such of the company as choose cards; at 12:30, there shall be a picnic supper, succeeded by catches and glees. The Ladies and Gentleman who have kindly accepted the offices of Lady Patronesses and Manager are:

Patronesses:

Duchess of Devonshire   Viscountess Melbourne
Duchess of Gordon   Viscountess Dungannon
Marchioness of Salisbury   Lady Templetown
Countess Cholmondeley   Lady Campbell
Countess Buckinghamshire   Hon. Mrs Damer
Countess Mount Edgecumbe   Mrs Crewe

Managers:

Earl Cholmondeley   Wm. Spencer Esq
Earl Mount Edgecumbe   T. Sheridan Esq."

All the old friends were still involved together in this venture, but they were getting older, and the proposal must have come to nothing, as there is no record of the private theatre opening.

Besides sculpting Nelson and arranging for amateur dramatics during 1800 and 1801, Anne had further work for her chisel. She was working on a bust of Charles James Fox, while at the same time producing two further dogs, exhibited at the Royal Academy in 1799 and 1800. The 1799 exhibit was possibly the marble version of Anne's own whippet, Fidele, referred to by Horace as in terracotta in 1787. Of the 1800 exhibit, a lapdog, nothing is known other than its exhibition number 1009. She may, of course, have completed other works which were not exhibited but given away to friends. If so, there is no record of them. She was by now aged over 50, and largely working in marble, which is hard physical toil. It is not surprising that output was limited.

The temporary cessation of war, ratified by the Peace of Amiens for which preliminaries were signed in October 1801, and which received its final signatures on 27th March 1802, was the signal for an outing to France. The Whig Foxites, including their master Charles Fox, and followed by others including Bess Foster, Mary Berry together with Anne, and Joseph Farington and a party of artists, made for France and an opportunity to view Napoleonic Paris and to meet and assess the new First Consul and his entourage. Most of those returning felt that they had not witnessed the triumph of democracy, rather the burgeoning of a new, if different, autocratic regime.

Anne Damer and Mary Berry, as good Foxites, keen travellers and enthusiastic shoppers, made a joint visit to Paris in March 1802. Their stated primary purpose was to present Napoleon with a terracotta bust of Charles James Fox sculpted by Anne. This gift of a model of the greatest English advocate of democracy would be a reminder to the First Consul of a champion of freedom, and might even encourage him to act in like fashion. Anne believed that she was giving her present to a Frenchman who, in the traditions of Rousseau, also believed in democratic rule. It may well be that they took with them two busts, one of Fox and another of Nelson, an opponent for whom Napoleon had the greatest admiration.

To be successful in her venture Anne would almost certainly need to be introduced to Napoleon himself. She had not found it difficult on previous visits to make the acquaintance of the *ancien régime*, and she was confident that there would be no problem with its successor. She also intended to visit the theatre and art galleries, whilst at the same time enjoying a shopping trip. Events during their stay were recorded by Mary in her journal.

They left London at 11.30am on Monday, 8th March 1802. By 7pm, they had arrived at Sittingbourne, where they spent the night. The journey was muddy, foggy and very cold. The following day they arrived at Dover in the early afternoon. They had missed the tide for that day and on the following morning, went aboard the *Swift*, commanded by Captain Blake. By 4pm on 10th March they were in Calais, where they cleared Customs without a problem. They spent a comfortable night at Dessein's Inn, which they found clean; however neither food nor wine proved satisfactory, and the bill was "immoderately dear".

They left Calais after breakfast the following day. The country people and their villages looked more prosperous than on previous visits, and the crops better grown and tended. Churches had often been desecrated by the revolutionaries, though they were still attended by the public. *Châteaux*, passed *en route*, were often damaged, almost always empty. The great *château* at Chantilly had been razed to the ground. On Sunday 14th March they entered Paris and drove to the Hôtel de l'Empire where they had taken an apartment.

Here they found the French hotelier enjoying the time-honoured national pastime of fleecing the English tourist. They were offered the choice of paying eighteen louis for fifteen days, or thirty for a month, meanwhile noting that Mr Caulfield, a wealthy young Irishman, was occupying a very superior apartment for ninety louis a month. "After a little consideration, a little murmuring, and a good deal of regret at losing time", the maid and the courier were dispatched to the St Germain quarter of Paris in search of better value. St Germain was an area that Anne and Mary knew well, but which was not then as fashionable as during their last visit. After a tedious but worthwhile wait, the negotiators returned with an offer of the first floor of the Hôtel d'Orléans, Rue des Petits Augustins, at the more competitive rate of five louis a week. The offer was promptly accepted. They moved to their new quarters as early as possible on the following day. On arrival, they found the hotel hardly changed since Mary's last visit sixteen years previously. Furniture and decoration showed signs of wear.

The formalities of arrival continued from 16th to 18th March. On the 16th they delivered letters of introduction to potential hostesses. On the 18th they went to the *Préfecture de la Police Générale* to register their presence. The Gallic propensity for form-filling had not been lessened by revolution. In a bare, drab room, lined with shelves containing round hat boxes, in which the records were stored, their names were entered in six books by polite, methodical and slow clerks. The scene resembled more a milliner's shop, than a police headquarters.

In the meantime, on 15th March Anne and Mary had gone to the gallery of the Louvre, where they were able to gain entrance by showing a passport at the door. The gallery was so long that the perspective ended almost in a point. Here were displayed a myriad of the finest paintings, including many that they had already seen in other countries. But this was not a travelling exhibition – these were the spoils of war. The smaller pictures, and those taken from palaces, were in their original frames, but the larger ones and those removed from churches were, if only as a temporary measure, contained in flat frames of yellow wood. Mary Berry noted that "exquisite pictures that one had formerly admired in their separate countries .... appeared in very good order, and not as if they had been varnished or worked upon." This latter opinion she subsequently revised in respect of the early Italian paintings where "their reparations are destroying ... the identity of the picture and the touch of the master."

On the ground floor were the statues and sculpture, shown off to advantage by the background walls being painted to resemble red and green granite. Mary noted that the statues were very much better placed in Paris than ever they had been in their native Italy, including the Apollo, standing in a niche at the end of the rooms and admirably lit.

During their tour, Anne and Mary met up with their friend the artist Maria Cosway, who introduced them to the gallery secretary, M. de la Vallée. Maria was engaged in cataloguing and sketching each exhibit, a Herculean task she probably never completed. They had expected to see each other as Anne, before leaving England, had asked Maria's husband, Richard, whether she could take anything to Maria for him. It is possible that they deposited two of Anne's busts, one of Charles Fox and one of Admiral Nelson, with the gallery for safekeeping, either on this occasion or on 22nd March, when they paid a further visit to the statue gallery. They returned for a final visit on Wednesday 7th April, when they again met Maria Cosway in the Louvre gallery, ostensibly to see David's painting, *The Rape of the Sabines*, but possibly also using this occasion to retrieve the busts, intended to be taken to Josephine Bonaparte whom they were due to meet on the following day. The gallery was closed to the public, as it was the day of the '*décade*', a holiday in the new French calendar, so it would have been a suitable time to arrange for collection.

On the evening of 15th March, and whenever the opportunity occurred during their stay, Mary and Anne visited the theatre. On this night, their seats were in the front row of a box, where they found a plainly-dressed man sitting in the front row, chewing tobacco. He neither offered them his seat nor asked them to join him, as would have been polite. He took absolutely no notice of them, and continued to chew, periodically spitting to one side. They quickly changed boxes. Subsequently they were to find that this experience of informal dress and bad manners was not unusual in the theatres they visited.

On 16th March, they paid their first visit to the Opera, at the enormous cost of 57 livres. The dancing was much admired, with Mlle Clothilde as Calypso, with a supporting cast of women dancers dressed in thin petticoats of white muslin, "allowing the whole form to be fairly perceived", above flesh-coloured *tricot,* with a little strap over one shoulder. In contrast, the audience left much to be desired. "Where one used to see brilliant groups of all the young people of fashion...... is now the strangest collection of odd, black-guard-looking people that can be conceived." Despite the shortcomings of their fellow theatregoers, Anne and Mary attended various theatres on nine further occasions.

On 31st March, they had a grander experience when they went to the Opera in the box of the Swedish Minister, the husband of Mme de Staël. In general, they found the acting good, the ballet superb, and French opera awful. They noted that on leaving the theatre, the transport which they had booked would eventually arrive, but that there was no social gathering prior to departure, as there had been in France prior to the revolution, and which still existed in England.

Shopping was also an important, if subsidiary, part of the expedition. They noticed that most of the shops were shut on Sundays, as in the days of the *ancien régime*, and also on the French revolutionary decades, the tenth day of every 10 day week. This required a little arithmetic agility to ensure that the shops were actually open when they visited. They noted that the Parisians still wore their best clothes on Sunday, though not necessarily on *décades*, and that on a fine day the gaiety of the street scene could make even Mary feel cheerful.

The first visit, on 16th March, was to Mme le Roi, the best dressmaker in town. However, the Paris fashions of 1802 were not for Mary. She was shown nothing that she would have liked to have worn, not because it was too young or too "singular" for her, but because everything had a "common vulgar look". Anne, ever practical, ordered a bonnet at a price of 2 louis, to be modelled on a similar piece made entirely of lace, which cost 72 louis. Mary did admire the mahogany furniture with hangings of purple silk with an orange fringe.

On the morning of Friday 19th March the shopping spree gained pace. They visited Vaché, a leading silk mercer, and Ligneureuse, who dealt in furniture and Sèvres china. They saw a lot of mahogany decorated with ormolu, new-style candelabra and new-look Sèvres, in dark tortoiseshell colours with steel rims and gold edging, again not to Mary's taste. The next day they went to look at wallpapers at M. Robert's shop. All the papers on show were mono-coloured flock, which were excellent, though again not entirely to Mary's personal taste. On Monday 22nd some *brocante* shops found favour; there were bargains to be had – Sèvres china selling at a quarter of its former price, and on Saturday 3rd and Tuesday 6th April they revisited these outlets for a shop-up before returning home.

The finale to the retail therapy was a visit to the celebrated Mlle Martin to buy rouge, thinking that the great-grandchildren of the founder would now be selling her wares. However, not at all: the founder herself, large and fat, with a huge bonnet over long powdered hair and dressed in the fashion of 20 years ago, served them herself.

On their arrival in Paris, Anne and Mary had lost no time in delivering their letters of introduction. By 19th March the delivery had borne fruit, and that afternoon they dined with Mme Chabot de Castellane, to whom they had taken a letter of introduction from Mme de Starhemberg. She was of the old pre-revolutionary school, living in a pretty house with a garden in the Faubourg Saint Germain. Mary observed the differences between old and new money and fashion, and noted the opinion of Mme Chabot de Castellane that never the twain would meet. Mary herself was clearly on the side of the old.

They were also fortunate to be able to make full use of the services of Mr Jackson, the British Consul, with whom they arranged a sequence of visits to call upon the wives of various senior members of the current French government, where they hoped to – and in fact did – meet their husbands, the generals and ministers. The first occasion resulted in an introduction to General Berthier, the War Minister. He was small, dark and ill-looking, in the uniform of a Minister of State, blue cloth with broad silver embroidery. Mary noted that standards of tailoring had slipped: all the gentlemen's clothes looked as if they were too large for them, and made by the village tailor. Cambacérès, the Second Consul, was also there. He surpassed Berthier by being still more uncommonly ill-looking, short and thick-set, wearing a consul's undress uniform of blue velvet with gold embroidery, fustian breeches and turn-down boots.

On Wednesday 24th at 11pm they called on the wife of the Minister of Justice, Mme Fouché. They found that the guests were all leaving as they arrived. However they were presented to a fair, vulgar woman in a yellow wig and gold muslin gown. The visit lasted 10 minutes, and in the anteroom as they made their departure they were able to curtsy to Fouché himself. They noted a little man with small penetrating grey eyes in a very pale face.

The following evening they went with Mr Jackson to be presented to the Second and Third Consuls. Cambacérès was in a large room hung with fine Gobelins tapestries depicting tales of the Turkish harem. Anne and Mary were presented to him. He received them politely and invited them to his next assembly on Sunday. They then proceeded to meet Le Brun, who was lodged in the Pavillon de Flore in the Tuileries. Among the company there was General Lafayette "in a plain blue coat, round hat, and cropped head." Le Brun had the manners and appearance of an educated man, and endeared himself to Anne by recalling having seen her in Paris at a sale of the Prince of Conti's pictures in 1775.

On the following day, Friday 26th, they walked in the Champs Elysées before dining with Mr Jackson. He had a number of guests including General Marmont, recently returned with Napoleon from Egypt, and much in the latter's confidence. Mary found him "rather short with black hair out of powder, and much beard; a sensible, intelligent, grave countenance: he put me something in mind of the second daughter of the Archbishop of York."

On Sunday evening at Cambacérès's assembly, they saw still more of Napoleon's generals. Brune, who had commanded in Holland, was one of the tallest men they had ever seen, while Masséna, who was not in uniform, was short, broad, with thick black hair and an intelligent, if vulgar, face. There were several other generals in full uniform, whose names they were unable to discover. The room was covered in beautiful carpets, not improved by all the men indiscriminately spitting on them. There were also many more women present than at other meetings, all of them either foreigners or members of the new society, some strange and uncouth, all meaning to be smart and loaded with finery.

On Saturday 3rd April they went to another ministerial assembly where Mme de Staël was noticed trying, as always, to talk to the most important man in the room, which may have been somewhat trying for Mary and Anne, attempting to do the same. On Wednesday 7th April they dined out again with a new face in Decrès, the Minister of the Marine. Although a naval hero, who had put up a remarkable resistance on the two decker ship *Guillaume Tell* against three British ships of the line in 1800, his appearance brought out all the superlatives in Mary's repertoire. He was "one of the fattest, vulgarest, ugliest black men I ever saw. I had no opportunity of judging more of him than his appearance."

Private dinners and public receptions were frequently followed by dances, large and small, private and public. No mention is made of either Anne or Mary taking to the dance floor, though on one occasion Mary did turn down a request from an unknown gentleman. The first of these was on the evening of 22nd March. They had attended a diplomatic reception until 10pm, returned to their hotel for supper by midnight, and then went onto a ball at the Cercle des Étrangers. This was said to be for the *nouveaux riches*, and there was no shortage of them, with 300-400 guests. The dress, or undress, of the women was not to Mary's taste: "Loads of finery in gold and silver, excessively fine laces, bare necks and shoulders more than halfway down the back, with the two bladebones squeezed together in a very narrow backed gown; arms covered with nothing but a piece of fine lace below the shoulder." Mary described it as an endless vista of bad taste without a single figure to give any pleasure to the eye. Men also were said to be unsmart. They could hardly believe that they were in Paris; their guide hastily informed them that the principal part of the company was actually only the second division of the *nouveaux riches*. They watched a well-danced French country dance and were home by 2am.

On Thursday 25th March, after half an hour at Le Brun's, they returned to meet up with M. Barrois, their guide, and after changing to dress down to less smart attire, went on to a public dance. The long hall, well lit with patent lamps suspended from the ceiling, was half full of shabby-looking people; one third were masked, with some men dressed as ladies, and vice versa. The dances were principally waltzes, and all the ladies who danced were "*sensées* to be of bad character", despite the apparent decency of their dress and manners. They remained at the ball for nearly an hour, and left the room much fuller than when they had entered. On Tuesday 30th, there was another small ball at General Berthier's, where General Moreau and a pretty young wife were present.

On Wednesday 31st March, after the Opera, they went to the Comte de Crillon's, where Mme de Crillon gave a *souper dansant* for a very select party of about 70 or 80 of the *ancien régime*. The ladies' dresses appeared simple when contrasted with those of the new society seen previously. Plain chemises of muslin and no bosom displayed more than it would have been in England were the order of the night. An excellent supper was provided at one o'clock with seating for all. M. de Crillon was the youngest son of the Duc de Crillon, who by prudence and remaining at his post, had successfully survived the revolution and retained his Paris house and servants. Mary had, of course, "remarked him at Mme de Castellane's dinner as a particularly gentleman-like man."

Friday 2nd April saw Anne and Mary attending a grand ball given by M. Demidoff, an extremely wealthy young Russian. All the *jeunesse de Paris* were there, both the old and the new world. Mary found the differences between the two cultures unbridgeable: the former brought up to protocol and politeness, the latter either unaware or neglectful of social conventions. She believed that "it is impossible that these two worlds should ever amalgamate in society: their children may. Till I saw them both, I blamed the old world; but it is still more the fault of the new." She might more accurately have reflected that the real world will always follow power and money, whether drawn from new or old.

At the ball were the best dancers of the day, some of the men in powdered wigs, others with the cropped hair favoured by Napoleon. They made a motley crew, though the girls were generally better-dressed. In the antechamber a *bouquetière* gave each lady a large bunch of forced flowers, roses and carnations, worth at least 12 or 18 livres apiece, which they were able to renew as often as they desired. The Russian servants' liveries were dark green, with vast amounts of gold lace. There were as well liveried huntsmen, couriers and jockeys, blacks and small boys dressed as Tartars, all of these last clad in scarlet and black. In addition, the waiters were all kitted-out in brown coats with gold embroidery, much resembling the uniform of the National Assembly tribunes. Despite all the splendour, the servants were thought by Mary to be poorly organized. Although M. Demidoff received the guests in person, many bypassed him, giving up their tickets at the door and heading straight for the action. Mary was convinced that the host did not know at least half the guests.

The next day the scene switched back to the *ancien régime*, this time an assembly given by the Duchesse de Luines. Three rooms were taken up with the old-world occupation of gambling. Those attending were better and more simply dressed than the new world, none more *décolletée* than in England, hair arranged with flowers, all in all a number of very pretty women. Once again there was no question as to which sort of society Mary preferred.

On Sunday evening the scene again changed from private to public. Anne and Mary visited a public garden open for dancing, formerly the house and garden of the Duchesse de Bourbon. The dancers were mainly shopkeepers, seamstresses, Mantua-makers and the like, all well-behaved and having an enjoyable time. They sat in the open air on 4th April without feeling cold, and with the green buds of spring bursting over their heads. It was more like the end of May than the beginning of April, but despite this feeling of spring in the air, Mary refused to dance with an unknown man who came up and requested that pleasure – tamely replying that she did not dance.

As well as the extremely crowded night-time schedule, Mary and Anne also found time for various daytime excursions. On their first Sunday in Paris they walked in the Tuileries; they found the visitors there much less colourful than before the revolution; however the gardens had been substantially improved, forming a series of grass *plats* surrounded by borders enclosed with rough treillage, and pretty plants and shrubs within. Several statues had been moved to this area, which was to its advantage.

On Thursday 25th they visited the Musée des Monuments Nationaux, close to their hotel, in the rooms and grounds of the previous Convent des Petits-Augustins. Here, saved from the ravages of revolution, an extensive collection of religious statues, tombs, sculptures and monuments to the great men and women of France had been assembled, under the direction of Alexandre Lenoir, described by Mary as the only violent Jacobin (in conversation) that she met during their stay. The sculptures had come from all parts of France, and were placed according to their time, 13th century, then 14th century, and so on. The principal attraction was the tomb of Francis I, designed by Philibert de l'Orme, and sculpted by Jean Goujon. It had been transported in sections and re-erected under a majestic dome. As with many of the other historic statues on display, Lenoir, obedient to the revolutionary code, displayed it for its worth as a historic piece of French sculpture, designed and executed by masters of their art, rather than as a tomb of a discredited monarchy.

Lenoir designed his gallery as a series of rooms around the former cloisters. In his own words, he had built "a museum devoted to history and chronology in which the different ages of French sculpture will be displayed in individual rooms, with each room decorated exactly in the style of the particular century." In the middle of the cloisters, he designed a garden in the English style, his Elysian Fields, in which were placed memorials to distinguished French artists and writers. The most notable was a memorial to Eloise and Abelard (now removed to Père Lachaise Cemetery). Mary recorded that Lenoir claimed that in these *champs Elysées* could be found the heart of Molière and the bones of Racine. Anne found it particularly interesting to observe the decline in the art of sculpture from the time of Francis I to Louis XIV. Their shared view was that provided the visitor could suppress any regret or indignation arising from the events that had brought all these treasures together, there was much to be admired, both on artistic and educational grounds.

They also visited the National Library, where nearly every seat was occupied by visitors reading or copying from books in longhand. Then on Sunday 28th March they drove through the Bois de Boulogne to Bagatelle. The little pavilion was now managed, and probably owned by, a businessman, who kept it well, as a popular and profitable attraction. Of course it could not compare with the previous occasion on which Mary had seen it, in 1785, as a breakfast guest of the Duke of Dorset, the British ambassador. On their return, they stopped in the Champs Elysées to witness a balloon take off, and after returning to the hotel saw it pass overhead.

A less exhilarating experience was a visit to a demonstration at an institute for the deaf and dumb. From the pupils, about twenty of them, dressed in uniform of a pepper and salt coloured material faced with blue, their tutor selected one to receive the first lesson, and then demonstrated that the more advanced could understand passages read to them and write these down, using the correct grammar. This section was of interest, but was followed by the tutor giving a monologue proving that "if he had the powers of giving others clear ideas he had not left a single one for himself." This professor was so boring that having sat there from 11am to after one o'clock, Mary and Anne crept away, leaving him still in discourse, and resolved never again to listen to a teacher of the deaf and dumb, "till we had become the first ourselves, and had no objection to remain the second." They had been recommended to this institution by Lord Henry Petty, whom they had met at a supper given for English visitors in Paris. He would go on to succeed his brother in 1809 as the Marquis of Lansdowne, and to become a successful statesman. Other guests at this party had included Lord Cowper and Mr Lutterell, a celebrated wit.

This procession of shops, assemblies, dinners, balls and excursions, though time-consuming, interesting and pleasurable, was incidental to the main purpose of getting to see the First Consul, Napoleon Bonaparte. With the help of the British Consul, Mr Jackson, Mary and Anne established contact with a Swiss tailor, called Sandoz, who did a lot of work for Josephine, and who, as a special favour, had obtained permission to show them Napoleon and Josephine's private rooms in the Tuileries. There, recovered from their morning experience at the institution for the deaf and dumb, they arrived on the afternoon of 29th March.

Their initial reaction was that it was a good thing that simple Republicans were not permitted to see the First Consul's magnificence. Mary had formerly seen Versailles, the Little Trianon, and many palaces in other countries, but never anything as magnificent as Napoleon and Josephine's quarters. These were composed of a set of rooms looking towards the garden from the Pavillon de Flore. The tour commenced with a large antechamber which was "hung and furnished with blue-lilac lustring embroidered in the honeysuckle pattern with *maron*, in the best taste possible." There was a beautiful picture of St Cecilia with a turban, playing the harp, by Domenichino, originally in the Borghese Palace.

The next room, which was the highlight, was furnished in yellow satin with brown and *sang de boeuf* fringes. The mirrors were all draped around with silk, rather than being framed, with marble and porphyry tables beneath, surmounted by great vases of Sèvres or granite, mounted in ormolu, with wonderful candelabra. In the middle of the room hung a huge chandelier of English crystal again mounted with a great deal of ormolu. The chairs were covered in exquisite tapestry.

The third room was the bedchamber, all in blue silk with white and gold fringes. The bed, recessed under a canopy of silk drapes, was of mahogany, richly and heavily ornamented with ormolu. Beyond was a small bathroom where Napoleon shaved, before ascending by a private staircase to his study above. Beyond the bathroom and on the same floor, a passage led to a small reading room, leading to Josephine's dressing room decorated with white muslin with embroidered and white lustring curtains with white and gold fringes. It contained a large rosewood cabinet which held everything required for ladies' work. Beyond the dressing room was a small bedroom, where Hortense de Beauharnais, Josephine's daughter by her first husband, had slept prior to her own marriage. Sadly, the door at the top of the stairs, accessing Napoleon's study, was locked. The following day, still under the mantle of Mr Sandoz, they tried again to obtain access to the study, but with no greater success. Apparently no one was admitted to this *cabinet de travail*, which they had been most curious to see.

On Thursday, 1st April, the duo enlisted the help of Maria Cosway to be presented to Napoleon's mother. Mary immediately recognised the house where she lived as one which she had frequented often on her first visit to Paris. Her friends who had lived there had emigrated, and the house had suffered during the Terror. The beautiful garden had been partially turned into a *potager,* and the rest was poorly tended. However, inside the house, under Mme Bonaparte's occupation, no expense had been spared.

Mme Bonaparte led her guests around her whole house, through the salon with chairs of crimson velvet laced with gold and curtains with gold-coloured fringes, to the room where they were introduced, clad in purple striped satin. All rooms were lit by the finest candelabra with floors covered with most magnificent carpets.

Mme Bonaparte herself was a woman of over 50 with large dark eyes and an intelligent face, who must formerly have been beautiful. She was said to be devout, and concerned to protect convents in newly-conquered countries. However she was unlikely to carry much influence; Napoleon came to see her when she was ill, and ensured that she lived well, but probably had little more to do with her. She was not going to be the route to meet the First Consul, but if the opportunity arose, it would be useful to be able to say that they had met her.

Again the Swiss tailor, Sandoz, proved himself invaluable by arranging for Anne and Mary to meet Josephine, as two distinguished ladies from England who had come over particularly to meet the First Consul and his wife. At 3pm on 2nd April they went to the Tuileries, and on asking for Sandoz, were shown into a salon. After a ten-minute wait, Sandoz arrived, and trusting that they did not mind a little détour, led them to the small waiting-room adjoining Josephine's dressing room. Guarding the door were two or three small black boys in waiting, and a Mameluke in Turkish dress. Josephine met them at the dressing room door, and the tailor disappeared.

Mary noted that she was slim, dark, of genteel appearance and not at all unlike Lady Elizabeth Foster, but less of a coquette, combining dignity with good manners. They talked about the furnishings of her apartment, about Malmaison, and of her garden. They discussed plants ordered from the nurserymen Lee and Kennedy in England, and more of which she was anxious to obtain. She went on to enquire whether they had reserved places for the Parade, and when they described these, she said that they were not good ones, and that she would get them placed in a better position. They thanked her, curtsied and took their leave. "Whom she took us for – whether the tailor had ever explained who Mrs. D. was – Heaven knows! But it is certain she had no idea of Mrs D's talent, or at least did not take the least notice of it, though I gave her a fair opportunity by asking if the little bust of Buonaparte, which stood upon a coin in the room, was like; she said it was very little like, but without relevéing the subject at all."

Monday 5th April was the day of the much-vaunted Parade. Sandoz led Anne and Mary to a window on the *entre-sol* of the Tuileries, which looked into the courtyard where the Parade would take place. It was, as promised by Josephine, the best viewpoint, with the eye-level over the heads of the infantry and just above those of the cavalry. Josephine's own party was at another window at the same level in these rooms.

The troops marched in, and took up their positions for review. Napoleon appeared, mounted on a pale dun horse with white mane and tail, accompanied by generals of infantry, cavalry, and artillery. They rode along the lines, inspecting the troops, passing Anne and Mary's viewing position twice. As far as could be seen beneath his hat, Napoleon appeared a good horseman, with a sallow complexion and serious expression. He wore infantry dress, blue with a broad white lapel, and a plain hat with a small national cockade.

A march-past followed, with Napoleon taking the salutes of the commanding officers, bands playing and colours flying. The troops departed, Napoleon dismounted and disappeared. Mary noticed that the troops' drill left much to be desired by English standards. They never marched in straight lines and their muskets pointed in a variety of directions. Even the colonels of English country militia would have been horrified. The Consular Guard were physically impressive, both cavalry and infantry, and were regarded as the élite of the Army. The other regiments looked small in comparison. The hussars, their officers' horses with tiger-skin trappings, looked very pretty, but in no way compared with any of the English regiments of dragoons or light horse.

On Thursday 8th April, the opportunity to meet Napoleon arrived at last at Josephine's official reception at the Tuileries for foreign ministers' wives and distinguished foreigners who wished to be presented. About 40 women and as many men, all foreign ministers, assembled; the ladies were invited to sit on chairs placed around the outside of the room, the gentlemen remaining standing in a group. When Napoleon, in his undress consul's uniform, and Josephine entered together through the bedchamber door, the ladies stood, while the couple, Napoleon first, proceeded around the room in an anticlockwise direction talking to each lady in turn for about 2 to 3 minutes.

Anne and Mary were on the further side of the room, and had time to observe the First Consul's progress. He asked one lady if she rode on horseback, another if she had been long in France. He addressed Italians with much the "same sort of royal nothings", though in Italian. When he got to Mary, he asked whether she had been long in Paris.

"Just over three weeks."

"What do you think of the Opera?"

"Oh! Very fine, but we have seen a lot of the Opera."

He continued on to Anne, who answered the question "Do you have such good dancers in England?" more diplomatically:

"Oh no, that's why we come here."

"But you have a lady with a very beautiful voice, Mrs Billington, I have heard her in Italy."

"Yes, certainly. She has a very fine voice, and it is an English one."

"Yes it is an English one, but she is married to a Frenchman and studied in Italy, so, in a way, she belongs to three nations."

Having made his point, Napoleon moved onto the next lady, a Russian, and again asked: "Do you ride on horseback?"

Mary regretted that Napoleon, like Josephine, seemed neither to have heard of Anne's talents as a sculptor, nor be aware that the prime reason for their visit was to offer a bust of Charles Fox to the First Consul. If the offer had already been made through a third party, and if it had reached the ears of the intended recipient, there was no mention of it. The opportunity for Anne or Mary to raise the subject directly simply did not arise. Mary was not a little piqued to be asked about the Opera, feeling it a subject that might have been "reserved for younger women".

Napoleon, having completed the round of ladies, joined the group of men, spoke briefly about this and that, and then left by the way he had entered. Josephine, meanwhile, had gone around the room a little behind her husband, and on his departure sat down and invited everyone else to do likewise. She talked to both ladies and men, and after about ten minutes got up and left the room.

Josephine's resemblance to Lady Elizabeth Foster was even more marked on this occasion. She had worn a pink silk gown with round velvet spots, a small white silk or satin hat with three small white feathers, which was tied under her chin, and a handkerchief in her hand – in Mary's opinion "a decided half-dress", whilst those attending had come in their most fashionable attire. Napoleon, too, had been in undress consular uniform. His hair was very dark and cropped short, lying awkwardly upon his head. He was not as small as popularly reported, nor as he had appeared on his horse. Broad shoulders lent importance to his figure. His complexion, though pale yellow, still seemed healthy; his teeth were good, and his smile appealing. His eyes were light grey, and he looked straight in the face of whoever he was speaking to. He had a peaceful air of quiet intelligence, which did not seem to square with the stern soldier seen on parade, nor the warrior general with fire darting from his eyes in the moment of victory.

Anne and Mary did not know that later on the same afternoon the British scientist, Sir Charles Blagden, introduced by letter from Sir Joseph Banks, was presented to the First Consul and his wife after dinner. Josephine had spoken to him "admiringly of Mrs Damer and Miss Berry, specially mentioning the former's skill as a sculptor." The first lady of France had evidently taken in more about the visitors than they had realised.

From Mary's diary it would seem that the purpose of the voyage had not been completed, and that Napoleon and Fox's bust had not been introduced to each other.

However, the diary may not have told the whole story. Joseph Farington's diary for 1802 gives a detailed description of a visit to Paris four months later. He had left for Paris on 27th August, in company with another painter John Opie. Fox was in Paris at the same time: "Mr Fox was lately at the Opera when Bonaparte was there; he leaned forward in his box to look at him." The visitors were not over-impressed by Paris; talking about its women, Opie had opined that he had seen "more handsome women in walking from Berners Street to the end of Oxford Street, than in all Paris in a fortnight he has been here."

On Saturday 11th September Farington went with the portrait painter John Hoppner and his wife to the Tuileries. Like the Berry/Damer party before him, Farington had arranged for a private view of the First Consul's private apartments. "They are on the left side of the Palace. They are not large but make a very handsome appearance, being furnished with taste and elegance united with solidity. Eight of the rooms are in line succeeding each other, and looking into the Garden of the Tuileries. The great dining room is on the opposite side, and looks into the court of the Tuileries. Of the eight rooms, the first is an ante-room… The next is a sitting room, which leads to what is called the ambassadors' room. The walls are covered with light blue satin festooned, and large glasses let in. The whole has the appearance of the inside of a tent. The next is a small library: but… the next room is a bedchamber very handsomely furnished in which the Chief Consul and Mme Bonaparte sleep. The next is a room which appears to be used as a dressing room ….The next was a bedchamber sometime occupied by the daughter of Mme Bonaparte, now married to Lucien Bonaparte. On a table in this room there were two busts, one of Charles Fox, the other of Lord Nelson, both executed by Mrs Damer, not very good likenesses, but they might be known."

So somehow Anne had managed to produce not only one bust of Fox, but also a second of Nelson. They are both likely to have been in terracotta, and the route by which they found their way to Napoleon and Josephine's private apartments remains a mystery. The physical position of the two busts would perhaps suggest that they were in a section of the apartments more used by Josephine than by Napoleon, and perhaps it is the former, who corresponded with Anne on her plant requirements shortly after the latter returned to England, who holds the key to the mystery. When and how the busts arrived in Paris, or whether they were left by Anne with Mr Jackson the Consul, or with Maria Cosway at the Louvre, history does not reveal. Certainly Anne later told Joseph Banks, in connection with the transportation of plants to Paris, that she had an excellent courier whom she knew to be efficient.

Having achieved their goal of meeting Napoleon and Josephine, the travellers prepared to return home, and started to say their goodbyes. However, there was one more visit that they were determined to make before departure. On the afternoon of 1st April, they had dined with Mme de Staël, the daughter of Louis XVI's one-time

Minister of Finance, M. Necker. She was very plain, but incredibly bright. Her marriage to Baron Gustav de Staël, Swedish Minister to the French court, had made a virtue out of necessity by giving him the financial stability of the Neckers, and her diplomatic rank and precedence at court. During the Terror in France she had emigrated to England, taking up residence in Juniper Hall in Surrey. When her husband was recognised by the new régime, she had returned to Paris as ambassador's wife, with a bolt-hole in her native Switzerland, if things should get tricky. She was a successful author and hostess, already well-known to Mary, who had met her first in Lausanne in 1784 when Mary was 20 and she 16.

Among the guests on this particular evening were General and Mme Marmont, M and Mme Necker, the hostess's parents, and Mme Recamier, the *soi-disant* leader of current Parisian fashion. Although Mary and Anne had left early, after being up late the previous night, they were already fascinated by Mme Recamier. They had met her again, dining with Mr Jackson, and had been informed that this rich banker's wife, a great beauty of the new world, had the finest house in Paris in the new style. They were determined to see it.

Due to depart for England on 11th April, Anne and Mary called on Mme Recamier the day before leaving. They found the house fitted extremely expensively in what was then called "*le gout antique*". Chairs were mahogany enriched with ormolu, covered in cloth or silk in good taste. Her bed, by repute the finest in Paris, was again of mahogany enriched with ormolu and bronze, and raised upon two steps, also of mahogany. Over the bed was thrown a cover of white muslin with rows of gold lace at either end, and the muslin embroidered as a border. The bed curtains were muslin, trimmed and worked like the cover, suspended from a carved crown of roses and tied back against the wall against which the bed stood.

Leading directly from the bedroom, a small bathroom had walls inlaid with satinwood and mahogany with arabesque patterns in black upon the satinwood. The bath was disguised as a sofa in a recess, covered with a scarlet cushion embroidered with black lace. Beyond was a small boudoir entirely lined with quilted pea-green lustring, drawn together in a bunch in the middle of the ceiling. Mary gives no hint as to whether they approved of the décor. If she had disapproved, she would certainly have said so; therefore the inference must be that they were actually, and for them surprisingly, impressed by this dramatic new world display. Perhaps, after all, it would not take a generation for old and new to become mutually acceptable.

Anne and Mary left Paris in the early afternoon of Sunday 11th April. Their journey was somewhat delayed by a drunken postilion, who fell off when a wheel horse stumbled on the slippery paviours. He lay on the ground unable to get up, more from the effects of alcohol than from his fall. A crowd quickly assembled, declaring that either his legs or his head were broken, and generally giving advice. Eventually he sat up, and declared himself ready to remount. However, the redoubtable travellers had seen and heard enough, and ordered the coachman to proceed without him. The journey continued with minor upsets, including a stop to repair the carriage, where they waited in the blacksmith's cottage. They were very pleasantly surprised by the cleanness and comparative prosperity of the household – plates and dishes on a dresser, hams hanging from the ceiling, and plenty of eggs. A week after setting off they arrived safely back in London.

Chapter 17

BELMOUR

In 1801 Anne's only novel, *Belmour*, was published by J. Johnson at St Paul's Churchyard, and printed by Luke Hanford of Lincoln's Inn Fields. Like Georgiana Duchess of Devonshire with her novel, *The Sylph*, Anne chose to remain anonymous, and it was not until December 1802 that the *Morning Chronicle* reported that "when the lately published novel *Belmour* is mentioned in the higher circles, it is unanimously ascribed to the Hon Mrs Damer". The novel had been a long while in gestation. It had been started in the winter of 1790-1791, when Anne had wintered in Portugal; she had obviously consulted Mary Berry on its contents, as in *Anne's Notebooks* for 1797 Mary writes: "Dear soul, I am indulging myself in idleness, of body, I mean, and not coming to you tonight, as this <u>indulging</u> myself in <u>not</u> coming to you has an odd sound to my ears … but you ought not to be affronted at it when I tell you I am going to pass an hour with Lord Belmour. I daresay we shall both of us think of you."

The actual name 'Belmour' may have been borrowed from William Congreve's play *The Old Bachelor*, where the elderly banker Fondlewife is cuckolded by the handsome Bellmour. Horace Walpole, writing to both Miss Berrys and addressing them as his joint wives, in the early days of their friendship, had referred to himself as Horace Fondlewives, a probable allusion to the same play. It was Anne who over the next few months was to steal Mary's friendship from Horace, as Bellmour stole Laetitia from the banker. The play's origins might well have been hatched as a conceit between Anne and Mary around this time.

The book starts with Belmour returning home from Italy to the family seat of Belmour Castle, somewhere in the West of England. This was a stately home set in rolling acres of parkland. The neighbouring villages were part of his father's estate, and their inhabitants were well-pleased with their landlord, his family and their position in life. The young Lord viewed this terrestrial paradise with a darkened and melancholy spirit. He had been infatuated with the world-ripened charms of Lady Roseberg, and she by his youth, education, conversation and good looks. The elderly Lord Roseberg, who had been kind and generous to Belmour, had been cuckolded by him. But time and Lady Roseberg had moved on, leaving the young Lord wiser and sadder. He had decided that a trip to Italy, to relive the delights of art and music gained previously on his Grand Tour, would be therapeutic. However, his melancholic thoughts had not been assuaged, and since it was fashionable in England to be melancholic, his brow remained furrowed and his mood dark.

Belmour goes for a walk after dinner, alone and melancholy, and hears a "soft female voice" go through a favourite Italian ballad, with the most touching expression. "The well-known words were melancholic and brought a thousand recollections to his mind, while the plaintive tone in which they were uttered appeared to sympathise with his own feelings." He meets the singer and discovers her name, Emily Melville. She comes to the Castle, and then vanishes. Belmour pursues her, but loses any trace of her.

Belmour's father, the Earl of Delavere, wishes him to marry his cousin Clementina, which Belmour is unable to do, as, charming though she is, he does not love her. The father dies having first signed papers creating him a Marquis. Still depressed and melancholic, although by this time more on account of Emily Melville than of Lady Roseberg, Belmour escorts his sister Caroline to Portugal. She too has had an unfortunate romance, with the married Derville, who turns up with his wife to accompany them. In Portugal Caroline, suitably chaperoned and attended by a doctor, and the Dervilles go off together to Spain *en route* for the winter in Italy. Belmour wanders in Spain for six months before returning to Portugal, where he stumbles across a church full of pots of cascading flowers. Here he meets a friar praying with his arms around an urn which contains the ashes of his late beloved, Rosaura. In the meantime, Belmour receives letters from England, one of which tells him that his steward requires his presence on business, while another informs him that his cousin Clementina is engaged to be married shortly. This news cheers him considerably, as the field is now clear for Emily.

Belmour returns to England and eventually meets with Emily's guardian, Dr. Stanmore, who tells him that while he has been in Portugal, Emily has married. "Her undeserved sufferings are, I trust, at an end. Mr Courtenay, to whom she is now married, sensible of her merit, will, doubtless, reward her virtues: and if my most earnest prayers can aught avail, my child will be happy!" He goes on to relate Emily's tragic orphan background. Her father, wrongfully disinherited from his family estate, had fallen in love with Emily's mother, another Emily, who had been employed as a companion to his half-sister. He had secured a commission in the army and a posting to the West Indies for two years, leaving two Emilys, the mother and now a daughter, in the care of Dr. Stanmore. Her husband expected home on leave, Emily and her daughter went to Falmouth to await his arrival. When the boat docked, they were waiting on the quayside. But only Melville's servant disembarked; he bore the sad news that shortly before embarkation his master had died of yellow fever. A year later the mother had died of a broken heart, leaving Emily, a small child, in the care of Dr. Stanmore.

By this time night has fallen, and Belmour accepts Dr Stanmore's invitation to stay. He is put into a white painted bedroom with drawings of Italy hung around the walls, including a Venetian scene with a figure in a white cloak at the Church of the Mendicanti. Belmour becomes certain that this was Emily's room. "Belmour was no sooner alone than on casting his eyes round the room, he was convinced that he was actually in the very apartment formerly occupied by Miss Melville. The sudden sensation, the long train of ideas which this circumstance excited in his mind, are not to be described – every part of the room was carefully examined by him, stepping lightly on the floor lest his footsteps should be heard in the small and thin-built house. The drawings in particular attracted his attention: they were views, evidently original, of different parts of Italy, and various buildings, both ancient and modern, of that country, enlivened with figures, and executed in a free and masterly style. Among many of Venice, the church of the Mendicanti was often repeated, and various views given of the inside of the building. On further examination among the figures in the foreground, one always presented itself so like his own that he thought – could it have been possible – but it must be fancy – yet it was always represented in the very cloak he wore, on the very bench he sat, where he had often passed a whole hour in listening to the divine music repeated from the grated gallery above. Yet he had sitten for no portrait while in Venice – and again it must be fancy."

Next day Dr. Stanmore is not well enough to see him, and he departs once more plunged in melancholy. "To me, she is lost forever! – Yet. I must see her again – I must assure her of my respect, my admiration, since I dare not, alas! of my regret."

Belmour knows that Courtenay's estate, Dean Abbey, is in Gloucestershire, with well-known and remarkable ruins in a neglected park. He goes there and while waiting on a terrace sees Emily at an upstairs window. She tells her servant to say that she is out, and Belmour goes away without seeing her. However he learns that she is going to Cheltenham to take the waters. Belmour goes there and meets up with Clementina now married to Lord Melford. Emily arrives, they meet again, and he sees her daily while she paints watercolours. They all go to a ball given by the nabob Seeres. Emily and Belmour are the talk of the ball, so handsome and so beautiful. Courtenay, who has hitherto been absent on business, arrives in Cheltenham, is introduced and invites Belmour to Dean Abbey. There, Emily and Belmour acknowledge their love that cannot be, and Belmour departs for London where he is laid low with a desperate fever for three weeks. Once again, he goes abroad, determined to seek solace in Greece.

The narrator tells of Emily's youth, as she had described it to Belmour during their time together at Cheltenham and Dean Abbey. She had spent her childhood with Dr. Stanmore, who had also attended to her education. At a local dance she had met Mrs Stainville, who had taken her under her wing to educate her with a tour of France and Italy. In Paris they met Lord Raymond, who fancied Emily. They had travelled on to

Italy followed by Lord Raymond. They had been in Rome for three months before Lord Raymond appeared. When he did arrive he had added indifference to indolence, and had been entirely uninterested in the classical sites, artists or writers. Gradually Mrs Stainville, who found classical antiquity *"ennuyant"* – and also liked a Lord – had decided to transfer Lord Raymond's affections from Emily to herself. They had moved on to Naples, where Mrs Stainville, worried that Lord Raymond might return to Emily, decided to leave for Venice. *En route* in Bologna Emily had noticed a handsome English stranger at the Opera, who had taken her fancy.

In Venice, Emily was placed in a music school, the de' Mendicanti, which she enjoyed, while Mrs Stainville and Lord Raymond were left to their own devices. Here she sang solos in the choir in an area made private from public view by a screen. Through gaps in the woodwork she was able to see the handsome English stranger appear again in a white cloak and sit down to listen. She sketched the scene. Mrs Stainville returned to England and delivered Emily to Dr. Stanmore, where she hung her drawings of Venice in her bedroom.

A further year elapses and Stanmore has to go on business to Cornwall while his house is redecorated. He therefore sends Emily to the Reverend Mr Rycroft, Rector at Belmour.

At last Emily sees her mysterious stranger again, but is wary of him, as Dr. Stanmore has told her that she should keep away from the proud people in the Castle. She believed that, as the Reverend Mr Rycroft had informed her, Belmour and Clementina were engaged, and therefore that it was improper for him to chase her. Emily is sent on to lodgings with Mr Enstine by Dr. Stanmore, while he remains away. She meets Courtenay there, and accepts his proposal having read a false newspaper report that Belmour and Clementina were married. She goes to live at Dean Abbey.

By now, the reader has been aware for some time that Belmour and the handsome stranger are one and the same, and that Belmour, trying to forget Lady Roseberg, was in Italy at the same time as Emily and Mrs Stainville. Indeed Belmour and Emily must have been aware of this when he set off for Greece, as Emily herself had recited her life history to him whilst in Cheltenham and at Dean Abbey.

Belmour's latest absence abroad lasts for nearly 3 years. He visits Greece and then goes on to Syria and the Levant. In Syria he meets the Portuguese friar, who tells him that while Rosaura is dead, Emily is still alive. This inspires Belmour to return to England. He visits Dean Abbey in a thunderstorm, where during a flash of lightning he sees mourning hatchments over the entrance door. Having fallen asleep in a ruined barn, he wakes next morning and hears Emily singing. Courtenay had been ill for two years before dying. The way is now open for the happy couple to wed. Dr. Stanmore marries them; Belmour's sister Caroline returns in good health and is married to her faithful former local suitor, Mr Mortimer. All live happily ever after.

The book makes full use of Anne's travel experiences in Portugal and Italy and contains lyrical descriptions of the beauties of Lisbon, Naples and Venice. The Portuguese section very much tallies with Anne's letters to Mary Berry in 1791. At one stage, before the decision that all her works should be burnt, Anne had seen herself as a travel writer, and she is almost certain to have retained notes made on site at the time of her travels. These she put to very good use in *Belmour.* It is equally likely that she would have kept similar records of her journeys in Italy.

In forming the book's characters Anne drew extensively on her own life's experience. The kindly and learned Dr. Stanmore is drawn from the Horace Walpole remembered from childhood days. The smooth and shallow St Fort is drawn on Augustus Fawkener (note the similarity in the sound of the names). Lady Roseberg draws many parallels with Lady Melbourne. The intended landing at Falmouth of Emily's soldier father fresh from the West Indies, only for his family to discover that he had died of fever, echoes the return of Mr Lennox, another army officer, awaited by Todle, at Goodwood in 1794, also from the yellow fever-afflicted Leeward Islands.

Anne's mother certainly recognised her daughter in the book's characters. The following poem was found within the covers of the Lewis Walpole library's copy of *Belmour.* It is described as having been written by the Countess Dowager of Ailesbury (then above eighty years of age) on a novel called *Belmour,* written by her daughter, the Hon. A.S. Damer. The poem is entitled *"The author is supposed to speak."*

> *Tis well known I can speak Greek*
> *As naturally as pigs squeak;*
> *Latin's for me no more difficile*
> *Than for blackbirds 'tis to whistle.*
> *Yet that don't make me melancholy*
> *I still retain my taste for folly.*
> *In proof of which peruse my book,*
> *Which when you honour with a look,*
> *You'll see the follies of the times,*
> *With some account of foreign climes;*
> *Lovers expert in dance and song,*
> *With reason weak, and passion strong.*
> *The damsels tho', as well as lovers,*
> *Are true to friends and love their mothers.*
> *Don't think me a conceited elf,*
> *I took the models from myself.*

She had certainly recognised, as a mother might, many similarities between Anne herself and Belmour, her hero. Both were born into aristocratic households, and both were great admirers of the arts in all forms. Both were attracted by naval feats, Anne by her sailor uncle, Lord William Campbell, Belmour by his gallant deceased friend, Captain Harcourt.

Belmour has recently been re-issued with a masterly and detailed commentary by Jonathan Gross. He follows the analysis by Andrew Elfinbein, laid out in his book, *Romantic Passion*, which sees the story of Belmour and Emily as a thinly disguised re-run of Anne and Mary Berry, with Anne in the role of Belmour. Her parents would certainly have liked her to be a man. Her father was a soldier, and her first recorded drawings, which she sent to Horace Walpole, are of soldiers in Germany. She was physically courageous; she had helped on deck whilst the trans-Channel packet on which she was travelling in 1779 had been attacked by a French privateer; she had crossed great wastes of Spain and Portugal, with only a mule driver as a companion; she certainly had a masculine side to her character.

However the obedient, well-behaved Emily, with the voice of an angel, does not square up with Mary Berry, who was argumentative with a voice like a foghorn. She was certainly no fair St Cecilia. Lytton Strachey, whilst intensely admiring her intelligence, described her as having a masculine mind, being "scolding and loud-voiced", and referred to her "frowns and hootings".

Whatever might have been going on in the author's mind concerning the real origins of her hero and heroine, the book, after a slow start, is still a very good read. Characters are carefully drawn, locations, whether in England or abroad, tellingly described, and highlights in the action dramatically depicted. The night-time scene at Dean Abbey, where Belmour sees the mourning hatchment above the door lit up by a flash of lightning, has true Gothic horror, beautifully contrasted the next morning with Emily singing in the stillness after the storm. Sometimes one feels that the characters are a little stilted, that real people would not have talked or acted as they do. Other than Lady Clementina, there is little of gaiety or laughter in the book, and melancholy rules supreme. That probably reflects the author's real-life personality and slight awkwardness. The words of Lady Sarah Lennox spring to mind: "A want of sweetness in her disposition; she is too strictly right ever to be beloved."

Contemporary reviews of the book criticised Belmour's morality in pursuing both Emily and Lady Roseberg, both ostensibly happily-married ladies. However, the book does portray society as it was, not necessarily as it should have been. By and large Belmour contains his passion for Emily, parting from her to lead a melancholy life abroad, and by his constant and charitable attentions to the poor and needy, and his care for family and friends, shows himself fit for the purpose of hero.

The book took Anne some ten years to write and complete. Large parts of it were drawn from her own life and experience, and from most of the places and countries which she had visited. Its contents had drained her supply of experiences and taxed her imagination to the full. It is not surprising that she did not attempt a second novel.

Chapter 18

SCULPTURE FROM LIFE

The disruptions to normal life caused by family deaths and by the traumas of the Berry and O'Hara engagement had left Anne little time for sculpture. She exhibited two busts in the Academy exhibition in 1795, and then nothing until 1799. In March 1797 *The Oracle*, reporting on the Royal Academy exhibition, commented that "Mrs Damer does not exhibit this year". In January 1798 *Lloyds Evening Post* stated that "the Hon Mrs Damer is exercising her admirable chisel upon an ornament for the new pyramid to be erected near Plymouth. It is a head of the gallant Lord Duncan." It is doubtful whether this was ever completed. In May 1799 Anne started to exhibit again at the Royal Academy. This year she returned to the portrayal of a dog. Carved from Carrara marble, it was described by *The Oracle* as charming, and "an elegant portraiture of fidelity from the hand of taste and beauty."

By December 1800 Anne was busy with her bust of Nelson. She was inspired and excited by the victor of the Nile, newly returned to England, man of the hour and national hero. She believed fervently in the part of sculpture as a historical record of a great man. Classical heroes of Greece and Rome had survived the years, contemporary proofs in stone of their sitters' qualities; as her contemporary Falconet put it in his *Reflections on Sculpture*: "elevating our soul to the virtues which have prevented these great men from being forgotten by mankind". A statue of a hero was important, both as a reminder and an inspiration to the viewer.

If the hero, like Nelson, was physically small, lacked an arm and an eye, and was not an heroic model, the sculptor had to rise above it the 18th century solution, as expounded by Winckelmann, was sculpture on the "Greek" model, requiring every gesture to be eliminated to produce tranquil works, "sedate but active; calm, but not indifferent or drowsy." Winckelmann encouraged sculptors to generalise anatomy and facial features.

Reynolds had echoed this, stating in addition in December 1780: "The desire of transmitting to posterity the shape of modern dress must be acknowledged to be purchased at a prodigious price, even the price of everything that is valuable in art."

To Anne, moving from 18th century neo-classicism to 19th century reality, her portrayal of Nelson was to be a halfway house. The head, though clearly recognisable as that of the hero, followed Winckelmann's precepts. Abandoning Reynolds's dictates the dress was naval uniform, as worn by Nelson. The medals and decorations are accurately recorded: the riband of the Order of the Bath falls across his chest from the right shoulder, the naval gold medals of St Vincent and the Nile are suspended over it; to the left the stars of the Bath, St Ferdinand, and the Turkish Crescent are attached. The bust was truncated from both shoulder epaulettes, avoiding the necessity to show only a single arm.

Anne's ambition was to produce a model of the world's greatest hero and present it to the world greatest city. On 21st January 1799 the Lord Mayor of London informed the Court of Common Council, meeting at the Guildhall, that he had received a letter from Mrs Damer offering her services to execute a portrait of Nelson either in bronze or marble for the city. The court had unanimously accepted her offer, and asked the Mayor to inform her of this decision.

It was one thing to have gained the approval of the Lord Mayor; it was another to persuade the hero of the Nile to sit to her. Anne's nephew and heir, Sir Alexander Johnston, said that Nelson had sat to Anne as long and as often as she had requested, because of his friendship with her uncle Lord William Campbell, and indeed they had briefly served together in the West Indies on HMS *Bristol*, under Admiral Sir Peter Parker, during the period 1766-8. In a later letter to Emma Hamilton, written in 1809, Anne claimed that it was through the influence of the Hamiltons that she had won Nelson's approval. Whatever his reasons, Nelson consented with pleasure, and as a thank you to Anne, presented her with the coat he had worn that day and night in Aboukir Bay, uncleaned, and still bearing the stains and powder marks of war.

The task of sculpting took its time. On 11th October 1800 the *Evening Post* reported that the bust intended as a present for the City of London was almost completed. In November the *Whitehall Evening Post* reported that Nelson was still attending for an hour every day or more, as Anne requested. Then disaster struck; as reported in the *Morning Post* of 11th December 1800, with an excruciating pun: "The admirers of fine arts will regret to hear that in finishing the bust of Lord Nelson, Mrs Damer has unfortunately broken off a part of the nose, which it is thought will spoil the whole of the capital performance."

The first model must have been completed by spring 1802, a cast made and copies completed by the figure-maker, B. Papera. In March 1802 Anne and Mary Berry set off to France intent on offering Napoleon a bust of Charles James Fox, the English proponent of freedom, and possibly one of Nelson, an enemy for whom Napoleon had the greatest respect and admiration. As we have seen, it is unclear whether they took a bust or busts with them, or whether they were intent on offering to send them in the future. By June 1802 the bust and its cast must have been completed, as the Wedgwood pottery account book has the following entry:

```
Mr Byerley        June 19 1802
Bought of B. Papera
Figure Maker to her Majesty
One bust of Mrs Deamour        0.12.0
One ditto of Lord Nelson       0.12.0
```

Also by summer, a delivery had been made to Paris. In August 1802 Joseph Farington recorded in his diary that he had seen two busts of Nelson and Charles James Fox, worked by Anne, exhibited in the Tuileries. From the above, it would seem that Papera had also completed models from casts of Fox and of Anne herself – the last possibly from a cast of the self-portrait presented to the Uffizi Gallery and brought back with her from Italy.

However it was not until spring 1804 that the marble bust commissioned by the City of London was first seen by the public. It was shown at the Royal Academy exhibition for that year. It took pride of place among the sculpted busts exhibited, being displayed in prime position at the top of a pyramid of exhibits. The *Morning Post* of 5th May 1804 described it as follows: "Among the number of busts that people this year's Exhibition, stands pre-eminent in merit as it does in situation, that of Lord Nelson. It was entirely finished as well as conceived, by the Honourable Mrs Damer; for while most of the modern Statuaries, Modellers strictly speaking, rather than Sculptors, confine their own labours to shaping the ductile clay, and suffer what little fire they may have instilled in this pliant material, again to evaporate under the mechanical process of the journeyman, who then copies the fragile form in the more stubborn marble, simply by rule and compass. The fair hand of a female artist remains as yet almost unrivalled in the arduous task of singly defying every difficulty opposed by the hardest produce of the Parian quarry.

"Notwithstanding its modern costume, this portrait of Lord Nelson displays more of the true spirit of the antique than most of the sculpture worthies that grace the circle formed around its base, in spite of all the advantages they enjoy of Roman togas or bared bosoms. It possesses that breadth of style which carefully discarding every incidental minutiae of the features, unworthy of record, as unconnected with the effect of the countenance or expression of the mind, prevents the truth of the resemblance from being diminished, instead of increased by a confusion of unmeaning details, cavities and protuberances, dimples and pimples, not mellowed by any assistance of colours, not smoothed down by any touch of the pencil. It exhibits moreover, a simplicity of attitude inseparable from real dignity."

The bust was finally delivered to the Guildhall in London in 1805, some five years after its commissioning. On 28th December a report in the *Ipswich Journal* recorded that Mrs Damer's offer to execute a statue of Lord Nelson for the Guildhall had been declined. Perhaps the worthy councillors of the City had considered that if a bust took five years, a statue might require ten.

Four years later, on the 31st October 1809, Anne wrote to Emma Hamilton. She had heard that a fine edition of Nelson's life was soon to be published, and very much hoped that the fact that Nelson had sat to her, and to no one else, for a sculpture should be mentioned, and that thus her name might be linked to "the most brilliant name that England ever gave birth to." Emma's reply, if indeed she did respond, is not recorded, but the sculpture is not mentioned in either Clarke and McArthur's *Life* of 1809, nor in Southey's famous and successful *Life* of 1812.

Portraying Nelson had given Anne a taste for the sculpture of contemporary heroes. She was also to produce a bust of Charles James Fox. Fox was a friend as well as a "hero". He had brought her the news of John Damer's death in 1776, and she had been an enthusiastic supporter of his candidature in the Westminster election of 1784. For 22 years thereafter it was Fox's lot to be in opposition to the government, for the great majority of that time led by William Pitt. These years spanned the Revolution in France, the rise of Napoleon, and the Napoleonic Wars up to Pitt's death. Charles Fox had supported the initial years of the Revolution in France, and the triumph of democracy over the perceived despotic tyranny of the Bourbon monarchy. Though he had baulked at the excesses of the Reign of Terror, he had thought it a lesser evil than the previous government of Louis XVI. He had welcomed the arrival of Napoleon, unprepared to admit that one form of tyranny was giving way to another. In Anne's simplistic view both Fox and Napoleon were fellow travellers, representing the Whig principle that in pursuit of political liberty, the power of the Crown should be diminished.

Fox probably sat for Anne around 1801. A first terracotta model must have been completed by late 1801 or early 1802, as, in whatever way it had reached its destination, a cast was seen by Farington in Paris in August 1802. The original terracotta bust was then exhibited at the Royal Academy in 1803. There seems to be no record of Fox sitting on any occasion. Two undated letters from Fox to Anne from St Anne's Hill record that she had written to him at Clarges Street, which he and Mrs Fox had long left, and that they would call on her at Strawberry Hill in a week's time.

A second model in marble was made by Anne probably from the original terracotta. Fox died in 1806, so it could not have been done from life after that. This was intended to be a personal gift from Anne to the Emperor Napoleon, in a durable material that would stand the test of time. Whenever it was finished, there was no immediate opportunity to present it personally, owing to the return of war with France. It seems most likely that Anne arranged for it to be delivered to Paris in 1812, where it remained in storage until the opportunity arose in 1815, during The Hundred Days, for Anne to present it herself.

Fox himself, by the year 1800, was dark, corpulent and grubby. Like Nelson, he did not naturally display a hero's physique for the benefit of the sculptor's chisel. Anne applied the same principles of draughtsmanship for Fox's features as for Nelson's; his features were portrayed as a recognisable likeness, shorn of all traces of a life of prodigious consumption. His clothing, coat and waistcoat and knotted cravat were accurately shown in contemporary, if slightly dishevelled, style; if the odd wine stain or trace of snuff were apparent, they would indeed be lifelike. Fox's features, jowly, with prominent eyebrows, broad forehead and lips set in a quizzical smile, have more than a hint of the lived-in look that his lifestyle demanded, but at the same time demonstrate vision and intelligence. If anything the treatment is more naturalistic than Nelson's, and it would be interesting to have been able to compare the terracotta model of 1802 with the marble version of 1812.

The next of Anne's heroes came from a very different mould, though like Nelson and Fox, from her own generation. Joseph Banks was born in 1743, the son of William Banks, an influential country squire and member of the House of Commons. Educated at both Harrow and Eton, and Christ Church Oxford, he did not want for tuition. While he was at Oxford his father died, leaving him squire of Revesby in Lincolnshire, and a wealthy man. While at Eton he had been painted studying a botanical illustration, and at Oxford too he developed his interests in the natural sciences at the expense of the conventional classical curriculum. Not finding a botanical tutor to his satisfaction among the Oxford dons, and perhaps thinking that "educated at Harrow, Eton, Oxford and Cambridge" might appear a trifle excessive, he imported and paid for a Cambridge botanist, Israel Lyons, to deliver a course of lectures at Oxford.

After Oxford, which he left without taking a degree, Banks divided his time between Lincolnshire and London. At the British Museum he met Daniel Solander, plantsman and disciple of Linnaeus. In 1766, a newly elected member of the Royal Society, Banks travelled across the Atlantic to study the flora of Newfoundland and Labrador, following which he published a Linnean description of the flora and fauna of that region. In 1768 he joined Captain Cook on the *Endeavour*, bound to Brazil, the Straits of Magellan, Tahiti, New Zealand and the eastern coast of Australia. The voyage was sponsored jointly by the Royal Navy and the Royal Society, and Banks's remit, along with his assistants, the botanists Solander and Spöring, and the illustrator Sydney Parkinson, was to collect and record botanical specimens, almost all of them new to the civilised world. On his return in 1771 the success of the expedition, with some 800 new specimens of the flora of Australia, ensured that Banks became a national celebrity. His scientific work with plants continued throughout his life, and in 1778 he was elected President of the Royal Society, a position which he held for the next forty-one years.

Banks divided his time between his house in Soho Square, London, where he established a scientific and literary salon, and which housed his botanical collections and library, and a house at Isleworth, standing in 34 acres and well watered by a natural spring, which he called Spring Grove. Here he developed an outstanding garden, featuring a wide botanic collection of live plants from home and abroad. At nearby Kew Palace, Banks advised King George III on his Royal Botanic Gardens, and under his direction Kew became a plantsman's Mecca.

Anne knew Banks socially; they moved in the same circles, they had Sir William Hamilton in common as a great friend, and they had co-operated in sourcing plants for Josephine Bonaparte following Anne's trip to Paris in March 1802. Not only was Banks an eminent botanist, but as President of the Royal Society, and as a senior trustee of the British Museum, he was at the pinnacle of two peaks, science and the future, and conservation and learning from the past. Anne's first bust of Banks was shown at the Royal Academy in 1806; this was modelled in terracotta, and its current whereabouts are unknown. A second bust cast in bronze was exhibited at the Royal Academy in 1813, and is now on prominent display in the British Museum. The viewer's first impression is of a massive dark head, a bull of a man, combining presence and authority behind a stern countenance. The head is much more lifelike than the two previous heroes, Nelson and Fox, and the coat, bearing the insignia of the Order of the Bath, and cravat, cleaner and more sharply delineated than Fox's. This is a man used to having authority, prepared to listen and to make his own judgements.

Most, if not all, of Anne's work in marble and bronze was preceded by a similar piece of the same sitter in terracotta. Presumably Anne had casts made from her terracotta models, and these could have been used to make moulds for bronzes, or further copies in terracotta to act as a master copy for works carved in marble.

Anne's fourth hero was also to be drawn from the world of science. Her bust of Sir Humphrey Davy is signed and dated 1813. It is a terracotta model, covered with a black paint to give the appearance of a bronze. It is a treatment which is very effective. Davy was 35 when the bust was sculpted. He appears younger, though a portrait of him by Sir Thomas Lawrence, completed some 10 years later, also makes him look a lot younger than his years. He has an open neck with a large collared coat, buttoned below. There is a hint of eyebrows over eyeballs with irises; hair curls over his forehead and sideboards descend down cheeks. The head is slightly inclined downwards, and underneath the long nose there is a determined half-smile. The chin is forceful, the forehead deep. Here is a man who is confident of his own abilities.

Davy was younger than the previous heroes. He was born in 1778 and Anne was already thirty at the time of his birth. He had obviously impressed her, and his record was indeed impressive. His early years had been spent in his native Cornwall, where he was an especially precocious child, combining a love of poetry and its composition with a bent for scientific experiment, surprisingly encouraged by a Cornish saddler and Quaker called Robert Dunkin. In 1795 he was apprenticed to a surgeon in

Penzance, where he took to chemistry in the apothecary's dispensary by day, and in a garret in his guardian's house by night. In 1798 he joined the Pneumatic Institution in Bristol, with the task of superintending experiments, notably with laughing gas (nitrous oxide). He himself became addicted to it, and he formed friendships with James Watt, Robert Southey and Samuel Taylor Coleridge, all of whom were users of it. Watt financed the building of a gas chamber, and experiments included the use of nitrous oxide as a cure for a hangover, apparently with some success.

In 1799 he first visited London where he attracted the attention of, among others, Anne's previous hero, Sir Joseph Banks, and in 1801 he was appointed Assistant lecturer at the newly formed Royal Institution. His lectures combined the gift of the gab with spectacular experimentation and were an immediate success. Davy was able to record that over 500 people had attended his June lecture, which included "Respiration, Nitrous Oxide, and unbounded Applause. Amen!" Youth and good looks assisted his popularity as a lecturer, and Anne, whose interest in chemistry had been evident in the laboratory at Goodwood, may well have been among the large number of female attendees. In 1804, at the age of 25, Davy was elected a member of the Royal Society. In June 1812 the Princess of Wales and Mary Berry visited Sir Humphrey Davy together; the Princess, Charlotte Campbell, and others had taken in small doses of the Imperial Gas, and all had been intoxicated for around three minutes They had then come back for further doses until the supply of gas was finished. Mary had apparently not succumbed to the temptation. No record exists of how Anne's sculpture came to be commissioned, or where and when Davy sat to her. Both sculptress and model had a talent for self-publicity, and would have believed such a bust to be to their mutual benefit. It was exhibited at the Royal Academy in 1814.

The last of Anne's naturalistic human busts, is of a heroine rather than a hero, Princess Caroline of Brunswick, later to become Queen Caroline, wife of George IV. In 1794 she was engaged to George Prince of Wales. She was a German Protestant princess and politically a suitable bride. George agreed to marry her in order to increase his annual allowance voted by Parliament, and thereby help to pay off his debts. She was physically unattractive and lacked style; but she was courageous and not afraid of speaking her mind. Wellington described her as a woman "of indelicate manners, indifferent character and not very inviting appearance", chosen by the Prince's mistress, Lady Jersey, in the "hope that disgust with a wife would secure constancy to a mistress." On being introduced to her the Prince had called for a brandy. They were married on 8th April 1795. George was drunk at the ceremony; a brief sexual encounter had followed, ending with the groom asleep in the fireplace. His new bride had summed it up succinctly. "Judge" said she, "what it was to have a drunken husband on one's wedding day, and one who passed the greatest part of his bridal night under the grate, where he fell, and where I left him."

Remarkably, this coupling, followed by another on the following night, resulted on 7th January 1796 in the birth of an heir to the throne, Princess Charlotte. Subsequently the royal couple lived apart. Towards the end of 1811 the Prince of Wales was appointed Regent, and directed that Caroline's access to Princess Charlotte be strictly limited. She had tolerated other slights and restrictions, but her relationship with her daughter was a close one, and she was determined to fight to secure it. She enlisted the help of Henry Brougham, an ambitious radical politician, and gained a considerable degree of public sympathy. Jane Austen wrote of her: "Poor woman, I shall support her as long as I can, because she is a Woman and because I hate her Husband." Anne felt a similar sympathy. She had met the Princess of Wales when she came to visit Strawberry Hill on two occasions in July 1809 and August 1810; her cousin, Lady Charlotte Campbell, was lady-in-waiting to the Princess, who had become an especially close friend of Mary Berry. The sittings took place in late 1813 and in January 1814, at a particularly difficult time for the Princess. She was distraught by the efforts of the Prince Regent to marry their daughter Princess Charlotte, the heir to the throne, to the Prince of Orange. Influenced by his prospective father-in-law, and not by his intended bride, the Prince had been ill-mannered and disdainful to the Princess of Wales, and thereby incurred her enmity.

The figure that Anne sculpted in terracotta is clad in a high necked shirt buttoned to the collar, with a fine frill of crinkled material which just shows above the collar. The Princess's head is circled by a long headband which hangs down either side of her head; crossing over beneath the top collar button, one end curls back over the left shoulder, the other stretches across her bosom. Daylight shows on either side between the falling bands and the tight-collared head. Joshua Reynold's precepts on the clothing of statues have given way to current fashion, not only in the clothing of the body, but in head gear as well. The hair too is shown in the fashion of the period; the two concentric curled locks at the centre of her forehead could well have graced a Lawrence portrait. Large eyes complete with pupils, eyebrows and lids, stare straight at the viewer; the mouth is firm, possibly truculent; the features are too square to be beautiful, but dumpy would be unkind, and she is recognisable as the lady in the red coat and bonnet painted by Romney. However the first and last general impression of this work is solid and stolid. The bust lacks grace – but then so did the sitter.

At the time that she sculpted the Princess of Wales Anne was aged 66, and her physical abilities were on the wain. Carving in marble requires strength and stamina, and she had not used this medium since finishing Charles James Fox in 1812. Joseph Banks was cast in bronze, the casting completed in a foundry from Anne's model in plaster or terracotta. Humphrey Davy too was worked in terracotta, albeit painted black to resemble bronze. She exhibited twice more at the Royal Academy; two of her favoured models of dogs, one in 1816 and one in 1818. Thirty-four years had elapsed between her first dog sculpture, shown at the Academy in 1784, and her last in 1818. They were much appreciated in their time, and it is sad that so few remain today. It would be thrilling if this book might encourage a reader somewhere to find a missing Damer dog.

The rest of her recorded works seem to have been bronzes, produced in the foundry from casts of earlier works. An 1823 self-portrait, probably a copy of her Uffizi bust, signed, dated, and inscribed as a present to her friend Richard Payne Knight, is described as being in marble, but is more likely to have been in bronze. It formed part of his bequest to the British Museum, but came to an untimely end during the 1940 Blitz of London. She also commissioned two further bronzes of Nelson. The first was presented to the Rajah of Tanjore, a self-governing Hindu province at the south-east of the Indian continent. Anne's nephew by marriage, Sir Alexander Johnston, was the Chief Justice of the island of Ceylon, immediately to the south of Tanjore on the Indian mainland. Johnston had experimented with the introduction of an English judicial system to the Hindu law courts, and especially with the concept of trial by jury. This had been adopted enthusiastically by the anglophile Rajah of Tanjore, who had also erected a monument to the British successes in the late war against the French. Between them Johnston and Anne agreed that a bust of Nelson would be a suitable token of thanks to this willing supporter of the Raj. The Admiral's victory at the Battle of the Nile had shattered French lines of communication, averted a French invasion of India and upheld British supremacy on the subcontinent. The bust would be an artistic reminder of Imperial reality. Like the Indian Empire, it has disappeared.

A second bronze of Nelson was given as a present to the Duke of Clarence, Lord High Admiral of England, in return for a commission in the Navy for Anne's great-nephew Frederick Erskine Johnston. With the bust she also offered to present the Duke with the coat that Nelson had worn at the Battle of the Nile, which he had given to her after sitting to her. The bust was completed shortly before Anne's death in 1828. It was mounted on the stump of the *Victory's* foremast, used as a pedestal, and placed in the library at Bushey Park. Mr Johnston got his commission; the coat is now to be seen in the Royal Naval Museum in Greenwich, and the bronze bust is in storage at Windsor Castle.

Sir Alexander Johnston's description of this event appears below:

"The late Lord William Campbell, a post-captain in the British Navy (the father of Lady Johnston and the grandfather of Lt Frederick Erskine Johnston, now first lieutenant of HMS *Terrible*), who had known a great deal of Lord Nelson when he first entered the Navy, had formed, even at that time, a high opinion of his bravery, zeal, and activity, and had been accustomed to speak of him frequently as a distinguished and a rising young man, to his niece, the Honourable Mrs Anne Seymour Damer (the daughter of his sister, the Countess of Ailesbury and her husband, Field Marshal Henry Seymour Conway), who had devoted herself from her childhood to the study of different branches of the Fine Arts, particularly to that of sculpture, in which she had attained at an early period of her life the greatest proficiency, as is shown by the very fine and numerous specimens of her genius and talents, in the collection now in the possession of her cousin, Lady Johnston, to whom she left them at her death.

"When Lord Nelson, by his victory of the Nile, had become an object of interest throughout all Europe, Mrs Damer, who, from what she had previously heard of him from her uncle and others, had formed the most enthusiastic idea of his character as a Hero, made an offer, which was gladly accepted by the City of London, to execute at her own expense, and present to the City a colossal bust in marble of Nelson, who, in consequence of the friendship, which he bore to her uncle, the late Lord William Campbell, very willingly sat to her as often and as long as she wished, in order to enable her to make the very striking likeness which she did of him. Having finished the bust, she, at the request of the City, placed it in that part of the Council Chamber in Guildhall in which it still stands, and in which she thought, as an artist, it would be seen to the greatest advantage.

"The last time he sat in to her, he good-humouredly asked what he could give her for the high honour which she had conferred on him, and for all the trouble which she had taken on the occasion. She answered, 'One of your old coats,' on which he replied, 'you shall immediately have one and it shall be the one which I value the most highly – the one which I wore during the whole day of the Battle of the Nile, and which I have never worn, nor even allowed to be brushed, since, in order that my Naval as well as other friends may know, from the streaks of perspiration and hair powder which are still to be seen on it, the exertions which I made and the anxiety which I felt on that day to deserve the approbation of my king and country.'

"Shortly after Mrs Damer had presented the bust to the City of London, His late Majesty King William IV, then Duke of Clarence, who had known her uncle, Lord William Campbell, in early life, and who had always been an admirer of her talents for sculpture, requested her to give him (which she did) a cast in plaster of Paris of that bust. Some years afterwards, when he was appointed Lord High Admiral of England, he called on her, and told her that he wished to show her, now that he had the power of doing so, how sincere the respect was which he entertained for her uncle's distinguished conduct as a naval officer, and for her own enthusiastic zeal for Nelson's heroic acts, and that he was therefore most anxious to place in the Navy the grandson of her uncle, Lord William Campbell, the present lieutenant F.E.Johnston of the *Terrible*, and to put up the finest bronze bust which you could execute of Nelson, along with his Coat, on the stump of the foremast of the *Victory* which stood in his library at Bushey. Mrs Damer, having obtained the consent of the parents, Sir Alexander and

Lady Johnston, of her cousin, young Mr Johnston, to her doing so, accepted the offer of His Royal Highness to place him in the Navy, and at the same time promised to execute for and present to His Royal Highness, for the purpose for which he intended it, the finest colossal bust of bronze which she could make of Nelson.

"Notwithstanding Mrs Damer's great age, she being at the time nearly 80 years old, she finished this bronze bust a few days before her death, but not having been able to present it to His Royal Highness herself, left directions that her cousin, young Mr Johnston, should present the bust and the Coat to His Royal Highness as soon as possible after her death.

"Upon His Royal Highness hearing of Mrs Damer's directions with respect to the bust and Coat, he immediately appointed a day on which he was to receive Mr Johnston with them; and having invited Sir Alexander and Lady Johnston and their son to Bushey, the bust was placed by His Royal Highness in their presence on the stump of the foremast of the *Victory* in the library; and the Painted Chamber in Greenwich Hospital having, on further consideration, been deemed a more appropriate place than Bushey for the Coat, it was put into the case in which it is now seen, with a glass over it, and sent to the Painted Chamber at Greenwich Hospital."

One final note remains to be added concerning Anne's later statuary – the bust that might have been – of the Empress Josephine. In 1969 there was an exhibition at the Musée Ernest Rupin in Brive to mark the 200th anniversary of Napoleon's birth. A description of Exhibit No 174 translates into English as "Cup and saucer in Sèvres china, given by the Empress Josephine to Anne Seymour Damer to thank her for a bust that she had made of the Empress at her request – explanatory plaque "given by her Majesty – the Empress Josephine of France. To Anne Seymour Damer. 1811." The exhibit was described as being from the collection of Mme G. Campbell-Johnston. Germaine Campbell-Johnston, or Campbell, as she sometimes described herself, was the widow of Diarmid Campbell-Johnston, a direct descendant of the Lady Johnston to whom Anne bequeathed her estate and works of art.

Was the Josephine bust an accurate record handed down by word of mouth through the Campbell-Johnston family? Or was it a wistful fancy dreamed up by Mme Germaine Campbell-Johnston? Certainly there seems to be no earlier written mention of it, and at first sight there seems to have been little opportunity for sittings. England and France were at war, Josephine was at Malmaison, Anne in Brook Street.

However apart from a christening in March 1810 in London, and a meeting with the Princess of Wales at Strawberry Hill in August 1810, there is little mention of Anne in England until the gift of the Sèvres china in January 1811. For the 1810 Royal Academy exhibition Anne produced a bronze of "A Muse". Nothing more is known about this piece. It is tempting to think that following Josephine's divorce from Napoleon in 1809 Anne had been able to slip across the Channel under a safe passage authorised by

Napoleon to meet up with her friend and sculpt her. The original terracotta model would have remained at Malmaison, and a cast, brought back to England, might have been sent to the foundry to reappear as a bronze "Muse" at the RA.

Such an enterprise would fit in with Anne's character, her disdain for authority if it was not old-fashioned Whig, her sense of adventure, and her willingness to support a fellow woman in distress, as shown by her later support of the Princess of Wales. She was to demonstrate in 1815 that a passage to France in wartime was not a problem for her. She would not have wished to draw public attention to such an escapade, and so the omission of any reference to Josephine in her portfolio would seem natural. She would have found exquisite amusement in watching Farington and his friends deliberating over the failings of a nameless Muse. Sadly the bronze has now vanished; the terracotta, if it ever existed at Malmaison, is unlikely to have survived the house's occupation by succeeding generations of Prussian, German, and English soldiery.

Chapter 19

THE MARCH OF TIME

No sooner had the Paris expedition of 1802 returned to England than Mary's play, *Fashionable Friends,* was produced at Drury Lane, with Charles Kemble in the role of Sir Dudley Dorimant, and Marie Thérèse du Camp as Lady Selina Vapour. Mary was still not revealing herself to the theatregoing public. The prologue, spoken by Charles Kemble, ended:

> *"This night our unknown author will produce*
> *Old subjects modernis'd for present use;*
> *If you're displeas'd, be cautious how you show it,*
> *Perhaps your nearest neighbour is the poet;*
> *but if you're pleas'd and anxious to befriend us,*
> *Like Fashionable Friends, in crowds attend us."*

Sadly, and to the great disappointment of Mary and her friends, the audience was not pleased, and the play ran only two nights.

Mary's health remained indifferent and it was not long before the Berry family started planning to return to the continent. On Tuesday 26th October 1802 they again left North Audley Street for the warmer climes of winter in Nice. By December they had arrived, and Mary wrote to Anne: "I remember your telling me that you thought you should feel comfortable and pleased at Strawberry if you could fancy me quietly settled, or taking a quiet walk at least. Be comfortable and be pleased then, dear soul! *Car enfin m'y voici."* The Berrys were to remain abroad until September 1803.

Anne meanwhile had plenty to occupy herself at home. Her novel *Belmour* was circulating in fashionable literary circles, and Farington noted that although published without the author's name, it was generally ascribed to Mrs Damer. In addition to sculpting Nelson for the City of London, she had entered into an exchange of letters with Josephine Bonaparte, with regard to the latter's horticultural requirements for the garden at Malmaison.

A letter from Josephine in 1802 acknowledged receipt of some seeds which Anne had given her, thanked her and asked her to pass on her thanks to *"le chevalier* Banks" as well. She recalled with great pleasure her short meeting with Anne, and impressed by her character and talents, looked forward to renewing their acquaintance. She went on to ask for Anne's help in obtaining seed of *banksias serrata*, and of any other new plants discovered by Banks and bearing his name.

This is likely to have been an ongoing correspondence, as on 9th December 1802 Anne wrote from Strawberry Hill to Sir Joseph Banks, asking him whether he could provide, from his nursery at Spring Grove, a "*strelitzia albiflos* or any other rare plant" for Josephine Bonaparte. She instructed that she should be given notice of the plant's arrival at her house in Upper Brook Street, so that she could make arrangements to send it on to Josephine in the manner that she had directed. Anne enquired after Sir Joseph's health and sent her compliments to Lady Banks and his sister. She said that if the weather continued to be mild it was unlikely that she would be in town until Christmas. She would let him know when she intended to arrive, and reminded him that, though not neighbours in London, they certainly were very close to each other in the country.

Banks must have replied swiftly, as on 20th December Anne wrote to him again, telling him that she had written to Josephine Bonaparte, saying that the much desired *strelitzia* would soon be hers, and in addition promising some seed from New South Wales. She expected to hear very soon from the captain of the trans-Channel boat, whom she trusted to take anything to Calais (including possibly the earlier despatch of the busts of Nelson and Fox), and suggested that in the meantime Banks should send to her the carefully wrapped package of seed. She would await the arrival of the *strelitzia* and promised to ensure a safe and speedy delivery to France. This horticultural business was still unfinished at the turn of the year.

At the same time Anne had to look after two houses, Upper Brook Street and Strawberry Hill, whilst also caring for her ageing mother Caroline, whose strength, which had been gradually weakening, finally gave out. On 17th January 1803 she died in Upper Brook Street. Anne was responsible for the funeral arrangements. It was the height of winter and very, very cold. Anne decided that her mother should rest not with her late husband, Harry, in the Seymour Conway family church at Ragley, but with her Campbell relations. Scotland and Inveraray were obviously too far, and so she decided on the church at Sundridge, near Combe Bank, where Anne herself had been born and where there was a Campbell vault. She described the events in a series of letters to Mary Berry in Nice.

On 16th January 1803 she wrote: "It is not possible for me to express to you what I have suffered for these last days. At my poor mother's age the sad idea of losing her must frequently, constantly almost, have occurred to my imagination, accompanied by a train of melancholy reflections. Unprepared, it is true, therefore, I could not be. But the scene now before me is rendered doubly distressing by my dearest mother's gentleness under her frequent sufferings and her extreme desire for life, and life, alas! alas! I too plainly see, cannot long be granted her. ... She breathes now with extreme difficulty and distress, and that difficulty and distress can but increase under a miracle. The weather is so sadly against her. Oh! Were she in your plain of Nice. But it is one of these despairing black dismal frosts, with a high wind, that now and then, indeed, give from a heavy atmosphere the hope of change, and then it resumes its chilling rigid state. Still is my mother's pulse and other powers of existence, as both Sir Walter and Chilvers affirm, such as might allow this dear good soul years of existence, but that one wheel, so he calls it, is nearly stopped, and little if any hope remains. Last night even was, to appearance, so favourable in a great degree, and I had gone to bed at about one o'clock having sat up the other nights very late and only had a few hours' heavy rest, Anne, as usual, coming up and giving me frequent reports, when, at about seven this morning, she was alarmed by my mother's throwing herself into her arms and saying she was dying. Chilvers (whom I have near in the front drawing-room) was instantly called, and afforded what assistance could be given. (I of course throwing over my Spanish cloak, was down in an instant.) The struggle was for some moments severe, but this time her strength still conquered!"

Two days later on Tuesday 18th January Anne continued: "Your mind will have anticipated what must be the sequel of my story! My dearest, kindest of mothers expired yesterday morning without a groan, without even a sigh. Her countenance instantly became placid, and her fine features made her beautiful in death! Such I am convinced can be the end only of one possessing a virtuous mind and a conscience without reproach, and such a one, I am proud to think, was my mother! A scene more affecting, more impressive than her end it were not possible to see. My grief is extreme, and much as I ever thought I should regret this dear mother, I find that regret more painful and deeper than I expected. All the arrangements, every little improvement at Strawberry Hill, this house, all (sometimes imperceptibly at the moment to myself) tended wholly to procure her amusement and comforts, and all these have lost their value to me. But never more to behold that benign countenance brighten up at the sight of me! This does give me the feeling of an almost broken heart, but I will not go on, tho' I know you would forgive me, nay, I know you like that I should speak – and with you why should I not! – from the first impression of my heart.

"I have, too, as you may suppose, melancholy duties to perform and melancholy business to settle, therefore, must not linger nor indulge in writing to you or enter further at present into details. I am not, I assure you, ill, and today am equal to all that may be required of me to do or settle.

"One thing I must add, my good kind uncle Frederick is in the house with me. He arrived on Sunday, the day before yesterday, and enters so much into all my feelings and all my ideas on this melancholy subject that he is a real support and comfort to me. He begs kindly to be remembered to you, and said just now, as he often does, that there is no one he loves or admires more than you. My dearest life, believe me, I feel amidst all my suffering for you, and I know the pang you will feel at not being with me on such an occasion. But better even now do I think it that you should be where you are in health and composed spirit (at least comparatively) than here with all the sufferings, of your own I mean, I feel convinced you could not have escaped, had you remained in England. I must end. May heaven preserve and bless you."

On Friday 21st January Anne continued to Mary: "First, as I know how anxious you will be for me, I must tell you I am not bodily ill, but equal to give every necessary order, to do all that is required of me, and that my mind is what may be called composed, tho' I feel my spirits weaken and my tears flow faster than on any similar occasion I have had the misfortune to witness. It cannot be otherwise. Every tender partial affection of my dearest mother towards me wakes in my recollections, and I feel a regret even for the moments I may have lost when she perhaps wished me to be with her, or at the remembrance of a single word or expression that the quickness of my temper or feelings may have made me utter when, poor soul! I ought to have spared her! Yet much, I trust, I have not to reproach myself with, and I do trust that I have not only contributed to the comfort of my dear mother, but made that comfort such as rendered life desirable to her, even to her latest moments.

"I think I told you (and if I did not, you will have no doubt that must be my intention) that I was determined to attend the last sad ceremony, say the '*ultimo vale*,' but I am not certain that I did tell you, as after considerations we had, when I last wrote, but just decided that the remains of my mother are to be deposited in Sundridge church in the chancel. Combe Bank was her father's place; there she lived, there she married, and in the same spot where she will be, my uncle Frederick, when fate calls him, will be himself deposited. There too I may at leisure raise a small monument to the memory of a beloved mother, and still have the power to drop over it a silent tear … I must add, on this sad subject, that Lord Tom called on me yesterday (rather I saw him yesterday for he and Lord John had been constantly at our door), and I am sure you will think it affecting and pretty in so young and gay a man when I tell you that he offered, with his brother, Lord John, to attend with us at the ceremony if, he said, I thought my uncle would like it. I answered for him and for myself, accepted his offer with thanks, as everything pleases me that I consider as a mark of affection, or a mark of respect for the memory of my mother…

"Madame de Starhemberg, the only person I have hitherto seen that I was not in a manner obliged to see, has been all kindness to me, her heart is so feeling, her attentions to my mother were so marked and so pleasing to her, good soul!…"

The midwinter journey to Combe Bank was long and hard. The cortège left London on Wednesday 26th January. The weather was intensely cold, and a sudden fall of snow had made the cobblestones of London so slippery that they could only proceed at walking pace. On the open road, progress was easier as they jumbled and jolted along, but the cold, if anything, was even worse. Anne felt so ill on arrival that she feared she would be incapable of attending the funeral on the following day. "But with resolution, I believe we always find strength to do what we decidedly think right."

On the following day her two nephews, Lords Tom and John Campbell, arrived between 10 and 11am, together with the clergyman who was to officiate, an old friend from London, Dr Vise. About an hour later the funeral procession started from Combe Bank. In driving snow, accompanied by the melancholy toll of the church bell, they followed the neatly-decked coffin, Anne on the arm of her uncle Frederick in front of Lord John and Lord Tom. The route was up a steep hill to the church which was entirely unheated. Despite this, the service was conducted impeccably and feelingly; Anne, in a state of grief, "saw and heard, but imperfectly," but once or twice when she looked up, she thought she saw tears in the eyes of Dr Vise. Anne summed up the service from her point of view. "It is sufficient to say I was miserably affected, but got through with the ceremony. ... Could the dear soul look down she would be pleased with this last tribute, so every way due to her."

The funeral party returned to the cold of Combe Bank. Anne was immediately seized with dreadful rheumatic pain in her back, which was so bad that for some minutes she could scarcely speak; she retired to her own room, where she remained until the pain lessened and she felt well enough to go down to dinner. She remained at Combe Bank for several days after the funeral. Her uncle and aunt were kind to her; she found it quiet and restful; and she could be at peace and alone without the necessity of seeing people. However, eventually the fear of becoming ill through cold drove her back to the warmth of London, with the intention of returning to the solitude of Strawberry Hill when the weather improved.

Preoccupation with her own grief did not preclude Anne from thinking of others, and especially of Mary and her health problems. She wrote to Mary that she had consulted Dr Moore, who had been of the opinion that the air in Nice would not entirely suit Mary's condition. Anne suggested that if they decided to move, they should not be constrained by financial worries. "What earthly object have I to think of but yourself, and you know how easily I can place a few hundreds into your account into Coutts' hands to serve, and you need not then be obliged even to good Hoper." Anne went on to suggest that possibly Spa would be better for Mary. However she did not suggest that she should join the Berry family there.

There was also the unfinished business of Josephine Bonaparte's plants to which to attend. On 24th February Anne wrote to Sir Joseph Banks reminding him that some months ago he had promised to provide the much-wanted *strelitzia*, when the weather was suitable for it to be lifted. She told him that she now had "a certain and quick conveyance" for the plant, provided it was not too early in the season. She hoped that he could send it to Upper Brook Street by the following night, as the intended transporter was leaving for Paris at 5am the next morning. She enquired after his health, and in a postscript, also as to that of Lady Banks and Miss Banks. The plant was presumably at Banks's nursery at Spring Grove, some 10 miles away, and this was a demand that would tax the patience and abilities of the most dedicated nurseryman. History does not relate whether Sir Joseph rose to the challenge.

Correspondence between Mary and Anne continued unabated, though somewhat delayed after war between France and England broke out again in May 1803. The correspondence remains one-sided as Mary retained Anne's letters, while Anne either did not keep or later caused Mary's to be destroyed. Mary had evidently suggested that they meet again, and Anne whilst not rejecting this outright, hedged her bets. She counselled Mary not to return to the English climate before June. Anne herself was thinking of leaving England in early June and was happy to consider meeting the Berrys in Spa or Paris or Brussels or anywhere "in a good climate where I can be quiet and near you, and do not wish to travel about by way of seeing anything or any place. I have not recovered my love of travelling, but I am convinced that the change of scene, continuing my route leisurely and alone, and resting a day or two as I find myself inclined, and knowing that I am going towards you, will of all other plans best tend to restore my mind and make me sensible I have still much to thank Heaven for."

Anne told Mary that she should expect to see her with two dogs at heel, for she refused to leave behind "my poor Hylass and Miss Mary, I conclude you would not have me leave her behind. She is a dear little thing, is grown broad backed and what you would call impudent."

By 28th March Anne had received several more rather querulous letters from Mary, mainly devoted to where they should meet. In reply she started by laying down where they should not; she did not want to name the exact day, nor to meet at an inn, nor anywhere where they would then have to bustle on to somewhere else. She suggested that she should join the Berrys wherever they had decided to settle quietly for the balance of summer, and then they could decide where to pass the winter together, whether in Italy or in France. The following day she wrote again, finishing a letter: "How I do long this seeming misunderstanding should cease in our letters and we not be answering each other at cross purposes."

By 7th April, as the political situation deteriorated, Anne gave up hope of meeting during the summer. The Berrys seem to have been planning to go to Switzerland, accompanied by a new male acquaintance, an intention which attracted Anne's displeasure. "To be sure, I should not have thought you would have taken a new Englishman from Nice with you for fear you should not find enough of them at Geneva, as I never saw the place yet where they did not abound, and how Mr Smyth could be 'useful' on the road. I am at a loss to guess." The same letter went on to record the news of the death of Sir William Hamilton. Another correspondent and friend of

Mary's, Mrs Howe, added information that Sir William had left Emma £700-£800 a year, and a few hundred pounds, his London house and furniture, the rest of his estate being left to his nephew, Charles Greville.

Anne's life continued quietly without the Berrys. She did not wish to see the world and its wife, confining her attentions largely to old friends such as Georgiana Devonshire and Elizabeth Melbourne. A letter from Georgiana to Anne, following the death of Elizabeth Melbourne's daughter Harriet Lamb, dates from this time.

"I was so extremely tired, dear Mrs Damer, and my spirits so worn out that I could not write to you last night. Lady Melbourne had wished me to tell you that she was as well as could be hop'd and that she would see you when you pleas'd. Poor little Harriet died at 10 yesterday morning at Kensington. Lady Elizabeth had gone there at 8 in the morning and was with her! ... For some time we have known there was no hope. But for the past week, or at least since Wednesday, it was very rapid – one of us has always been with dear Lady M who has suffered so much anxiety that I must look on her relief as a blessing. She was much agitated yesterday but is I hope calmer today.

God bless you, Mrs Damer
Yours ever, G.Devonshire"

Three days later Anne had seen Elizabeth Melbourne, who had been "miserably affected". She wrote to Mary Berry that "the melancholy deaths one hears of daily are quite shocking". 'Mother Fanny', the aged mother of Elizabeth Farren, now Countess of Derby, had also died; her daughter had been much attached to her, and Anne pitied her in her loss.

Anne still had to finish Nelson's marble bust for the City of London. This she completed during the year, in time for it to be shown at the Royal Academy exhibition of 1804, where it occupied pride of place among the sculptures. Farington noted that he had been to the Exhibition, which had been very full and very hot. He had met Anne, and they had spoken to Lawrence about the painter Bourgeois. Anne had remarked on the danger of admitting inferior artists into the Society, "as they might do mischief".

During 1805 and 1806 Anne found a new correspondent, her half-brother-in-law, the Duke of Richmond. Now a lonely and elderly widower, he found in Anne a listening ear, in whom he could confide and whose judgement and confidentiality he trusted. In June 1805 he had left his beloved Goodwood to come to London to see his dentist with regard to stopping, or alternatively removing, an aching tooth. He bemoaned the fact that the rigours of the journey from Sussex to London had caused him to lose the use of his legs. He hated having to be carried everywhere, but much looked forward to seeing Anne again, and felt that he might be able to call on her. If she would give him a time and date, he could probably be unobtrusively lifted into his carriage at his back door. Alternatively, he would be very happy if she called on him in the morning, when he felt better than in the evenings.

History does not record whether a meeting took place, but shortly afterwards Anne must have left London to visit her Campbell cousins at Inveraray. Her uncle, the fifth Duke of Argyll, Caroline's brother, was in his 80s, and had become frail. He was to die the following year, and perhaps Anne thought she should pay him a last visit. Whilst there, she might well have met up again with her cousins Augusta and Charlotte, the former of whom had married Brigadier General Clavering, and whose daughter would later seek Anne's literary advice. The latter, who still retained her family name of Campbell, having married John Campbell of Shawfield and Islay, MP for the Burghs of Ayr, will appear in a later chapter.

Anne had obviously returned to London from Scotland by 18th October, two days before the Battle of Trafalgar, when Richmond wrote again, this time from Goodwood, saying how pleased he was that she had returned from her long journey, "and that you find the Duke of Argyll in that comfortable way that is the only one fit for old men, living quietly at home with a few friends and amusing himself with his country concerns." Richmond himself was, perforce, in a similar condition at Goodwood, "very well content to pass the remainder of my days within the small circle of this neighbourhood for though I can just hobble from one room to another and can ride out very much to my own comfort, yet I am so subject to returns of gout which seize me suddenly and confine me for months together, that I dread being caught anywhere from home, where in such a situation, I have still resources that no other place would afford me." Sadly, there would be no more expeditions to London or to Strawberry Hill, but he very much hoped that Anne would visit him at Goodwood.

As already noted, following Nelson's death at the Battle of Trafalgar, Anne had suggested in the autumn of 1805 that she produce a full-blown statue of Nelson as a present for the City of London. Her offer was turned down on the grounds that a competition to design a memorial statue for St Paul's Cathedral had been proposed and agreed. This decision was relayed to Anne, who replied that she entirely approved of the decision to throw it open to the world and to afford an opportunity for competition, at the same time signifying that she intended to be one of the competitors. Farington noted in his diary on 7th December that he and Boydell looked over the list of subscribers to the British Institution to select a committee to inspect the design submitted for the competition. He had named Lords Dartmouth and Northwick & the Marquis of Stafford, Sir Abraham Hume, Sir George Beaumont, William Smith and William Fitzhugh.

Nelson's State Funeral was due to be held on 9th January 1806 in St Paul's Cathedral. Nelson mania was rife. Everybody wanted a memento of England's saviour. The firm of B. Papera, previously referred to as copiers of Anne's busts of Nelson and Fox, were not slow in coming forward. On 11th December 1805 an advertisement appeared in the *Morning Chronicle*, offering "Casts from the original bust of Lord Nelson, executed in marble by the Hon Anne Seymour Damer, presented by her to the City of London are to be had at B.Papera's, Plaster figure-maker to Her Majesty, No 16 Marylebone Street, Golden Square – the above portrait is perfectly original and the only one executed in sculpture for which Lord Nelson ever sat." History does not relate whether Anne received any royalties from sales. As an amateur, she may have believed it beneath her dignity to accept payment; as the keeper of the increasingly expensive Strawberry Hill, she might have found additional income helpful.

Shortly after Nelson's funeral, Anne received a letter from Edinburgh from her cousin Lady Charlotte Campbell, saying that her brother John had arrived bearing with him casts of Anne's bust of her. "Many thanks for them and I'm sure I shall now put an additional value upon my head since you have thought it worthwhile to make a copy of it." She must have sat for her bust the previous year, when Anne was staying at Inveraray. A further cast had also been given to Lord John Campbell, who kept it in his rooms where it was immediately recognised by all his visitors. This bust had never been exhibited in public, and was therefore unrecorded, other than in the contents of this letter. Although Horace had believed that he had recorded all her earlier work, some of her later modelling may never have been catalogued.

A fortnight after Nelson's burial service another great Englishman died, worn out by the age of 46: the Prime Minister, William Pitt. Whereas Nelson was mourned by the world, Pitt had become a focus of universal criticism. The French victory at Austerlitz in December had smashed the Continental alliance against them; England might rule the seas, but France controlled the continent. A new government was formed with Grenville as Prime Minister and Charles Fox as a Secretary of State. Richmond wrote to Anne on 16th March 1806 noting her enthusiasm to see her old favourites at last returned to power: "They have it now all to themselves and God grant that they may use it well and that this country may once more feel its independency secure from that French Dominion that seems to be spreading itself over all Europe. But our new ministry has much to do; many difficulties of the first magnitude to struggle with, both at home and abroad. It seems to be composed of a coalition of men whose notions, habits and principles are of very opposite natures. Whether public good or private interest has brought them together, or will keep them united, time and their actions will show." The remaining five pages of his letter complained of lack of consultation by Fox and the Prince of Wales, whom he had consistently supported, in the appointment of placemen in the new government. It was the cry of the old lion cast out from his pride by a younger usurper; Richmond, confined to Goodwood by ill health, and despite his great wealth, was now yesterday's man.

Fox was back in power after 15 years in the wilderness; for Anne, this was a triumphant moment. However, her happiness was short-lived. In late March, another great Fox supporter and Anne's bosom friend, Georgiana Devonshire, fell ill. Anne was extremely concerned, though a letter to her from Georgiana's physician, Sir Alexander Farquhar gave some encouragement. "Sir Walter Farquhar presents his compliments to Mrs Damer. The Duchess of Devonshire has certainly been very ill and is still so – but upon the whole this has been a favourable day – Sir Walter will have the honour of waiting upon Mrs Damer tomorrow. He would have written to her more but has been out of town." Sadly, there would be no more favourable days; Georgiana's condition deteriorated rapidly, and she died on 30th March 1806, at the early age of 48, from an abscess on the liver.

Anne's friends and relations realised what the loss of Georgiana would mean to her. The same day the Duke of Richmond wrote: "I sincerely condole with you, my dear Mrs Damer, on the loss of certainly one of the most amiable of women and best of friends. There is nothing to be said that can give any consolation on such occasions. We must bear as well as we can the griefs inseparable from such misfortunes, the necessary attendants on human life."

A letter dated 5th April 1806 from Fox to Anne refers to Georgiana's death: "I write you one line to say I shall be in town at dinner on Sunday and should like to see you in the Treasury very much, but as the Prince dines there, of course I cannot come out of the dining room early, not till near 10, but if you should have no objection to that hour, perhaps you will come then, or if not about one on Monday morning, or if neither of these are suitable to you I will call upon you in the course of the morning. … I really doubt whether I shall ever speak to the Duke of Georgiana; her manner at Lord Derby's when she spoke to me gave me a sensation I shall never forget, and what you tell me has brought it back to my recollection with additional force … God bless you, Mrs D.

"There have been several letters found to Lady Elizabeth [Foster] … written at different times; Lady Elizabeth says those to her nearly kill her from the love they express to her. If you are asked, you may say that she had left directions about everything with Lady Elizabeth, not in the last fatal illness, but before, and some a long time ago … I see people more by their faces, not by their words to me, express doubts about Lady E. And therefore I really think it only common justice to say that as it is … for I do not believe it possible for any person to have always behaved more honourably than Lady E. behaved to the Duchess … even my friends here enquired very closely … but you shall hear more when I see you. How miserably cold the weather has been."

A little later Lord John Campbell wrote to Anne from Scotland: "Alas the poor Duchess of Devonshire! Tho' I did not know her, I was truly sorry for her death. To be torn from youth, beauty and happiness in this world, yet surely to a better, or what would be the use of this short existence here, even in the longest life and transient happiness as it is, at best."

Fox for a short time proved an excellent minister. He needed to be pragmatic because Napoleon, his one-time hero, now all-powerful in Europe was in no mood to make peace. However it was to be a short tenure of power; by July he was ill, by September he was dead. Anne would have attended his funeral in Westminster Abbey on 10th October.

On 19th April 1806 Farington recorded that Sir George Beaumont with Mr William Smith and Mr George Hibbert had examined the entries for the competition for a statue of Nelson for St Paul's cathedral. They had placed their votes. It is not clear for whom they had voted, but it was evident that it was not for Mrs Damer, as Sir George was said to be worried by Anne's probable reaction when she discovered that he had not voted for her. He also considered that Mr William Lock, another judge, was unlikely to cast his vote for the same reason.

A few months later, on 30th December 1806, Farington indulged in a further round of Damer-bashing. He recorded that he had been sitting for a portrait by Henry Edridge. The latter had recalled a conversation with William Pitt, whom he had been painting, in which Pitt had wondered why more women did not study the arts, as their dispositions seemed well-suited to such pursuits. Edridge had said that Michelangelo and Raphael had shown that to reach the top required the greatest skills. Pitt had then mentioned Anne as a fine example, to which Edridge had replied that he was not impressed by her, and that Angelica Kaufmann had shown far greater skill in the more difficult art of painting; he had added that her work too, was weak in comparison with her male counterparts.

Six months later, Farington was at it again. On 7th June 1807 he had gone "to the Academy at two o'clock, and met Lady Thomond...... who had a Private view of the Exhibition through my means. Lady Thomond laughed much at a small model for a Monument to Lord Nelson. I told her it was by Mrs Damer." Again in February 1808, he noted a favourable description of Anne's bust of Lord Nelson by the antiquary and art collector, Thomas Hope. The latter's description, which did not accord with Farington's views, was described as "most extravagant and false and ridiculous." Anne had been so delighted with it that she had ordered 50 copies to be printed to be given away. Clearly, as far as Farington was concerned, Anne, the amateur lady artist intruding into a male professional world, could do no good. The bias against her, and the ill will which he bore her, should certainly be taken into account when assessing his criticism.

Gradually, as seasons and years followed each other, the relationship between Anne and Mary Berry cooled. The Berrys had made their own mark on society and collected their own friends. Mary was a published author and the sisters' company and conversation were eagerly sought by their new friends. Anne was no longer a key to open social doors for them; Anne herself, with advancing age, was less given to society. However, they remained good friends and neighbours at the two Strawberry Hills. They saw each other frequently and corresponded intermittently, though not at the prodigious rate of the 1790s. They would, for instance, swap notes on Madame de Staël's novel, *Delphine*. In September 1808 Anne wrote to Mary in celebration of the British Peninsular War victory at Vimiera. "Poor, mistaken O'Hara! Had he lived, which I think he would, had you lived with him, how should we not have at this moment exulted and rejoiced! I say we, for surely you would both have let me creep on your Rocks, while I could creep on Earth! But no more of this: perhaps too much already!"

In August 1807 Mary and Anne stayed with Mary's friends, the Greatheeds, at Guys Cliff in Warwickshire. They visited Warwick Castle and after dinner strolled together by the riverside, "where the whole scene is deliciously inducive of quiet, calmness and repose." On Monday 24th August Mary took her leave of the Greatheeds, having spent nearly 3 weeks with them. Before breakfast she took a quiet solitary walk by the river, giving the impression that Anne had only been there for part of the visit. On Wednesday 9th September Mary set off to stay at Combe Bank with Lord Frederick Campbell, with no mention of Anne being present. They were together again on Tuesday 15th September, when Mary went with Anne to Wedgwood's, where she had not been for three or four years. She noted the blue and white ware made in imitation of China was better than the Coalbrookdale of the same sort. Mary went on to Tunbridge Wells without Anne.

On 27th September Mary based herself at Little Strawberry Hill and started to look over Mme du Deffand's papers, which she was to publish the following year. The work was long and arduous, and her health suffered as a result. On Tuesday 10th November she felt too unwell to dine downstairs, leaving Prince Starhemberg to dine with her father and Anne. On Sunday 22nd she had recovered; Prince Starhemberg called again and they sent for Anne. On Christmas Eve Anne and Mary, by now in London, were entertained in return by Prince Starhemberg.

A similar pattern continued through the first months of 1808. On Saturday 5th March Anne joined the Berrys in North Audley Street, with Sir Henry Englefield as the other guest. On Sunday 6th Mary went to Anne's after church. Anne would have been saddened to hear of another death three days later. On 8th March George Damer, Earl of Dorchester and Lord-Lieutenant for Dorset, died at his home in Park Lane, to be succeeded by his brother Lionel. He was reputed "to have died immensely rich."

Anne's relationship with George had always been friendly, and unlike his father, he bore her no grudges. On Wednesday 9th March Mary again went to Anne and read Sir Walter Scott's newly published *Marmion* to her. On Thursday 31st March Mary and Anne and Lord Frederick Campbell went to the British Museum together to see the new wing and the disposition of Mr Townley's marbles and other things taken by the British Army in Egypt.

On 27th April Anne and Mary spent the evening together. On 6th May they read together. In July the Berrys set off for a roundabout tour starting at Guys Cliff and going through Cheshire, Lancashire and the Lake District to Scotland, returning to London in mid-October.

Chapter 20

PRINCESS CAROLINE
AND A DASH TO PARIS

In January 1809 Mary Berry arranged that Longman's should publish her translation and editing of Mme du Deffand's letters, at whatever price her business manager, Mr Edwards, should agree. At the end of the month she received a letter from Anne, telling the news of Sir John Moore's death at Corunna.

It was Mary Berry who was to be the catalyst for the next new episode in Anne's life. On 31st May 1809 Mary was introduced to the Princess of Wales. She recorded in her journal that the meeting had not been a success. The Princess had asked Lady Sheffield to introduce Miss Berry to her and had noticed Mary making a face when Lady Sheffield proposed that she should introduce her. "Such an overdressed, bare-bosomed, painted eye-browed figure one never saw," said Mary later. However, three days later she was at a breakfast party given by Lady Glenbervie for the Princess of Wales at the Pheasantry. A few weeks later, on 7th July, Mary went to Lady Fordyce's where again the Princess of Wales was present. Lady Charlotte Lindsay, the Princess's lady-in-waiting, shortly to succeed Anne as Mary's confidante, escorted her to a room where the Princess was surrounded by her usual court.

On 10th July Anne called on Mary in London, but by 7th August she was back at Strawberry Hill awaiting a "surprise" visit. It would seem that Mary had probably set up the occasion. Anne had received notice of the impending visit two to three days beforehand, with the instructions that the visit would be informal, that the Berrys should be present, and that they should all feign surprise at the Royal arrival. The Princess of Wales, attended by Lady Charlotte Lindsay, arrived at about three o'clock, and asked for the Berrys. They joined the party in the Holbein Room, and Mary recorded the visit: "The Princess talked a great deal more than she looked at anything, and seemed pleased to have more people to talk to; the pictures, etc, of the house, and observations on them came merely to fill gaps and give new matter for discourse. She was in her very best manner, and her conversation is certainly uncommonly lively, odd, and clever. What a pity that she has not a grain of common sense! Not an ounce of ballast to prevent high spirits, and, of course, a mind without any degree of moral taste, from running away with her, and allowing her to act indecorously and ridiculously whenever an occasion offers! Were she always to conduct herself as she did here today, she would merit the character of having not only a remarkably easy and gracious manner, but natural cleverness above any of her peers that I have seen, and a good many have at different times fallen under my observation. After walking over the house, she was carried into the library, where refreshments were prepared. Of these, she did not taste, but proposed us all sitting down, which we did for about half an hour, then departed with a thousand thanks to Mrs Damer, and shaking us all by the hand."

She had been accompanied by William Austin, known as "Willikins", a small boy, the son of a Deptford pauper, whom she had adopted, and whom, Mary noted, "she would do well to put to school, but does very ill to take about with her during his holidays. She is not of a disposition to want either the amusement or endearing tenderness of a child; and, after all that has been said of her, one may easily guess what may be said of this little boy about seven or eight years old." Here, Mary alludes to a rumour prevalent since 1805, that the small boy was the Princess's illegitimate son. She had adopted a number of other children, whom she had placed with foster parents, but only William Austin had been selected to live under her roof. A high-powered investigative committee, meeting in secret, had interviewed witnesses, servants, and William Austin's mother, Sophia, and come to the conclusion that the rumour was baseless, and that William was indeed, Sophia's son. However, news of the investigation had leaked into the public domain, and as in all of rumour's fires, the ashes proved difficult to dowse.

The visit must have been a success, as the following day Lady Glenbervie called at Strawberry Hill with a proposal from the Princess that she and Anne should share a box at the Opera House at Covent Garden. Mary thought it ridiculous that the Princess of Wales should not have her own box, paid for by an annual subscription by the King. Whatever her earlier opinion, Mary was from now on a firm supporter of and a regular attendant upon Princess Caroline.

On 9th September Anne went with Prince Starhemberg and Mary Berry to Astley's Amphitheatre, where they saw *The Arab*, culminating in an onstage battle with twelve live horses which, Mary thought, might have been more convincing on a larger stage. Astley's, which survived till the end of the 19th century, was a curious mix of circus and theatre. A conventional stage stood behind a circus ring, the spectators being seated in tiers on either side of the ring. The spectacle in the ring was probably more important than the acting on the stage, which provided the framework for the spectacles. The same trio were again at the theatre on 12th September.

On 31st October Anne wrote to Emma Hamilton asking for her good offices in providing for a picture of her bust of Nelson to appear in a new biography of Nelson, but does not seem to have received a reply.

On 29th November the Berrys, having returned from a protracted autumn visit to East Anglia, dined with the Princess of Wales at Kensington Palace, where Anne's cousin Lady Charlotte Campbell had just been appointed a Lady of the Bedchamber. On Saturday 9th December they went to dine again, and on Monday 11th they were once more at the Princess's, where they witnessed a sparsely-attended gathering, which was supposed to be an Assembly.

January 1810 opened with a further visit to the Princess of Wales. On Thursday 11th January Mary went to Strawberry Hill and walked over to Little Strawberry, where she found the garden looking tidy. She reflected that everything about Twickenham "now wears, to me, a melancholy aspect: its charms are no longer for me." Fond memories would be more pleasant than the expense of possession, and she had already decided that such reflections would be followed by action. To provide additional income, she had decided to let the property. The new tenant was the Rev Dr Bell, a Prebendary of Westminster Abbey.

The Berrys' departure from Little Strawberry marked another stage in the loosening of ties between Anne and Mary. They remained good friends, but inevitably saw less of each other, and Anne's place as Mary's chief confidante was increasingly taken by Lady Charlotte Lindsay, another lady-in-waiting to the Princess of Wales. One occasion when Anne and Mary did get together was on Sunday 4th March, when they were both godmothers to the daughter of Mr Hoper, their lawyer and business adviser. They went to St James's Church at one o'clock, but were kept waiting until three, because there had been over 300 communicants, largely people obliged to qualify for their various employments by proving that they had attended church. Anne might have been thinking of further theatrical performances, as she asked Mary to enquire to Mr Hoper about the cost of theatre props. However it seems to have come to nothing as no further performances were recorded.

The year 1811 started with a surprise gift for Anne. The Empress Josephine had sent her a present of a fine Sèvres porcelain cup and saucer. The gift was most probably a thank you for Anne's efforts on Josephine's behalf to secure plants and seeds for her garden at Malmaison. It is also possible, though unlikely, that it was also a thank you for a bust of Josephine which Anne may have sculpted (see Chapter 18). Mary was invited to meet M. de Bréhan, the Frenchman who had brought the gift. He also brought a large order for plants and seeds for Lee and Kennedy, the London nurserymen. It was hoped that he might also have produced payment for a previous large consignment. M. de Bréhan, who had a mother and uncle living in Hampstead, would have been pleased and fortunate to be able to see them. War with France had made England a no-go area for Frenchmen, and anyone leaving France for England required a passport signed twice personally by the Emperor. The French had obviously not lost their propensity for form filling, nor Josephine her influence over Napoleon.

In March Anne, worn down by the strain and expense of Strawberry Hill, decided to relinquish her life tenancy and handed the house and its collection over to the dowager Lady Waldegrave. She was sad but relieved to leave, but the house had lost its magic for her and the departure of the Berrys from Little Strawberry Hill in the previous year had severed one of the few remaining ties. Keppel Craven wrote charmingly to Mary Berry, asking her to remember him most particularly to Anne. "You cannot conceive how much I regret her giving up Strawberry Hill, for I must ever remember with pleasure the happy rainy days I occasionally passed there; our embarkations, disembarkations, eating strawberries, the wet grass that adorns the Bay of Biscay, and the terrific adventure of my boat, driven by a gale of wind into Mr Somebody's garden."

Another reminder of the golden past was provided by a nostalgic visit that Mary paid to Park Place. On 30th June she wrote to Anne: "I was at Park Place yesterday. It had rained much in the night, and was a grey, damp, melancholy day, suiting well with the feelings I carried to it." She found the garden in a state of decay, seats falling to pieces, trees overgrown, or dead and left standing; the small flower garden with its fountain dry and borders empty, the pergola damaged and smothered by foliage, and the thorn tree at its centre unpruned and spreading rampantly. "Oh, how every step of it affected me! I saw you and O'H. sitting under this thorn tree in its trim days, and myself having left you merely to enjoy the delicious sensation of knowing you were expressing for me every sentiment I could wish to inspire. I saw him following me into the laurel walk, and in giving me a letter (which I had accidentally dropped) in a joking manner, first convincing me of the seriousness of the sentiment I had inspired." Mary had also visited the library and seen again Anne's figure, perched on a ladder, arranging the bookshelves, and she had remembered Anne's expression, when she had come back into the room and found Mary and O'Hara still sitting where she had left them…. "I am so glad I have seen Park Place once more, in spite of all the melancholy it inspired, but I should be sorry to see more of it."

Mary went to Tunbridge Wells for the months of August to October 1811. She wrote from there to Anne with reference to a book, *The Memoirs of Colonel Hutchinson*, by his wife Lucy, that she was currently reading. Mary expressed herself delighted with the book; she found Mrs Hutchinson's description of her husband's attachment to her as being "the truest, the most elevated and admirable picture of love and true affection from and to a superior mind that can be imagined. It fills up every line of that ideal picture long ago traced by imagination, and now engraved by reason on my heart. … Farewell, or I shall grow romantic." Anne must have visited her during her stay, as she wrote from Combe Bank on 23rd September telling Mary that if she had feared she might lose Anne's affection, "were it wandering, wavering, or on the wing," she was certainly mistaken. They had obviously had a row, as Anne told Mary that it was not the minor problems at Tunbridge which had vexed her, so much as Mary's manner, and what she had said to her. There was nothing wrong with Anne's health, though old age and a weakness in the lungs made it more difficult for her to walk uphill or through sand in the midday sun. Anne looked forward to seeing Mary again, but as always their mutual affection was better expressed on paper than on actually in person. Anne ended the letter by asking Mary whither she should address her next letter. Their warm correspondence would still continue, even if less frequently than hitherto. Agnes too kept in touch, describing herself as wading through the mud and filth of the streets of London to see Mrs Damer on New Year's Day 1812. Occasionally a little encouragement was needed. On 12th August 1812 Charlotte Campbell wrote to Mary Berry: "You are a good Girl, though, Dear Berrina, to go to Mrs Damer. I rejoice at it, and I'm sure that seeing each other will do you both good. I sometimes wonder why one ever consents to be absent from the Friends one loves most. Is there anything that compensates for the absence of a beloved object? I know of none. Berrina, Dear Berrina, I shall never be wiser or better." In September 1813 the Berrys signed a seven-year lease for Little Strawberry Hill with Alderman Wood, the protagonist of the Princess of Wales, at a rental of 150 guineas. Although this seemed to be a breach of the terms of Horace Walpole's will, Anne did not place any obstacle in their way.

As Anne's relationship with Mary gradually cooled, she turned her attention increasingly to her mother's Scottish roots and her Campbell cousins. Seymour Conway and Hertford relations, her father's family, remained out of touch. It is worth at this stage recalling who all these cousins were. There were the children of the fifth Duke of Argyll, Lord George Campbell, who had succeeded his father as sixth Duke in 1806, and his younger brother, Lord John Campbell. They had two sisters: the first, Lady Augusta Campbell, born in 1760, had married Brigadier General Clavering. They had produced an only daughter, Charlotte, who in 1817, married Miles Fletcher at Ardincaple Castle. The second and much younger Lady Charlotte Campbell, born in 1775 had retained her maiden name by marrying Colonel John Campbell, who died in 1809, leaving her a widow with nine children, five of whom survived into adulthood. They were Walter, Eliza, Emma, Eleonora, and Harriet Beaujolais. There was also Lady Johnston, formerly Louisa Campbell, the daughter of Anne's uncle, Lord William Campbell, the gallant sailor and rescuer of the drowning man in the Thames. In 1799, Louisa had married an Indian civil servant and lawyer, Sir Alexander Johnston. These cousins, and their older children, moved closer to Anne as she grew older.

As all female Campbells at Inveraray had enjoyed a fine education in English literature, and several had their own literary aspirations, Anne, herself an author, bibliophile, and possessor of a fine library, found that she was required as a literary consultant, and if not so required, appointed herself. In February 1810 Susan Ferrier, daughter of the Argyll's family solicitor, and childhood friend of Charlotte Clavering, wrote to her about a book, probably called *Self Indulgence,* on which the latter was co-operating with her aunt, the recently widowed Lady Charlotte Campbell. Susan advised that she show her work to a literary friend of which her aunt had many, including Anne. "Is not Mrs Damer *un bas-bleu?*" (blue stocking).

Susan and Charlotte Clavering were themselves co-operating in a literary venture which, after a long gestation, was eventually to appear in 1818 as Susan's first novel *Marriage*, in which social satire mixed with keenly observed caricature. In another 1810 letter from her home Ardencaple Castle, Charlotte wrote to Susan about characters in the book:

"First of all I must tell you that I approve in the most signal manner of 'Lady Maclaughlan'. The sort of character was totally unexpected by me, and I was really quite transported with her. Do I know the person who is the original? The dress was vastly like Mrs Damer, and the manners like Lady Frederick (widow of Lord Frederick Campbell), tell me if you did not mean a touch at her. I love poor Sir Sampson vastly, though it is impossible in the presence of his lady to have eyes or ears for anyone else. Her kissing Lady Juliana and holding her at arms length is capital." It is worth quoting the first appearance in the book of Lady Maclaughlan. "The heavy rumble of a ponderous vehicle now proclaimed the approach of the expected visitor; which pleasing anticipation was soon changed into blissful certainty by the approach of a high-roofed, square-bottomed, pea-green chariot, drawn by two longtailed white horses, and followed by a lackey in the Highland garb. Out of this equipage issued a figure, clothed in a light-coloured, large-flowered chintz raiment, carefully drawn through the pocket holes, either for its own preservation, or the more disinterested purpose of displaying a dark short stuff petticoat, which with the same liberality afforded ample scope for the survey of a pair of worsted stockings and black leather shoes, something resembling buckets. A faded red cloth jacket, which bore evident marks of having been severed from its native skirts, now acted in the capacity of a spencer. On the head rose a stupendous fabric, in the form of a cap, on the summit of which was placed a black beaver hat, tied *à la poissarde.* A small black satin muffin in one hand, and a gold headed walking stick in the other, completed the dress and decoration of this personage."

Lady Maclaughlan was introduced to the heroine Lady Juliana: "'So – you're very pretty – yes, you are very pretty!' kissing the forehead, cheeks, and chin of the youthful beauty between every pause. Then, holding her at arms length, she surveyed her from head to foot, with elevated brows, and a broad fixed stare."

By evening Lady Maclaughlan had changed. "She was now arrayed in a pompadour satin negligee, and petticoat trimmed with Brussels lace. A high starched handkerchief formed a complete breastwork, on which, amid a large bouquet of truly artificial roses, reposed a miniature of Sir Sampson, *à la militaire.* A small fly cap of antique lace was scarcely perceptible on the summit of a stupendous frizzled toupée, hemmed in on each side by large curls. The muff and stick had been relinquished for a large fan, something resembling an Indian screen, which she waved to and fro in one hand, while a vast brocaded work bag was suspended from the other."

Undoubtedly the description of morning and evening dress is exaggerated for the benefit and amusement of the reader. However, it is indicative of the fact that in old age Anne's appearance had certainly become eccentric.

On 20th December 1812 Charlotte wrote to Susan telling her that she had just received a copy of *Self Indulgence* from Lady Charlotte Campbell. A few days later she had received another parcel five times the size from Lady Charlotte, which she opened with some excitement, only to find that it was a further copy of the same work, but with a difference. Anne Damer had read *Self Indulgence*, published anonymously, decided that Lady Charlotte was the author, summoned her, and told her that it needed improvements to make it fit for a second edition. Anne had made her sit down and read the book slowly to her, while she marked with a pencil the passages that required improvement. The second parcel had contained this annotated copy, with instructions to Charlotte from her aunt to make the required improvements. She had not objected to this imposition "as I am not obliged to look out for faults, but those that are marked with a pencil…".

As well as the Campbell cousins, Anne also kept up with other old friends in an ageing world. On 3rd May 1813 she was reported as having been present the previous day at "a grand entertainment" given by the Melbournes at their house in Whitehall. Other guests included His Royal Highness the Prince Regent, the Duke of Devonshire, the Earl and Countess of Bessborough, Lord and Lady Morpeth, the Earl of Egremont, the Earl of Fife, the Earl of Stair, Lord Maynard, Colonel Bloomfield, and Mrs George Lamb.

In the world beyond that of literary correction and grand entertainment, the year 1812 was to see Napoleon's fortunes take a decisive turn for the worse. The French were fighting on two fronts, under Marshals Soult and Marmont against Wellington in the Spanish peninsula, whilst Napoleon himself led an army of 700,000 into Russia. 400,000 soldiers of the Grand Army were conscripted from the subjugated states in Italy, Poland and Germany. Their revolutionary ardour, wherever it might have existed, was long subdued, and their supplies and equipment utterly unequal to the rigours of a Russian winter. Although Napoleon occupied Moscow on 14th September, following the indecisive Battle of Borodino, the Russian policy of refusing to meet him either in battle or negotiation left him no alternative but to retreat by the way he had come. When he reached Paris on 5th December, he had lost 400,000 men dead or wounded, and a further 100,000 taken prisoner. The Grand Army had ceased to exist. In Spain, Wellington had won the battle of Salamanca before retiring into Portugal for the winter, and it seemed only a matter of time before he would force the French out of Spain.

The following year, 1813, saw the slow collapse of Napoleon's empire. Wellington swept through Spain to Bayonne. The monarchies of central Europe gradually recovered some of their nerve to combine forces and evict the French from their countries, and by the end of 1813 Napoleon had been driven back nearly to the Rhine. By the Treaty of Chaumont, Russia, Prussia, and Austria each agreed to maintain 150,000 troops in the ongoing war with France. This was to be partially financed by an English subsidy of £35 million, divided between them. By March 1814 Wellington's troops reached Bordeaux, where the populace rose up against Napoleon demanding the restitution of the Bourbon monarchy. On 28th March the allied leaders drank a toast to Louis XVIII and the expulsion of Napoleon Bonaparte. Their armies pressed on into France and on 31st March Paris capitulated. The ensuing Treaty of Paris, masterminded by the English Foreign Secretary, Castlereagh, saw Napoleon exiled to Elba and a Bourbon monarchy restored to France with Talleyrand at the head of the French administration. It was intended that the Prince of Orange, the heir to a strengthened and independent Holland, should marry Princess Charlotte, the heir to the English throne.

At home, as George III lapsed into total madness, the Prince Regent had assumed the duties of king. Among his first acts was to forbid the Princess of Wales access to Princess Charlotte, her only child and heir presumptive to the throne. As previously noted, a war of attrition commenced between the estranged couple, in which both Mary Berry and Anne took the part of the Princess of Wales. The latter's ladies-in-waiting included the two Charlottes, Anne's cousin Lady Charlotte Campbell, and Lady Charlotte Lindsay, Mary's new bosom pal. Politically the Princess was assisted by Henry Brougham, an ambitious Whig member of Parliament. She also had the support of her daughter, Princess Charlotte. Following Napoleon's defeat in 1814, the royal families of Europe gathered in London to attend victory celebrations, from which the Princess of Wales was specifically excluded. Cut off from her daughter and friends and ostracised by the Court, Caroline determined to seek comfort abroad. A deal was negotiated with Lord Castlereagh and she agreed to leave the country on payment of an annual allowance of £35,000. On 8th August 1814 Caroline left England, taking Lady Charlotte Lindsay as lady-in-waiting.

While the problems of the Princess of Wales mounted, Anne was engaged in sculpting her bust. The Princess herself, encouraged by Anne, modelled in clay as a hobby; and this must have given Anne a further impetus to produce a fine likeness. Mary Berry's journal for 15th January 1814 records that in the morning she "went to Mrs Damer's to meet the Princess of Wales, who was there for her last sitting for a bust." In the meantime, Mary had taken on the role of confidante and adviser to the

Princess, which she was to continue through early spring 1814, while at the same time conducting an almost daily session of dinners and soirées with Madame de Staël, where they argued and debated away with entire satisfaction to themselves, and hopefully, on some occasions, to others. For the first three months of the year, Mary had the assistance and close friendship of Lady Charlotte Campbell, as lady-in-waiting to the Princess, to help her; but by the end of March Charlotte, exhausted by the work, "going out, morning, noon and night," and fed up with the Princess's undignified conduct, resigned her position, and took her children to Geneva, where the cost of living was much less expensive, and where she too would come under the spell of Mme de Staël, freed by Napoleon's abdication to return to her native Switzerland. Mme de Staël was a former *inamorata* of Charlotte's brother, Lord John Campbell, who had escaped both from her and from Napoleon's police by dressing up as a maid to Mlle de la Chaux, more lately governess to Lady Charlotte Campbell's children. The Campbell clan took up residence at a house called Les Grottes, where they remained for six months. However, if she believed that she had escaped the Princess of Wales, she would have to think again.

The decision of both Mme de Staël and the Princess of Wales to leave the country meant that they would be no longer available to Mary, and the Berrys decided on a long trip to Raith with their cousin Ronald Ferguson, departing in July and not returning until just before Christmas 1814. Mary told Anne that she missed Madame de Staël, but that "she will never think more of me till we meet again. I know her well, with all her faults, ridicules, and littlenesses; and yet she is a very superior creature." Actually the boot was on the other foot, as it was not long before Madame de Staël was to write to Mary wondering why she had not heard from her. The following March she wrote again, with an accompanying note from her daughter Albertine, inviting Mary to visit once more to celebrate Albertine's engagement to M. de Broglie.

Meanwhile the Princess, *en route* from her native Brunswick to the warmer climes of Italy, ensured that Les Grottes in Geneva was included in her itinerary. To Charlotte's chagrin, she arrived and demanded that a celebratory ball be arranged. The Princess appeared on the night more undressed than dressed, and when she began to waltz, the earth moved. By the time of the Princess's departure, and perhaps to facilitate it, Charlotte had promised that she would rejoin her at Genoa and go on with her to Naples and Rome. In October 1814 Charlotte left Geneva and travelled to Nice, where she was living in March 1815.

With the Princess and Lady Charlotte on the continent and the Berrys in Scotland, Anne had temporarily lost her cause of the moment. However it was not to be long before world events gave her another outlet for her energies. On 10th March 1815 news reached London of Napoleon's escape from Elba. He had landed at Cannes with around 600 soldiers and two pieces of cannon. He had returned, and announced his proclamations for the liberation of his faithful subjects: "The eagles are on the wing, will perch from spire to spire and soon reach those of Notre Dame"; there would be constitutional reform and democratic government.

Mary Berry, by then back in London, received a letter from the Princess of Wales on board HMS *Clorinda,* dated 23rd March. The royal party had left Naples in confusion, made their way to Leghorn, and boarded the frigate. The Princess wrote that she planned to return to England as soon as possible after the death of George III, whenever that might be. In the meantime: "if everything goes on quiet in France, I shall go to Nice and be with dear Lady Charlotte Campbell, to meet Mrs Damer, and to pass our summer at the Lago di Como." By 31st May a very long letter from Keppel Craven to Mary Berry told her, at the end of a fascinating account of events in Naples, that they had heard from the Princess "who is touralising at Milan, on the Lake of Como with Lady Charlotte Campbell. I conclude the other Charlotte [Lindsay] is arrived [in England]; if so, let her read the history of our campaign."

For Anne, the news of Napoleon's return to Paris came as a clarion call. Her usual advisers were not to hand: the Berrys and Campbells in Scotland, Lady Charlotte Campbell on the continent. She took a decision and acted on it. On 1st May 1815, at the Elysée Palace in Paris, she personally presented the Emperor Napoleon with a marble bust of Charles James Fox, carved by herself. England and France had been at war since Napoleon was outlawed by the international community on 5th March. The channel between the warring countries should have been blockaded, with a passport system in force, likewise the land frontiers. So how did Anne get to Paris? The details of her journey are not recorded, but it would seem that her usual allies, courage and determination, would have seen her through. It is unclear whether or not the bust had preceded her to the French capital and she had simply been waiting for a suitable opportunity to present it to Napoleon, or whether she brought it with her at the time.

The Times newspaper of 9th May included a report from Paris, dated 4th May, which stated that Mrs Seymour Damer had had the honour of presenting to the Emperor a marble bust of Charles Fox, which she herself had sculpted. She had already presented a similar bust, modelled in plaster, after the Peace of Amiens. She had the honour of an interview with the Emperor, who on this occasion told her that "if this distinguished man had lived, there would have been peace; the debt of England would have been less than 1 million, and many thousands of men would still be alive."

Another French report added that Anne had been encouraged to produce the marble version for Napoleon because of his approval of its plaster forebear, and by the high opinion which she knew that he had of Fox. This version of the story also stated that the statue had been completed by 1812, and that Anne had entrusted it to a Frenchman who brought it to Paris, but, for undisclosed reasons, it had not reached its destination. Mrs Damer had come to Paris, and bearing the bust, inscribed 1812, in her hands, had asked Marshal Bertrand's permission for her to deposit the bust in the manner which he considered most appropriate. This report noted that Mme Damer had stayed at the Hotel De Wagram in the Rue de St Augustin.

A further description appearing in a much later list of Anne's works, written in French, stated that she had the honour to present it in person to the Emperor on 1st May 1815 at the Elysée Palace. This bust had been promised during Anne's visit after the Peace of Amiens. This version also stated that Anne left Paris shortly after the presentation, but not before receiving from the hands of Marshal Bertrand a magnificent box, the cover of which bore a portrait of Napoleon, surrounded by diamonds. Bertrand had asked her to accept this as a souvenir, adding that Napoleon had instructed that the bust should be placed in the Gallery of Great Men at Fontainebleau.

At the same time, on a different note, *The Times* published a separate paragraph based on a report from a French paper, *Le Moniteur*, noting that some idiotic Englishwoman had presented the Corsican with the bust of Charles Fox.

What induced this 66-year-old lady to make such a dramatic lone journey? She had certainly become more eccentric in old age. She was living alone with her maid in Upper Brook Street, the summer charms of Strawberry Hill no longer available to her. She had recently seen all that Charles James Fox had stood for disappear in front of her eyes. The French experiment with democracy, which had gone so disastrously wrong, had resulted in the restoration of the Bourbon monarchy in France and the collapse of the Whig party in England. In Anne's mind, her marble bust of Fox represented the old value of liberty.

Furthermore she had finished the bust, started in time of peace, in 1812, when England and France were again at war. Entry to France was forbidden and there had been no opportunity to make the presentation until peace in 1814, when Napoleon had been immediately deported to Elba. May 1815 when perhaps, after the brief peace, passport restrictions were more lax, was Anne's first opportunity to visit France and see Napoleon. From the latter's point of view the visit would have been an unexpected but welcome public relations triumph, at a time when it was much needed. He may also have seen in Anne someone whose courage and ability to seize the moment, reflected some of his own strengths. He would certainly have had as much pleasure in giving her his miniature diamond encrusted portrait as she had in receiving it.

The world and Mary Berry did not approve of Anne's dash to Paris. Fraternising with the commander of an army about to do battle with that of your own country was not popular. For the average Englishman, the only good Frenchman was a dead one. Mary caught the national mood when she wrote reproving Anne, in Lausanne, on 23rd July 1815, a month after the battle of Waterloo. Napoleon was about to be landed, a prisoner, at Torbay. "The rapid course of public events, each one more wonderful than the other, which have taken place within this last month, leave all comment, as well as all calculation, at a distance. You little thought that your friend at Paris would be in England before yourself, and that your bust may return to that country it never ought to have left, without going out of the possession of the person to whom you gave it."

However others were less censorious. The *Plymouth and Cornish Advertiser* on 18th January 1816 listed 4th May, when "Mrs Seymour Damer presented Bonaparte with a bust of Charles Fox" as one of the significant and remarkable dates of the year 1815. Since the article was likely to have been syndicated to all the provincial press, it is probable that this record of Anne's journey, sandwiched neatly between 2nd March: "Bonaparte landed with 1000 men at Cannes", and 17th-18th June: "The glorious Battle of Waterloo", would have been published across England.

Immediately after receiving her gift, Anne made her departure from Paris. Travelling south eastwards towards Switzerland, she avoided the military manoeuvres starting on the Belgian frontier, crossing the frontier and arriving at Lausanne, where she joined forces with Lady Charlotte Campbell and family, who had recently left the Princess of Wales in Milan. Together they returned to England.

In the meantime, the Princess of Wales had become infatuated with a six-foot-three hunk of moustachioed Italian named Pergami, a former soldier fighting for Napoleon's armies, who swiftly belied early rumours that a war wound had incapacitated his virility. Starting his acquaintanceship with the Princess as her courier, he quickly became inseparable from his mistress. They were noticed together in Genoa; she, plump, red-faced, in befeathered pink hat and short white skirt displaying legs clad in pink topped boots, was lounging on blue velvet in a phaeton, shaped like a seashell, covered with mother of pearl, and drawn by two small piebald horses. He rode in front, also on a small piebald horse. Together Caroline and Pergami set out on a Mediterranean pleasure trip, pursued by spies employed by the British government to gather evidence of marital infidelity.

Following the defeat of Napoleon, Paris once more became a fashionable venue for English visitors. In February 1816 Mary Berry left England at the invitation of the Earl and Countess of Hardwicke, to stay with them in Paris, where she remained until the end of May. She wrote extremely frequently to Agnes, less often to Anne. Early in May, Anne fell ill. Mary wrote to Agnes that the letters she had had from Anne confirmed what Agnes had told her: "Her ills of every sort are everyday increasing and are alas absolutely without remedy." Mary regretted that she had sealed a letter to Anne precipitately, and asked Agnes to tell her that she was forwarding Anne's enclosures in her letters, as requested. Mary returned to London for June and July, following which the Berry family left for an extended stay in Genoa from August 1816, arriving back in England in August 1818. During this time they attended the marriage of Lady Charlotte Campbell to her son's tutor, the Rev Edward Bury. In March 1817 Mary's father Mr Berry died in Genoa, and Anne wrote in sympathy.

Meanwhile, back in England after her dash to Paris, Anne, tired of Upper Brook Street in summer, was searching for a country house in the vicinity of Twickenham. Temporarily she rented a house at East Sheen, belonging to the newly-widowed Lady Buckinghamshire. In July 1817 York House at Twickenham was advertised for sale in *The Times*. It was described as a spacious freehold mansion. Anne, with a very substantial library and collection of sculpture to house, had no intention of downsizing in old age. In the estate agent's words, it was "most delightfully situate on the bank of the Thames" it had "coach houses, stabling, conservatory, greenhouse, theatre, beautiful lawn and pleasure grounds in the highest order, capital kitchen garden and meadow, the whole containing about 10 acres." It had once been the country home of Lord Clarendon, Charles II's Lord Chancellor. Anne had known it of old, when it had been the home of her great friends, the Austrian ambassador Prince Starhemberg and his wife. It had been the latter who had comforted Anne after the death of her mother and she had attended their family amateur theatricals there. Starhemberg had left in 1810, since when the house had either remained empty or for a short time had been rented by Euseby Cleaver, Archbishop of Dublin, who "from mental disease was unable to discharge the duties of the see." The sale was completed in September 1818.

At the same time as negotiating for a new house, Anne found herself named jointly with the Marquis of Cholmondeley in a court action in which they were opposed by Lord Clinton. The case was based on estates in Devon and Cornwall that had at one time belonged to the Rolle family, from whom Horace Walpole had been descended. These estates, which were currently in the possession of Lord Clinton, had been claimed by the Marquis of Cholmondeley, supported by Anne, citing some very complicated laws concerning mortgages and ownership of property. The case rumbled on for two years, before judgement was finally made. On 16th August 1820 the Master of the Rolls declared that the Marquis Cholmondeley had, in no event, any interest whatever in the estate in question, and that if the Marquis Cholmondeley and Mrs Damer, or either of them, had ever had any title, they were for ever barred by the Statute of Limitations, and therefore he dismissed their claim. The real winners, as always, were the lawyers.

In addition to matters of law, Anne had a sculptural remedial to which to attend. *The Morning Chronicle* of 24th March 1820 reported that the Lord Mayor of London had received a letter from Mrs Damer with regard to the restoration of Lord Nelson's bust, which she had completed, following which it would be restored to "its previous dignified situation".

In January 1820 George III finally died, and the Prince Regent succeeded him as George IV. The news reached Mary and Agnes Berry in Paris on Monday 31st, and they set about buying their clothes for a mourning period of three weeks, halved by order of the King from the usual six. In early March the Berrys set out again for Italy, passing through Switzerland *en route*. It was here, in Geneva, that they met Queen Caroline, no longer Princess of Wales, on her way back to England. It was the last time they were to see her. A letter from the Queen to Mary Berry from Geneva, dated 25th May, communicated what she described as good news. Alderman Wood, the man to whom the Berrys had rented Little Strawberry Hill, and Lady Anne Hamilton would meet her at Dijon, and Henry Brougham near Calais. She hoped to be living at Blackheath and would send Mary Berry news when she got there.

The Queen landed at Dover on 4th June, accompanied by Lady Anne Hamilton and her self-appointed adviser, Alderman Wood. She arrived in London on 6th June, and took up residence at Alderman Wood's house in South Audley Street. The King, who had already instructed that Caroline's name be removed from the Prayer Book, was furious at her arrival and instructed his prime minister Lord Liverpool to take proceedings against her on the grounds of her adultery with her Italian lover and companion, Pergami, over the previous two years. The proceedings would take the form of a select committee enquiry in both Lords and Commons.

Henry Brougham prevailed on the Queen to leave South Audley Street and take up lodgings with Lady Anne Hamilton in Portland Street. Here she was visited by a few of her male friends, but the only lady of fashion to call on her was Anne Damer. Perhaps, considered Lady Charlotte Lindsay, she "thought this visit a respect due to the station of a Queen, against whom nothing has as yet been proved. The only inconvenience that may result to her is, that no other woman of character (except Lady T) having made this visit, it acquires greater consequence than should naturally belong to so simple an action, and she will be reckoned a decided partisan of the Queen's, when she probably only disapproves of the proceedings against her."

As Parliamentary proceedings rumbled backward and forward, the Queen took up residence in August at Brandenburg House. On 10th November, 1820 the House of Lords passed the bill approving the divorce by 108 votes to 99, the majority being the exact number of ministers in the Lords. With this slender majority and no hope of getting the bill through the House of Commons, Lord Liverpool, the Prime Minister, withdrew it. Lady Charlotte Lindsay was in the Lords all day and was able to recount the news to Anne, with whom she dined that evening.

For a short while the Queen's star was in the ascendant. Fêted by radicals as their future leader, the Queen was seen to stand for reform and for the triumph of the will of the people over the crown. The truth was that she was exhausted both by failing health and by the rigours and strains of the recent trial. She had no real bent for politics, the pleasures of life were sufficient for her. Badly advised by Alderman Wood, she accepted Liverpool's offer of £50,000 a year, but only on condition that her name was restored to the Prayer Book, a condition which the King refused to accept. Gradually the revolutionary fervour subsided; a new magazine, *John Bull*, supported the Government and denigrated Caroline and her colleagues. It particularly aimed its darts at the ladies who visited the Queen. Speaking of Mrs Brougham, *John Bull* noted that "her marriage and that of the birth of her child followed one another much more closely than has been usual in well-regulated families." Anne was once again accused of being "strangely susceptible to the charms of her own sex". Lady Jersey was also attacked, whilst it was inferred that the Queen living at "Brandyberg House" had an undue liking for the cordials. These friends continued to visit Caroline, but the rest of Society stayed away. The Queen became determined to attend George IV's coronation, which took place on 19th July 1821. The King was even more determined that she should not. The Queen, accompanied by Lord Hood and Lady Anne Hamilton, attempted four times to enter Westminster Abbey by different entrances. Finally, at the door nearest to Poets' Corner, she was met by Sir Robert Inglis, Gold Staff, who told her that there was no room for her within. He escorted her back from Poets' Corner to her carriage, and she left defeated, to calls of "Go back to Pergami!".

Anne had dined with the Queen at Brandenburg House at the height of her popularity, on 11th February 1821. The other guests included Thomas Creevey, Henry Brougham and Keppel Craven, and these three collected Anne from Upper Brook Street. Creevey was most impressed by Anne, whom he had not previously met. "She is 70 years of age and as fresh as if she was 50". When they reached Brandenburg House, they were shown to "a very handsome, well proportioned room, from 40 to 50 feet long, very lofty, with a fine coved ceiling, painted with gods and goddesses in their very best clothes". The room looked onto the River Thames. When they entered, the Queen went up to Anne, and welcomed her, then to Brougham, and then to Creevey. The last named, was concerned, as "I am not sure whether I did not commit the outrage of putting out my hand without her doing the same first; be it as it may, however, we did shake hands." He found her more agreeable than on previous meetings, and she had taken him aside after dinner, to explain her worries about her financial situation.

Keppel Craven had made the party laugh by remembering an Italian ball given by the Duke of Caparo, where the Queen had appeared as the Genius of History, being preceded by Fame with a fanfare on the trumpet. As the moment of entry approached, Fame was found to have mislaid the trumpet. After a brief hiatus, they made their entry, Fame to the front, blowing a horn belonging to one of the Duke's keepers. They had gone down to dinner with Craven partnering the Queen, Brougham accompanying Anne, whilst the diminutive Mme Felice put her arm through that of Creevey.

Sadly, the Queen was not to give many more dinner parties. On the night of the Coronation, she had attempted to appear in good spirits, but "while she laughed the tears rolled down her face – tears of anguish so acute that she seemed to dread the usual approach of rest." That night she had taken a mixture of magnesia and laudanum, to relieve pain, and by the end of the month it was clear that she was seriously and incurably ill. She died, delirious and in pain, on 7th August.

Brandenburg House, where she had died, was in Hammersmith, not far from Twickenham and York House. The Queen's coffin was laid out in the marble hall. Friends, neighbours and the general public were permitted entry to pay their last respects. The neighbouring gentry were let in at 3pm, the crowd at 6pm. Anne, as a close personal friend, was permitted to enter early with another dear colleague, Lady Anne Hamilton. Anne was reported as approaching the Royal coffin, kneeling in front of it, and fervently kissing it. She had appeared so absorbed in grief that Lady Anne had found it difficult to persuade her to rise and leave.

In death, the Queen was as popular as she had ever been in life. In her Will, she had desired that she should be buried in her native Brunswick, and the King and Government had every reason to agree that her final resting place should be as far from England as possible. Their immediate problem was how to get her there. Lord Liverpool thought the best solution was to take the coffin by boat down the Thames, and thence into the open sea and on to Brunswick. However the Admiralty were unable to guarantee that the seamen, who had vigorously supported Caroline during her trial, would not bar the way. An alternative route by land was chosen, passing through Kensington and Bayswater north-east towards Harwich, and avoiding the city. At 7.30am on 15th August the cortège of hearse and 16 coaches, escorted by a squadron of the Blues, set off. By the time the procession reached Kensington it was clear that the surrounding and growing crowd was intent that it should pass through the City. A squadron of the Life Guards was summoned to assist. The procession moved slowly forward as far as the Cumberland Gate exit to Hyde Park, when it was brought to a halt in driving rain, and a hail of bricks and stones. Amidst casualties both to troops and to the crowd, an *impasse* was reached. Eventually, to save further bloodshed, the Chief Metropolitan Magistrate ordered that the Queen's body be taken to the City, whence it passed without further confrontation to Harwich. As she had wished, her tomb in Brunswick bears the inscription "Caroline of Brunswick, the injured Queen of England."

Anne Damer was too old to have played an active part in the last years of Caroline's life. However, to have the courage to support, and be seen to support, the unpopular and unfashionable was one of her most desirable traits. In the case of Napoleon, six years previously, her actions had been eccentric, even misguided. In supporting Caroline, like her the subject of abuse, whether deserved or not, she had upheld the old Whig principle of lessening the power of the monarchy. Like her, the Queen was a woman in a man's world; another sculptress denigrated by those in power.

Chapter 21

THE FINAL CURTAIN

The last ten years of Anne's life would be spent between Upper Brook Street and York House. At the latter she gradually collected together her own sculptures. She was too old to travel far and her last years were spent in a quiet but steady decline. In March 1825 Mary Berry became very ill in London, Agnes being extremely worried as to whether she would survive. She took five weeks to recover, "without a spark of life either in body or in mind." During her recovery period, she visited Anne at York House for a short stay. This may be the last time that they saw each other.

Like many people who feel the proximity of the Grim Reaper, Anne spent some time in making and correcting her Will. Her latest Will, dated 1st December 1825, followed another, now lost or destroyed, to which a previous codicil dated 1818 was attached. This codicil was carried forward and attached to the 1825 Will.

Anne appointed her cousin John Campbell, Accountant General of the High Court of Chancery, and Moses Hoper, her lawyer, as her executors. She directed that all the Campbell pictures in her possession be left to the Duke of Argyll and all her plate to her cousin, Lord John Campbell. Specific requests to other cousins included £100 to Lady Augusta Clavering and to Lady Johnston, and £500 to her executor John Campbell. Her faithful servant and lady's maid Anne Weaver received £500. Her houses, No 9 Upper Brook Street, London, and York House, Twickenham, were to be sold. From the proceeds an annuity of £250 per annum was to be paid to Anne Weaver, and she directed that this payment take precedence over all others. The residue of the estate, including the proceeds of the houses, was left to John Campbell.

The previous 1818 codicil, which was attached to this edition of the Will, included gifts of one year's wages and a mourning suit for all her servants, and, in addition, legacies of £50 to Anne Thorle, a former servant, and Thomas Smith her coachman. In addition, Anne Weaver would receive all Anne's cloaks and her silver watch and chain.

The next codicil, dated 16th February 1826, added annuities of £10 a year for additional former servants Ann Brantham and Mary Bland. This codicil contained specific instructions concerning Anne's own burial. Her remains were to be deposited in Sundridge church in the special vault prepared to receive them, alongside those of her mother. The vault would be found in the chancel of the church by taking up the flagstones at the foot of the monument which Anne had erected in memory of her mother. Here Anne's uncle Lord Frederick Campbell had prepared a plinth for Anne herself, on which she instructed the following inscription should be placed:

HIC PROPE JACET
UNO CLARA CUM MATRE LOCO
ANNE SEYMOUR DAMER
SCULPTRIX ET STATUTARIA ILLUSTRIS FEMINA
HENRICI SEYMOUR CONWAY ET CAROLINE CAMPBELL FILIA

Anne also requested that within her coffin should be placed the bones of her favourite dog Fidele, which would be found in a small box wrapped up in a silk handkerchief, and her mallet and some of her chisels as well. Wherever she was going, she wished to take the tools of her trade, and her dog, with her.

A morbid fear of being buried alive caused her to request that her body be thrown into quicklime, or alternatively be opened to prevent any possibility of her being buried alive, "an idea which has always presented itself to my imaginations with peculiar dread and horror."

On 16th March 1826 she appointed a new executor, giving her reasons: "My particular reason for the appointment of my friend, Sir Jonathan Wathen Waller, Bart. as my sole executor is principally that I have given to him my confidential directions concerning all my papers, manuscripts etc, and I do not choose any other person to have anything to do with them." Anne's new executor, to replace both John Campbell and Moses Hoper, was her neighbour, oculist to the king and the owner of Pope's Villa in Twickenham. Moses Hoper was removed from his place as executor but to ensure no hard feelings was left £500. "As a proof of my regard and that he may not feel himself hurt at the appointment of another trustee in his place."

Another codicil, dated 31st July 1826, was required, owing to the precipitate death of Anne's cousin, former executor and heir, John Campbell. Her new heir was another cousin, John Campbell's sister Louisa Johnston, the wife of Sir Alexander Johnston.

The bequest in favour of Moses Hoper was not to survive long. In a final codicil dated 5th August 1826, Anne acted again. "Whereas I have lately been informed by my faithful servant Anne Weaver that Mrs Moses Hoper is indebted to her in the sum of £500 lent by her the said Anne Weaver to him the said Mrs Moses Hoper, I hereby direct that in case the above named sum of £500 be not paid by Mrs Moses Hoper to Anne Weaver before the period of my death, then that the legacy of £500 left by me to the said Mr Moses Hoper in a codicil to my last Will and Testament bearing the date the 21st day of December 1825 shall to all intents and purposes become null and void and I hereby direct and empower my executors to pay the whole sum of the said £500 or such part or parts thereof as may remain unpaid and all such interest as may be due thereon to the said Anne Weaver on her giving to Mr Moses Hoper a proper receipt and release for the said sum of £500 or such part thereof as may still be due to her with the interest therefrom." Interestingly, Anne's solicitors' clerk originally attributed the debt to Moses Hoper himself. A later correction added the word "Mrs", but failed to alter the "him" to "her".

Anne died at about one o'clock in the morning on 28th May 1828. Sir Jonathan Waller and the Duke of Argyll were present at her death, along with others of Anne's friends and attendants. Immediately after her death, Waller asked that a particular box in Anne's bedroom be given to him. He knew that this contained her Will and all relevant codicils, and he and the Duke of Argyll made sure that it was secured in a closed position, and applied their seals over the closure. About 12 o'clock that morning in the presence of the Duke of Argyll and of various relations, friends and servants, Waller broke the seals and opened the box with a key which had been found in the deceased's pocket. The Will was read, the various codicils and amendments to them noted, and eventually on 9th June the Will was proved and Sir Jonathan Waller was free to start its Administration.

The confidential instructions with regard to Anne's papers and manuscripts were simple. All were to be destroyed. Sir Jonathan seems to have carried out his instructions swiftly and thoroughly. He retained *Anne's Notebooks*, with their extracts from Mary Berry's letters and little else. All letters to Anne, both from Horace Walpole, Mary Berry, and other correspondents were burned. The reasoning behind these instructions died probably with Anne, and certainly with Sir Jonathan. It is probable that Anne had considered that destruction would ensure that they could not be used in any publications after her death either to confirm or refute the "abuse" she had suffered during her life. In the words of her cousin, Lady Charlotte Campbell: "It would be difficult to account for this 'abuse' were it not an established fact that all women who meddle with literature, especially those in the higher ranks of life, place themselves in a pillory, at which every impertinent idler conceives he has a right to throw his rotten eggs."

The following notices of Mrs Damer's death appeared respectively in the *Morning Post & Times* of 29th May 1828 and in the *Gentleman's Magazine* May to July 1828

Morning Post and Times
"Early on Wednesday, 28 May, died, at her house in Upper Brook Street, Grosvenor square, the Hon. Anne Seymour Damer, the only child of the late Right Hon. Field Marshal Conway (brother to Francis, Earl of Hertford), and the Lady Caroline Campbell, daughter of John, fourth Duke of Argyll, and widow of Charles, Earl of Ailesbury."

Gentleman's Magazine.
Obituary
Hon. Mrs Damer, May 28th.

"In Upper Brook Street in her 80th year, the Hon Anne Seymour Damer, celebrated as an amateur sculptor, and as legatee of Horace Walpole, Earl of Orford, of Strawberry Hill. She was the only child of the Right Hon Henry Seymour Conway, brother of Francis, first Marquis of Hertford, by Lady Caroline Campbell, daughter of John, fourth Duke of Argyll and widow of Charles, Earl of Ailesbury and Elgin. She was married June 14th 1767 to the Hon John Damer, eldest son of Joseph, first Lord Milton, and brother of George, Earl of Dorchester. Her marriage was an unhappy one. Mr Damer was heir to an expectancy of £30,000 a year, but was a turn too eccentric to be confined within limits of fortune. He shot himself at the Bedford Arms, Covent Garden, August 15th 1776, leaving Mrs Damer a widow without issue. From this period Mrs Damer appears to have devoted herself to the cultivation of her talents, particularly to her chisel, and became afterwards as eminent in Sculpture as her contemporaries Maria Cosway and Angelica Kaufmann were in Painting. In 1797, on the death of her father's intimate friend Horace Walpole (for by that name he is better known than by the Earldom, which he possessed the last six years of his life), Mrs Damer found herself the owner of the pretty Ivy-house, called Strawberry Hill, with a legacy of £2000 to keep it in repair, on condition she resided there and did not dispose of it to any person, unless it were to his great niece the Countess Dowager Waldegrave, on whom and her heirs it was entailed. All his prints, books, and furniture were made heirlooms. His niece, the Duchess of Gloucester, preferred £10,000 to this Villa. Mrs Damer's portrait by Hamilton is at Strawberry Hill. Mrs Damer resided at the celebrated house from Lord Orford's death to about the year 1810, when she gave it up to the late Countess Waldegrave, who died there in January 1816. When the Duke of Richmond patronised private theatricals, he was glad to avail himself of Mrs Damer's assistance. She was the Thalia of the scene. She appeared in the character of "Wonder", when Lord Henry Fitzgerald supported the part of "Don Felix". She also was eminent as Mrs Lovemore in *The Way to Keep Him*, and Lady Freelove in *The Jealous Wife*.

"At a later period, during her residence at Strawberry Hill, she herself fitted up an elegant theatre. Here the comedy called *Fashionable Lovers* (which has been attributed to the part of Lord Orford), was presented. Mr Kemble obtained permission to transplant this comedy to Drury Lane, but it was not successful.

"In the art of Sculpture, Mrs Damer undoubtedly took the lead of all amateurs. In early life, she received lessons from Ceracchi and the elder Bacon, and she even followed the example of professional artists in taking a voyage to Italy to improve herself. Her elegant, tasteful and classical productions are widely scattered as presents.

"At the suggestion of Sir Alexander Johnston, her relative, with a view to aid the advancement of European Arts in India, she sent a bust of Lord Nelson to the King of Tanjore, and she presented another bust of Nelson to the Corporation of London, which is placed in the Common Council Room at the Guildhall. A statue of George III by Mrs Damer adorns the Register Office at Edinburgh, and her beautiful bust of Sir Joseph Banks at the British Museum is well known. But perhaps the most public of her works are the colossal heads of 'Thames' and 'Isis' on Henley Bridge. Several of her busts are in the hands of private individuals. Mrs Damer possessed one of the best selected and most valuable libraries ever formed by a female collector. She had, we hear, directed that her apron and tools should be buried with her: as also the bones of her favourite dog that died before her."

Anne's life would be further recalled by the sale of her library, which took place in her old home, No 18 Upper Brook Street, from July 18th-23rd 1828. The sale was conducted by Mr Rainy, auctioneer, of No 8 Berkeley Square. The lots were sold at the rate of 180 per day for five days, many lots containing 20-30 books. The total sales value was £1541-4s-6d for the books, and £652-16s-6d for furniture. Glancing down the auctioneer's catalogue, the reader is drawn back inevitably to scenes and episodes from Anne's life. Among the works on Day 1 was Rousseau's *La Nouvelle Héloise, Lettres de Madame du Barry*, Hume's dialogues on religion, a collection of English prologues and epilogues, *Sense and Sensibility, Pride and Prejudice* and Edwards' *Natural History of Uncommon Birds*. Day 2 saw the *Works* of Buffon, Blaine on dogs, O'Meara's *Napoleon in Exile*, Normand's *Memoirs of Josephine*, and Madame de Staël's *Considérations sur la Révolution Française*. The last three, plus several more, were bound uniformly into 38 volumes, to provide *A Succinct History of the Rise and Decline of Napoleon*. Latin texts from Virgil and Ovid featured prominently on this day and the remaining three.

Day 3 featured Horace Walpole's gothic novel *The Castle of Otranto*, as well as the same author's *Anecdotes of Painting*. Darwin's *Botanic Garden* was also evident, splendidly bound in yellow morocco. Day 4 saw M. Dutens' *Itinéraire de l'Europe*, the works of Voltaire, Rousseau and Rabelais, *Les Lettres de Mme Sévigny*, 61 volumes of classical authors, and Thucydides, Herodotus and Xenophon in Greek. Curtis's *Botanical Magazine* and the works of Linnaeus provided a reminder of Anne's gardening interests. The last day included Fox's speeches, Miss Baillie's plays, Montfaucon's *L'Antiquité Expliquée*, a first edition of Shakespeare's works dated 1623, Gray's poems, and Sir William Hamilton's *Observations on the Volcanoes of the Two Sicilies*. A special reminder of the newspapers, whose reporting of her activities had been both her delight and horror, was provided by *The News*, a Sunday paper from 1805-1828, neatly half-bound in 22 volumes.

Her life had been as rich and varied as her library. She was a widely-educated woman of many talents, happy to display them in an age when an ostentatious show of female prowess in the arts was generally frowned upon. Happy as hostess and friend to actors and actresses, in whose theatres her contemporaries were happy to be seen, but whose acquaintance they were content to ignore, Anne knew that she would provoke criticism, yet was unprepared to ride it when it came. Capable of close friendships with friends with common interests, she found it difficult to come close to persons of inferior abilities, who in turn resented her disdain.

ENVOI

FRIENDSHIP

The translations of the passages from Cicero which follow are taken from *Anne's Notebooks:*

"And without virtue friendship can in no way exist."

"Who can have a true life, as Ennius says, who does not find pleasure in a friend's reciprocal friendship? What is sweeter than to have someone to whom you can dare to say everything as to yourself? What would be the great advantage of prosperity, if you did not have someone to rejoice in it as much as you yourself do? Adversity indeed would be difficult to bear without one to take it harder even than you … And I am not speaking now of an everyday or ordinary friendship (though that gives pleasure and profit), but of a true, perfect friendship, the kind of the few celebrated ones. For friendship makes prosperity more distinguished and makes adversity easier by splitting and sharing it. … But indeed watching a friend is like watching a likeness of oneself. For this reason they are both present when absent, and abundant when lacking, and strong when weak, and something that is difficult to express, alive when dead."

Cicero Laelius

PERSONAE DRAMATIS

Ailesbury, Countess of 1721-1803 Daughter of John Campbell later 4th duke of Argyll. m 1.(1739) Charles Bruce 3rd Earl of Ailesbury (1682-1747). 1 daughter Lady Mary Bruce b.1740. (See Duchess of Richmond). 2. (1747) Henry Seymour Conway. (see). 1 daughter Anne Seymour Conway b.1748.

Albany Mme d' 1752-1824 Self styled Countess of Albany. German princess Louise de Stolberg had married Charles Stuart "Bonnie Prince Charlie", in 1772. She was 19, he over 50, with limited prospects and dependency on alcohol. They lived in Florence, where in 1776, she met the Italian poet Alfieri. They became lovers, and in 1786 after a legal separation from Charles, they set up home in Paris. Louise's maternal grandmother had been a Bruce, a daughter of Caroline Ailesbury's first husband's father. She was thus a relation to be entertained when she visited England in 1791. The couple fled France to Italy in 1792 where they lived till Alfieri died 1803.

Arabin Major Will Soldier and dilettanti comedy actor. Regular in AD's Richmond House Theatre. He also appeared in amateur theatre at Brandenburg House, belonging to the Margravine of Ansbach, formerly Lady Craven, and at Hinchinbrook for Lord Sandwich.

Argyll 4th Duke of 1693-1770 Grandfather of AD. Father of Lady Ailesbury. Successful soldier, inheriting Dukedom of Argyll unexpectedly. Married Mary Bellenden.

Argyll 5th Duke of 1723-1806 Eldest son of John Campbell 4th Duke of Argyll. Uncle of AD. Married 1759 Elizabeth dowager Duchess of Hamilton (nee Gunning). 5 children. 1. Augusta. 2. George John (1763-64) 3. George (1768-1839) 6th Duke of Argyll 4. Charlotte (1775-1861) 5. John (1777-1847) 7th Duke of Argyll. Home Inverary Castle.

Bacon John (the elder) 1740-1799 Sculptor. Son of a London clothworker. Trained in modelling china. Developed large studio. Elected RA 1777. AD learned to carve marble at his studio.

Balbi Madame de 1758-1842 Mistress of the Comte de Provence, the future Louis XVIII. Noted for her acerbic wit.

Banks Sir Joseph 1743-1820 see main text p.230.

Barrymore Countess of 1749-1780 Born Amelia Stanhope daughter of 2nd Earl of Harrington. m.1767 6th Earl of Barrymore. Contemporary of AD. Topped the Bon Ton chart of Society hostesses in 1775.

Beauharnais Josephine de 1763-1814 Born in Martinique as Rose Tascher, a member of a wealthy white Creole family of plantation owners. Married in France in 1779 to Alexandre de Beauharnais. He went to the guillotine in 1794. She became Napoleon's mistress 1795. Married in 1796 she became known as Josephine. Crowned Empress 1804. Divorced as childless in 2010. Moved to Malmaison. D1814. A keen gardener, AD assisted her to obtain seeds and plants for Malmaison.

Beaumont Sir John, 7th Baronet 1753-1827 Taught to draw at Eton by Alexander Cozens, the landscape artist. A leading amateur artist and exhibitor at the RA. Assembled a fine collection part of which he offered to the Nation in 1824, on condition that Parliament purchased further pictures, resulting in the creation of The National Gallery. A supporter of Uvedale Price and the Picturesque movement. Friend of Wordsworth.

Beckford William 1760-1844 Inherited great wealth from sugar plantations in Jamaica. In Italy in 1782 where he met AD in Naples. m.1783 Lady Margaret Gordon. However he was bisexual and ostracised from England to Europe when his homosexual relationship with William Courtenay was made public. Built Fonthill Abbey in Wiltshire. Eclectic art collector. Author of gothic novel *Vathek*. In Portugal 1787. His Portuguese journals echo AD's description 1790-91, and also the Portuguese sections of Belmour.

Berry Mary 1763-1852 Protegée of HW. Daughter of Robert Berry and great niece of Robert Ferguson of Raith 1690-1781. Writer and literary salon hostess. Bosom friend of AD.

Berry Agnes 1764-1852 Younger sister of Mary. Amateur water colourist. Experienced a series of unsuccessful romantic dalliances.

Berry Robert Father of **Mary and Agnes**. m.1762 Miss Seton who died in childbirth 1767, leaving them to be brought up by their father. Nephew and heir of Robert Ferguson of Raith, he was disinherited in favour of his brother William. Travelled extensively on the continent with his daughters. Died in Genoa 1817

Bertrand Henri-Gatien 1773-1844 French General and aide to Napoleon from Egypt in 1798, through all campaigns, with him in Elba in 1815, during the 100 Days, and with him in exile in St Helena until Napoleon's death in 1821. Created Grand Marechal du Palais in 1813. Pardoned by Louis XVIII, he returned to France. In 1840 he was a member of the mission to return Napoleon's ashes to France.

Bonaparte Mme de 1750-1836 Napoleon's mother. Born Letizia Ramolino, she married, aged 13, Carlo Buonaparte in Ajaccio, Corsica in 1764. She had 13 children, 8 of whom survived infancy, most becoming European monarchs. She was a strict mother. Her husband who was Corsican envoy to Louis XVI died in 1785. She lived in Paris till 1815 when she moved to Rome, where she remained till her death.

Bonaparte Napoleon 1769-1821 m. Josephine de Beauharnais 1796. First Consul of France in 1799. Cultivated English Whigs after the Treaty of Amiens 1801. Emperor of France 1804-14. Mistakenly admired by AD as being in the mould of Charles James Fox, a supporter of liberty. 1810 Divorced Josephine, as childless and married

Archduchess Marie Louise of Austria to secure an heir. Banished to Elba 1814, before returning to France for The 100 Days, culminating in the battle of Waterloo Subsequently banished to St Helena where he died.

Boydell John 1720-1804 Publisher and print engraver. Successful businessman exporting engravings to France. Lord Mayor of London 1790. Opened his Shakespeare Gallery in 1789 for which all leading artists of the day produced works from Shakespeare for Boydell to sell as prints. AD contributed two bas relief sculptures. Print sales beneath expectations partly due to French wars depressing home and destroying continental markets. Gallery failed and sold by lottery in 1805.

Brougham Henry 1778-1868 Eloquent lawyer and Whig politician, educated in Edinburgh, where he helped found and contributed to the Whig Edinburgh Review. Fellow of Royal Society at age 25. Returned to the Commons in 1815 as MP for Winchilsea. A radical Whig, his views were not consistent, and he was more popular with the public than with his fellow MPs. Appointed attorney to Princess Caroline in 1812, he made his name in her defence in the House of Lords Divorce debate of 1820. Later became Lord Chancellor, helped found London University, and was responsible for seeing the Great Reform Bill (1832) and The Abolition of Slavery Act (1833) through the Lords.

Brune General Guillaume 1763-1815 French general responsible for driving Anglo Russian army out of Holland in 1799. Ambassador to Constantinople 1802-03. Joined Napoleon during the 100 Days in 1815, to command the army in southern France to resist the Austrians. Following the Bourbon restoration he was murdered by royalists at Avignon.

Buccleuch 3rd Duke of 1746-1812 (also 5th Duke of Queensberry) Henry Scott. His mother, Lady Dalkeith, had been a daughter of the 2nd Duke of Argyll, and therefore a Campbell relation of AD. Her husband had died before inheriting the ducal titles. A leading Scottish landowner, AD's parents considered him a suitable match for their daughter. However he married 1767 Lady Betty Montagu, daughter of the Duke Montagu, and an heiress. Tutored by Adam Smith he accumulated even greater wealth and a reputation for meanness.

Buller Mrs 1744c.-1812 Born Mary Coxe of Ston Easton, Somerset. Widow of James Buller of Downes, Devon. London neighbour and friend of HW. Witty, well educated, and a Greek scholar. Known to HW as Mrs B. Neighbour of AD at 44 Upper Brook St.

Butler Lady Eleanor 1739-1829 The elder of the two Ladies of Llangollen. The younger was Sarah Ponsonby 1757?-1832. Irish neighbours from Kilkenny. Met in 1768 and became close friends. Moved from Ireland and settled together at Plas Newydd Llangollen in 1780. Lived a reclusive life immersed in literature and their garden. Visited by Wordsworth, Byron, Shelley and Walter Scott. Lady Eleanor Butler's attendance at The Richmond House production of *The Wonder* was a rare venture out.

Cambacérès Jean-Jacques Régis de 1753-1824 Trained as a lawyer. Moderate revolutionary who was appointed 2nd Consul 1799, and drew up the Code Napoleon legal system.

Cambis Mme de 1729-1809 Gabrielle-Francoise-Charlotte d'Alsace Hénin Liétard. French aristocrat. m.1755 Vicomte de Cambis. Friend of HW and Mme du Deffand. Mistress of the Duke of Richmond, and probably mother of Henrietta Leclerc, Richmond's illegitimate d. Emigrated to England 1789. Niece of the Marquise de Boufflers. Mme du Deffand referred to the Boufflers family as "les oiseaux". – the birds of passage, a reference to their marital inconstancy. The Marquise (oiseau mère), Mme de Boisgelin (oiseau fille), and Mme de Cambis (oiseau nièce). The two latter were early friends in France of AD. Died in Richmond.

Campbell Lady Augusta 1760-1831 Daughter of 5th Duke of Argyll. AD's 1st cousin. Returned from Paris with AD 1782. m. Brigadier Clavering 1785.

Campbell Miss Caroline 1765c.-1789 Elder daughter of Lord William Campbell. Died unmarried. Travelled to Italy 1785 with AD. Took part in Richmond House plays.

Campbell Lady Charlotte 1775-1861 Youngest child of 5th Duke of Argyll. 1st cousin to AD. m.(1) 1796 Colonel John Campbell. 9 children. In 1809, recently widowed, she became lady in waiting to Caroline Princess of Wales. m.(2) 1818 Rev Edward Bury, tutor to her son. 2ds. Prolific authoress and mother.

Campbell Lord Frederick 1729-1816 Son of John Campbell 4th Duke of Argyll. Uncle to AD. AD was born at his house Combe Bank, Sundridge, Kent. MP for various Scottish constituencies. Appointed Lord Clerk Register for Scotland. He commissioned Adam to build the Register House in Princes Street, Edinburgh, and asked AD to sculpt a statue of George III. m. 1769 Mary, widow of Earl Ferrers, who had been hung for shooting his steward. She died 1807 in a fire at Combe Bank. He is buried, as AD and her mother, in Sundridge church.

Campbell Lord George 1768-1839 Son of 5th Duke of Argyll. 1st cousin to AD. Succeeded his father as 6th Duke 1806. Known in family as Lord Tom.

Campbell Lord John 1777-1847 Youngest son of 5th Duke of Argyll. 1st cousin to AD. Succeeded as 7th Duke of Argyll 1839.

Campbell Miss Louisa 1766-1852 Younger daughter of Sir William Campbell 1st cousin to AD. m.1799 to Sir Alexander Johnston. Ultimate beneficiary of AD's will.

Campbell Lady William c.1737-1784 Born Sarah Izard, daughter of Ralph Izard, a South Carolinan plantation owner and early supporter of American independence. Mother of Caroline and Louisa. Travelling companion of AD.

Campbell Lord William 1731-1778 Son of John Campbell 4th Duke of Argyll. Captain RN. Last Governor General of South Carolina. m. Sarah Izard 1763. 2ds, 1 s. Driven from S.Carolina by rebel American colonists he joined Admiral Sir Peter

Parker on board HMS *Bristol*. Died as a result of wound received at Battle for Fort Moultrie in 1776. Favourite uncle of AD who regarded him as a hero.

Carlisle Frederick Howard 5th Earl 1748-1825 In his youth a man of fashion. Married 1771 Margaret Leveson-Gower. 10 children. Responsible for much of the Castle Howard picture collection.

Caroline of Brunswick Princess of Wales 1768-1821, 1st cousin to the Prince of Wales. Her mother was George III's sister. Chosen from a shortage of German Protestant princesses to marry the Prince of Wales, already married to Mrs Fitzherbert, in 1795. The marriage was a disaster, and the behaviour of both partners disastrous. See Chapter 20.

Ceracchi Giuseppe 1751-1801 Sculptor. Trained in Italy, he arrived in London 1773. Trained AD in sculpture, and modelled her, at the instigation of her uncle Lord Frederick Campbell, as the Muse of Sculpture. This work now in the British Museum. Returned to Italy 1781. A keen Jacobin he was arrested, after a plot to kill Napoleon, in 1801 and subsequently condemned to the guillotine.

Chatham 1st Earl of (William Pitt the Elder) 1708-1778 Architect of British success in the Seven Years War (1756-1763) by a Prussian alliance tying down French armies in Europe, thus freeing British troops for colonial success in Canada, India and the West Indies. As Lord Privy Seal led the government from 1766-68 with Henry Seymour Conway as Secretary of State for the North. Brilliant orator.

Cholmeley Mrs Daughter of Sir Henry Englefield 6th baronet. m.1792 Francis Cholmeley of Brandsby in Yorkshire. Patron and friend of John Sell Cotman. Friend of Mary Berry and Yorkshire neighbour of Mary Berry's Seton relations.

Cholmondeley 1st Marquis of 1749-1827 Descendant of Sir Robert Walpole and cousin of AD. Lord Steward of the Household 1812-21.

Clavering Brigadier General Henry Mordaunt 1759-1850 m. 1785 Lady Augusta Campbell. Their son Douglas Clavering was an Arctic explorer.

Clavering Charlotte 1794-1831 Daughter of AD's 1st cousin Augusta Clavering (née Campbell). m.1817 Miles Fletcher.

Clive Mrs Kitty 1711-1785 Actress in comedy with Garrick's company in Drury Lane. Married to and separated from George Clive, barrister. Retired from stage 1769 to live as neighbour of HW at Little Strawberry Hill, known by HW as Cliveden.

Coke Lady Mary 1727-1811 Distant Campbell cousin to AD. Youngest daughter of 2nd Duke of Argyll. m.Viscount Coke 1747; separated 1750. Widowed 1753. Never remarried. Kept a daily journal of events.

Colebrooke Sir George Bt 1729-1809 MP and merchant banker. Inherited family bank and ownership of one of the pocket borough parliamentary seats of Gatton. Chairman of East India Co. He was in financial difficulty 1772. Speculated in commodities, hemp, flax and especially alum, which led to financial collapse Declared bankrupt 1777. Probably a bad influence on John Damer.

Combe William 1742-1823 Writer and satirist, who continually lived beyond his means, spending frequent periods in debtors' enforced accommodation. Lampooned AD for which he subsequently apologised. Best remembered for Dr Syntax series (1812-22) where Combe's verses accompanied Rowlandson's drawings in a satire on The Picturesque movement.

Conway Anne Seymour (see Damer Anne) 1748-1828

Conway Field Marshal Henry Seymour 1721-1795 Father of AD. Second son of the 1st Lord Conway and his wife Charlotte (née Shorter). Her sister Catherine had been the wife of Sir Robert Walpole. Walpole's younger son HW was therefore his 1st cousin. School friend of HW at Eton. Professional soldier and politician. m.1747 Caroline Countess of Ailesbury. 1 daughter. AD.

Connolly Lady Louisa 1743-1821 3rd daughter of 2nd Duke of Richmond. After her parents' death she went to her sister Emily (Lady Kildare) in Ireland. m. 1758 Tom Conolly, Irish landowner and English MP till 1780. In 1802 he inherited Wentworth Castle.

Cosway Maria 1760-1838 Born in Florence with an Italian mother and English father, a wealthy inn keeper to tourists on the Grand Tour. Trained as an artist in Italy. Arrived in England 1779. 1781 m.fellow artist Richard Cosway. Society Hostess and friend of AD. Separated from R.Cosway and lived in France. Became a friend and lover of Thomas Jefferson. During the Consulate 1801-03 she copied the paintings in the Louvre, an unfinished project. After returning to England in 1821 to nurse her husband she sold his painting collection to help finance her school for catholic girls at Lodi in Italy where she died.

Cosway Richard 1742-1821 Artist. Friend of AD whom he frequently painted. Married Maria, 18 years his junior. A libertine.

Craven Keppel Richard 1779-1851 Son of Lady Craven, free loving playwright, who following the death of Lord Craven, her first husband, married her lover to become Margravine of Brandenburg Ansbach Bayreuth. Following his death she lived in Italy with her son Keppel. In 1814 he was appointed a chamberlain to the Princess of Wales in Italy for 6 months. Subsequently gave evidence for Caroline in her divorce trial. Afterwards lived largely in Italy with his friend Sir William Gell. Author of Italian travel books with sketches by himself. Bon viveur and popular host.

Creevey Thomas 1768-1838 Whig MP and follower of Fox, net working gossip and correspondent. His papers, published after his death, are a valuable source for early 19th century England. "Old Creevey is a living proof that a man may be perfectly happy and exceedingly poor."

Crewe Mrs Frances Anne 1748-1818 Whig political hostess. Daughter of Fulke Greville. m.1766 John Crewe MP. Friend and supporter of Fox, especially at the 1784 Election. Renowned for beauty. Sometime mistress of Sheridan who dedicated *School for Scandal* to her.

Cruikshank William 1745-1800 Born in Edinburgh. Studied anatomy at Glasgow University. Went to London 1771 as anatomical assistant to William Hunter. Ran an anatomical school in Windmill St London. Taught AD rudiments of anatomy.

Cumberland Duke of 1721-1765 Younger son of George II. Henry Seymour Conway's commanding officer at the defeats of Fontenoy and Lauffeldt, and in Scotland following the 1745 rebellion. A brave man, but a largely unsuccessful strategist and general.

Czartoriski Princess Izabela 1746-1835 Austrian heiress, daughter of Count Fleming. Married Polish Prince Czartoriski. 1761. Patron of the arts. Met Benjamin Franklin, Rousseau and Voltaire in Paris 1772. Founded Czartoriski Museum.

Damer Hon Mrs Anne (AD) 1748-1828 Daughter of Henry Seymour Conway and Caroline Countess of Ailesbury. First cousin once removed and god daughter of HW. Niece of 5th Duke of Argyll, Lord Frederick Campbell and Captain Sir William Campbell RN. 1st cousin of Louisa Campbell, Caroline Campbell, Lady Charlotte Campbell, Lady Augusta Campbell, Lord George (Tom) Campbell and Lord John Campbell. 13 other first cousins, children of the 1st Marquis of Hertford.

Damer Lady Caroline 1752-1829 Only daughter of 1st Earl of Dorchester. On death of her brother George she inherited his estates. After her death the estates devolved to her Dawson cousins, children of Mary Damer sister to 1st Earl of Dorchester. This family changed their name to Dawson-Damer and became Earls of Portarlington.

Damer Hon George 1746-1808 Second son of 1st Earl of Dorchester. MP for various constituencies 1768-1798, when he succeeded his father as 2nd Earl of Dorchester. Privy Councillor 1794. Lord Lieutenant of Dorset 1803-1808. He was unmarried and the titles became extinct after his death.

Damer Hon John 1744-1776 Eldest son of 1st Earl of Dorchester. Educated Eton and Trinity Cambridge. 1767 m. AD. Separated 1774. Committed suicide 1776.

Damer Hon Lionel 1748-1807 Youngest son of 1st Earl of Dorchester. Whig MP for Peterborough 1786-1802 under patronage of Earl Fitzwilliam. High Sheriff of Dorset 1786. Home: Came House Dorchester.

Damer Joseph 1676-1737 Second son of John Damer, and nephew of Joseph Damer, of Came Dorset, Cromwellian cavalry officer, who had later made a fortune in Ireland. The latter died in 1720 at a great age leaving his Irish estates to Joseph's older brother John, and his Dorset estates to Joseph. MP for Dorchester 1722-27. m Mary Churchill 1714.

Progeny: Joseph Damer 1st Earl of Dorchester, and Mary who married William Dawson, 1st Viscount Carlow.

Damer Joseph 1718-1798 See Dorchester 1st Earl of.

Dashkova Princess 1744-1810 Very able Russian aristocrat (née Vorontsov) m. Prince Mikhail Dashkov 1759. Assisted in the 1762 coup, which installed Catherine the

Great. Her husband died 1764. Relations with Catherine cooled, and in 1768 she went on an extended European progress. In 1782 she met AD in Naples with her teenage son, who sat to AD, before returning to Russia, where she was appointed Director of the Imperial Academy of Arts and Sciences. Patron of the wider use of the Russian language.

Davy Sir Humphry 1778-1829 For early life see main text p.231. Knighted 1812. Married a wealthy widow. Went on European tour 1813-14 with Michael Faraday as his assistant. Returned to England following Napoleon's escape from Elba. In 1815 produced the Davy Safety Lamp for miners, aimed at halting coal pit fires caused by naked flames, by using wire gauze to trap the flame within the lamp. In 1819 he was created a baronet. 1820 President of the Royal Society. Died of heart disease 1829 in Switzerland. Buried in Geneva.

Decrès Denis 1761-1820 French admiral, minister of the Navy 1801-1814, and again during the 100 days in 1815.

Derby 12th Earl of 1752-1834 Succeeded to the title in 1776. Lord Lieutenant of Lancashire 1776-1834. He named two classic horse races The Derby, which he won with Sir Peter Teazle in 1787, and the Oaks named after his house at Epsom. Amateur actor and colleague of AD in the productions of the Richmond House players. m. 1 (1774) Lady Elizabeth Hamilton, whose mother had been Elizabeth Gunning, before marriage to the Duke of Hamilton. 2. 1797 (Following the death of his first wife (from whom he had been long separated) Elizabeth Farren the actress.

Devonshire 4th Duke of 1720-1764 William Cavendish Whig Grandee. Lord Lieutenant of Ireland with Henry Seymour Conway as his No 2. Briefly First Lord of The Treasury 1756-7. Enjoyed poor health and died young, leaving Henry Seymour Conway £5000.

Devonshire 5th Duke of 1748-1811 William Cavendish Whig politician whose wealth and influence were his greatest assets. m(1) 1774 Lady Georgiana Spencer, (2) 1809 Lady Elizabeth Foster. A dog lover.

Devonshire Duchess of 1757-1806 Georgiana Cavendish Born Lady Georgiana (rhymes with "trainer") Spencer, d. of Earl Spencer. m.1774 William 5th Duke of Devonshire. by whom she had 3 children Georgiana (1783), Harriet (1785), William (1790) and 1 child by Lord Grey Eliza (1792). Society and political hostess. Close friend of AD.

Dorchester 1st Earl of 1718-1798 Joseph Damer MP various constituencies 1741-62. m. 1742 Lady Caroline Sackville, d. of 1st Duke of Dorset. 1762 created Lord Milton of Milton Abbey in Dorset. 1792 Created 1st Earl of Dorchester. 3s. 1d. Rebuilt Milton Abbey as a private residence and created model village of Milton Abbas.

Dowdeswell William 1721-1775 Tewkesbury land owner. Educated at Westminster, Christ Chuch, Oxford and Leyden University. MP for Tewkesbury 1747-54, and for

Worcestershire from 1761 until his death. Prominent Whig, made Chancellor of the Exchequer in Rockingham's 1765 administration, along side Henry Seymour Conway as Secretary of State. A competent financier, he refused to join Pitt's government in 1766, and thereafter led the Rockingham faction in the Commons.

Downman John 1750-1824 Welsh artist. Art education at RA Schools and studio of Benjamin West. Exhibited 148 works at the RA between 1769 and 1819. Painted portraits for theatrical sets of Richmond House Players.

Du Barry Adolphe Vicomte de 17? -1778 Nephew of Louis XV's mistress Mme du Barry. m. 1773 Helene de Tournon. Invited to England 1778 by AD. Killed in a duel with his associate the Comte de Rice at Bathampton.

Du Barry Vicomtesse Helene 1757-1782 (see above) Following the duel she fled to France with AD. Later remarried and reappeared at the court of Louis XVI.

Du Deffand Mme 1697-1780 Of noble birth, she was educated in a Paris convent where she was brilliant yet cynical. She had an arranged and unhappy marriage to her cousin the Marquis du Deffand which lasted from 1718-1722. She then had a succession of lovers. Friend of Voltaire and Montesquieu, her salon in Paris was where the smart set met. In 1754 she went blind, and in 1764 her salon was discontinued. In 1766 she met HW visiting the Duke of Richmond, then ambassador to France. He was captivated by her wit and wisdom. They started a correspondence in French which lasted till her death.

Duncannon Lady 1761-1821 Born Henrietta (Harriet) Spencer, younger daughter of Earl Spencer, and sister to Georgiana, the duchess of Devonshire. m. 1780 Lord Duncannon, who became 3rd Earl of Bessborough, on his father's death in 1793. It was a Whig arranged marriage which did not work. The couple separated.

Dutens Louis 1730-1812 Frenchman who spent most of his life in England. Sometime tutor to the younger son of the Duke of Northumberland, and English chargé d'affaires Turin on three separate occasions. In 1778 he was in Bath when AD arrived with the du Barrys.

Englefield Sir Henry (Harry) 1752-1822 7th baronet. Eminent antiquary and scientist. FRS 1778. Roman Catholic faith debarred him from public office. Friend of C.J.Fox. Lived at Whiteknights Park, Earley, near Reading. Brother of Mrs Cholmeley.

Farren Elizabeth 1759-1829 Leading actress from 1777, when she first appeared on the London stage to her last performance in 1797 as Lady Teazle in *School for Scandal*. Specialised in comedy. Friend of AD and directed the performances of the Richmond House players, who included her admirer the 12th Earl of Derby, whom she married on retiring from the stage. She had a son and two daughters and died at the Derby family home at Knowsley in Lancashire. There is a famous painting of her by Sir Thomas Lawrence hastening across a windy landscape in a white fur trimmed cloak.

Farington Joseph 1747-1821 Topographical artist and diarist. Studied under Richard Wilson. Elected RA 1785. Kept a diary from 1793 until his death. Visited Paris in 1803 after the Treaty of Amiens. Disliked AD as a sculptress and as a person.

Fawkener William Augustus 1750-1811 Diplomat. Appointed a clerk to the Privy Council 1790. Sent on government missions to Tuscany, Russia and Portugal. His mother was a Walpole relation. Frequent visitor to Lady Melbourne's Brocket Park with AD. Relationships with women left a trail of debris. First marriage to Georgiana Poyntz ended in divorce and a duel. Married secondly Elizabeth Wright (Wight?). Lover of AD, and subsequently proposed marriage to her, although apparently already married at the time.

Ferrier Susan 1782-1854 Scottish novelist with a fresh and witty style. Wrote 3 novels *Marriage, The Inheritance* and *Destiny*. Friend of Charlotte Clavering.

Fitzgerald Lord Henry 1761-1829 Younger son of the1st Duke and Duchess of Leinster (née Lady Emily Lennox). Soldier and talented amateur actor. Took leading parts in Richmond House productions.

Fitzpatrick Richard 1748-1813 "The charming Mr Fitzpatrick" (HW) Younger brother of Lord Ossory. Noted for his wit. Whig MP. Unmarried.

Fordyce Dr George 1736-1802 Fashionable Scottish doctor treating AD. Physician to St Thomas's Hospital 1770-1802. FRS 1776.

Foster Lady Elizabeth 1759-1824 Daughter of Frederick Hervey 4th Earl of Bristol. m.(1) 1776 John Foster; 2 sons. Separated 1781. In 1782 met Duke and Duchess of Devonshire in Bath and became part of a ménage à trois. Daughter Caroline born in Italy in 1785, where she met up with AD. They visited Venice together. m.(2) Duke of Devonshire 1809, 3 years after death of first duchess.

Fox Lady Caroline 1723-1774 Eldest daughter of 2nd Duke of Richmond. m.Henry Fox 1st Lord Holland. Mother of Charles James Fox. Sister of Lady Kildare.

Fox Charles James 1749-1806 Prominent Whig politician. Rake and gambler. Gave AD news of John Damer's suicide. AD supported him in 1784 election and looked on him as a hero. Sculpted by AD. m.1796 Elizabeth Armistead, former courtesan. Settled at St Anne's Hill, Chertsey. Joined Ministry of All Talents in 1806 as foreign secretary. Opponent of slave trade. Died in office.

Fouché Joseph 1759-1820 Jacobin revolutionary, infamous as the Butcher of Lyons. Engineered the coup of 9 Thermidor to overthrow Robespierre. In 1799 appointed minister of Police. From then until his final dismissal in 1816, he plotted with and against Napoleon. His network of spies was feared by all. Cunning and unprincipled he was a remarkable survivor.

Freeman Miss Probably the daughter of Sambrooke Freeman of Fawley Court, a neighbouring estate on the opposite bank of the Thames to Park Place. Sculpted by AD in terracotta and marble 1789, now at the V and A., and the model for Isis (1784-5) on Henley Bridge.

Gardner Daniel 1750-1805 Society portrait painter. Taught by George Romney, Gardner came to London 1767. 1770 entered Royal Academy Schools. 1773 joined Sir Joshua Reynolds' studio for a short time. Developed his own busy style using a mixture of gouache, pastel and oils.

Glenbervie 1st Lord 1743-1823 Sylvester Douglas. Scottish lawyer. m.1789 Catherine, daughter of ex PM Lord North. MP for various constituencies 1794-1806. In charge of Woods and Forests 1803-14. Diaries and papers an historical source.

Gloucester Maria Duchess of 1736-1807 Illegitimate daughter of Sir Edward Walpole, younger son of Sir Robert Walpole. 1st cousin to HW. m.(1)1759 2nd Earl Waldegrave (d.1763) m.(2)1766 Prince William, Duke of Gloucester.

Gosset Isaac 1713-1799 Member of a Normandy Huguenot family who had fled to Jersey at the end of the 17th century following confiscation of their estates. Isaac became a modeller of wax portrait cameos working in London. Among his sitters were Henry Seymour Conway and Lady Ailesbury.

Graham the Hon Mrs 1757-1792 Born Mary Cathcart, daughter of Lord Cathcart, ambassador to St Petersburg. m.1774. Scottish landowner Thomas Graham. Famously painted 1777 by Gainsborough. Her portrait is in the Scottish National Gallery, Edinburgh. Became a dear friend and steadying influence on Georgiana Devonshire after death of John Damer. Emigrated to Italy for health reasons and died young of TB.

Gray Thomas 1716-1771 Eton contemporary of HW. Cambridge scholar 1734-38. Grand Tour with HW 1739-41, including learning French at Rheims joined by Henry Seymour Conway. Quarrelled with HW in Italy, but reconciled 1745. HW published his works through the Strawberry Hill Press. His Elegy Written in a Country Churchyard was written in 1750 to immediate acclaim.

Greatheed Bertie 1759-1826 Owner of Guy's Cliffe near Warwick. Literary lion, but poet and playwright of little distinction. m. his cousin Ann Bertie. 1 son, who predeceased him. Friend of Mrs Siddons and Mary Berry.

Greville Charles 1749-1809 Younger son of 1st Earl of Warwick. Nephew of Sir William Hamilton. MP for Warwick 1773-90. Emma Hart was his mistress 1782-6. He exchanged her with Sir William Hamilton in return for being named as Hamilton's heir. He never married. Friend of Sir Joseph Banks, a keen gardener and co founder of the Royal Horticultural Society. The plant genus grevillea is named after him.

Hamilton Lady Anne 1766-1846 Eldest daughter of the 9th Duke of Hamilton. She never married. Lady in waiting to Princess and Queen Caroline. 6 feet high Creevey noted that "she bears a striking resemblance to one of Lord Derby's great red deer."

Hamilton Emma Lady 1765-1815 Born Amy Lyon, d of a Cheshire blacksmith. Mistress of Charles Greville who sent her to his uncle the recently widowed Sir William Hamilton, as a present in return for declaring him his heir. Acted as hostess for Sir William and married him 1791. Nursed Nelson after the Battle of the Nile 1798 and became his lover. After Sir William's death in 1803, she lived with Nelson and their daughter Horatia at Merton Place Wimbledon. After Nelson's death in 1805, she accrued debts, and moved to France to avoid her creditors. Died at Calais in penury.

Hamilton Sir William 1731-1803 Ambassador to the Kingdom of Naples and Sicily 1764-1800. Collector of antiquities. Vulcanologist, made FRS for his studies of Vesuvius and Etna. m.(1) Catherine Barlow 1758. She died 1782. Admirer of AD and her sculpture. m.(2) Emma Lyon 1791. After leaving Naples, lived together with Nelson and Emma until his death.

Harrington 2nd Earl of 1719-1779 William Stanhope. General, politician and roué. m. 1746 Lady Caroline FitzRoy, daughter of the 2nd Duke of Grafton. They had 3 daughters of similar age to AD. Isabella (Bell), m. Lord Molyneux, Amelia m. 6th Earl Barrymore, and Henrietta (Harriot) m. 2nd Lord Foley.

Hertford 1st Marquess of 1718-1794 Henry Seymour Conway's elder brother and AD's uncle. Privy Councillor, Ambassador to Paris, Viceroy of Ireland he was created Marquess of Hertford in 1793.

Hervey Mrs Elizabeth 1748-1820 Friend of AD. Stepsister to William Beckford. m. Col Thomas Hervey, grandson of 1st Earl of Bristol. Novelist.

Hobart The Hon Mrs 1739-1816 Born Albinia Bertie. m.1757 Hon George Hobart, who succeeded as 3rd Earl of Buckinghamshire 1793. Prolific amateur actress, if somewhat overweight. Acted in Richmond House plays and acted in and produced *The Jealous Wife*.

Hoper Moses c. 1762-1842 Solicitor and man of business to AD and her friends. Son of Rev John Soper of Steyning. Practised in London.

Hotham Sir Charles 1729-94 Yorkshire squire and soldier. m. 1752 Dorothy Hobart, daughter of 1st Earl of Buckinghamshire. On active service in Seven Years War. Retired from army as lieutenant general 1775. Friend of AD, though considerably older. Patron and friend of actors and actresses William and Sarah Siddons, Elizabeth Farren, and John Kemble.

Hume David 1711-1776 Scottish philosopher and historian. Published a *Treatise of Human Nature* 1739. 1763-1765 Secretary to Lord Hertford in Paris. 1766-1767 Secretary to Henry Seymour Conway, Secretary of State for the North.

Jerningham Edward 1727-1812 Second son of a Roman Catholic Norfolk baronet. A very moderate playwright and poet. Welcomed at Park Place by AD's parents. Known by AD's family as "the charming man." Not a marrying type, but a reliable escort.

Jersey Lady 1753-1821 m.1770 George Villiers, 4th Earl of Jersey. The Prince Regent became infatuated with her, and they started an affair in 1793. In 1796 she was associated in the public's mind with the Prince Regent's poor treatment of his wife Caroline of Brunswick. She was hissed by the London mob, and sought refuge at

Bognor where she met AD and Mary Berry. Intelligent, beautiful and witty, she had several other lovers including William Augustus Fawkener.

Johnston Sir Alexander 1775-1849 Brought up in Madras where his father worked in a civilian occupation. Spoke 3 Indian languages at an early age. Returned to England with his parents 1792. Trained as a lawyer and called to the bar 1800. In 1799 married Louisa Campbell, AD's 1st cousin (see). Went to Ceylon as advocate-general, and promoted to chief justice 1805. Recognised as expert on Indian native customs and procedures. 1809 recalled to England to advise on reforms of East India Co. 1810 knighted and elected FRS. 1811 returned to Ceylon as president of the Council. 1811-19 introduced universal popular education, religious tolerance, and trial by jury – western measures carefully crafted to accord with Hindu, Moslem and Buddhist beliefs. Having returned to England helped to found East Asiatic Society. 1832 Privy Councillor and 1833 member of its judicial committee specialising in the interpretation of native Indian law. In 1837 on death of an uncle, succeeded to family estate of Carnsalloch Dumfriesshire. His great great great granddaughter Marigold is married to the author of this book.

Kauffman Angelica 1741-1807 Fine Austrian artist. After working in Italy she came to London in 1766 and her first portrait in England was of AD. In 1769 became one of the first members of the RA. In later years she retired to Rome.

Kildare Lady 1731-1814 Born Lady Emily Lennox, daughter of 2nd Duke of Richmond. m.1747 James Fitzgerald 20th Earl of Kildare. In 1766 her husband became Duke of Leinster. 19 children. Sister of Lady Caroline Fox. Following Kildare's death in 1783, she married her childrens' tutor, the Rev Mr Ogilvy, and produced a further 3 daughters.

Kirgate Thomas 1734-1810 Printer and secretary to HW from 1765-1789. Not reemployed by AD on HW's death.

Lamb Peniston 1770-1805 Eldest son of Lady Melbourne. Sculpted by AD around 1780. Became an MP. Died young.

Leclerc Henrietta 1775 circa-1846 Illegitimate daughter of the Duke of Richmond, her mother was probably Mme de Cambis. m.1808 Col John Dorrien. Nicknamed "the Poor Orphan" she lived at Lavant House, near Goodwood, provided by her father.

Leinster Duchess of *and* **Lennox Lady Emily (see Kildare Lady)**

Lenoir Alexandre 1761-1839 Ardent revolutionary, who was appalled by the wanton destruction of monuments connected with the French kings. Secured permission to collect them in the Musée des Monuments Nationaux. After the Bourbon Restoration he became responsible for returning much of his collection to its former owners and sites.

Lennox Colonel Edward 1764-1819 Soldier. Nephew of 3rd Duke of Richmond. m. 1789 Lady Charlotte "Todle" Gordon, a great gambler. Succeeded his uncle 1806.

Founding member of the MCC. He and his wife gave the famous ball in Brussels on the eve of Waterloo. Lord Lieutenant of Ireland 1807-13. Governor General of British North America 1818-19.

Lennox Lady Louisa (see Connolly)

Lennox Lady Sarah 1745-1826 Daughter of 2nd Duke of Richmond, and sister-in-law to AD's half sister. A wayward lady. m.(1)1762 and divorced 1769 Sir Charles Bunbury. m.(2)1781 Hon. George Napier.

Lindsay Lady Charlotte 1770-1849 Daughter of Prime Minister Lord North. m.1800. Colonel Hon John Lindsay (d 1826). 1800 appointed Lady in waiting to Caroline Princess of Wales. Close friend and confidante of Mary Berry. No children.

Lubomirski Prince Henry 1770-1850 Son of Duke Josef Lubomirski. Adopted by his wealthy childless aunt at the age of 6. A very beautiful boy, he was taken around Europe to be painted and sculpted by leading artists, including Greuze, Elizabeth Vigée Lebrun, Angelica Kauffman and Canova. He was in London 1787, and probably sculpted then by AD.

Lybbe Powys Mrs Caroline 1738-1817 Born Caroline Girle, daughter of a surgeon. m. 1762 Philip Lybbe Powys. Lived at Hardwick House near Whitchurch, Oxon. Neighbours of the Conways at Park Place. Diarist. Her brother-in-law was rector of the neighbouring parish of Fawley, home of the Freeman family

Lysons Daniel 1762-1834 Son of a Gloucestershire clergyman. Educated Bath Grammar School and Oxford. 1789-1800 curate at Putney. Chaplain to HW. Published *The Environs of London*, a topographical survey in 4 vols 1792-96. Inherited estate in Gloucestershire 1800 to which he retired.

Lyttelton Lord 1709-1773 George Lyttelton created 1st Lord Lyttelton 1744. Whig politician. Chancellor of the Exchequer 1755-1756. Friend of HW and Henry Seymour Conway. Only son Tom, (2nd and "bad" Lord Lyttelton 1744-1779) was childhood playmate of AD at Strawberry Hill.

Mann Sir Horace 1706-1786 Diplomatic representative of the British Government to the Grand Duchy of Tuscany. Resident in Florence from 1737-1786. Correspondent with HW.

Marmont General Auguste de 1774-1852 Soldier and friend of Napoleon. Skilful commander who stood by Napoleon till 1814, when he realised that further resistance was useless and surrendered to the allies.

Masséna General André 1758-1817 Fine soldier. Served successfully in Italy and then through central Europe. Retired by Napoleon after losing Peninsular war battles in 1811.

Melbourne Viscountess 1751-1818 Close friend of AD. Née Elizabeth Milbanke. m.1769 Sir Peniston Lamb, afterwards Viscount Melbourne. Neighbour of AD in Melbourne House, London. Frequent hostess to AD at Brocket Hall, Hertfordshire.

Montagu Lady Elizabeth (Betty) (see Buccleuch Duke of)

Mount Edgecumbe 1st Earl of 1720-1795 George Edgcumbe created Viscount 1781, Earl 1789. Admiral and courtier. Family seat Mount Edgecumbe in Cornwall, overlooking Plymouth Sound. AD visited. 1777.

Mount Edgecumbe 2nd Earl of 1764-1839 Richard Edgecumbe, son of 1st earl. Amateur actor in Richmond House plays and also played at Blenheim. Acted at Strawberry Hill in 1800 after succeeding to the earldom.

Nelson Admiral the Viscount 1758-1805 Sculpted by AD 1800-01. Served as a young officer in the W.Indies where Lord William Campbell, AD's uncle was also present. His victory at Aboukir Bay in 1798 brought him into contact with Emma Hamilton, and inspired AD to sculpt him as a hero. Killed at the Battle of Trafalgar 1805.

O'Brien Lady Susan 1744-1827 Niece of Lord Holland and 1st cousin to Charles Fox. Close friend and correspondent with Lady Sarah Lennox. m. 1764 William O'Brien, an actor.

O'Hara General Charles 1740-1802 Professional soldier. Handed the sword of surrender to George Washington at Yorktown 1781. Captured by Napoleon at Toulon 1793. Imprisoned France 1793-5. On release, proposed to Mary Berry whom he had met in Italy previously. Appointed governor of Gibraltar, he sailed away without Mary, who would not leave England. Died in Gibraltar.

Ossory Countess of Upper 1738-1804 Born Anne Liddell, daughter of a wealthy Northumbrian coal mine proprietor. m.1756 heir to Duke of Grafton, who succeeded 1757. Duke disliked her life style and losses at cards and they separated 1765. An affair with the Duke of Portland ended in her humiliation, when he got engaged to Lady Dorothy Cavendish. Rejected by London society, she was introduced by HW to the 2nd Earl of Upper Ossory. They became lovers and in 1768 an illegitimate daughter, Anne was born. Grafton divorced her in 1769. She immediately married Ossory, and retired from London for his country estates, mainly at Ampthill in Bedfordshire. She started a lengthy correspondence with HW in 1769 that continued until January 1797, a few weeks before his death.

Pepys William 1741-1825 Lawyer. m. 1777 Elizabeth (d.1830) daughter of William Dowdeswell, Chancellor of the Exchequer. Neighbours of HW at Twickenham.

Pergami Bartolomeo 1785-1842 Italian ex soldier. Chamberlain and reputed lover of Princess Caroline in Italy and around the Mediterranean 1814-19.

Petty Lord Henry 1780-1863 2nd son of Prime Minister, the Earl of Shelburne (created Marquis of Lansdowne 1784). Educated at Westminster School, Edinburgh and Cambridge Universities, he was groomed for political stardom. In Paris after the Treaty of Amiens he met Fox and Lafayette. Whilst there he was elected to the Commons in his absence. By 1806 he was Chancellor of the Exchequer. He was a staunch Whig and espoused their reforming policies throughout the first half of the 19th century. On his elder brother's death, he succeeded as Marquis of Lansdowne in 1810. Conciliatory by nature, and not overly ambitious for preferment, he never achieved the highest offices of state, but was respected as a wise and conscientious statesman.

Pitt William 1759-1806. Prime minister 1783-1801 and 1804-06. Arch rival of Charles Fox and the old style Whigs. Disliked by AD.

Ponsonby Lady Charlotte 1750-1782 Daughter of 2nd Earl of Bessborough. m.1770 Earl Fitzwilliam.

Recamier Mme Juliette 1777-1849 Her salon was attended by the political and literary leaders of post revolutionary French society for around 30 years from 1800. She was married to a rich banker 30 years her senior, though the marriage was never consummated. She was beautiful, witty and level headed. A good friend of Mme de Staël.

Rice Joseph Louis Count 1732?-? Irish adventurer from Dingle peninsula. Son of a wine importer. Educated in a Jesuit seminary, the Irish College at Louvain. Joined the Imperial Austrian army, and became a friend of the Emperor Joseph II, brother of Marie Antoinette. Created a Count of the Holy Roman Empire by Joseph. Fought duel with Vicomte du Barry 1778 Bath. Reputed to have attempted to arrange the escape of Marie Antoinette from the Temple prison to be shipped to Dingle on a vessel carrying wine. However the Queen refused to leave her husband and children.

Richmond, 3rd Duchess of 1740-1796 Née Lady Mary Bruce, only d. of 3rd Earl and Countess of Ailesbury. Half sister to AD who was a frequent Goodwood visitor.

Richmond, 3rd Duke of 1735-1806 Charles Lennox, educated Westminster School. Succeeded his father in 1750. Opponent of North's policy on the American colonies. A radical thinker 1770s. More conservative as a member of Pitt's government 1780s. Dismissed from government 1795. Lord Lieutenant of Sussex. London address Richmond House, where he sponsored the Richmond House plays organised by AD. Country seat Goodwood House. m.1757 Lady Mary Bruce elder half-sister to AD. No children.

Rockingham 2nd Marquess of 1730-1782 Wealthy landowner in Yorkshire, Northamptonshire and Ireland. Formed Rockingham Club of Whig supporters of Duke of Newcastle, disaffected from the Grenvilles. Formed government 1765-66 with Henry Seymour Conway as Secretary of State. Resigned over cabinet disagreements and spent next 16 years in opposition. Recalled as Prime Minister for short spell in 1782 with Shelburne and Fox to end the American War of Independence, with Henry Seymour Conway as titular commander in chief of the army. Died of influenza after 14 weeks in office. Noted for probity and diffidence.

Sefton 1st Countess of 1748-1818 Born Isabella "Bell" Stanhope, daughter of Lady Harrington. Friend of AD. Married Viscount Molyneux 1768. The Molyneux family had been staunch R.C.s and substantial land owners in Ireland and England. In return for agreement to convert to the Anglican church, Molyneux was rewarded with the Earldom of Sefton in 1771.

Siddons Mrs Sarah 1755-1831 Actress and friend of AD who sculpted her bust. Adviser to AD on theatrical matters.

Smith Adam 1723-1790 Scottish pioneer of economics. Educated at Glasgow University and Balliol College Oxford he returned to Edinburgh. Became a friend of David Hume and a leading member of the Scottish Enlightenment. In 1751 Professor teaching logic at Glasgow University. In 1753 elected Head of Moral Philosophy at Edinburgh University. From 1763 to 1766 he travelled Europe as tutor to the young Duke of Buccleuch, and his younger brother, a better paid job. Best remembered for his *Wealth of Nations* published in 1776.

Spencer Lord Robert 1747-1831 Younger son of 2nd Duke of Marlborough. Whig MP for various seats. Celebrated gambler. Lost a fortune, took to the bank at faro, and made a fortune in 1791. Never touched a card afterwards.

Staël Mme de 1766-1817 Daughter of Jacques Necker, Louis XVI's Swiss minister of finance. Saloniste, writer and champion of "sensibility". Her husband was Swedish ambassador to France which allowed her some level of diplomatic immunity until his death in 1802. During the worst excess of the Revolution she retired to the safety of her Swiss chateau of Coppet. Her most notable work was *Delphine* (1802).

Starhemberg Prince Austrian ambassador to England. Bought York House Twickenham 1796. He and his wife became great friends of AD, especially following her mother's death.

Strafford Countess of 1721-1785 Born Lady Anne Campbell, daughter of 2nd Duke of Argyll. Elder sister of Lady Mary Coke, and distant cousin of AD. Married Thomas Wentworth, 2nd Earl of Strafford and lived at Wentworth Castle, near Barnsley, in Yorkshire. Fine landscape visited by AD.

Thrale Mrs Hester 1741-1821 m.1763 Samuel Thrale, a rich brewer. She was a friend of Samuel Johnson and Fanny Burney. Literary figure, writing and publishing several works. Disliked by HW and AD. After Thrale's death she married (1784) Gabriel Piozzi, an Italian music teacher.

Townshend The Hon Charles 1725-1767 Grandson of Turnip Townshend. MP for various constituencies. Brilliant but lightweight and erratic. Paymaster General in Rockingham's 1765 administration. Chancellor of the Exchequer to Chatham in 1766. Reduced Land Tax from 4s to 3s in the £, and voted in taxes on tea and other commodities to be raised in the American Colonies precipitating The Boston Tea Party and American War of Independence. Died shortly afterwards.

Townshend The Hon. John 1757-1833 Younger son of 4th Viscount Townshend and great grandson of Turnip Townshend. MP variously for Cambridge University,

Westminster and Knaresborough. Eloped with Georgiana Fawkener (née Poyntz) 1786. Their son John became 4th Marquess Townshend.

Waldegrave Maria Dowager Countess of (1736-1807) Born Maria Walpole, illegitimate daughter of HW's brother Sir Edward Walpole and his mistress Dorothy Clement. m.1. (1759) 2nd Earl Waldegrave (d.1763). 3 daughters Elizabeth, Charlotte and Anna, painted as the 3 Waldegrave Sisters by Reynolds. m.2 (1766) HRH the Duke of Gloucester. This marriage of a royal duke to a commoner of illegitimate descent led to the Royal Marriages Act 1772, whereby in future royal dukes would have to obtain the crown's permission before marriage.

Waldegrave Lady Elizabeth 1760-1816 The eldest of the three sisters (see above) married her cousin the 4th Earl Waldegrave (1751-1789), and inherited Strawberry Hill, moving there after AD vacated the house in 1811. Her husband having predeceased her, she succeeded to Strawberry Hill as the Dowager Lady Waldegrave.

Wales Caroline Princess of 1768-1821 German princess. Born Caroline of Brunswick, first cousin to future George IV, to whom she was married 1795. Couple lived apart after two nights. Princess Charlotte born 1796. In 1814 Caroline went to Italy and took her servant Bartolomeo Pergami as a lover. In 1820 she returned to England as Queen, unwanted and unrecognised by George IV. Attracted the sympathy of AD. Died 1821.

Waller Sir Jonathan Wathen 1769-1853 Born Jonathan Phipps, he became an eminent eye doctor. In 1804 started London's first eye hospital. Created a baronet 1814 by George III. Subsequently eye doctor to George IV and William IV. Lived at Popes Villa Twickenham. Close neighbour to AD at York House. AD's Executor.

Walpole Horace (HW) 1717-1797 Youngest son of Lady Walpole, wife of Sir Robert Walpole PM. His father may have been Sir Robert though physically he more resembled Lord Hervey, his mother's lover. First cousin once removed and Godfather to AD. Built and lived at Strawberry Hill. Prolific letter writer and publisher through The Strawberry Hill Press.

Wilkes John 1725-1797 Radical politician. Supported freedom of the press, and championed the cause of the colonists during the American War of Independence. Popular with the London mob 1768-1778. Edited the North Briton Newspaper. Member of the HellFire Club.

Wood Sir Mathew 1st baronet 1768-1843 Born in Devon, he had come to London as a young man, becoming a partner in a lucrative hop merchanting business. He became a member of the Fishmongers Company, and Lord Mayor of London 1815-16. In 1817 elected an MP for the City of London. A radical Whig, he was an unlikely champion for Queen Caroline in her fight for recognition. Certainly their political views were very different. Later he persuaded the Duke and Duchess of Kent to return to England for the birth of Princess (later Queen) Victoria. After her succession in 1837 she created him a baronet, the first hereditary title awarded by her.

MAIN SOURCES USED

A bibliography of The Strawberry Hill Press by AT Hazen and JP Kirby 1973

Anne Damer's Notebooks Lewis Walpole Collection Farmington

Anne Damer's Will National Archives

Anne Seymour Damer: Art and Fashion 1748-1828 by Percy Noble

Anne Seymour Damer (1748-1828) Sculptor. By Susan Benforado. University of
New Mexico 1986

Aristocrats by Stella Tilyard 1994

A Sapphick Elegy by Jack Cavendish 1782

Belmour by Anne Seymour Damer edited by Dr Jonathan Gross 2011

Byron's Corbeau Blanc, The Life and Letters of Lady Melbourne: ed Dr Jonathan
Gross. Pub Rice University Press 1997

Christies Sale Catalogue of John Damer's goods at Tilney St 1777

Dorset County Archives. Hand written note: To the Child (probably by Lord Milton).

Edward Jerningham and His Friends edited by Lewis Bettany 1919

England's Mistress The infamous life of Emma Hamilton by Kate Williams pub
Hutchinson 2006

Extracts of the Journals and Correspondence of Miss Berry 3 vols: edited by Lady
Theresa Lewis 1866 (Originals in British Library)

Fields of Fire by David Constantine pub Phoenix Press 2001

Georgiana Duchess of Devonshire by Amanda Foreman pub Harper Collins 1999

Horace Walpole's Will National Archives

Hotham family letters Hull History Centre

Italy with Sketches of Spain and Portugal by William Beckford pub Richard Bentley
1834

John Damer's Inquest Proceedings Westminster Abbey 1776

Letters of Horace Walpole edited by Mrs Paget Toynbee 1905

Letters of Horace Walpole edited by WS Lewis Lewis Walpole Library

Life of Nelson by Robert Southey Folio Society 1956

Madame du Barry by Joan Haslip Tauris Parke Paperbacks 2008

Napoleon's British Visitors and Captives 1801-1815 by J.Goldsworth Alger pub
AMS New York 1970

Memoirs of a traveller, now in retirement by Louis Dutens 1806

Peace in Piccadilly by Sheila Birkenhead pub Hamish Hamilton 1958

Rebel Queen The Trial of Caroline by Jane Robbins pub Simon and Schuster 2006

Romantic Genius by Andrew Elfinbein pub Columbia Univ Press 1999

Sarah Siddons by Roger Manvell pub. William Heinemann Ltd 1970

Strawberry Hill Horace Walpole's Gothic Castle by Anna Chalcraft and Judith Viscardi pub Francis Lincoln Ltd 2007

Temples of Thespis by Sybil Rosenfeld 1978 pub The Society for Theatre Research 1978

Ten Dorset Mysteries by Roger Guttridge. Ensign Publications 1989

The Berry Papers edited by Lewis Melville pub John Lane The Bodley Head 1914

The Burney Collection of Eighteenth Century Newspapers British Library

The Creevy Papers edited by Sir Herbert Maxwell 1903

The Diary of Joseph Farington 8 vols British Library

The Diaries of Sylvester Douglas Lord Glenbervie. 2 vols. edited by Francis Bickley pub Constable 1928

The Diary of Mrs Philip Lybbe-Powys ed Emily Cleminson Longmans Green 1899

The Empress of Pleasure Teresa Conelys by Judith Summers pub. Simon and Schuster 2003

The First of April by William Combe 1777

The Grace of Friendship Horace Walpole and the Misses Berry by Virginia Surtees pub by Michael Russell (Publishing) Ltd 1995

The Harlot and The Statesman Elizabeth Armistead & Charles James Fox by I.M. Davis The Kensal Press 1985

The Letters and Journals of Lady Mary Coke ed Hon. JA Home pub David Douglas 1889

The Life and Letters of Lady Sarah Lennox Anon

The Memoirs of Princess Dashkova translated edition 1995

The Naples Despatches of Sir William Hamilton ed John Davis and Giovanni Capuano pub I.B.Tauris 2008

The Nelson Portraits by Richard Walker pub Royal Naval Museum 1998

The Sylph by Georgiana Duchess of Devonshire. Edited by Jonathan Gross 2007

The Trial between William Fawkener Esq;plaintiff, and the Honourable John Townshend; defendant. 1786 Reproduction from British Library

The Whig Club: or a sketch of modern patriotism by Charles Piggott printed for W.Priest 1794

Three Generations of Fascinating Women. By Lady Russell pub Longmans Green and Co 1905

Travels through Spain in the Years 1775 and 1776 by Henry Swinburne pub P.Elmsly 1787

Waller Papers. Sale of Mrs Damer's Library Warwickshire County Archives Westminster Coroner's Records; John Damer's Inquest 1776

WALPOLE CONWAY FAMILY TREE

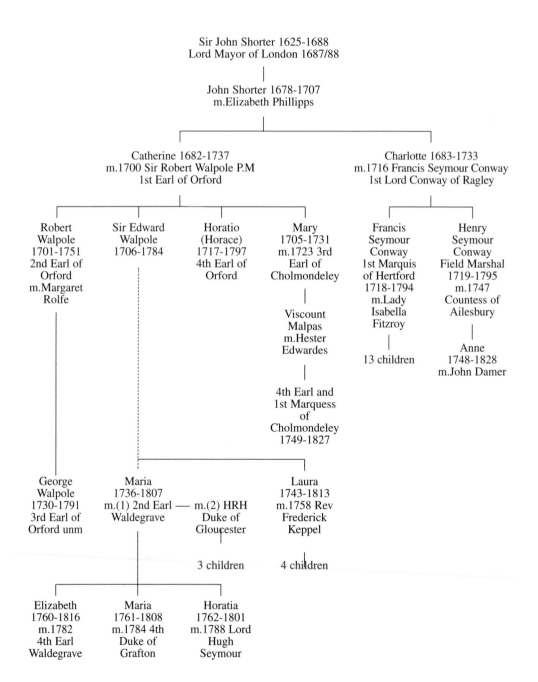

Sir John Shorter 1625-1688
Lord Mayor of London 1687/88

John Shorter 1678-1707
m.Elizabeth Phillipps

Catherine 1682-1737
m.1700 Sir Robert Walpole P.M
1st Earl of Orford

Charlotte 1683-1733
m.1716 Francis Seymour Conway
1st Lord Conway of Ragley

Robert
Walpole
1701-1751
2nd Earl of
Orford
m.Margaret
Rolfe

Sir Edward
Walpole
1706-1784

Horatio
(Horace)
1717-1797
4th Earl of
Orford

Mary
1705-1731
m.1723 3rd
Earl of
Cholmondeley

Francis
Seymour
Conway
1st Marquis
of Hertford
1718-1794
m.Lady
Isabella
Fitzroy

Henry
Seymour
Conway
Field Marshal
1719-1795
m.1747
Countess of
Ailesbury

Viscount
Malpas
m.Hester
Edwardes

13 children

Anne
1748-1828
m.John Damer

4th Earl and
1st Marquess
of
Cholmondeley
1749-1827

George
Walpole
1730-1791
3rd Earl of
Orford unm

Maria
1736-1807
m.(1) 2nd Earl — m.(2) HRH
Waldegrave   Duke of
              Gloucester

Laura
1743-1813
m.1758 Rev
Frederick
Keppel

3 children

4 children

Elizabeth
1760-1816
m.1782
4th Earl
Waldegrave

Maria
1761-1808
m.1784 4th
Duke of
Grafton

Horatia
1762-1801
m.1788 Lord
Hugh
Seymour

CAMPBELL JOHNSTON FAMILY TREE

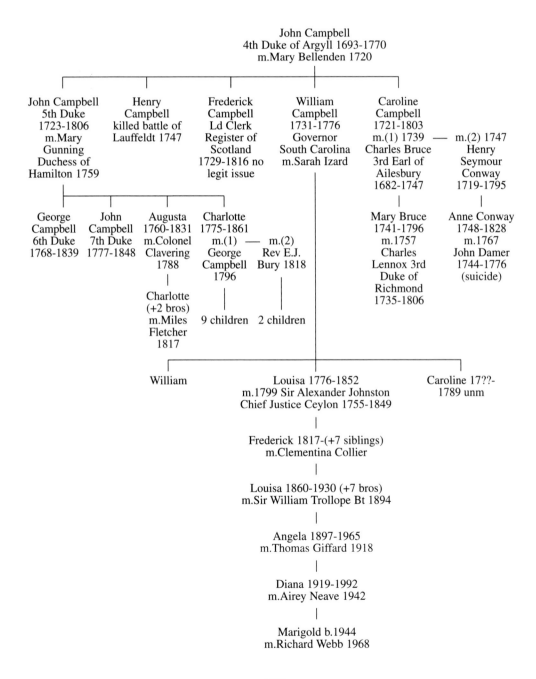

John Campbell
4th Duke of Argyll 1693-1770
m.Mary Bellenden 1720

John Campbell
5th Duke
1723-1806
m.Mary
Gunning
Duchess of
Hamilton 1759

Henry
Campbell
killed battle of
Lauffeldt 1747

Frederick
Campbell
Ld Clerk
Register of
Scotland
1729-1816 no
legit issue

William
Campbell
1731-1776
Governor
South Carolina
m.Sarah Izard

Caroline
Campbell
1721-1803
m.(1) 1739 —— m.(2) 1747
Charles Bruce   Henry
3rd Earl of   Seymour
Ailesbury   Conway
1682-1747   1719-1795

George
Campbell
6th Duke
1768-1839

John
Campbell
7th Duke
1777-1848

Augusta
1760-1831
m.Colonel
Clavering
1788

Charlotte
1775-1861
m.(1) — m.(2)
George   Rev E.J.
Campbell   Bury 1818
1796

Mary Bruce
1741-1796
m.1757
Charles
Lennox 3rd
Duke of
Richmond
1735-1806

Anne Conway
1748-1828
m.1767
John Damer
1744-1776
(suicide)

Charlotte
(+2 bros)
m.Miles
Fletcher
1817

9 children   2 children

William

Louisa 1776-1852
m.1799 Sir Alexander Johnston
Chief Justice Ceylon 1755-1849

Caroline 17??-
1789 unm

Frederick 1817-(+7 siblings)
m.Clementina Collier

Louisa 1860-1930 (+7 bros)
m.Sir William Trollope Bt 1894

Angela 1897-1965
m.Thomas Giffard 1918

Diana 1919-1992
m.Airey Neave 1942

Marigold b.1944
m.Richard Webb 1968

LIST OF ANNE DAMER'S SCULPTURES

Date	Sculptures	Medium	Location
	* exhibited Royal Academy		
1776	Shock dog	wax	
1777	Miss Caroline Campbell	wax medallion	Private Collection
1777	Lady Ailesbury	wax medallion	Private Collection
1777	Voltaire	wax medallion	Private Collection
1777	Emperor Augustus	wax medallion	
1780	Seated woman	terracotta	
1780	Sketch for monument to Ld W.Campbell		
1780?	Georgiana Duchess of Devonshire	terracotta bust	
1780?	Ideal head	marble by Nollekins from model by ASD	Rhode I. School of Design Museum
1780?	Lady Melbourne	Terracotta bust	
1780	Miss Caroline Campbell	Terracotta bust	
1780?	Son of Ly Melbourne as Mercury	Terracotta	
1780	Princess Dashkova's daughter	Terracotta profile medallion	
1780	Shockdog	Terracotta portrait	Private Collection
1780	Niobe	Terracotta bronzed	
1781?	Niobe	marble (her first)	Private Collection
1782	Ceres	terracotta	
1782	Medallion head of Jupiter		
1783	Greyhound	terracotta	
1783	Princess Dashkova's daughter	marble profile medallion	sent to Russia 1783
1784	Lady Melbourne*	marble bust	
1784	Head of Mercury*	cast	
1784?	Cupid catches a butterfly on his knee*	terracotta?	
1784	Two dogs asleep	grey terracotta (clay)	Private collection
1784	Two dogs asleep	terracotta	Knowsley
1784	Two dogs asleep*	marble	Goodwood House
1784	Model for mask of Isis on Henley Bridge*	grey 'terracotta (clay)	Private Collection

Date	Sculptures	Medium	Location
	* exhibited Royal Academy		
1784	Model for mask of Thames*		
1784 to 86	Masks of Thames and Isis	portland stone	Henley Bridge
1784	Bust of son of Rossi the	terracotta	
	dancer as young Paris*		
1785	self portrait	terracotta	
1785	Head of General Conway	terracotta	
	in a helmet		
1785 (?)	Duke of Richmond		
1785	Two small kittens*	terracotta	
1785 to 86	Lady Elisabeth Foster	wax? profile medallion	
1785 to 86	Self portrait	marble	Uffizi Gallery
1785	Lady Melbourne's son as Mercury*	marble	
1786	Osprey Eagle*	terracotta	
1786 to 89	The death of Cleopatra	terracotta bas relief	
1786 to 89	Scene from Coriolanus Act 2 scene 1	terracotta bas relief	
1786 to 89	Scene from Coriolanus Act 4 scene 5	terracotta bas relief	
1786 to 87	Hygeia*	plaster small	
1787	Caroline Countess of Ailesbury	terracotta	
1787	Elizabeth Farren	terracotta	
1787	Nephew of Princess	terracotta	
	Lubomirski, a boy		
1787 to 88	Son of dancer Rossi as Paris*	marble	
1787	Terrier*	terracotta	
1787	George III	terracotta model	
1787	Restoration of antique	cast in bronze on white	
	bust of Jupiter Serapis	marble plinth	
1788	Terrier	marble	
1788	Prince Lubomirski as	marble	Ashmolean Museum
	a young Bacchus*		
1789	Two Kittens*	marble	Private Collection
1789	Lady Elizabeth Foster	terracotta	
1789	Miss Freeman as Isis	terracotta	
1789	Miss Freeman as Isis*	marble	V & A Museum
1789	Apollo	?	
1789	Miss Farren as Thalia*	marble	National Portrait Gallery
1789	Caroline Countess of Ailesbury	marble	Sundridge Church
1790	Portrait of a lady of quality*	marble	

Date	Sculptures	Medium	Location
	* exhibited Royal Academy		
1790	Eriynnis	terracotta	
1790 to 94	George III	marble	Edinburgh Scottish National Register Office
1791	Restoration to antique eagle		
1793	Mary Berry	terracotta painted bronze	
1794?	Mary Berry	bronze	National Portrait Gallery
1794	Mrs Siddons as Melpomene*	plaster?	
1794 to 95	bust*	marble	
1799?	a dog*	marble	
1800?	a lap dog*		
1801 to 02	Charles James Fox*	terracotta	
1802	Lord Nelson	terracotta or plaster	
1803	Lord Nelson*	marble	Guild Hall London
1804 to 05	Bust of Master WH Betty*	terracotta	
1806	Sir Joseph Banks*	terracotta	
1806	Lady Charlotte Campbell	terracotta or plaster	
1805 to 07	Sketch for monument to Lord Nelson*		
c1810	Head of a muse*	bronze	
1812	Charles James Fox	marble	Malmaison Musee Nationale
1812 to 13	Sir Joseph Banks*	bronze	British Museum
1813	Sir Humphrey Davy*	terracotta bronzed	Royal Institution London
1814	Princess Caroline of Brunswick	terracotta	Rangers House Blackheath
1816	Dog*	terracotta	
1818	Dog*	terracotta	
1823	Self portrait	marble	
1825 to 26	Lord Nelson	bronze for Rajah of Tanjore	
1827 to 28	Lord Nelson	bronze for Duke of Clarence	Windsor Castle

INDEX

Index Note: HC = Henry Conway; AD = Anne Damer; JD = John Damer; HW = Horace Walpole. Locators in roman numerals refer to gallery page numbers.

actors' rest houses, 104, 106
Ailesbury, Charles Bruce, 3rd Earl, 5, 8
Ailsbury, Countess (née Campbell, AD's mother), 92, 116, 274
    character and appearance, 23, 25, *I, XXIV*
    death, 239-42
    letters and gifts to HW, 21, 26
    married life, 5-6, 8-9, 12-13: HC's death, 166, 185
    needlework, *XXIV*
    personal fortune, 9
    The author is supposed to speak, 224
    visits AD in workshop, 140
Albany, Mme d', 142, 274
Almacks Assembly Rooms, St James's, 30-31, 37, 61
amateur theatricals, 83, 98-106, 202-3
American War of Independence, 48, 61, 86
Ampthill, 101
Amsterdam, Stadt household, 10
anatomical drawings, 74, *X, XI*
Anglo-French Wars (1744-1748), 10: (1778-1782), 61, 67: (1793-1802), 171, 197-9, 204: (1803-1814), 257-8; *see also* France
Arabin, Major Will, 100, 274
Aranjuez, 129
Argyll, George Campbell, 6th Duke, 277
Argyll, John Campbell, 4th Duke (AD's maternal grandfather), 1, 6, 7, 274
Argyll, John Campbell, 5th Duke (AD's uncle), 24, 245, 274
Armitage, John, 50
Ashmolean Museum, 108
Astley's Amphitheatre, 252
Austin, William "Willikins," 252

Bacon, John, 73-4, 274
Bacon, John the Younger, 108
Badajoz, Spain, 127
Baillie, Jonanna, 203
Balbi, Mme de, 131, 274
Banks, Joseph, 230-31, 232, 239, 242-3, 274, *XXVI*
Barrymore, Countess, 47, 48, 274
Bath, 62
Bayonne, 130-31
Beauharnais, Josephine de, 213, 214, 216, 236-7, 238-9, 274-5
Beckford, William, 70
Bells Weekly Messenger, 195
Belmour, 96, 123, 124, 220-5
Berry, Robert, 113, 190, 275
Berry, Agnes, 111-12, 135, 138, 162, 177, 255, *XIX*
Berry, Mary, 77, 201, 206, 232, 262, *XVIII, XIX,*
    character, 111-12, 137-8, 167
    early life, 112-13, 169
    Fashionable Friends, 202-3, 238
    friendship with Mme de Staël, 259-60
    health and injury, 129, 135, 167, 267
    HW's literary legacy, 190
    meets and befriends Princess of Wales, 251-2, 258-9
    relationship with AD, and letters, 116, 117, 118-33, 136-50, 161, 242, 243, 254
        on Charles O'Hara, 172-3, 174-7, 249
        confidences, 120-21, 122, 136-8, 139, 141, 151, 155-7, 159-60, 161, 177-8, 220
        cooling of relationship, 162-5
        on family and acquaintances, 140, 141-50, 157-8, 173: AD's mother's final days, 239-41
        in later life, 249-50, 251-3, 254-5
        on Fawkener's marriage proposal to AD, 152-4
        seen through the character of Emily in *Belmour,* 225

relationship with Charles O'Hara, 169, 170, 171-81, 182-3, 184, 254
relationship with HW, and letters, 113-17, 121, 134-5, 139-40, 142, 148-50, 161, 167-8, 174-5, 186-7: distress over implications of, 149-50, 156-7
Berthier, General, 208
Bertrand, Henri-Gatien, 261, 275
Blagden, Sir Charles, 216
Blue Stockingers, 4
Bognor, 184
Boissy, *Les Dehors Trompeurs ou l'Homme du Jour (False Appearances),* 103-4, 105
Bonaparte, Mme de, 214, 275
Boydell, John, 106-7, 276
Bréhan, M. de, 253
British Museum, 230, 231, 250
Brocket Park, Hertfordshire, 42, 96-7
Brooks, 40
Brougham, Henry, 264, 276
Brown, Lancelot 'Capability,' 35
Bruce, Mary, Dutchess of Richmond (AD's half-sister), 8, 23, 24, 25, 40, 59
Brune, General Guillaume, 209, 276
Buccleuch, 3rd Duke of, 31-2, 144, 145, 276
Buller, Mrs, 135, 140, 142, 276
Burgos Cathedral, 130
Burgoyne, General, 99, 101
Burke. Edmund, 87, 88
Burnet, blind fiddler, 49-50
Butler, Lady Eleanor, 102, 276
Buxton, 106

Cambacérès, Jean-Jacques-Régis de, 208, 209, 277
Cambis, Mme de, 146, 277
Campbell, Lady Augusta (AD's cousin), 142, 177, 245, 255
Campbell, Caroline (AD's cousin), 76, 92, 94, 142-3, 277
Campbell, Caroline (AD's mother) *see* Ailsbury, Countess

Campbell, Charlotte (AD's cousin), 142, 143-4, 145, 245, 246, 253, 255, 256, 259-60, 277

Campbell, Lord Frederick (AD's uncle), 108, 132, 190, 240-41, 277

Campbell, Lord George, 6th Duke of Argyll, 277

Campbell, Harry (AC's uncle), 9

Campbell, Colonel John, 4th Duke of Argyll (AD's maternal grandfather), 1, 6, 7, 274

Campbell, John, 5th Duke of Argyll (AD's uncle), 24, 245

Campbell, John, 7th Duke of Argyll (AD's cousin), 122, 246, 259, 267

Campbell, Louisa (AD's cousin), 146, 277

Campbell, Mary (née Bellenden, AD's maternal grandmother), 8

Campbell, Lady Sarah (née Izard), 9, 66, 69, 94

Campbell, Lord William, 27-8, 92, 227, 234-5, 277-8

Campbell-Johnston, Germaine, 236

Carlini, Agostino, 73, XXX

Carlisle, Frederick Howard, 5th Earl, 44-5, 278

Caroline of Brunswick, Princess of Wales (later Queen Caroline), 8, 232-3, 251-3, 258-60, 264-8, 278, 291

Cavendish, William, 5th Duke of Devonshire, 77

Ceracchi, Giuseppe, 72-3, 278, IX

Chambers, Sir William, 35

Charlotte, Princess, 258

Cholmeley.Mrs, 138, 139, 157-8, 163, 165, 167, 278

Cholmondeley, Marquis of, 263, 278

Christie's, 56-7, 106, 107

Clarence, Duke of, 234, 235-6

Clavering, Augusta (née Campbell, AD's cousin), 142, 177, 245, 255

Clavering, Charlotte, 255-6, 278

Clive, Kitty, 17, 103, 121, 148-9, 278

Cliveden, Twickenham, 121, 148-9, 165, 190, 253, 255

Coke, Lady Mary, 14, 26, 30-32, 38, 40, 41-2, 43-4, 45, 47, 278: on JD's death, 51, 55

Colebrooke, Sir George, 39, 49, 56-7, 278

Colman, George, *The Jealous Wife,* 102-3

Combe Bank, Sundridge, Kent, 1, 11, 241-2, *II*

Combe, William, 79, 141, 143, 160, 279

Congreve, William, *The Old Batchelor,* 220

Connolly, Lady Louisa, 55, 279

Conway, Caroline (née Campbell, AD's mother) *see* Ailesbury, Countess

Conway, Charlotte, (née Shorter, AD's grandmother), 5, 6

Conway, Field Marshall Henry 'Harry' Seymour (AD's father), 5, 103, 108
   birth and education, 6
   career, military and parliamentary, 7, 12-13, 19, 22, 46
   as Commander-in-Chief of the Army, 86
   command of Oxfordshire militia and German posting, 25-6, 27
   created Field Marshal, 157
   as Governor of Jersey, 61, 67-8
   opposes parliamentary privilege, 27, 28
   retires from politics, 89, 90-91
   returned as member for Gatton, 39
   Rochefort expedition and aftermath, 22-3
   as Secretary of State for the North, 28-9, 39
   as secretary to Marquess of Hartington, 20-21
   character, 39
   courtship and marriage, 7-11: earlier affections, 43, 92
   death, 165-6
   Ecchardt portrait, *I*
   family life, 11-12, 23-4, 38: estate work and improvements, 24, 58, 110
   health, 48, 68, 135-6
   relationship with HW, 7-8, 11-12, 13-14, 19, 26, 28, 60, 68, 90-91, 92

Conway, Francis Seymour, 1st Marquis of Hertford (AD's uncle), 5, 28, 29

Conway House, Warwick Street, Soho, 11, 185: robbery and fire, 38

Cook, Captain James, 230

Cookham property owned by JD, 57

Corbet, Moses, Lieutenant-Governor of Jersey, 67

Cosway, Maria, 206, 279

Cosway, Richard, 139, 279, *XXI*

Creevey, Thomas, 265, 279

Crewe, Frances Anne, 89, 204, 279

Crillon, Mme de, 210

Cruikshank, Dr William Cumberland, 74, 280

Cumberland, Duke of, 9-10, 19, 22, 280

d'Albany, Madame, 142, 274

Dalkeith, Lady, 31, 32

Dallaway's *Anecdotes of the Arts in England,* 76

The Damerian Apollo (cartoon), 85, *XXII*

Damer, Anne (1748-1828)
   appearance and portraiture, 33, 45, 47-8, 96, 201, *VIII,* *XVII, XIX,*
      Carr, Cosway and Downman portraits, *XXI*
      Cerrachi's *The Muse of Sculpture, IX*
      depicted in Farrier's *Marriage,* 256-7
      Ecchardt portrait, *I*
      Gardner portrait, *VII*
      and jewellery, 56
      Kauffman portrait, 30, *IV*
      Reynolds portrait, 103, *XVII*
   artistic career
      as amateur and intruder, 75, 185, 248
      criticism and ridicule, 84-5
      education and growing reputation, 68-9
      first intimations of, 24, 26, 72: artistic beliefs, 76
      as Royal Academy exhibitor, 75, 76-7, 201-2, 203, 226, 228, 231, 233, 236, 244, 248
      training, 72-4
   artistic works
      anatomical drawings, 74, *X, XI*
      bas-reliefs, 106-8, *XXII*
      bozzetti, 73
      bust of Caroline Ailesbury, *XXIV*
      busts of Campbell cousins, 246
      bust of Joseph Banks, 231, 233, *XXVI*

bust of Mary Berry, *XVIII*
bust of Princess Caroline, 232, 233, 258
bust of Humphrey Davy, 231, 233
busts of Elizabeth Farren and Miss Freeman, *XV*
busts of Charles Fox, 151, 204-5, 229-30, 260-62
bust of Empress Josephine (no provenance), 236-7
busts of Prince Lubomirski and Rossi, 108
bust of Nelson, 200, 226-9, 235, 244, 246, 248, 263: and bronzes, 234-5, *XXIX*
bust of a niobid, 76, *XV*
dogs, cats and birds, 77-8, 88, 96, 201, 226, 233-4, *XIII*: Fidele, AD's own dog, 77: shock dog, 26, 77, *XII*
masks for Henley Bridge, 87-8, 93-4, 96, *IX, XVI*
model of Ceres, 69, 70
in Napoleon and Josephine's private apartments, 217
sculptures, list of, 296-8
self portrait, 95, *XIV, XV*
statue of King George III, 84, 108-9, *XX*
Strawberry Hill collection, 193-4
terracottas and marbles of friends (1780s), 76-7
wax head, *IX*
Belmour, 96, 123, 124, 220-5
Mary Berry, relationship with, and letters, 118-33, 136-50, 242, 243
  confidences, 120-21, 122, 136-8, 139, 141, 151, 155-7, 159-60, 161, 177-8, 220: on Fawkener's marriage proposal, 152-4
  cooling of relationship, 162-5
  on family and acquaintances, 140, 141-50, 157-8, 173; mother's final days, 239-41
  in later life, 249-50, 251-3, 254-5
  on Charles O'Hara, 172-3, 174-7, 249
birth, childhood and adolescence, 1, 11
  intellectual stimuli and attainments, 17-18, 29, 45

pet 'Jeriboo' and life at Park Place, 18-19
relationship with father, 7
under HW's care, 13, 14, 17-18
visits Ireland, 20-21
witnesses saving of drowning man, 27-8
character, 23, 29, 48, 55-6, 60, 66, 68, 70, 224: as Lady Anne Parker in *The Sybil,* 54
death of father, 165-6
declining years and death, 118, 235, 236
  dash to Paris, 260-62
  death, 269: notices of, 269-70
  moves to York House and court action, 263-4
  relationship with Campbell cousins, 255-7
  Will and codicils, 267-9
health, 45, 68, 93, 140, 144, 167-8, 262
HW's will and AD's duties as executrix, 187-8, 190-91: removal to Strawberry Hill, 191-5
marriage and widowhood
  AD takes a lover, 97, 98
  engagement and pre-nuptial arrangements, 32-3, 35
  JD's death and reaction to, 50-51, 54: moves to Sackville Street, 60-61, 161-2: returns to father's house, 58, 59
  JD's debts and reaction to, 48, 49, 55, 57-8
  marriage and early adaption to, 36-7, 38, 39-40: Sarah Lennox on, 55
  later marriage proposals, 91, 151-3
  separates officially from JD, 46-7
social and public life
  abusive conjecture on AD's sexuality, 79-83, 122, 141, 143, 160, 163
  appearances at masquerades, 44, 47, 68
  befriends Duchess of Devonshire, 46-8
  befriends Mary Berry, 115-17
  befriends Princess Dashkova, 69-70
  befriends Sir William Hamilton, 69, 70-71

befriends the du Barrys and gives aid after duel, 62, 64-6
Continental trips and journeys, 45-6, 69-70, 95, 119-32, 204-5, 260-62: aboard boat taken by French privateer, 66: Lisbon to London 126-32
correspondence with Lord Hotham, 104-6
introduction to society, 30-32
meets and befriends Josephine Bonaparte, 214, 216, 236, 238-9, 242-3
meets Napoleon Bonaparte, 215-16, 260-61
participates in amateur dramatics, 98-9, 100, 102-3, 104
as patroness of Ottoman Street theatre, 203-4
political support for Fox, 89, 229
Princess of Wales and, 251-2, 264, 265-6
social group and meetings, 41-3
Damer, George (JD's brother), 51, 249-50, 280: involvement in murder at Florence, 33-4
Damer, John
  character, 45, 51
  Cookham property, 57
  debts, 48-9
  engagement to marry Anne, 32-3: separation, 46
  family and education, 33, 34-5, 280: library, 56-7
  portraiture and appearance, 56, *VI*
  suicide at Covent Garden and aftermath, 49-51, 55: possibility of fake, 52-3
Damer, John (JD's great-uncle), 41
Damer, Joseph, Lord Milton (JD's father), 33, 34-5, 41, 52, 280
Damer, Lady Caroline, 280
Damer, Lionel, 55, 249, 280
Darwin, Erasmus, 76
Dashkova, Princess, 69-70, 95, 280-81
Davy, Humphrey, 231-2, 281, *XXVIII*
Decrès, Denis, 209, 281
Derby, Edward Smith-Stanley, Lord, 83, 100, 103, 281

Devonshire, Georgiana Cavendish, Duchess of, 37-8, 46-7, 68, 76, 89-90, 95, 247-8, 281, *VIII*

letters to AD, 81-2, 244

The Sylph, 54

Devonshire, William Cavendish, 5th Duke of, 77, 95, 102, 281

Dorchester House, Park Lane, 35

Dorchester, Joseph Damer, 1st Earl of, 33, 34-5, 41, 52, 281

Dowdeswell, William, 29, 281-2

Downman, John, 99, 282, *XXI*

Drury Lane Theatre, 67: Thomas Greenwood, scene painter, 99, 102

du Barry, Adolphe, Vicomte, 61-6, 282

du Barry, Hélène, Vicomtesse, 46, 61-6, 80, 282

du Barry, Mme, 61-2

du Deffand, Mme, 35, 40, 45-6, 65, 114, 251, 282

duels, 63-6, 98

Duncannon, Lady, 145, 282

Dutens, Louis, 62-5, 282

East India Company, 86-7

Edgecumbe, Mr, 100

Edinburgh, 108

education system, 3-4

election (1784), and run-up to, 86-91

Elvas, Portugal, 126-7

Englefield, Sir Henry, 100, 201, 249, 282

Falconet's *Reflections on Sculpture,* 226

Fane, Frederick, 52-3

Farington, Joseph, 185, 187, 190, 201, 217, 248, 283

Farquhar, Sir Alexander, 247

Farren, Elizabeth, 76, 82, 83-4, 99-100, 101, 104-6, 166, 244, 282

Fawkener, Georgiana (née Poyntz), 97

Fawkener, Sir Everard, 97

Fawkener, William Augustus ("Dorimont"), 97-8, 151-4, 158, 172, 224, 283, *XXIII*

Featherstonehaugh, Harry, 196

Felpham, Sussex, 144-5, 146-7

Ferrier, Susan, *Marriage,* 255-7, 283

Fidele, AD's dog, 77, 124

Fitzgerald, Lord Henry, 101, 102, 103, 283

Fitzpatrick, Richard, 45, 283

Foldson, Miss, 121

Fordyce, Dr George, 144, 283

Foster, Elizabeth "Bess" (née Hervey), 77, 81, 95-6, 247, 283

Fouché, Joseph, 208, 283

Fox, Charles James, 45, 50-51, 54, 87, 89-90, 217, 229-30, 246-7, 283, *XXIII, XXVII*

Fox, Lady Caroline, 23, 283

France, 120, 121, 130-32, 154, 171, 204-19, 229, 260-61, 262; *see also* Anglo-French wars

Freeman, Miss, of Fawley Court, 76, 83-4, 283, *XV*

Gardner, Daniel, 47, 284

The Gentleman's Magazine, 186, 270-71

George III, King of England, 87, 89, 103, 263: AD's statue of, 84, 108-9, *XX*

George, Prince of Wales (later George IV), 90, 102, 232-3, 258, 263, 265

Glenbervie, Lady, 251, 252, 284

Gloucester, Duchess of (AD's cousin), 102, 190

Gloucester, Duke of, 102

Goldsmith, Oliver, 44

Goodwood, 59, 96, 104, 146, 164, 245

Gosset, Isaac, 26, 72, 284

Graham, Mary, 54, 81, 284

Granada, 128-9

Gray, Thomas, 6, 16, 17, 284

Greatheed family, 104, 105, 160, 201, 249, 284

Greville, Charles, 95, 196, 244, 284

Grimaldi, Princess, 70-71

The Guardian, 101, 102

Gunning, Elizabeth, Duchess of Hamilton, 25

Guttridge, Roger, *Ten Dorset Mysteries,* 52

Hamilton, Emma (née Hart), 95, 145, 196-7, 199-200, 229, 244, 284-5

Hamilton, Lady,(1st wife of Sir William) 67, 70

Hamilton, Lady Anne, 264-5, 266, 284

Hamilton, Sir William, 69, 70-71, 88, 145, 196, 198, 243-4, 285, *XXIII*

proposes to AD, 91

proposes to, and marries, Emma Hart, 95, 196-7, 199

Harley, Lady Margaret, Duchess of Portland, 3-4

Harrington, Lady, 43, 44, 50-51, 92, 285

Hart, Emma *see* Hamilton, Emma

Hartington, Marquess of, 19-20

Hastings, Warren, 86-7

Haymarket Theatre, 158

Henley bridge, 93-4, 96, *XVI*

Hertford, Francis Conway, 1st Marquis (AD's uncle), 5, 28, 29, 285

Hertford, Lady, 92

Hervey, Mrs Elizabeth, 158, 171-2, 285

Hillsborough, Lord, 67

Hobart, Mrs, 102-3, 285

Hoper, Moses, 268-9, 285

Hoppner, John, 217

Hotham, Sir Charles, 104-6, 285

Howard, Mr, 31

Hume, David, 7, 28, 72, 285

Hunter, John, 92

Hutchinsons' *Memoirs of Colonel Hutchinson,* 254

Hyde Park, 98

India, 234

India Bill, 87

Irish independence question, 20

Italian Principalities, 66-7, 69, 70-71, 95-6, 129, 135, 138, 170, 196, 198, 260: Neapolitan Royal Family, 198

Jackson, Mr, British Consul, Paris, 208-9

Jerningham, Edward, 59, 126, 139, 141, 143, 285: *The Siege of Berwick,* 159

Jersey, 61, 67-8, 110

Jersey, Lady, 184, 285-6

Johnson, Samuel, 83

Johnston, Lady Louisa (née Campbell), 236, 255

Johnston, Sir Alexander, 234-6

Jordan, Mrs Dorothea, 84

Josephine, Empress of France, 213, 214, 216, 236-7, 238-9, 274-5

Kauffman, Angelica, 30, 95, 286, *IV*

Kemble, Charles, 203, 238

Keppel Craven, Richard, 254, 260, 279

Kew, 231
Kildare, Lady, 23, 286
Kings Theatre, Haymarket, 68
Kirgate, Thomas, 188-9, 286

Lamb, Elizabeth (née Milbanke), 42
Lamb, Harriet, 244
Lamb, Peniston, 42, 76, 147, 286
laughing gas (nitrous oxide), 232
Le Clerc, Miss, 145
le ton, 3, 30, 37, 39, 40, 44-5, 61,
    97-8: *bon ton*, 48, 83
Lee, Nathaniel, *Theodosius*, 103
Leinster, Duchess of, 55, 66
Lennox, Colonel Edward, 164, 286-7
Lennox, Lady Sarah, 30, 55, 60, 287
Lenoir, Alexandre, 212, 286
Leverian Museum, 108
library of AD, 271
Liège, 9
Lindsay, Lady Charlotte, 264, 287
Lisbon, 120, 122-5
Little Strawberry Hill (Cliveden),
    121, 148-9, 165, 190, 253, 255
Lloyds Evening Post, 200, 226
London mob, 102, 104
Louis XV, King of France, 61-2
Louis XVI, King of France, 138
Louvre, 296
Lubomirski, Prince Henry, 108, 287,
    XXV
Lybbe Powys, Mrs Caroline, 103,
    185, 287
Lysons, Daniel, 185, 287
Lyttelton, Lady, 41, 42
Lyttelton, Lord "Tommy," 14, 19,
    287
Lyttelton, Lord George, 19, 43, 287

Madrid, 129
Malthus, Thomas Robert, 1
Mann, Sir Horace, 33-4, 48, 69, 95,
    96, 287
marble as a medium, 74
Marie Antoinette, Queen of France,
    81, 82, 138, 154
marital misbehaviours, 37-8, 81, 97-8
Marmont, General Auguste de, 209,
    218, 287
masquerades and *macaroni*, 40, 44,
    47, 68
Masséna, General André, 209, 287
medicine, 92-3, 167
Melbourne, Lady Elizabeth, 37, 44,
    46-7, 54, 61, 81, 96-7, 98, 144,
    147, 224, 244, 287, *VII*

Melbourne, Peniston Lamb, Lord,
    42, 76, 147, 286
Melbourne House, Piccadilly, 42
Merry, Captain, 101, 103
Milton Abbey, Dorset, 34-5, 52-3, 73
Milton, Lord (JD's father), 33, 41,
    73: blames AD for son's death,
    51, 54-5, 57-8
Minorca, 12
Molyneux, Lady Isabella, 43
Montagu, Elizabeth (née Robinson),
    3-4, 76
Montagu, Lady Mary Wortley, 13-14
Montague, Lady Betty, 31-2
Montfaucon's *L'Antiquité Expliquée
    et Representée en Figures*, 76
More, Hannah, 148, 184
Morning Chronicle, 220, 246
Morning Post, 227, 228
Mount Edgecumbe, George, 1st Earl,
    59-60, 288
Mount Edgecumbe, Lady, 141
Mount Edgecumbe, Richard, 2nd
    Earl, 202, 204, 288
Murphy, Arthur, *The Way to Keep
    Him*, 98-9
The Muse of Sculpture, 72, *IX*
Musée des Monuments Nationaux,
    211-12
Musée Ernest Rupin, Brive, 236
Mutiny Bill, 87

Naples, 66-7, 69, 196, 198-9
Napoleon Bonaparte, 171, 204, 213,
    215-16, 257, 259-62, 275-6,
    XXXII
National Assembly (Revolutionary
    French government), 121, 132,
    138
Neapolitan Royal Family, 198
Nelson, Horatio, 197-200, 229, 288
    AD's bust of, 200, 226-9, 235,
    244, 246, 248, 263: Duke of
    Clarence's bronze, 234-6,
    XXIX
    coat worn at Aboukir Bay, 227,
    234, 235, *XXXII*
    memorial statue, 245
nitrous oxide (laughing gas), 232
Notebooks, 119, 136, 151, 152, 155,
    165, 175, 176, 273

O'Brien, Lady Susan, 30, 55, 66,
    288
O'Hara, General Charles, 122, 126,
    142, 167

description of and death, 182-3
relationship with Mary Berry,
    169, 170, 171-81: letters to
    Mary, 179-81
youth and military career, 169-71,
    288
Opera House entertainments, 47
Opie, John, 217
Ossory, Anne, Countess of, 78, 94,
    96, 100, 101, 111, 114, 149,
    186-7
Ottoman Street Private Theatre, 203-
    4
Oxford, 162-3

Pantheon, 44, 61, 139
Papera, B., figure-maker, 227-8, 246
Paris, 131-2, 205-19, 260-61, 262:
    National Assembly, 121, 132,
    138
Park Place, Remenham, 13, 18-19,
    21, 43, 104, *III*
    AD and JD marry, 36-7
    AD's visits to, 58, 59, 109-10,
    142, 157
    at HC's death, 166, 171
    disposal of, 166-7, 173, 185, 254
    distillery, 58-9, 157
    grounds and farms, 24, 58-9:
    Jersey's stone circle, 110
    HC's retirement to, 90-91
    visitors to, 24, 92, 116, 162
Pepys family, 115, 116, 184, 288
Pergami, Bartolomeo, 262, 264, 288
Perry, James, *Mimosa; Or, The
    Sensitive Plant*, 80
Petty, Lord Henry, 212, 288-9
Piggott, Charles, *The Whig Club or A
    Sketch of Modern Patriotism*, 83
Pigott, Charles, 109
Pitt, William (The Elder), 3, 22, 278
Pitt, William (The Younger), 87, 88-
    9, 97, 246, 289
politics, 1-2, 26-7, 86-91
Ponsonby, Lady Charlotte, 30, 289
Powys, Rev Thomas, 94
Prince Frederick, mail packet boat, 66

Ragley, Warwickshire, 25-6, 166
Recamier, Mme Juliette, 218, 289
Reynolds, Sir Joshua, 44, 226, *V, VI,
    XVII*
Rice, James Louis, 62-3, 289
Richmond, Charles Lennox, 3rd
    Duke of, 24, 38, 54, 66, 73, 87,
    104, 145, 244-5, 246, 289

Richmond, Charlotte Lennox, 4th Duchess of, 164

Richmond, Mary, 3rd Dutchess of (AD's half-sister), 8, 23, 25, 40, 59, 96, 164, 185-6, 289

Richmond House players, 83, 99-104, 143: AD on, 104-5

Robinson, John (publican), 49-50

Rockingham, 2nd Marquess of, 2, 28, 29, 86, 289

Rouquet, Jean, 3

Rousseau, Jean-Jacques, *La Nouvelle Héloise,* 82

Royal Academy, 75, 76-7, 165, 185, 201, 226, 228, 229, 231, 236, 244, 248

Royal Institution, 232

Sackville Street, 162-3

Sackville, Lady Caroline (JD's mother), 35

Sandoz, Anne and Mary's Paris guide, 213, 214

"A Sapphick Elegy", 80-81

scandalmongering, 79-82

sculptures of AD, listed, 296-8

Sefton, 1st Countess of, 44, 45, 68, 289-90

Self Indulgence, 256, 257

Seven Years War, 21-3, 25

Seville, 127-8

sexuality, 82-3

Shelburne, Lord, 86

Sheridan, Richard Brinsley, 103-4

Siddons, Sarah, 100, 105-6, 107, 290

Sierra Morena, 127

smallpox and inoculation, 13-14, 92

Smith, Adam, 34, 290

soldiering, 6

Spa, Belgium, 61, 62, 66

Spain, 127-9

Spencer, Lord Robert, 24, 45, 89, 290

Stadt household, Amsterdam, 10

Staël, Mme de, 207, 209, 217-18, 249, 259, 290

Stanhope, Lady Harriot, 43-4, 50-51

Stanley, Edward, 12th Lord Derby, 45

Starhemberg, Madame de, 241

Starhemberg, Prince, 203, 249, 252, 263, 290

Strafford, Lady Anne, 43, 290

Strawberry Hill Press, 17, 188, 193

Strawberry Hill, Twickenham, 13, 16-17, 25, 42, 60, 87, 96, 113-14, 142, *II, III, XXXI*: under

AD's ownership, 187-9, 191-5, 202, 251, 253-4

Stubbs, George, 74

Sundridge, Kent, 1, 11, 241-2, 267-8

Terni, 170

Thrale, Mrs Hester, 82-3, 160

Tilney Street, Mayfair, (AD's marital home), 36, 49, 55-7

Toulon, 171

Townshend, John, 97-8, 290-91

Trafalgar, Battle of, 245

Tregonwell family, 34

Tuileries, 213, 215, 217

Tyrawley, Lord, 169

Uffizi gallery, 96, *XIV, XV*

Upper Brook Street, 163, 185, 271

Upper Ossory, Countess of, 78, 94, 96, 100, 101, 111, 114, 149, 186-7

Valladolid, Spain, 129-30

Valletort, Lord, 59-60

Vardy, John, 35

Venice, 96

Villiers, Lord, 43

Waldegrave, Dowager Lady Elizabeth, 253, 270, 291

Waldegrave, Lady Laura, 97

Waldegrave, Lady Maria (née Walpole, AD's cousin), 41-2, 254, 291

Waller, Sir Jonathan Wathen, 268, 291

Walpole, Catherine, 6

Walpole, George, 3rd Earl of Orford, 148

Walpole, Horace, 4th Earl of Orford, 6, 7, 42, 224, 291, *V, XXIII*

birth, early life and education, 15-16

career in parliament, 27, 28, 39

character and constitution, 16, 132

A Description of the Villa at Strawberry Hill, 190

final illness and death, 148, 186-7: terms of Will, 187-90

letters, 16

on 1874 election, 88

on the Berry sisters, 111-12

to the Berry sisters, and relationship with, 113-17, 121, 134-5, 139-40, 142,

148-50, 161, 167-8, 174-5: on speculation concerning Mary, 156

on AD, and relationship with, 13, 14, 17-18, 32-4, 40-41, 45-6, 68, 70, 78, 132-3, 146, 147, 158-9, 163, 167: AD's intellect and attainments, 68, 72, 93-4, 96

to HC, and relationship with, 7-8, 11-12, 13-14, 19, 28, 60, 68, 90-91, 92

on elevation to Earldom, 148

on household affairs at Strawberry Hill, 87, 96

on JD, 39, 48-9, 51

on Charles O'Hara, 170-71, 174

on old age and heath, 41, 93, 114, 135

on Park Place, 110, 116

on Richmond House players, 100-101, 102

literary legacy, 190

Reminiscences of the Courts of George I and George II, 115

Walpole, Robert, 1st Earl of Orford, 6, 15

wax as a medium, 72

Wedgwood, 227-8, 249

Wellington, Duke of, 257-8

Wentworth, 24

Westminster, 90

Westminster Abbey, 157

Whitehall Evening Post, 187, 200, 227

Wilberforce, William, 88

Wilkes, John, 26-7, 291

Windsor, 147

Wood, Sir Mathew, 255, 264, 291

The World, 143

Wyatt, James, 99, 102

York House, Twickenham, 263, 267, *XXXI*

York, Duke of, 102